THE GESTAPO AND GERMAN SOCIETY

THE GESTAPO AND GERMAN SOCIETY

Enforcing Racial Policy

1933–1945

ROBERT GELLATELY

CLARENDON PRESS · OXFORD

Oxford University Press, Walton Street, Oxford OX2 6DP
Oxford New York
Athens Auckland Bangkok Bombay
Calcutta Cape Town Dar es Salaam Delhi
Florence Hong Kong Istanbul Karachi
Kuala Lumpur Madras Madrid Melbourne
Mexico City Nairobi Paris Singapore
Taipei Tokyo Toronto
and associated companies in
Berlin Ibadan

Oxford is a trade mark of Oxford University Press

Published in the United States by
Oxford University Press Inc., New York

British Library Cataloguing in Publication Data
Data available

Library of Congress Cataloging in Publication Data
Gellately, Robert, 1943-
p. cm.
The Gestapo and German society: enforcing racial policy 1935-1945/
Robert Gellately.
Includes bibliographical references.
1. Jews—Germany—History—1933-1945. 2. Germany. Geheime
Staatspolizei. 3. Jews—Germany (West)—Unterfranken—Persecutions.
4. Germany—Ethnic relations. 5. Unterfranken (Germany)—Ethnic
relations. I. Title.
DS135.G3315G45 1990
943'.004924—dc20 89-26534
ISBN 0-19-820297-0

5 7 9 10 8 6 4

Printed in Great Britain
on acid-free paper by
Biddles Ltd.
Guildford and King's Lynn

PREFACE

THIS book began to take shape one day several years ago in the Würzburg state archives. After reading through a number of Gestapo (secret state police) case-files on the persecution of the Jews, I began to wonder how it was possible for the Gestapo to detect the smallest signs of non-compliance with Nazi doctrines, especially when the suspected 'crime' pertained to the most private spheres of social, family, and sexual life. The files were far from clear on that point, and often said nothing about why an investigation began. How could the police have been able to enforce policies with such scrupulousness and *apparent* ease? Although a great deal was already known to historians about the nature of the policies, their ideological inspiration, and the contributions of leading Nazis, little had been written about the process by which these doctrines had been transformed into reality inside Germany.

At the time many Germans believed that there was a Gestapo agent on every street corner. Nor was this belief limited to the Nazi era, but has continued, to a greater or lesser extent, to shape perceptions both inside and outside present-day Germany about the Nazi police state and terroristic regime which was eminently capable of enforcing the dictatorship's will. According to this kind of logic, the structure of everyday life was so overshadowed by the physical presence of the secret police, one operating beyond the reach of conventional civil and legal justice, that the most innocuous forms of disobedience could be placed under surveillance and control, politicized, characterized as opposition, and therefore criminalized. An extensive police force, which could perhaps call on an army of agents and spies, would ensure that disobedience could readily be spotted and that popular compliance with and accommodation to the dictates of the regime would follow. Put another way, in such a police state there would have been few, if any, relatively secure social enclaves in which any real resistance or opposition could have crystallized. We have been telling each other this story, in its several variants, for over fifty years. It is no longer convincing.

In many respects I am surprised that this book turned out to deal so much with the police. As with most social historians, my inclination has been to avoid discussion of the police or the state administration. I was interested in the Gestapo case-files as sources of information about popular responses to various Nazi measures, especially the anti-Semitic ones, and hitherto I had only a secondary interest in histories of the Gestapo or the SS. As I read the Gestapo files I was convinced that the material contained in them was extremely important, but I also soon came to see that I could make sense of it only by extending the investigation to include social-historical, organizational, and even personnel issues of the Gestapo itself. As I presented the results of my research at various gatherings of specialists, my impression was reinforced that much less was known about the everyday workings of the police than might be supposed. Given that my intention in writing this book was to appeal not only to such specialists, but to a wider readership, I felt it was essential to show just how the police apparatus emerged, how it was organized and operated on a routine basis. Instead of writing a book on the German people's reactions to Nazi anti-Semitism, which was my original intention, I ended up examining how racial policy was enforced.

Specialists on the German police and the Gestapo may wish to skip over the first two chapters, although I have tried to show how the Gestapo emerged and was related to German society in ways that are not always made clear in the literature. I have also raised several issues that should interest them, such as the extent to which the political police from the days of the Weimar Republic was 'purged'.

Geographically, the book focuses primarily upon the city of Würzburg and the district of Lower Franconia in Bavaria. I have tried to justify the 'German society' in the book's title by looking at both similar and different districts elsewhere in the country, and this book is certainly not intended to have only local or regional implications.

Just as I was beginning my research, the Institute for Contemporary History in Munich, in co-operation with Bavarian archives, inaugurated the 'Bavarian Project'. While I was not part of that project, I benefited immensely from it, and especially from the information offered to me by several persons associated with it. My sincere thanks to Martin Broszat, director of the Institute, as well as Falk Wiesemann and Anton Grossmann. Elke Fröhlich offered especially valuable advice. Ian Kershaw, a non-German participant in the project, has encouraged my work from the outset, and I am happy to record my gratitude. I would like to make special mention of the late Reinhard Mann (1948–81), whose work on the Gestapo remained unfinished on his untimely death. This book owes a great deal to his research findings.

It would be impossible to name all those archivists who helped me, but I would like to make special mention of several. Dr Hermann Rumschöttel pointed out where I could find important materials not only in Munich, but in other archives in Bavaria as well. In the Würzburg archive I received the kindest co-operation from Dr Siegfried Wenisch. His colleagues in the reading-room responded with good cheer (most of the time) to my repeated requests for more and more files. They never made me feel guilty about my *Aktenhunger*, and I thank them for indulging what Dominick LaCapra would call my archival fetishism. In the Düsseldorf archive I was warmly received by Dr Anselm Faust, who assisted my work. At the federal archives in Koblenz Dr Wilhelm Lenz has provided both help and encouragement, and his friendship and hospitality over the years make me look forward to a return visit to Koblenz.

Some of the material in Chapters 2 and 5 is also dealt with in an article 'The Gestapo and German Society: Political Denunciation in the Gestapo Case Files', which has been published in the *Journal of Modern History* (December 1988). Mary Van Steenberg, the managing editor of the journal, offered numerous suggestions for improving that piece and I want to record my gratitude here. One of the anonymous readers of the article asked several challenging questions. He turned out to be Gerald Feldman, and without wishing to hold him responsible for the views expressed in this book, I want to thank him for an especially probing analysis of the paper. The book's organization was influenced by his comments and queries.

At various times and places I have profited from discussions with colleagues. I owe thanks to Sarah Gordon for pointing out the importance of Gestapo case-files as social-historical sources, and for discussions at the very earliest stages of this project. As it has turned out, I have emphasized different themes and reached different conclusions, but I am sure we share common concerns about the history of racial persecution. I am grateful to my friend and colleague Gary Owens, who never failed to lend me a sympathetic ear as I struggled to find direction for this book. Lawrence Stokes of Dalhousie University has helped me from start to finish, and has been a constant source of information. Michael Kater of York University offered both criticism and encouragement on several occasions, and I certainly benefited from both. I am deeply indebted to Marie Fleming. I like to think my prose offered her a chance to hone her considerable abilities for spotting sloppy logic and dubious reasoning. She got plenty of practice in reading through the manuscript, and has saved me from countless infelicities.

I would also like to thank Tim Mason, William Allen, Rudy Koshar, Barbara Lane, Christopher Browning, Claudia Koonz, Kurt Düwell, Michael Geyer, Geoff Eley, Richard Bessel, Tom Childers, Jane Caplan, Marion Kaplan, Peter Hayes, Otto Dov Kulka, Hans Mommsen, Ulrich Herbert, Konrad Jarausch, Walter Struve, Eberhard Kolb, Reinhard Rürup, Lutz Niethammer, Detlev Peukert, Peter Alter, Gerhard Hirschfeld, Charles Maier, Czeslaw Łuczak, Klaus Drobisch, Roland Flade, and Sybil Milton. I am grateful to John Waś for improvements to the manuscript during copy-editing.

This book could not have been written without the support of Huron College and the financial assistance of grants from the Social Sciences and Humanities Research Council of Canada. The Alexander von Humboldt Foundation (Bonn) also provided funds at crucial times. It is a pleasure to acknowledge that support.

Official German guide-lines on accessibility to the archives, and especially Gestapo case-files, require that persons be referred to only in 'strictly anonymous forms'. Accordingly, the names of persons mentioned in the book from the Gestapo case-files and other archival sources have been changed. An exception has been made in Chapter 6, in the case of Ilse Sonja Totzke, for reasons that will become evident. Members of the Gestapo and other Nazi officials of various kinds are not protected by the guide-lines and are referred to by their real names.

R. G.

London, Canada
July, 1989

CONTENTS

LIST OF MAPS

LIST OF TABLES

ABBREVIATIONS AND GLOSSARY

For archival abbreviations see the first section of the Bibliography.

BPP	Bayerische Politische Polizei (Bavarian Political Police, after 1936 part of the Gestapo)
BVP	Bayerische Volkspartei (Bavarian People's Party)
DAF	Deutsche Arbeitsfront (German Labour Front)
DNVP	Deutschnationale Volkspartei (German National People's Party)
DVP	Deutsche Volkspartei (German People's Party)
Gendarmerie	the rural police
Gestapa	Geheimes Staatspolizeiamt (National headquarters of the Gestapo)
Gestapo	Geheime Staatspolizei (Secret State Police)
GL	Gauleitung (Nazi Party regional headquarters)
IfZ	Institut für Zeitgeschichte (Munich)
IMT	International Military Tribunal, held in Nuremberg (trial of the major war criminals)
KLB	*Kirchliche Lage in Bayern* (see bibliography)
KPD	Kommunistische Partei Deutschlands (Communist Party of Germany)
Kreisleiter	Nazi Party regional leader below the Gauleiter
Kripo	Kriminalpolizei (Criminal Police)
KZ	Konzentrationslager (Concentration camp)
LRA	Landratsamt (local district head office, state administration)
NS	National Socialist, abbreviated form to refer to a Nazi organization or to the times
NSDAP	Nationalsozialistische Deutsche Arbeiter Partei (National Socialist German Workers' Party, the Nazi Party)
NSV	Nationalsozialistische Volkswohlfahrt (Nazi Welfare Association)
Orpo	Ordnungspolizei (regular police, comprising also the Schutzpolizei (Schupo) or regular uniformed police, and gendarmerie)
Ortsbauernführer	local peasant leader
Ortsgruppenleiter	Nazi Party local leader, below the Kreisleiter
RSHA	Reichssicherheitshauptamt (the main security department formed in 1939 embracing, among other organizations, the Gestapo, Kripo, and SD)
SA	Sturmabteilung (Storm-troops, or 'Brownshirts')

Schupo	see Orpo
Schutzhaft	'protective custody', in effect arrest and internment
SD	Sicherheitsdienst (Security Service)
Sipo	Sicherheitspolizei (Security Police, eventually composed of Gestapo and Kripo)
Sopade	Sozialdemokratische Partei Deutschlands (exiled SPD executive, based in Prague, 1933–8; Paris, 1938–40; London, 1940); for underground SPD records see Bibliography under *Deutschland-Berichte*
SPD	Sozialdemokratische Partei Deutschlands (Social Democratic Party of Germany)
SS	Schutzstaffel (black-shirted organization led by Himmler)
Stapo	short form for Staatspolizei or Gestapo
VfZ	*Vierteljahrshefte für Zeitgeschichte*
YLBI	*Year Book of the Leo Baeck Institute*

Lower Franconia

Upper Franconia

Middle Franconia

Upper Palatinate

Swabia

Lower Bavaria

Upper Bavaria

—	Boundaries of administrative regions (*Regierungsbezirke*)
○	Towns/cities
—	Boundaries of administrative districts (*Bezirksämter*, from 1939 *Landkreise*)

```
0        25       50 Miles
├────────┼────────┤
0        40       80 Km
```

MAP I Bavaria, 1933 (excluding the Palatinate)

● Jewish community present here in 1933

○ Jews living here were attached to a neighbouring
Jewish community in 1933

★ No Jews lived here in 1933, but there exists
a Jewish cemetery

Unterri

●Brückenau

Schond

●Mittelsinn

●Völker

●Dittlofs

Unterert

We

Burgsinn

●Alzenau

Rieneck

Han

○Wasserlos

●Schöllkrippen

●Gemünden

●Hörstein

●Heßdc

●Adelsberg

○Hösbach

●Goldbach

Lohr●

●Aschaffenburg

Wiesenfeld

●Karlsta

●Schweinheim

Laudenbach●

Th

●Großostheim

●Urspringen

●Kleinwallstadt

●Karbach

●Marktheidenfeld

●Sommerau

Veitshöchheir

●Eschau

Wörth a. Main Fechenbach

●Homburg a. Main   Wü

Klingenberg

Hö

★ Reistenhausen

Re

Oberaltertheim

Kleinheubach●

Unteraltertheim●

Miltenberg

Geroldsha

Allersk

Büttha

| 0 | 5 | 10 | 15 | 20 Miles |

| 0 | 10 | 20 | 30 Km |

MAP 2 Lower Franconia

Weimarschmieden

Willmars

Neustädtles ★

Nordheim v.d.
Röhn

erelsbach Oberwaldbehrungen

Bastheim Mellrichstadt

Mittelstreu

Unsleben

Höchheim

ustadt a.d. Saale Eichenhausen Trappstadt

Kleineibstadt

Saale

Steinach a.d. Saale Kleinbardorf Königshofen i.
Grabfeld

Sulzdorf a.d. Lederhecke

Poppenlauer Oberlauringen Ermershausen

Maroldsweisch

Bad Kissingen Maßbach

Schweinshaupten

Aidhausen Burgpreppach Memmelsdorf
i. Ufr
Lendershausen Hofheim i. Ufr. Untermerzbach
Kleinsteinach

Ebern ★

ausen Niederwerm

ach

erbach Schweinfurt

Geldersheim

Schonungen Haßfurt Reckendorf

Göchsheim Ebelsbach

Westheim b. Haßfurt

Limbach

Theilheim

wanfeld

Zeilitzheim

Gerolzhofen

senheim

Frankenwinheim

Lülsfeld

feld Dettelbach Altenschönbach

Prichsenstadt

au

tockheim Kleinlangheim

ld

Großlangheim

Kitzingen Wiesenbronn

stadt Rödelsee

ausen Mainbernheim

larktsteft Marktbreit

orf Obernbreit

Gnodstadt Hüttenheim i. Bav.

usen

gshofen

rsheim

Introduction

EVEN to some astute political observers in Berlin, Adolf Hitler's grasp on power seemed at best tenuous on the day of his appointment as Chancellor of Germany on 30 January 1933. President Paul von Hindenburg, who agreed to accept him, had to overcome some last-minute qualms, but comforted himself with the knowledge that Hitler's cabinet would be dominated by a majority of conservative ministers. One of the men responsible for pressing Hitler's appointment, now named Hitler's Vice-Chancellor, the ex-Chancellor Franz von Papen, thought that he would be able to manage the upstart. Papen was in for a shock, but in January he was able to draw satisfaction from the fact that non-Nazis had control of the military and held such key ministries as Defence, Finance, Economics and Agriculture, Justice, and Foreign Affairs. Convinced that he and his conservative-nationalist colleagues would have an easy time of it with the new Chancellor, Papen exclaimed to Minister of Finance Count Schwerin von Krosigk, 'We have hired him!' Of a doubting acquaintance he demanded, 'What do you want? I have Hindenburg's confidence. Within two months we will have pushed Hitler so far into a corner that he'll squeak.'[1]

That day, 30 January, was also a momentous one for Joseph Goebbels, Hitler's chief lieutenant in the capital city and the man responsible for Nazi Party propaganda. At 3.00 a.m. on 31 January, after an eventful evening, Goebbels wrote in his diary another interpretation of events:

It seems like a dream. The Wilhelmstrasse is ours. The Leader is already working in [the] Chancellory. We stand in the window upstairs, watching hundreds and thousands of people march past the aged President of the Reich and the young Chancellor in the flaming torchlight, shouting their joy and gratitude... Germany is at a turning-point in her history... Outside the Kaiserhof the masses are in wild uproar. In the meantime Hitler's appointment has become public. The thousands soon become tens of thousands. An endless stream of people floods the Wilhelmstrasse... The struggle for power now lies behind us, but we must go on working to retain it... Indescribable enthusiasm fills the streets. A few yards from the Chancellory, the President of the Reich stands at his window, a towering, dignified, heroic figure, invested with a touch of old-time marvel. Now and then with his cane he beats time to the military marches. Hundreds and thousands and hundreds of thousands march past our windows in never-ending, uniform rhythm. The rising of a nation! Germany has awakened! In a spontaneous explosion of joy the people espouse the German Revolution... The new

[1] Both remarks are quoted in Karl Dietrich Bracher, *Die deutsche Diktatur: Entstehung, Struktur, Folgen des Nationalsozialismus*, 2nd edn. (Cologne, 1969), 213.

Reich has risen, sanctified with blood. Fourteen years of work have been crowned by victory. We have reached our goal. The German Revolution has begun![2]

Like other Nazi leaders, Goebbels fully believed that real changes were possible. As Hermann Göring stated in a radio broadcast on the night of Hitler's appointment, 'We are closing the darkest era of Germany's history and are beginning a new chapter.'[3] Within weeks what was left of the Weimar constitution was laid to rest and the rule of law suspended. By the middle of 1933 all political parties had been abolished and virtually all organized opposition was eliminated in the process of 'co-ordination' or *Gleichschaltung*.

There was a determination to Nazify Germany, but, given the 'anti-practical nature' of Nazi ideology, it was not quite clear what this entailed; in the event 'the most radical steps on any issue were always those which could be presented as "most national socialist"—there was no practical yardstick for judgement'.[4] Even if the new holders of power were not as united as sometimes supposed, they could in general agree on the 'desirability' of making the country 'more National Socialist'. Politically it was expeditious to begin by removing from the body politic the parts that were at once damned by the Nazi *Weltanschauung*, and already on the margins of the existing society. The new masters, whether in Berlin or out in the provinces and small towns, thus proceeded by what has been called a 'negative selection process'; with campaigns not only against the democratic system and old enemies, but those people who were to some extent already vulnerable—the Jews, Marxists (Socialists and Communists), pacificists, anti-social elements, Jehovah's Witnesses, homosexuals, criminals, and so on.[5]

---

[2] Joseph Goebbels, *My Part in Germany's Fight*, trans. K. Fiedler (1940; New York, 1979), 207–9.

[3] Quoted in R. J. Overy, *Goering: The Iron Man* (London, 1984), 22.

[4] Timothy W. Mason, 'Intention and Explanation: A Current Controversy about the Interpretation of National Socialism', in Gerhard Hirschfeld and Lothar Kettenacher (eds.), *Der 'Führerstaat': Mythos und Realität. Studien zur Struktur und Politik des Dritten Reiches* (Stuttgart, 1981), 27. For introductions to the literature (apart from Bracher and works cited below in n. 50) and the controversies see Pierre Ayçoberry, *The Nazi Question: An Essay on the Interpretations of National Socialism (1922–1975)*, trans. R. Hurley (New York, 1981), 109ff.; Eike Hennig, *Bürgerliche Gesellschaft und Faschismus in Deutschland: Ein Forschungsbericht*, 2nd edn. (Frankfurt, 1982), 19ff; Ian Kershaw, *The Nazi Dictatorship: Problems and Perspectives of Interpretation* (London, 1985), 1ff.; John Hiden and John Farquharson, *Explaining Hitler's Germany: Historians and the Third Reich* (Totowa, NJ, 1983), 83ff.; Michael R. Marrus, *The Holocaust in History* (Hanover and London, 1987), 31ff. The *Historikerstreit* also continues to produce a substantial number of important books and essays, with promises of still more to come. Among the latter will be a book by Richard J. Evans. The best place to begin is with Charles S. Maier, *The Unmasterable Past: History, Holocaust, and German National Identity* (Cambridge, Mass., 1988).

[5] Martin Broszat, *Der Staat Hitlers: Grundlegung und Entwicklung seiner inneren Verfassung* (Munich, 1971), 433–4. Cf. Michael H. Kater, 'Die ernsten Bibelforscher im Dritten Reich', *VfZ* 17 (1969), 181ff.; Donald Kenrick and Grattan Puxon, *The Destiny of Europe's Gypsies* (New York, 1972), 59ff.; Ernst Klee, *'Euthanasie' im NS-Staat: Die 'Vernichtung lebensunwerten Lebens'* (Frankfurt, 1983), 15ff. See also Richard J. Evans, 'Introduction: The "Dangerous Classes" in Germany from the Middle Ages to the Twentieth Century', in Richard J. Evans (ed), *The German Underworld: Deviants and Outcasts in German History* (London, 1988), 1–28, for an introduction

The 'new order' was hammered out in part by the use or threat of violence, and accompanied by an avalanche of laws, decrees, ordinances, or simply appeals and demands by local Nazis claiming to be acting in Hitler's name. It was uncertain for a time which organizations would be entrusted with implementing the policies hatched in the distant capital. There was, of course, the civil service, which for the most part dutifully stayed at its desk, but it was distrusted. The Nazi Party (NSDAP) itself was a prime candidate, with massive numbers (about 850,000 in early 1933) already enlisted. The sheer violence and numbers in Ernst Röhm's Brownshirts—the Sturmabteilung (SA)—advanced their claim to be a new and radical revolutionary army. From about 450,000 at the time of Hitler's appointment, it exploded to 2.9 million by August of the next year.[6] As will be seen, there were problems with both of these organizations.

In 1933 there was also the much smaller and more élitist SS under Heinrich Himmler (the Schutzstaffel), which had only 52,000 members.[7] Although in time the SS proved to be the ultimate victor, it grew to be too unwieldy and lacking in technical competence to operate as the enforcer in Nazi Germany. The result was that a novel executive machine 'was constructed from parts of the SS', a machine completely 'independent of the State administration and, as a matter of principle, subject to no official norms'.[8] The other 'parts' comprised the technically competent members of already existing police bodies able and willing to make the adjustment to changed circumstances. This 'machine' was then assigned tasks of various kinds, or took the initiative on its own, both inside Germany and later in the occupied territories.

Arguably the most important cog in this 'new machine' inside the Reich was the Geheime Staatspolizei (Gestapo) or Secret State Police. It became, in Karl Dietrich Bracher's words, 'the institutional basis of [the] innermost reality of the Third Reich'.[9] Just how that machine acquired and used its power is the subject of this book. From its central headquarters in Berlin's

---

to the literature; in the same volume see Wolfgang Ayass, 'Vagrants and Beggars in Hitler's Reich', 210ff. Also instructive is Götz Aly and Karl Heinz Roth, *Die restlose Erfassung: Volkszählen, Identifizieren, Aussondern im Nationalsozialismus* (Berlin, 1984), 13ff. Much of the recent literature on the persecution of the Jews is discussed in Eberhard Jäckel and Jürgen Rohwer (eds.), *Der Mord an den Juden im Zweiten Weltkrieg* (Stuttgart, 1985); Herbert A. Strauss and Norbert Kampe (eds.), *Antisemitismus: Von der Judenfeindschaft zum Holocaust* (Frankfurt, 1985). An East German perspective is provided in the work of Kurt Nowak, *'Euthanasie' und Sterilisierung im 'Dritten Reich'* (Weimar 1980), and Kurt Pätzold, *Faschismus, Rassenwahn, Judenverfolgung: Eine Studie zur politischer Strategie und Taktik des faschistischen deutschen Imperialismus (1933–1935)* (Berlin (East), 1975), 13ff.

[6] The figures are from Mathilde Jamin, *Zwischen den Klassen: Zur Sozialstruktur der SA-Führerschaft* (Wuppertal, 1984), 2, 5.

[7] For the figures and a brief introduction see George H. Stein, *The Waffen SS: Hitler's Elite Guard at War, 1939–1945* (Ithaca, 1966), p. xxvi.

[8] Hans Buchheim, 'Die SS: Das Herrschaftsinstrument', in Hans Buchheim *et al.*, *Anatomie des SS-Staates*, (Olten, 1965), i. 29.

[9] Bracher, *Die deutsche Diktatur*, 382.

Prinz Albrecht Strasse 8, the Gestapo became the key link in the terror system
and police state, and attained a reputation for ruthlessness and cruelty, so
that the very mention of the name filled the hearts of contemporaries with
dread and foreboding. Even today it remains a token of the most sinister
and horrific aspects of Hitler's dictatorship, including arbitrary arrest and
detention, endless interrogations, forced confessions under torture in police
basements, and wilful misuse of police authority.[10]

1. REVIEW OF THE LITERATURE

The literature which has appeared on Nazi Germany since 1945 is vast, but
the Gestapo, and particularly its everyday operations outside the gaols and
concentration camps, have received little attention. Part of the failure can be
attributed to the methods employed by historians. Much of the work to date
either employs the methods of legal or administrative history, such as the
examination of the SS state published by the Institute for Contemporary
History in Munich, or approaches the topic through the biographies of its
leading figures.[11] Useful as these works are, only rarely do they venture into
social history, so that they never really get close to exploring how the police
went about enforcing policy. But the problem goes deeper than questions of
methodology. Why is it that social historians of Nazi Germany have not got
round to studying institutions like the Secret State Police, which played such
a prominent role in Hitler's 'new order'?

David Schoenbaum's innovative social history provides detailed treatment
of the state and touches on nearly every branch of the civil service; yet the
Gestapo is not mentioned at all.[12] Even in many of the recent books to appear
on the 'history of everyday life' (Alltagsgeschichte) relatively little is said about
the enforcement process—granted that part of the problem can be traced to
the destruction, nearly everywhere, of many essential sources.[13] On the other
hand, why is it that oral-history projects have not explored this theme more

[10] For an introduction see Johannes Tuchel and Reinold Schattenfroh, Zentrale des Terrors: Prinz-
Albrecht-Straße 8. Das Hauptquartier der Gestapo (Berlin, 1987), 63ff., and Reinhard Rürup (ed.),
Topographie des Terrors: Gestapo, SS und Reichssicherheitshauptamt auf dem 'Prinz-Albrecht-Gelände'.
Eine Dokumentation (Berlin, 1987), 36ff.

[11] See Buchheim et al., Anatomie des SS-Staates. Some accounts turn into mini-histories of the
entire era: see e.g. Jacques Delarue, Geschichte der Gestapo, trans. Hans Steinsdorff (Düsseldorf,
1964); Edward Crankshaw, Gestapo: Instrument of Tyranny (London, 1956); Alain Desroches, La
Gestapo: Atrocités et secrets de l'inquisition nazie (Paris, 1972).

[12] David Schoenbaum, Hitler's Social Revolution: Class and Status in Nazi Germany 1933–1939
(London, 1967), 202ff. Police and political police are mentioned once each and not cited in the
index.

[13] An exception here is Detlev Peukert, Volksgenossen und Gemeinschaftsfremde: Anpassung, Ausmerze und Aufbegehren unter dem Nationalsozialismus (Cologne, 1982), 55ff. More attention might
have been devoted to policing in the project on Bavaria. See Martin Broszat et al. (eds.), Bayern
in der NS-Zeit, 6 vols. (Munich, 1977–83).

extensively? These experiences ought to have marked memories indelibly.[14] While it is reassuring that the Gestapo and the Nazi Party (in its policing function) turn up in some recent social-historical literature, there are few attempts to integrate the local 'inputs' into the examination of the routine workings of the police.[15]

There has been a tendency to suppose that the 'police state' relied on an extraordinarily large police force, which in turn could count on the collaboration of an army of paid agents and spies. It is true that even in the Weimar years Berlin, for example, had more policemen than comparable cities in the United States, such as New York.[16] Still, a detailed study of the local distribution of the Gestapo shows that the number of those involved was small.[17]

Moreover, it is fair to say that, given the increasing reach of the regime into social life, the ever-expanding claims to watch and modify behaviour, there were certainly far too few to have accomplished their tasks even with the collaboration of other elements in the police network.[18] Overestimation of those involved seems to have been a widespread contemporary misperception, in society at large and especially on the Left. One man otherwise knowledgeable of the situation in the mines around Bochum wrote in 1936, for example, that there was 'one works spy for every twelve to fifteen workers'.[19] Such a figure is almost certainly an exaggeration. How would the regime go about finding so many spies willing to go down the mines? In all likelihood such 'spies' were not the police plants often supposed, but insiders— at the very least, residents of long standing in the community who came

[14] The theme might have been explored more, for example, by Lutz Niethammer (ed.), *'Die Jahre weiß man nicht, wo man die heute hinsetzen soll': Faschismus-Erfahrungen im Ruhrgebiet* (Berlin, 1983). For an important analysis of the silence see in this volume the essay by Ulrich Herbert, '"Die guten und die schlechten Zeiten": Überlegungen zur diachronen Analyse lebensgeschichtlicher Interviews' (pp. 67ff.); see also Annemarie Tröger, 'German Women's Memories of World War II', in Margaret Randolph Higonnet *et al.* (eds.), *Behind the Lines: Gender and the Two World Wars* (New Haven, 1987), 285ff. Cf. Bettina Wenke, *Interviews mit Überlebenden: Verfolgung und Widerstand in Südwestdeutschland* (Stuttgart, 1980), 20ff., and 98ff.; Lothar Steinbach, *Ein Volk, Ein Reich, Ein Glaube? Ehemalige Nationalsozialisten und Zeitzeugen berichten über ihr Leben im Dritten Reich* (Berlin, 1983), 21ff.

[15] On the policing function of the NSDAP see Michael H. Kater, *The Nazi Party: A Social Profile of Members and Leaders, 1919–1945* (Cambridge, Mass., 1983), 190ff. Kater quotes Hermann Rauschning's remark that the Nazi system worked as it did because 'everyone is the other man's devil, everyone supervises everybody' (p. 208). See also Aryeh L. Unger, *The Totalitarian Party: Party and People in Nazi Germany and the Soviet Union* (Cambridge, 1974), 83ff.

[16] James F. Richardson, 'Berlin Police in the Weimar Republic: A Comparison with Police Forces in Cities in the United States', in George L. Mosse (ed.), *Police Forces in History* (London, 1975), 79ff. For useful remarks on the different meanings of the concept of 'police state' see e.g. Brian Chapman, *Police State* (London, 1970), 11ff.

[17] The exact figures are given in chs. 1 and 2.

[18] See ch. 2 for details.

[19] From a contemporary document by Franz Vogt, 'Die Lage der deutschen Bergarbeiter (August 1936)' repr. in Detlev J. K. Peukert and Frank Bajohr, *Spuren des Widerstands: Die Bergarbeiterbewegung im Dritten Reich und im Exil* (Munich, 1987), 140.

forward, more or less voluntarily, for all kinds of reasons, not necessarily or
even primarily because of allegiance to Nazism.[20]

Only rarely have historians and political scientists offered suggestions as
to how the Gestapo, in spite of its small numbers, attained its reputation
for efficiency. Franz Neumann noted that the police represented 'the most
important instrument of the Nazi system', but said little about how it operated
on a routine basis.[21] E. K. Bramstedt touched on several important aspects of
the problem, and suggestively pointed to the notion of 'control by fear'.[22]
Martin Broszat's renowned account of the Nazi state never mentions the
problem of enforcement as such, though he treats it by implication.[23] In a
neglected short essay on the political denunciations he discovered while
working in local archives on the history of Nazi Germany, he points to a
crucial feature of the enforcement process.[24] Various sections in the standard
work on the SS delineate the institutional evolution of the political police,
but, because they adopt an exclusively institutional approach, much that is
essential to questions raised here is not discussed.[25] Hannah Arendt offers
some ideas which pertain to the topic under examination and are worth
recalling.

While Arendt exaggerates the role of agents in the operation of the political
police, she highlights the significance of 'mutual suspicion' which came to
permeate 'all social relationships'; she claims that in turn there grew 'an all-
pervasive atmosphere even outside the special purview of the secret police'.[26]
'Collaboration of the population in denouncing political opponents and volunteer service as stool pigeons', while they were not without precedents in
earlier times and places, were in Hitler's Germany 'so well organized that the
work of specialists' was 'almost superfluous'.[27] If, by 'specialists' here, Arendt
meant to suggest the full-time members of bodies such as the Gestapo, she
was certainly correct. 'In a system of ubiquitous spying, where everybody
may be a police agent', but almost certainly is not, it becomes possible for the
police to work effectively.[28]

---

[20] G. R. Elton, *Policy and Police: The Enforcement of the Reformation in the Age of Thomas Cromwell*
(Cambridge, 1972), 331ff., suggests that enforcement relied on 'amateurs' earlier as well.

[21] Franz Neumann, *Behemoth: The Structure and Practice of National Socialism* (New York, 1966),
540.

[22] E. K. Bramstedt, *Dictatorship and Political Police: The Technique of Control by Fear* (1945; New
York, 1976), 137ff.

[23] Broszat, *Der Staat Hitlers*, ch. 10.

[24] Martin Broszat, 'Politische Denunziationen in der NS-Zeit: Aus Forschungserfahrungen im
Staatsarchiv München', *Archivalische Zeitschrift*, 73 (1977), 221ff. For the post-war legal problem
of dealing with the matter see Hans Carl Nipperdey, 'Die Haftung für politische Denunziation in
der Nazizeit', in H. C. Nipperdey (ed.), *Das Deutsche Privatrecht in der Mitte des 20. Jahrhunderts:
Festschrift für Heinrich Lehmann zum 80. Geburtstag*, i (Berlin, 1956), 285–307.

[25] Buchheim, 'Die SS', 13ff.

[26] Hannah Arendt, *The Origins of Totalitarianism* (New York, 1966), 430.

[27] Ibid. 431.

[28] Ibid.

An approach to the problem of enforcement is offered from another angle by Ian Kershaw's recent book on the role and social reception of the consciously produced 'Hitler myth', While giving due weight to the accomplishments of Joseph Goebbels and Nazi propaganda, Kershaw rightly points out that

propaganda was above all effective where it was building upon, not countering, already existing values and mentalities. The ready-made terrain of pre-existing beliefs, prejudices, and phobias forming an important stratum of the German political culture on to which the 'Hitler myth' could easily be imprinted, provides, therefore, an equally essential element in explaining how the propaganda image of Hitler as a 'representative individual' upholding the 'true sense of propriety of the German people' could take hold and flourish.[29]

Gestapo power was built upon many of the same pre-existing beliefs. As well, long-standing attitudes to crime, and the stigmas attached to those branded as criminals and delinquents, worked on behalf of whoever wore the police uniform, and against those whom they anathematized.[30]

This book combines administrative and social history and attempts to deal with the everyday interaction between the Gestapo, German society, and the enforcing of racial policy. It asks what were the preoccupations of the Gestapo? How was it organized locally, who served in it, how did it go about its tasks, and, most importantly, how did it initiate cases? What was its relationship to the Nazi Party and other elements in the police system? How and why do its tasks change over the course of the twelve-year history of the Third Reich? How, to mention but one example, was it quite evidently able to enforce decrees that encroached upon the most private sphere of personal, family, and sexual life? The regime could promulgate many kinds of anti-Semitic policies, but how were they enforced? Its racist 'intentions' have long been the subject of historians' research, but how it went about realizing them has not received the attention it deserves.

With the outbreak of war, when an army of 'racially inferior' peoples had to be brought to Germany to work, all kinds of race regulations were issued to ensure that no 'racial mixing' took place. How were these regulations policed? If Polish workers, for example, were sent in small handfuls about the rural landscape as workers and quartered in farmhouses, how could pro-hibited sexual or even friendship ties be prevented? How successful was the Gestapo in policing the vast array of measures in the whole field of racial policy? What were the limitations on the 'success'?

The theme explored throughout is that the enforcement of racial policies designed to separate the groups defined by the Nazis as 'racially foreign' required the co-operation or collaboration of 'ordinary citizens'. Given the

---

[29] Ian Kershaw, *The 'Hitler Myth': Image and Reality in the Third Reich* (Oxford, 1987), 4–5.
[30] See e.g. George L. Mosse, *Toward the Final Solution: A History of European Racism* (New York, 1978), 219ff.; Hans-Joachim Döring, *Die Zigeuner im NS-Staat* (Hamburg, 1964), 11ff.

small numbers of Gestapo agents and the often minute detail about private matters that was required for the successful execution of Nazi policies, these simply could not have been enforced without the support of those members of the population who came forward with the necessary information. It needs to be said that such participation, as referred to here, came from people not formally members of nor honorary or paid agents of the Gestapo and/or other Nazi organizations. Moreover, by no means were those who passed on information to the police invariably acting out of explicit loyalty to Nazism or Hitler as such. As will be seen, the issues surrounding motivational questions are far more complex than one might assume.

This book suggests that social historians ought to deal more systematically with institutions, particularly the Gestapo, which played such a profound social role, and at the same time it reminds those who are concerned with institutional histories and 'high politics' to consider shifting the emphasis somewhat away from decision-making and institutions. Until now few historians of Hitler's Germany have been prepared to focus on enforcement even though this is the sphere in which official 'intentions' run up against 'structures'. Far from any trivialization, which some might feel to be the consequence of moving away from a preoccupation with Nazi leaders in order to incorporate social-historical findings, such research indicates that responsibility for the criminal features of the regime cannot be dismissed as simply the work of a handful at the top.[31] It should not be forgotten that 'ordinary' citizens played a key role in their own policing and helped make possible the murderous deeds of the regime.

2. PERSECUTION, CONSENSUS, RESISTANCE, DISSENT

There are a number of fine works on dissenting opinion or behaviour, as well as resistance and persecution, and henceforth social-historical work on Nazi Germany must take 'popular opinion' into account.[32] Far from speaking with monolithic unanimity, the German people counted in its ranks numerous grumblers, malcontents, dissenters, and opponents. Displeasure with how things were going, of one sort or another, could be witnessed in virtually all groups in society, at least on occasion. Ian Kershaw points out that by 1939 (if not earlier), particularly on the 'Jewish question', there was a consensus 'based on the passivity and apathy of the vast majority of the population', behaviour which was nothing less than a 'deliberate turning away from any personal responsibility'. However, this moral abdication was reinforced by the more active participation of at least some people because 'the conditions

---

[31] See the examination of the charge in Mason, 'Intention and Explanation', 23ff.
[32] See Ian Kershaw, *Popular Opinion and Political Dissent in the Third Reich: Bavaria 1933–1945* (Oxford, 1983), 4ff.

of Nazism encouraged the full flourishing of denunciation as an effective form of social control, in which neighbours and workmates collaborated with "active" not "passive complicity" in building the climate of repression and apathetic compliance'.[33]

In their understandable efforts to uncover popular forms of resistance, historians have frequently lost sight of the broad field of consensus. As Marlis Steinert reminds us, the German government, like any other one, could not have carried on for very long without a good deal of consensus, 'whether forced or passive, of a broad social stratum'.[34] This book sets out to examine the bases of support on which the regime was able to rely. The theme pursued throughout is that the Gestapo, and, by extension, the regime, could not have enforced racial policy on its own. It is necessary to recall with Detlev Peukert that the 'fondly drawn pictures of everyday non-acceptance' that began streaming from the presses in the Federal Republic with the approach of the fiftieth anniversary of the 'seizure of power' took place 'against the background of the majority's passivity, conformity or even enthusiastic support'.[35]

The ability of the regime to carry on, at least until the middle of the war-years, was not seriously affected by the existence and persistence of dissent, which flared into opposition and even resistance on rare occasions. A close look at the way the regime isolated the Jews socially reveals that, in spite of a few stumbling-blocks and miscalculations which caused ripples of public consternation, it was able to enforce policies with remarkable 'success'. Kershaw has made a convincing argument for the 'indifference' and lack of concern most citizens entertained when it came to the fate of the Jews. But one has to ask whether 'indifference' is not a form of 'passive complicity'.[36] Regardless of the terminology, this stance was not incompatible with the relatively smooth implementation of public policies aimed at gradually separating Jews from other citizens.

But while this book is less concerned with dissent and resistance than with compliance and persecution, it will have implications for anyone interested in the former. If, as Barrington Moore would have it, the one prerequisite for expressions of disobedience to take place is the existence of 'social and political space within the prevailing order' in which a minimum of mobilization can occur, it can be said that the same process by which it proved possible for the

---

[33] Ian Kershaw, 'German Popular Opinion and the "Jewish Question", 1939–1943: Some Further Reflections' in Arnold Paucker (ed.), *Die Juden im Nationalsozialistischen Deutschland/The Jews in Nazi Germany 1933–1945* (Tübingen, 1986), 384–5.

[34] Marlis G. Steinert, *Hitler's War and the Germans: Public Mood and Attitude during the Second World War*, ed. and trans. T. E. J. de Witt (Athens, Ohio, 1977), 1.

[35] Detlev J. K. Peukert, 'Widerstand und "Resistenz": Zu den Bänden V und VI der Publikation "Bayern in der NS-Zeit"', *Archiv für Sozialgeschichte*, 24 (1984), 665.

[36] Kershaw, 'German Popular Opinion', 367. He quotes the latter concept from Otto Dov Kulka and Aron Rodrigue, 'The German Population and the Jews in the Third Reich: Recent Publications and Trends in Research on German Society and the "Jewish Question"', *Yad Vashem Studies*, 16 (1984).

Naxi regime to enforce its policies simultaneously had the effect of eliminating—or reducing drastically—the 'more or less protected enclaves within
which dissatisfied or oppressed groups have some room to develop'.[37] In so
far as the growing effectiveness of the Gestapo helped produce compliance,
the space for resistance was reduced.

3. TERROR, FORCE, 'BLIND OBEDIENCE', OPPORTUNISM

Much has been made in the literature of the general atmosphere of terror
and fear faced by contemporaries inside Nazi Germany. According to many
reports, from the first days of the 'new order' brutality was applied against
actual and potential enemies, not without considerable effect even on people
not personally at risk. William Allen states that 'in the atmosphere of terror,
even people who were friends' concluded that they had to betray each other
to survive.[38] He also points out the significance of the 'social reinforcement
of the terror system'—how people such as the (non-Nazi) school headmaster
began, without ever having been ordered to do so, to encourage changes in
students' behaviour more appropriate to the new state of affairs.[39] Much more
was involved than blind obedience, and even when people were ordered to
desist from giving knowingly false tip-offs to the Gestapo—in order, for
example, to get one's spouse placed in custody to obtain a more favourable
divorce settlement—such instrumental use of the police persisted.

Quite apart from the need to explore how the propensity ever arose for
people such as the school headmaster to become unofficial enforcers, the
motivation cannot be reduced to fear, as is often done (although not by Allen).
It is also misleading to mention only negative factors, because more positive
ones were also at work. The 'legal' façade surrounding the seizure of power
no doubt led many law-abiding citizens, out of respect for the legal norms, to
comply. Because the take-over was not patently illegal many could choose to
ignore its revolutionary character, especially after the radicals were subdued
following the purge in June 1934. That purge not only 'offered the Nazi
leadership a belated opportunity to rediscover its moral standards', as Richard
Bessel maintains, but beyond that allowed the 'unpolitical German' to see
'National Socialist institutions as a constituent part of his bourgeois normality'.[40] But even before the so-called 'night of the long knives' put an end to
Storm-trooper radicalism, the regime was welcomed by many.

[37] Barrington Moore, jun., *Injustice: The Social Bases of Obedience and Revolt* (White Plains, NY, 1978), 482.
[38] William Sheridan Allen, *The Nazi Seizure of Power: The Experience of a Single German Town 1922–1945*, rev. edn. (New York, 1984), 189.
[39] Ibid. 157.
[40] Richard Bessel, *Political Violence and the Rise of Nazism: The Storm Troopers in Eastern Germany 1925–1934* (New Haven, 1984), 139; cf. p. 140.

Hans Bernd Gisevius, a member of the Gestapo in 1933, later recollected that many people fell in line of their own acord: 'There was, to be sure, a tremendous amount of bitterness and distrust, and frequently open revolt appeared. But there was at least an equal amount of enthusiasm and devotion, not to say fanaticism. Seldom had a nation so readily surrendered all its rights and liberties as did ours in those first hopeful, intoxicated months of the new millennium.'[41] What struck him most forcefully was what he called 'individual *Gleichschaltung*', by which he meant a kind of willing self-integration into the new system. 'Not one of these zealots would confess to another whether his principal motive was idealism or opportunism. But all of them understood that they could no longer hang back.'[42] As Fritz Stern rightly points out, in an essay suggestively entitled 'National Socialism as Temptation', it is a mistake to think that the chief motive was opportunism when the 'voluntary, preemptive acceptance of the conformity ordered or expected by the regime' grew 'out of a whole range of motives'.[43]

Equal care should be taken to avoid placing too much weight on the use of compulsion or force. A modern industrial society as complex as Germany's cannot be enslaved entirely by 'force'. For Michel Foucault

the exercise of power is not violence; nor is it consent which, implicitly, is renewable. It is a total structure of actions brought to bear upon possible actions; it incites, it induces, it seduces, it makes easier or more difficult; in the extreme it constrains or forbids absolutely; it is nevertheless always a way of acting upon an acting subject or acting subjects by virtue of their acting or being capable of actions. A set of actions upon other actions.

The exercise of power therefore presupposes the existence of some degree of individual freedom.[44] He adds that while Nazi Germany suffered from a 'disease of power', that is, experienced a pathological form of power-relations, we should be aware that, notwithstanding its historical uniqueness, it was 'not quite original' but 'used and extended mechanisms already present in most other societies'. Beyond that, in spite of its 'own internal madness', it 'used to a large extent the ideas and devices of our own political rationality'.[45]

In Hitler's Germany a combination of positive and negative factors, continuities and discontinuities, contributed to the creation of a 'disciplined' or

---

[41] Hans Bernd Gisevius, *To the Bitter End*, trans. R. and C. Winstone (London, 1948), 101–2.

[42] Ibid. 105.

[43] The article is in his *Dreams and Delusions: The Drama of German History* (New York, 1987) 169–170.

[44] Michel Foucault, 'The Subject and Power', in Hubert L. Dreyfus and Paul Rabinow, *Michel Foucault: Beyond Structuralism and Hermeneutics*, 2nd edn. (Chicago, 1983), 220.

[45] Ibid. 209.

'carceral' society.[46] Not all members of such a society will lend a hand in policing, nor is it necessary that all of them do so.

4. ENFORCING POLICY

The term 'enforce' carries with it a wide range of lexical meanings, including 'urge, press home (argument, demand); impose (action, conduct, *(up)on* person etc.); compel observance of (law etc.)'.[47] The Gestapo certainly urged, imposed, and compelled, and also elicited much co-operation. The ways in which it proved structurally possible to enforce racial policy are the focus of this study.

The notion of 'policy-enforcement' (rather than 'law-enforcement') is used primarily because institutions such as the Gestapo and even the NSDAP took it upon themselves to enforce not merely laws (or decrees and ordinances), but the far broader range of behaviour thought by them to fall outside the spirit or ideology of the 'new order'.[48] For example, the Gestapo sought to enforce the anti-Semitic laws and various regulations, but also pursued a whole range of behaviour (such as 'friendship towards the Jews') made formally illegal only later.[49] Such deviations would constitute apparent non-acceptance of Nazi 'policies concerning the Jews' or *Judenpolitik*.

At the street level, effective enforcement required a minimal degree of popular co-operation. It was quite beside the point to ascertain whether the people who provided information to the Gestapo, the denouncers or informers, agreed with the decisions taken at the highest level (part of the time, or at all), let alone whether they shared their leaders' political or ideological views. Thus, it is important for historians to distinguish the regime's popularity or acclaim from the question of the degree to which it was actively or passively supported. Although many citizens, especially in the working class and/or Catholic-peasant milieux, might have been happy to see Hitler ousted, especially after the opening of hostilities against the Soviet Union, the regime's efforts in enforcing its racial policies to separate Jews from non-Jews (to keep to this example) were never jeopardized.

As will become clear, the regime was less dependent than one might have

---

[46] See Michel Foucault, *Discipline and Punish: The Birth of the Prison*, trans. A. Sheridan (New York, 1979), 293ff. For an analysis of the rise of the police see his 'Politics and Reason' in *Michel Foucault: Politics, Philosophy, Culture. Interviews and Other Writings 1977–1984*, ed. Lawrence D. Kritzman (New York, 1988), 58ff. Still useful is Georg Rusche and Otto Kirchheimer, *Punishment and Social Structure* (1939; New York, 1968), 177ff.

[47] *The Concise Oxford Dictionary*, 7th edn. (Oxford, 1982), 319.

[48] I have discussed further issues in 'Enforcing Racial Policy in Nazi Germany', a paper to be published in Thomas Childers and Jane Caplan (eds.), *Re-Evaluating the 'Third Reich': Interpretations and Debates* (New York: Holmes and Meier, forthcoming). Elton, 83ff., shows how a very broad notion of 'policy' was enforced earlier.

[49] Peukert, *Volksgenossen*, 221ff.

expected on an enthusiastic reception of the 'new order' by all, or even most, citizens. A crucial factor in the enforcement process was not the 'popularity' of the system; German society as a whole did not need to become thoroughly National Socialist, anti-Semitic, or racist. What was required was that the regime establish the official 'line', elicit co-operation, and act relentlessly on the basis of information received.

5. WHAT THE BOOK DOES NOT DO

A word needs also to be said about what the book does *not* do. It does not catalogue the many and various crimes, recounts little about the torture and beating inflicted on some who fell into the hands of the state police, and does not provide a detailed institutional history of the Gestapo as such. The book has something to say about arbitrary arrest and 'protective custody' (*Schutzhaft*), which provided the Gestapo with virtually unlimited powers of arrest and confinement, for it was precisely such sanctions that set the Gestapo apart from all earlier political police in Germany. The book deals with a small part of the Gestapo's full work-load. Little is said about the deportations and the death camps. The Gestapo came to concern itself with so many issues that no single monograph can deal adequately with all of them. The book is not a 'history of everyday life' if one understands by that term a reconstruction of the experiences of the people as they themselves would have understood them. I agree with Jürgen Kocka that 'it simply is insufficient to reconstruct experiences', a goal set by many authors in the studies of 'everyday life'; 'experiences can be false', he continued. 'Imagine if one were to reconstruct the experiences of peasants in the 1880s; they were sincere anti-Semites; I have not understood the phenomenon through reconstructing these experiences.' In order to achieve understanding, it is necessary to go beyond the immediate environment, to conduct research into numerous aspects of the problem 'totally hidden from the poor peasant'.[50]

[50] See Jürgen Kocka's remarks at the meetings whose transactions are printed in *Alltagsgeschichte der NS-Zeit: Neue Perspektive oder Trivialisierung? Kolloquien des Instituts für Zeitgeschichte* (Munich, 1984), 53–4. Cf. Michael H. Kater, 'Begrifflichkeit und Historie: 'Alltag', 'Neokonservatismus' und 'Judenfrage' als Themen einer NS-bezogenen Sozialgeschichtsschreibung', *Archiv für Sozialgeschichte*, 23 (1983), 688–705, and his 'Nazism and the Third Reich in Recent Historiography', *Canadian Journal of History*, 20 (1985), 85 ff. See the special issue of the *New German Critique*, 44 (Spring–Summer 1988) on the Historikerstreit, especially the article by Mary Nolan, 'The *Historikerstreit* and Social History', pp. 51–80; she is critical of approaches that emphasize the role of 'indifference or even opposition to the regime's racial policies' as decisive factors in the persecution of the Jews because of the tendency to 'ignore the pervasiveness of complicity' (p. 80). She is also right to insist that alternative approaches, such as the one adopted in this book, by no means represent 'a return to crude theories of collective guilt. Rather, they offer a way to link normality and terror, supporter/resister and victim, everyday life and Auschwitz.' I explore these issues in a paper entitled '"A Monstrous Uneasiness": Citizen Participation and Persecution of the Jews in Nazi Germany' for a conference on 'Lessons and Legacies: The Meaning of the Holocaust in a Changing World' at Northwestern University, November 1989. The transactions, edited by Peter Hayes, are to be published.

Many things were also hidden from citizens of Nazi Germany; yet the actions of some of these same citizens made possible the very tyranny under which they suffered. This is what the historian must recall and try to understand.

6. DOCUMENTARY SOURCES AND MATERIALS

The main materials drawn on in the book are Gestapo case-files. These were created by the police whenever a person was brought to their attention. Some of the files contain an insignificant half-sheet of paper, others run to hundreds of pages; some are very revealing, many of no apparent use to the historian. At best, they bring the study of Nazi Germany down to the grass roots, and the intentions of the leaders—whether Hitler as policy-maker or Himmler as chief of the German police—are left behind in the distant capital city. The files give clues about what the regime could actually accomplish, implement, or enforce out in the provinces. They are excellent sources for a study of the dynamic interaction between police, people, and policy. The strengths and weaknesses of these sources are discussed below, but here it can be said that, while flawed, they have not been laundered (that is, selectively cleansed of certain kinds of information).

Everywhere in Germany these materials were destroyed, with just two major exceptions; 19,000 or so survived for the small city of Würzburg, with its surrounding province of Lower Franconia, Bavaria. It is primarily these sources that are explored in detail, but the study also makes selective use of some of the 70,000 files that survive for Düsseldorf and the areas under its control. These rare materials are, to reiterate, heterogeneous and uneven. One starting-point for a study of them is the recent work on the social history of the Düsseldorf Gestapo by the late Reinhard Mann. The posthumous publication of a number of his articles and papers, even though some of them are bare sketches and not without weaknesses, makes available to a wider audience at least some of the efforts he made to quantify the workings of the Gestapo.[51]

The Gestapo materials from Würzburg and Düsseldorf permit some interesting comparisons. While it might be perfectly justified to maintain that the pattern was slightly different elsewhere, and that Würzburg and Lower Franconia or the Government District of Düsseldorf were 'exceptional', it is fortuitous that neither was a hotbed of Nazism. Since most of the sources elsewhere were distroyed there is no ultimate way to ascertain the degree of difference and similarity.

---

[51] Reinhard Mann, *Protest und Kontrolle im Dritten Reich: Nationalsozialistische Herrschaft im Alltag einer rheinischen Großstadt* (Frankfurt, 1987). Additional Gestapo case-files exist in the State Archive (LA Speyer) but cannot at present be used as they are unsorted. I understand that some case-files also survived for Stettin (Szczecin), and are presumably located in Poland.

Besides the Gestapo case-files, the study utilizes other kinds of Gestapo fragments that have come to light from around the country, and the whole range of national, regional, and local records. In addition, it draws upon the well-known underground records of the illegal SPD, the Sopade reports, as well as surveys of opinion and mood composed for the war-years by the Security Service (SD). Material from the post-war trials, especially from the International Military Tribunal held in Nuremberg, is utilized as well. Finally, much use has been made of autobiographies and diaries.

For a number of reasons the book makes little use of interviews with the survivors of persecution, for that would be a separate project in its own right. As noted above, the book does not set out to reconstruct their experiences in the manner of a 'history of everyday life'. Moreover, the people of the time would have had difficulty recounting how the surveillance and terror system worked, not least because the mystery and uncertainty about the system was deliberately exploited by the Gestapo.

7. THE BOOK'S ORGANIZATION

Part I deals with the evolution of the Gestapo. The first chapter indicates some of the continuities and discontinuities from earlier periods. The limits and possibilities of the new police powers and expanding spheres of activity are also discussed. Once the 'nationalization' of the political police has been clarified, the next chapter moves to the local level, for that is where routine enforcement takes place. It examines the local operation of the political police, and reveals its set-up and the people who worked for it. Because the Gestapo headed an extensive police network beyond the Gestapo proper, it is important to deal with this topic. It needs to be said that not only does the history of the Gestapo remain to be written, but much more work is needed on the social history of other elements in the police network at whose head it stood, such as the Security Service (Sicherheitsdienst), the Criminal Police (Kriminal-Polizei or Kripo), and even the ordinary uniformed police (Ordnungspolizei and its subsidiary part, the Schutzpolizei or Schupo). Even the Nazi Party's functioning as a local political watch-dog after 1933 requires more research.

Part II turns to German society, and to the concrete social context in which policing occurred. The book's geographical emphasis is the Bavarian region around the city of Würzburg, Lower Franconia, an area unique and exceptional in many ways—as are all the regions across the country. Chapters 3 and 4 discuss the problem of the representativeness of the area by drawing upon sources from similar and contrasting areas within Bavaria and across Germany, and by utilizing as wide a range of sources as possible. Given the complexity of German society, it is clear that most communities have specific structures (the urban–rural mix, or the industrial–agrarian one) and unique cultural characteristics (especially those of religion, attitudes to the central government, the degree of visibility of racial minorities) which influence the particular configuration of police–society relationships. The daily operation of the political police, which is tied to its local environment to some extent, was probably a little different in one area from the practice somewhere else. In Lower Franconia it would seem that the extent of co-operation attained by the Gestapo was in all likelihood towards the lower end of the spectrum rather than near the maximum which probably obtained in the Protestant parts of Bavaria, such as neighbouring Middle Franconia, centred around the city of Nuremberg.

Part III studies the enforcing of racial policy on the basis of Gestapo case-files. The transition to the examination of concrete practice at the local level is made by dealing, in Chapter 5, with what the book argues was the crucial mechanism in the routine functioning of the Gestapo, that of political denunciations or, simply stated, the provision of information or tip-offs.

Chapter 6 looks at how the Gestapo sought to enforce racial policies designed to separate Jews from non-Jews. In particular, it shows some of the ways in which the effort failed, and points to local examples of non-compliance of the racist message, even some rare heroic resistance to it.

Chapter 7 indicates that in order to overcome any such opposition or dissent, the Gestapo doubled its efforts to obtain compliance. The Gestapo interpreted its mandate in the broadest possible terms, and went about fulfilling it by applying pressure when necessary, at times by the use of extremely brutal methods. Although a reputation for brutality to some extent contributed to the effectiveness of the Gestapo, like the knowledge that anyone could be sent to a concentration camp for an indefinite period, such fears do not provide an entirely satisfactory explanation for how the Gestapo was able to carry out its mandate so 'successfully'. In the sphere of racial policies designed to isolate the Jews, policies that sought to encroach into the most private spheres of social and sexual life, the Gestapo—brutal or otherwise—was never in a position to accomplish its tasks on its own. It required the collaboration of many people in official or semi-official positions. It was also heavily dependent upon public participation in the enforcement process, specifically through the provision of information on suspected deviations from or disagreements with, the Nazi stand on the 'Jewish question'.

In Chapter 8 the emphasis shifts to the enforcement of another kind of racial policy, that aimed at Polish foreign workers, who, though considered 'racially foreign' and inferior, were brought to the Reich in ever greater numbers but rigorously segregated and, according to the letter and spirit of the law, subjected to the most radical kinds of apartheid measures. How the regime went about enforcing these policies in this area of social life helps fill out the picture of how racial policy was enforced. It goes without saying that any study of Nazi racism must deal with the persecution of the Jews. It is important to recognize that any explanation of the evolution of racial policy and its enforcement ought not to ignore the many other varieties of persecution that took place in the name of race inside Germany's borders.

As it turns out, in the last years of the Third Reich several factors combined to alter significantly the pattern of involvement of the German people in the process of enforcing racial policy inside the country, now largely aimed at the foreign workers, especially the Poles. This changing pattern of involvement, as will become clear, only serves to underline the crucial role played by ordinary citizens in the Nazi terror system.[52]

The conclusion of the book draws together the strands of the argument as set forth in each chapter. A brief epilogue outlines the results of the post-war trials of Gestapo officials and several key Nazi leaders in Würzburg and Lower Franconia.

---

[52] For an analysis of recent writing on the terror system see my 'Terror System, Racial Persecution and Resistance in Nazi Germany: Remarks on the Historiography', to be published in a special issue of *German Studies Review* (forthcoming).

I

THE GESTAPO

I

The Emergence of the Gestapo

THE Gestapo took shape in the context of a complex set of interacting social forces, personalities, and traditions.[1] Beginning in early 1933, in one state after another it was decided to tighten the organization of the police. As one telling phrase from a law of 26 April on the Prussian Gestapo stated, it was necessary 'to assure the effective battle against all endeavours directed at the existence and security of the state'.[2] Such aims were pursued vigorously and soon involved ever greater incursions by the police into the lives of citizens. The Gestapo grew unchecked not least because the definition of what constituted security and opposition was inflated and expanded beyond all previous boundaries. Legal and civil rights, which had been protected by the rule of law, were disregarded and often dissolved. Eventually, it came to function as the ultimate 'thought-police' about which rulers in earlier times with ambitions to control their subjects could only have fantasized.[3] After gradually working out spheres of influence with other organizations concerned with monitoring and controlling behaviour, the Gestapo became much more than an extension of the traditional state apparatus and enforcer of policy. At times it could become lawgiver, judge, jury, and executioner.

Like most Continental countries, Germany had a long tradition of police surveillance of political affairs. Though there had been no central control before the Nazis took over, local branches across the country had built up considerable expertise and were, by the beginning of 1933, sophisticated and highly professionalized. The hindrances which had for many years stood in the way of establishing a national political police force began to disappear during the phase immediately following Hitler's appointment, known as 'co-ordination' (Gleichschaltung). Much has been written on the upheaval, termed by one writer a 'legal revolution', because while paying lip-service to the constitution and keeping up the appearance of legality, the Nazis introduced

---

[1] See the remarks of Michel Foucault, 'Nietzsche, Genealogy, History', in Paul Rabinow (ed.), *The Foucault Reader* (New York, 1984), 83ff.

[2] Buchheim, 116.

[3] See *Runderlaß des Preuß. Ministers des Innern vom 26.4.1933*, given in full in Martin Hirsch, Diemut Majer, and Jürgen Meinck (eds.), *Recht, Verwaltung und Justiz im Nationalsozialismus: Ausgewählte Schriften, Gesetze und Gerichtsentscheidungen von 1933 bis 1945* (Cologne, 1984), 326.

[4] Bracher, *Die deutsche Diktatur*, 209ff.

a 'new regime'.[4] In a sense they did. However, this break with the past was not simply dictated to the German people by the handful at the top.

There was a remarkable degree of accommodation to the new exigencies. It needs to be remembered that the occupants of the various offices were not simply removed across the board and police headquarters turned over to the Nazis. To the extent that there was a purge of the police, as the next chapter shows, it was aimed more at the upper levels, and even there selectively, at those who failed to make adjustments to the new circumstances—in some cases at high-profile persons whose earlier political views were a clear liability. There was an important infrastructure already in place that supported the creation of a secret police. Martin Broszat, reflecting on the absence of resistance to the Nazi 'revolution', which made it unnecessary to employ massive violence to establish or maintain the 'new order', noted that the transition phase (co-ordination) took place generally so smoothly and speedily that 'often it was more a matter of accommodation than a revolutionary upheaval'.[5]

1. Political police in Europe and Germany up to 1933

The use of political police in Europe goes back at least to the French Revolution of 1789, and well beyond Germany's borders. It has been argued that policing the 'political' was invented as a result of the conjuncture of 'broad historical processes'—economic, juridico-political, and scientific—which Europe experienced in the period from the late eighteenth to the early nineteenth century.[6] For Michel Foucault it is in this period, as crime takes on an increasingly political dimension, that a 'general surveillance of the population' begins—to quote a French account from 1847, a 'silent, mysterious, unperceived vigilance...it is the eye of the government ceaselessly open and watching without distinction over all citizens, yet without subjecting them to any measure of coercion whatever... It does not need to be written into the law'.[7] Furthermore, 'the disciplining of society' since the eighteenth century should not be understood to suggest that people gradually became 'more and more obedient, nor that they set about assembling in barracks, schools, or prisons; rather that an increasingly better invigilated process of adjustment has been sought after—more and more rational and economic—between productive activities, resources of communication, and the play of power relations'.[8]

David Bayley's study of the police in Europe shows that their development was not simply the result of the growth of cities, population, industrialization,

---

[5] Broszat, *Der Staat Hitlers*, 426.
[6] Foucault, *Discipline and Punish*, 218, 273.
[7] Ibid. 280.
[8] Foucault, 'Subject and Power', 219. In 1884 a French writer noted with irony that 'the citizen is free to do whatever he likes, but under police supervision': I. Guyot, *La Police* (Paris, 1884), quoted in Tom Bowden, *Beyond the Limits of the Law* (Harmondsworth, 1978), 138.

or even 'criminality', but has more to do with political transformations, violent resistance to government, and the 'creation of new law and order tasks'.[9] The growth of 'political police' is seen as an integral part of the 'state-making' process in the modern era. Charles Tilly, in his account of France, remarks that in the course of the nineteenth century 'policing and political repression waxed and waned together'; generally revolutions were followed by increasing the number of police and expanding their budgets. 'The final effect was to lay down a uniform net of control over the entire country.[10] Still, there were enormous variations between the various European countries, in such matters as the tasks assigned the police, the national structures, nature of control over them, internal organization, role, behaviour, and public image.[11]

The evolution of the police in German lands was constrained by the late unification. However, even before 1871 the existence of local police had long been a fixture of life for most Germans, and there was a tradition of police involvement in issues well beyond concerns about public security and narrowly defined crime; as order could be disturbed by a wide variety of incidents, such as those which might arise from 'sanitation, foodstuffs, public amusements, economic regulations, information media, perhaps the maintenance of roads', and so forth, the relatively few police that existed, though spread thin, were involved in these as well.[12]

The issue of local-police powers was bound to arise in Germany with changing and conflicting expectations of the social role the police should play. How a newly created nation-state would respond was briefly discussed in the constitutional debates during the German revolution of 1848–9, when the liberal-dominated meetings voted to put control of local-police administration in the hands of the central state. The concern expressed was 'to strengthen state supervision of the villages that were too primitive to run themselves and the cities that were too complex'.[13] Nevertheless, there were some efforts to unify some aspects of police work before unification in 1871. For example, for a decade or so from the early 1850s the 'Police Association' (Polizeiverein) held regular conferences and eventually weekly exchanges of

---

[9] David H. Bayley, 'The Police and Political Development in Europe', in Charles Tilly (ed.), *The Formation of National States in Western Europe* (Princeton, 1975), 378. For a different emphasis see Clive Emsley, *Policing and its Context 1750–1870 (London, 1983), 162.
[10] Charles Tilly, *The Contentious French: Four Centuries of Popular Struggle* (Cambridge, Mass., 1986), 289.
[11] See the contrasts summarized in Bayley, 341.
[12] Mack Walker, *German Home Towns: Community, State, and General Estate 1648–1871* (Ithaca, 1971), 45–6. Reinhard Koselleck, *Preußen zwischen Reform und Revolution* (Stuttgart, 1975), 462, claims that in Prussia after 1815 'effective police control of everyday life' did not exist, for there were too few in the police. In the face of rising population, social unrest, poverty, and so on, demands were made for increases but these were rejected by the ministry.
[13] Walker, 381.

information.[14] However, the local particularism that survived the revolution continued to hold suspect any scheme to introduce a centralized police power. For the most part such powers remained with local states before and even after unification.

The instructions issued to the mid-century political police forces which sprang up nearly everywhere across the country have a twentieth-century ring to them. For example, in 1848, even before the outbreak of revolution in that year, King Ludwig I in Bavaria ordered Munich's police to put public opinion under surveillance—especially in the public houses. His Ministry of the Interior formalized and generalized that demand in March and instructed the main administrative governors in the monarchy henceforth to insist that 'the most exact continuous reconnaissance' be kept 'on the general mood and attitude of the people in the larger and smaller cities as well as in the countryside'.[15] By August 1849 local administrators were instructed to fill out a detailed questionnaire on the political behaviour of the people in their district. In twelve separate categories they were to compose monthly reports on political, social, and economic developments; soon more specific political questions were added, for example on attitudes to the person of the king and politics in general, and on the existence of democratic organizations or newspapers.[16]

Special sections in the bigger municipal police forces devoted to 'politics' were gradually created across the country from mid-century. Especially in the major centres they were highly sensitive and active, keeping a close tab on the most innocuous kinds of public activities that might somehow be deemed 'political'. In Bismarck's and Wilhelm's Germany the state was endowed with increased powers and, under special legislation from time to time (such as that aimed at the Social Democratic Party, the SPD), could prosecute 'political' criminality in the name of staving off revolution. While the variously named Politische Polizei (political police) remained largely decentralized, local organizations could act in concert and everywhere pressed their vigilance on the public.

In Imperial Germany surveillance of broadly defined political behaviour, including attitudes, became a responsibility of an increasing number of professionally trained police officials.[17] Just how far these officials were prepared to interpret their tasks may be gathered from the kinds of organizations

---

[14] Wolfram Siemann, *'Deutschlands Ruhe, Sicherheit und Ordnung': Die Anfänge der politischen Polizei 1806–1866* (Tübingen, 1985), 254ff.

[15] Ibid. 429.

[16] Ibid. 429–30. See also Hermann Reiter, *Die Revolution von 1848/49 in Altbayern: Ihre sozialen und mentalen Voraussetzungen und ihr Verlauf* (Munich, 1983), 5ff.

[17] For background to the professionalization of the political police in each German state see Siemann, 41ff. For remarks on the poor quality of police in Germany before 1848 see Richard Tilly in Charles, Louse, and Richard Tilly, *The Rebellious Century 1830–1930* (Cambridge, Mass., 1975), 218ff.

dutifully watched by the Hamburg political police before 1918. In this liberal and semi-independent 'city-state' of Hamburg, middle-class organizations such as the 'Fighting Community against Department Stores and Consumer Co-operatives' and the 'League for the Introduction of the Eight-o'Clock Closing in Retail Outlets' were routinely watched.

There was surveillance of all political parties and semi-political associations, and separate files were drawn up on their leading personalities. Even obscure and marginal politicians might end up with a very large file which recorded the details of their public lives (for the most part their private affairs were not of concern). The Socialists as the most radical party of the day were subject to particularly close scrutiny, but the Hamburg 'Association for the Fighting of Social Democracy' had files established on it as well.[18] The SPD continued to be watched even after 1918, when one of its members was President and another the Chancellor of the new Weimar Republic. The files of the Hamburg police run to many thousands of volumes. Similar vigilance by specific political police forces appears to have existed in most German states before 1918, although no national umbrella organization with any authority was in place. Instead, each state continued to guard its independence in police affairs as a kind of residual of German particularism. No doubt the police of the major centres, notably Berlin, played a dominant role because of the superior resources—expertise, money, and information—at its disposal.

The Weimar Republic, founded at the end of the war, did not create a new national police force, one it might have used to fight the many declared enemies, some of whom were on the Right and some on the Left. And even though the new 'insiders' had only recently suffered at the hands of a system of justice which had them as 'outsiders', a decision was taken not to tamper with the 'independence' of judges who had been appointed in the Kaiser's day.[19]

As is well known, the reluctant revolutionaries were loath to interfere with the law. In Berlin itself the Socialists 'officially' got rid of the political police, but, sensing that such an institution was needed to track the enemies of the new regime, they soon established a force under a new name: Department IA (in place of the older Political Department V). Jurisdiction of the new force did not extend beyond Prussia. Given the social, economic, and political instability of the Weimar Republic, it comes as no surprise that the surveillance by the police of political matters was 'vastly extended' after 1918 in Berlin. In most German states a parallel process took place, and for the

---

[18] For examples of the extensiveness of the political police see Robert Gellately, *The Politics of Economic Despair: Shopkeepers and German Politics, 1890–1914* (London, 1974), and Dirk Stegmann, *Die Erben Bismarcks: Parteien und Verbände in der Spätphase des Wilhelminishen Deutschlands* (Cologne, 1970).

[19] See Heinrich Hannover and Elisabeth Hannover-Drück, *Politische Justiz 1918–1933* (Bornheim-Merten, 1987), 21ff.

same reasons. There were more 'enemies' of the state than ever before and the atmosphere was marked by *putsch* attempts, strikes, riots, even foreign invasions, not to say by massive economic and social catastrophe.[20]

But despite this more or less covert reliance on the political police, the Weimar Republic also felt it had to live up to its own self-image as a highly democratic regime. It seemed in keeping with the new spirit that the police be kept under stricter control. There were a number of occasions, such as Hitler's abortive *putsch* attempt in 1923, when the lack of authority at the centre seemed nearly to herald the breaking up of the German state. In that context the enemies of Weimar could find support for their contention that one of its fundamental weaknesses was the nearly complete absence of any national police authority. There was a Reich Public Prosecutor, to be sure, but he could take action only through the individual prosecutors of the various states and their subsidiary organs.[21] The tasks of keeping track of the numerous extremist groups also lay to a large extent in the individual component states. While some negotiations reached agreements in the area of criminal law which pertained to the country as a whole, there was no central control and no unification of the police.

Dealing with the political police was complicated because of the marked political differences between the major states. There was, for example, 'red' Prussia, considered radical because of the large Socialist parliamentary representation and because of its 'red' capital, Berlin. At the other end of the political spectrum there was 'blue' Bavaria, conservative, royalist, and Catholic. Most of the states between these two extremes guarded their jurisdictions jealously and viewed suggestions for a central police authority with suspicion. Such a national body could not function without the necessary local infrastructure, and attempts at centralization failed.[22]

2. BURNING OF THE REICHSTAG AND EMERGENCY DECREES OF 1933

The crucial events that culminated in the emergence of the Gestapo began with the burning of the Reichstag building on 27 February 1933. The next day the so-called Reichstag-fire decree 'suspended until further notice' the guarantees of personal liberty as stipulated in the Weimar constitution.

[20] Hsi-Huey Liang, *The Berlin Police Force in the Weimar Republic* (Berkeley, 1970), 6. For an introduction to Bavaria see Johannes Schwarze, *Die bayerische Polizei und ihre historische Funktion bei der Aufrechterhaltung der öffentlichen Sicherheit in Bayern von 1919–1933* (Munich, 1977), 16ff.

[21] See Hans Mommsen, 'The Reichstag Fire and its Political Consequences', in Hajo Holborn (ed.), *Republic to Reich: The Making of the Nazi Revolution* (New York, 1973), 185.

[22] For Prussia see Christoph Graf, *Politische Polizei zwischen Demokratie und Diktatur* (Berlin, 1983), 5ff.; for Bavaria see Shlomo Aronson, *Reinhard Heydrich und die Frühgeschichte von Gestapo und SD* (Stuttgart, 1971), 94ff.

Section 2 of the decree made it possible for the national government to abolish the independence of the federal states and to begin introducing its appointees into the police and justice systems. Among other things, the decree gave the police the right to issue detention orders to hold suspects in 'protective custody', that is, without due process. The decree suspended freedom of speech, of the press, of assembly and association, and permitted violations of the privacy of postal, telegraphic, and telephone communications. Personal privacy and property rights were encroached upon when the police were given permission to exceed previous legal limits on house-searches and confiscations.[23]

There is continuing controversy over whether the Nazis set fire to the parliament buildings as part of a systematic and well-considered plan, or exploited a situation not of their own making, or just fumbled their way forward. However, there is little dispute about the net effect of the emergency decrees promulgated as a result of the fire.[24] Along with several earlier and additional follow-up measures decreed in short order (which made much more drastic punishments possible) they constituted a 'kind of *coup d'état*' and introduced into Germany the novel condition of 'permanent emergency' which lasted until 1945.[25] Though presented politically as necessary to fight Communism, the decrees provided 'the formal basis for the Lawless State [*Unrechtsstaat*]'.[26] The preamble to the measure which spoke of an alleged Communist threat 'without doubt legitimized' the state of 'permanent emergency' with the public at large, at least for the anti-Communist majority.[27]

The Reichstag-fire decrees had a dramatic effect on the formal-institutional evolution of the political police because they provided a new 'legal' basis. The developments which followed those measures need to be examined carefully. It is, however, important to keep clearly in view the ways in which the public responded in the circumstances because the participation, compliance, or accommodation of ordinary citizens plays such an important role in the creation of the 'police state'. Popular anxiety about Communist subversion, as well as a desire to see the end of what remained of the hated Weimar Republic, drew attention away from the arbitrary arrests and beatings, as well as the first 'wild' concentration camps established around the country in the days and weeks following the burning of the Reichstag.

In the campaign for what would be the last even remotely free elections of

---

[23] See Hirsch, Majer, and Meinck, 89–90.
[24] See Mommsen, 'Reichstag Fire', 130ff.
[25] Ibid. 199; see also Karl Dietrich Bracher, 'Stufen der Machtergreifung', in Karl Dietrich Bracher, Wolfgang Sauer, and Gerhard Schulz, *Die Nationalsozialistische Machtergreifung: Studien zur Errichtung des totalitären Herrschaftssystems in Deutschland 1933/34* (Cologne, 1962), 82–8.
[26] Aronson, 66.
[27] Ibid. On the popularity of anti-Communism see Timothy W. Mason, 'The Third Reich and the German Left: Persecution and Resistance', in Hedley Bull (ed.), *The Challenge of the Third Reich* (Oxford, 1986), 99.

5 March, the Nazis conducted what was termed a 'national uprising'; in its name they terrorized their opponents, made much of the threat from the Left, and appealed to the people to give Hitler a chance. As he had promised repeatedly, 'heads were rolling', as the state went after the Communists and others allegedly representing a danger to the nation. 'Brutality and repression in the interests of "peace and order"' increased Hitler's popularity and came to play an important part in the 'Hitler myth'.[28]

3. FROM SECRET POLICE TO THE GESTAPO LAWS OF 1936

From the perspective of 1936 a prominent official in the Berlin headquarters of the Gestapo could reflect on what he considered to have been the decisive change which resulted from the Reichstag-fire decree as follows:

Whereas hitherto the police, under paragraphs 112ff. of the Code of Criminal Procedure, could only make arrests as auxiliaries of the Public Prosecutor when he was instituting criminal proceedings, or could under certain conditions . . . take people briefly into police custody, they were now entitled, when combating subversive activities, to use the most effective means against enemies of the state—deprivation of freedom in the form of protective custody.[29]

The notion of 'protective custody' (*Schutzhaft*) was not without precedent in Germany even before 1914, although then it was designed to protect someone from a danger, such as being mobbed. That definition was soon broadened, but when applied, for example, towards the end of the Weimar days, the suspect person was to be released within twenty-four hours or brought before a judge. The concept was not specifically mentioned in the so-called Reichstag-fire decree, but the suspension of the legal right to personal freedom, central to the decree, opened the way for police to arrest and detain any suspect deemed a 'threat' to the state. In the absence of legal recourse, and intimately linked to the formation of the burgeoning concentration-camp system, this form of custody could easily be misused. Unlike imprisonment following judicial procedures or the police detention orders (limited in time), 'protective custody' could amount to an unlimited incarceration without trial. It was designed, moreover, not simply to deal with indictable offences, but also to be used in a preventive fashion, that is, to undermine 'threats from subversive elements' before they materialized.[30] The ability to order 'protective custody' was to become an extremely effective and important weapon in the hands of the Gestapo, one that set the Nazi police clearly apart from earlier periods.

---

[28] Kershaw, *The 'Hitler Myth'*, 53.
[29] Hans Tesmer of the Gestapo, quoted in Martin Broszat, 'Nationalsozialistische Konzentrationslager 1933–1945', in Buchheim *et al.*, ii. 11.
[30] Ibid. 11–13.

(a) Creation of the Gestapo in Prussia

Political police forces existed in most of the federal German states before 1933, so that the Gestapo did not have to be created from scratch, but resulted from a process of modification and transformation. The first organization explicitly called the Secret State Police, or Gestapo, was created by Hermann Göring in early 1933, in part to hold his own in the power-struggles inside the Nazi leadership, and also to deal with political opponents, especially the Communists. He was in an advantageous position to create a new political police because, as the Prussian Minister of the Interior, he was effectively in charge of Prussia's police. Göring found Rudolf Diels, a young and ambitious police official, and put him in charge of Department (Abteilung) IA of the Prussian Police. Diels, who had already ingratiated himself to Göring, notably by providing him with secret information on political enemies, was ordered at the end of January 1933 to begin a systematic search for Communist Party functionaries. Within the Berlin Police Presidency Diels created a special department 'For the Fight against Communism'.[31] At the beginning of May this department and the remainder of what had been Department IA moved into what would become the infamous No. 8 Prinz Albrecht Strasse near the government quarter of Berlin.[32]

'In order to assure the effective struggle against all of the efforts directed against the existence and security of the state', a new organization was created on 26 April 1933 by a special law for the establishment of a Secret State Police Office (Gestapa). The law was designed to provide the necessary preconditions for speedy and successful results.[33] By the end of that month Diels was effectively in charge, and spread the organizational network all over Prussia from Berlin headquarters.[34]

Another important organizational innovation was the creation in each Government District (Regierungsbezirk) of regional Secret State Police posts (Staatspolizeistellen, usually shortened to 'Stapostellen'), so that Berlin Gestapo headquarters spread its control to the rest of Prussia, the largest state in the country. A law of 30 November 1933 freed the Gestapo from the jurisdiction of the Prussian Minister of the Interior and gave local Gestapo posts, henceforth responsible to Berlin, a considerable degree of independence from the control of traditional police or administrative authorities. A significant step towards the extension of Gestapo competence and centralization had been taken, and it was well on the way to becoming an identifiable

---

[31] Rudolf Diels, *Lucifer ante Portas. . . . Es spricht der erste Chef der Gestapo* (Stuttgart, 1950), 166, Graf, 120.

[32] See Rürup (ed.), 30ff., and Tuchel and Schattenfroh, 63ff. For an introduction to Göring see Overy, *Goering*, 22ff.

[33] For a copy of the law see Hirsch, Majer, and Meinck (eds.), 326–7; also IMT xxix. 250–1, doc. PS 2104.

[34] See esp. the biography in Graf, p. 230.

institution. Any business that touched on 'the political' came under its aegis.[35] Local police were in effect subordinated, for they were to follow instructions issued from Berlin. The significance of this last point would later become clearer: in effect members of the Gestapo would operate as high-level officials who could commandeer such assistance as was required to carry out specific tasks.[36]

Furthermore, these new laws not only removed the Gestapo from the administration of traditional police authority but gave it a role no political police had hitherto performed in Prussia or anywhere else in Germany. Nevertheless, the second law left important issues unsettled so that it later proved necessary to add various provisions. Since some of these cancelled each other out, only the net results need be mentioned. Local Stapostellen were in the future to become 'independent organs of the Gestapo', that is to say, they were to sever ties with local/regional state authorities. Senior appointments were to be made from Berlin. Of course co-operation with the regular local administrative officials was to be continued. Yet, with the measures taken as of 8 March 1934 'the Prussian Gestapo with all its ramifications was now divorced from the rest of state administration' and had formally become an independent body.[37]

Göring remained the nominal head of the Gestapo until 1936, but already in 1934, as it grew stronger, he began to lose control. In January 1934 Prussia's police as a whole were subordinated to the Reich, and by 20 April, when Himmler was named Prussian deputy chief and inspector of the Prussian police, and (two days later) Heydrich became chief of the Prussian Gestapa, a separate Prussian police ceased to exist. Rivalries and conflicts continued within the organization, but it was nevertheless well on the way to becoming a crucial component of the dictatorship, especially because these two ambitious leaders had already established their control over the SS as well as the political police elsewhere in the country. Apart from Prussia and Berlin, important developments affecting the shape of the Secret Police during the early phase took place in Bavaria.

---

[35] See Buchheim, 38–40. In 1935 Werner Best commented that 'the Gestapo is an independent branch of the internal administration' (quoted by Buchheim, 40). Hans Bernd Gisevius said that from the point of view of the police system it was 'nonsense' to separate the Gestapo from the criminal and order police. See his testimony in IMT xii. 171.

[36] See the detailed analysis in Graf, 139ff. For the law of 30 Nov. 1933 see IMT xxix. 251–2, doc. PS 2105.

[37] Graf, 144. For the law of 8 Mar. 1934 see IMT xxix. 258–69, doc. PS 2113. Cf. the testimony of Gisevius, ibid. xii. 173.

(b) Creation of the Gestapo in Bavaria

The transformation of the political police in Bavaria followed a pattern broadly similar to that in Prussia, although there were important differences. The changes were effected in Bavaria as part of the co-ordination, or Nazification, of the state after the appointment of Hitler and in the days following the Reichstag fire. Because of the central importance of Bavaria to the present study, a brief word needs to be said about the ways in which the National Socialists 'seized' power there.

The 'seizure of power' in Bavaria

Even after Hitler was appointed Chancellor, and backed by the considerable powers conferred by the Reichstag-fire decrees, the Nazis were unable to win the nation-wide majority they had hoped for in the elections of 5 March 1933. Bavaria as a whole voted within a point (43.1 per cent in favour) of the national figure (43.9 per cent). But inside Bavaria there was considerable fluctuation in the support, with, for example, largely Protestant Upper and Middle Franconia voting respectively for the Nazis at 48.7 and 51.6 per cent, while the three districts with the highest percentage of Catholics gave the lower percentage of votes to the Nazis.[38]

The Bavarian government did what it could to resist the usurping of its powers by the national government, which was bent on centralizing power in its own hands and ending 'particularism' once and for all. Even before the March elections the emergency decrees made it possible for Berlin to 'take over the powers of the supreme authority' in states where it was considered 'necessary for the restoration of public security and order'.[39] Such open-ended provisions were bound to cause considerable anxiety in the south of Germany, with its traditional suspicion of Prussia and Berlin. During Hitler's interview with Bavarian Prime Minister Heinrich Held, on 1 March 1933—just before the March elections—the new Chancellor said he had no intention of intervening in Bavaria by (for example) taking over the police authority (as he would do in Hamburg, Bremen, Lübeck, and Hesse, between 5 and 7 March).[40] In the wake of the election, which did not settle matters one way or the other, Nazis in Munich, as in other parts of Germany, decided to treat the results as a victory and moved to take power.

At a meeting with Held on 9 March 1933, the head of the SA, Ernst Röhm, Gauleiter Adolf Wagner, and Himmler demanded that he agree to appoint General Ritter von Epp as Federal Commissar for Bavaria. Outside Held's headquarters the SA was threatening to erupt in violence; these were scenes

---

[38] See tables VI and VII in Kershaw, *Popular Opinion*, 24–5.

[39] Hirsch, Majer, and Meinck (eds.), 89.

[40] Geoffrey Pridham, *Hitler's Rise to Power: The Nazi Movement in Bavaria 1923–33* (London, 1973), 302. For a copy of the Hitler–Held discussions see Falk Wiesemann, *Die Vorgeschichte der nationalsozialistischen Machtübernahme in Bayern 1932/1933* (Berlin, 1975), 294ff.

reminiscent of the beer-hall *putsch* of November 1923, when Hitler and a
motley group of Nazis and allies sought to take power in Bavaria by force.
There were important differences the second time round, not least the existence of the Reichstag-fire decree, which could be readily applied to any local
situation threatening 'law and order'. Arbitrary interference in states' rights
by a determined Hitler government could not be stopped.

Bavarian Prime Minister Held made pre-emptive strikes of his own against
the Communists in Bavaria to prove that he had the situation in hand, and
appealed to President Hindenburg and Chancellor Hitler, but to no avail. By
the end of 9 March Held passed over the reins of power to Epp, who named
Wagner his Interior Commissar, gave Himmler the job as Commissar of the
Munich Police Presidium, and Hans Frank that of Minister of Justice. Nazis
had the strategically important positions and commenced immediately to
organize the terror.[41]

Across Bavaria, very much as elsewhere, local 'seizures of power' 'used the
tactic of pushing legally elected mayors out of office, accompanied by force,
or rumor of force, from assembled SA men. With a pseudo-legality provided
by Berlin, plus local NS will and action, the representatives of the old order
left protesting, but they did leave.'[42] There was less uniformity in localities
across Bavaria than such a statement might indicate. There were marked
contrasts from place to place in the political landscape. Districts with a
tradition of support for National Socialism—such as Middle Franconia—
reacted differently from places more reticent in their support. The smoothness
of the transition also depended on local Nazi attitudes and the willingness of
mayoral incumbents to leave. Strong-arm tactics and 'spontaneous' violence
from below were also used, approaches which served to intimidate opponents
'by adding to the atmosphere of fear necessary' for their suppression, which
in turn 'served the purpose of the party leadership for a while'.[43] In this
context it is important to look at the role of the SA in the co-ordination of
Bavaria, and then examine the less ostentatious manner in which the political
police were given vastly new powers in that state.

SA violence and its role in 'co-ordination'

The terror inflicted by the Storm-troopers (the Sturmabeilung or SA, sometimes called the 'Brownshirts') and SS (Schutzstaffel), Himmler's élite black-
shirted corps) in the early months of the Nazi regime served to intensify
the atmosphere of fear which accompanied the emergence of the Gestapo.
Disturbances were deliberately created and anxiety levels raised, and such
orchestrated scenarios were used as pretexts by Nazi leaders to 're-establish'
order. The climate was deliberately made more oppressive in the months

---

[41] For the background see Wiesemann, 272ff.
[42] Edward N. Peterson, *The Limits of Hitler's Power* (Princeton, 1969), 159.
[43] Pridham, 312.

immediately following Hitler's appointment and the burning of the Reichstag, as Germany was torn apart by violence inflicted particularly by the SA and to a lesser extent by the SS. These actions created both a massive number of new places of incarceration—the concentration camps—and, arguably, the condition for a general awareness of the unspeakable cruelties committed in them. After 30 January the SA acted as vigilantes as well. Not only was there an official crackdown on 'opponents' but patently illegal terror was meted out to enemies in large doses. The existing police stood idly by, and in some areas even played an active role in the early wave of repression.

Membership in the SA increased spectacularly after the (re)appointment of Ernst Röhm in January 1931, though this expansion was more a reflection of the worsening unemployment and sense of frustration than an indication of Röhm's organizational skills and leadership abilities. In the two key national elections in 1932, as well as in the daily struggles, the SA represented the violent side of the Nazis' efforts to obtain power. It was always on the verge of getting out of control, and even a few months after his appointment as head of the SA Röhm was faced with a mutiny of some of his north German followers.

Growth of the organization took off dramatically after Hitler's appointment.[44] Some wanted to get in on the spoils—sometimes just a job—and many were simply determined to start reckoning with their old enemies, especially Communists and Socialists. Avenues for revenge opened when SA (and also SS) were turned into auxiliary police (so-called 'Hilfspolizei'). In Bavaria this occurred 'spontaneously' on the night of the take-over of power (9–10 March), but it was made official on the 14th. One writer suggests that in part the deputizing of the SA was to balance off local police, not all of whom were by any means favourably disposed to the Nazis,[45] but it is clear that the SA was also used in struggles among the Nazis in power. The March election had gone sufficiently well for it plausibly to be called a victory, and now the results were treated as a mandate from the people to continue the 'struggle against Marxism'; far from being 'superfluous', the revolution was 'legitimized'.[46] The decision to employ the auxiliary police in Bavaria seems to have been reached by Röhm, Himmler, and Party Gauleiter Adolf Wagner, primarily because, whatever their differences, they could support the radicalism of the SA and were convinced that the momentarily influential persons in Bavaria (head of government Von Epp, Justice Minister Frank, and Finance Minister Siebert) were slow to push forward with the revolution.[47]

The 'revolution' which was to follow moved on two separate but not

---

[44] Jamin, *Zwischen den Klassen*, 2–5. For some self-portraits of SA members see Peter H. Merkl, *The Making of a Stormtrooper* (Princeton, 1980), 26ff.
[45] Wolfgang Sauer, 'Die Mobilmachung der Gewalt', in Bracher, Sauer, and Schulz, 866–7.
[46] Ibid. 868.
[47] Peter Diehl-Thiele, *Partei und Staat im Dritten Reich* (Munich, 1969), 75ff.

unrelated levels: 'co-ordination' actions—wrapped in semi-legalities, and generally surreptitious—and openly terrorist ones carried out in the public eye, aimed at the Marxists and 'enemies of the state' and the wide variety of opposition covered by such terms.[48]

Nazi violence against 'enemies' was deliberately fanned by the regime's leaders. The SA was not only deputized but in some areas given the legal right to carry firearms.[49] The demoralizing effect on old enemies was obvious; these were violent people, neither trained nor interested in the procedures of the law, so that when orders went out from Berlin on the night of 28 February to arrest leading Communists (with the help of SA/SS auxiliary police), to occupy strategically important positions, and so on, the resulting mistreatment of many was to be predicted. The first head of the Gestapo, Rudolf Diels, much later wrote of the 'revolution' of the SA in March 1933:

Unlike the Party, the SA was prepared for its seizure of power. There was no need for a unitary leadership; the Group Staff [Gruppenstab] set the example, but gave no orders. However, the SA formations [Stürme] had firm plans for the actions in the Communist quarters of the city. In those March days every SA man was 'on the heels of the enemy', each knew what he had to do. The formations cleaned up their districts. They knew not only where their enemies lived; long before they had also discovered their hideouts and meeting-places. Where the knowledge of the SA failed, it was supported by a flood of denunciations and an army of snoopers and tittle-tattlers (as thirteen years later, during the de-Nazification).[50] Not only the Communists, but anyone who had expressed himself against Hitler's movement was in danger. The police could only superficially keep up with the Revolution of the Berlin SA in March 1933.[51]

That such denunciations quickly became part of the social landscape can be seen in the provinces, in areas such as Bavaria as well. Of course, from the perspective of the Prussian Gestapo it seemed, as Diels put it, that 'the uprising of the Berlin SA electrified the most distant parts of the country. Revolutionary conditions prevailed in many big cities where the powers of the police were transferred to local SA leaders.'[52]

Much SA work was done 'spontaneously', that is, by individual actions allegedly carried out from below by groups of SA acting on their own initiative. A Gestapo insider remarked that 'our contemporaries have often and justly smiled at the adverbs "spontaneously" and "voluntary", words which soon became clichés of all Nazi journalism'.[53] He added, however, that the SA acted in every way as if it could do whatever it wanted. It left the policemen

---

[48] Diehl-Thiele, Partei und Staat in Dritten Reich, 75 ff.

[49] Allen, The Nazi Seizure of Power, 157.

[50] Cf. Wolfgang Krüger, Entnazifiziert! (Wuppertal, 1982), 97ff.; Lutz Niethammer, Die Mitläuferfabrik: Die Entnazifizierung am Beispiel Bayerns (Berlin, 1982), 593ff.

[51] Diels, 222.

[52] Ibid. 225.

[53] Gisevius, 101.

'behind at headquarters' and roamed the streets 'alone in search of "enemies of the state"'; it 'laughed at the administrative and judicial principles which dated from the days of the "system"', but 'the worst feature of all, so far as the helpless government authorities were concerned, was that the SA would not release its prey. Woe to the unfortunate who was caught in the clutches of the storm-troops.'[54] This insider does not, however, appreciate the usefulness of the violence of the SA and others in the auxiliary police, such as the SS.

The value of the SA to the Nazi state went well beyond what it might accomplish as part of the police force proper; its arbitrariness and brutality, word of which spread quickly, also helped consolidate power and carry through the 'co-ordination' process.[55] The actions of the SA gave constant cause for complaint, and though the ways in which local government was more or less cowed into submission all over the country were significant as well, the SA played an important part in the 'seizure of power', at the level of simply facing down opponents in the streets.

For a time the SA managed to create a system of special commissioners to parallel the state administrative set-up—a situation which was ultimately terminated as part of the 'Night of the Long Knives', when the SA leaders were killed off at the end of June 1934.[56] The 'auxiliary police' were disbanded in Prussia on 2 August 1933, a sign that the most violent stage of the revolution was over.[57] In Bavaria the institution was brought to a close at about the same time.

Even as early as a Cabinet meeting of 7 April 1933, the way the SA was going about its business gave cause for concern in Munich's government circles. In the context of a discussion of the problems resulting from the use of the SA as 'auxiliary police', Minister of Justice Hans Frank noted that already some 5,000 people had been taken into custody and that the number was sure to rise. Under the circumstances he advised the introduction of more formalized proceedings. His view of what needed to be changed gives a good idea of the atmosphere in Bavaria at the time:

Arrests on the basis of simple denunciations and arbitrary arrests by subordinate organs must cease. The interrogation of those taken into custody must be completed at once. When the reasons for the arrest are not adequate, the person concerned must be set free. Normal proceedings must be introduced to regulate responsibility and offer those arrested certain securities and opportunities for complaint. The police commandant must procure exact information on all those arrested... A committee

[54] Ibid. 112.
[55] Ortwin Domröse, *Der NS-Staat in Bayern von der Machtergreifung bis zum Röhm-Putsch* (Munich, 1974), 185ff.; Jochen Klenner, *Verhältnis von Partei und Staat 1933–1945: Dargestellt am Beispiel Bayerns* (Munich, 1974), 116ff.
[56] Domröse, 185ff; for the east see Bessel, 114.
[57] Bessel, 113.

should be set up to examine complaints and occupied by higher police officials and one or two judges from the administrative court after reference to the SA.[58]

Epp, the leading political figure in Bavaria, reiterated this demand on the very next day, and involved Hitler's name in support; nevertheless, local 'spontaneous' initiatives continued.

The Brownshirts showed their violent inclinations in Bavarian districts such as Middle Franconia. Nuremberg, administrative centre of the area, was known in this period because of Gauleiter Julius Streicher's radicalism, and especially his rabid anti-Semitism purveyed through the scandal-sheet *Der Stürmer*, and because Nazi Party rallies were held there. During those March days of 1933 the SA in Nuremberg was in its heyday. With the appointment there in September 1933 of the leader of the Franconian SA, Hans-Günther von Obernitz, as police president (even if, to be sure, he was the third one inside six months to hold the job) it seemed that the organization was finally reaping the spoils for which it had fought.[59] Targets for Storm-trooper violence in Nuremberg, as elsewhere, were the Leftist parties and the Jews. 'With the knowledge and frequently in the presence of regular police, the SA arrested, intimidated, and on numerous occasions tortured real or alleged opponents of the new regime.'[60]

4. HIMMLER, HEYDRICH, AND THE BAVARIAN POLITICAL POLICE

The actions in the streets prepared the ground for the emergence of a secret police in Bavaria, one which then linked up with the Prussian Gestapo. Bavaria too had had a political police before the First World War, albeit one very much centred on the Munich Metropolitan Police (the Polizeidirektion München). In Imperial Germany Munich's political police, like the one in Hamburg described above, regularly kept track of the political goings-on in the capital. But while there was a tradition that could be built upon, by the standards of the Third Reich this surveillance was limited and tame.

The Munich Metropolitan Police, which had acted as an official central body for all of Bavaria in many 'political' matters, particularly from the 1920s, was reorganized at the end of 1932. Under the new scheme the political police became Department (Abteilung) VI, divided in turn into five specific bureaux (Dienststellen) from the earlier 'desks' (Referate) of Department VI. Structurally, not much changed. There was surveillance of state-threatening groups such as Nazis and Communists, as well as public gatherings, elections, the press, and so on, some counter-espionage activity, and

---

[58] Hans Frank, quoted in Pridham, 314. Cf. Diehl-Thiele, 8off.
[59] Erich G. Reiche, *The Development of the SA in Nürnberg 1922–1934* (Cambridge, 1986), 179–80.
[60] Ibid. 179.

a central political intelligence service. These operations were backed by a card-index system. There were trained specialists, with detailed knowledge of their subject.

(a) The structure of the political police

In March Heinrich Himmler became provisional Police President of Munich, and he had the able assistance of Reinhard Heydrich, who headed the political police (in Department VI). These changes were part of Epp's initial transformation of the political and administrative set-up in Bavaria. The statement containing the official announcement of the new Himmler–Heydrich team also emphasized that the responsibility of the police for the maintenance of public security and order—a defensive mission—would henceforth be supplemented by an offensive political mission, namely the assurance of 'loyal adherence to the Reich Government of National Revival under the leadership of Adolf Hitler'.[61]

Himmler was named 'Political Police Commander' of Bavaria as of 1 April 1933. Given a special position in the Bavarian Ministry of the Interior, he received enormous new powers. A new Bavarian Political Police (Bayerische Politische Polizei, BPP) was at once established and removed from the authority of police headquarters in Munich, that is, it was given the kind of independence attained (later) in Prussia. Himmler could count not only on the political police, but also on the special Emergency Police, the ordinary uniformed police (those in blue), and the rural gendarmerie, 'for enforcement purposes'. Thus, within a month of the 'seizure of power' not only had the Nazis acquired official control over the police, but through Himmler they had linked it to the SS—for the time being, in marked contrast to Prussia—and the concentration-camp system.[62]

It was one thing to be officially awarded police powers, but quite another to exercise them, given the very real competition of the SA, particularly in Bavaria, which was to continue until the blood-bath of June 1934. In fact a peculiar situation existed in Bavaria, since at times the SS leader—acting as the commander of the (state) police apparatus—was in conflict with Röhm (SA head) and some of the latter's followers, while at other times the two would ally in order to cover up crimes (such as the murder of political opponents in the SS Dachau camp). A Gestapo insider commented later that 'right at the start of the Nazi regime an internal struggle raged over who was to exercise the chief police power', and this was especially the case in Bavaria; he added that of course 'there was no doubt that whoever eventually won would occupy a decisive position'.[63]

[61] The phrase is quoted by Buchheim, 40–1.
[62] See the document in Aronson, 323.
[63] Gisevius, 187.

(b) Exercise of police powers in 'co-ordination'

In the proclaimed emergency situation after the Reichstag fire the political
police were instructed in effect to treat the opponents of Nazism as the enemies
of the German state. They were be to ruthlessly dealt with, a business made
much easier for career specialists who had long wanted to do more but were
held back by the law: those constraints now virtually disappeared. In Bavaria
one group of opponents after another was systematically terrorized. The new
Bavarian police system—backed by 'spontaneous' actions in the street and
in the 'wild' concentration camps of the SA—made use of the double-edged
sword of 'preventive arrest' and confinement in a concentration camp.[64] In
spite of local variations, at least in retrospect a pattern seems evident, although
this should not be taken to mean that a carefully conceived plan was being
followed.

The campaign of repression began with the Communists. This was a
politically wise choice for any number of reasons, not least because they were
allegedly responsible for torching the Reichstag in Berlin. Moreover, actions
against KPD functionaries could play upon widespread anti-Communism.[65]
The police pursued Communists in the working-class districts of the larger
centres across Bavaria, often with the help of the SA drafted as 'auxiliary
police'. But even in a small provincial city like Würzburg (with a total
population of about 100,000) there were 108 house-searches conducted
between 9 and 20 March, with 51 arrests. While exact figures for all of
Bavaria are not available, it has been suggested on the basis of semi-official
data that already by 13 April as many as 3,000 Communists had been placed
in 'protective custody', with a grand total of 5,400 such arrests.[66] The
immediate impact on the KPD was catastrophic: the Bavarian Political Police
proudly reported on 25 May that the party and its affiliations 'had ceased to
exist'.[67] The police underestimated the resilience of the party, and only by
constantly snooping, planting agents, and carrying out arrests could the
KPD's activities be eliminated over the next few years.

To some extent other political opponents were also placed in 'protective
custody', and sent for a time to a concentration camp, though none of these
experienced the same range of persecution. The SPD, and particularly its
paramilitary organization—the Reichsbanner—and the associated free trade
unions, as Marxist-oriented Leftists, were certainly forbidden to exist, and
some of their members were arrested. A quantitative analysis of the case-files
of the Würzburg Gestapo indicates that as few as 126 of the thousand or so
SPD members in the city personally experienced the wrath of the police and

---

[64] Bay HStA: MA 106670, RP Oberbayern, 20 Mar. 1933.

[65] E.g. Bay HStA: MA 106682, RP Schwaben/Neuburg, 22 Mar. 1933.

[66] Hartmut Mehringer, 'Die KPD in Bayern 1919–1945: Vorgeschichte, Verfolgung und Widerstand', in Broszat *et al.* (eds.), *Bayern in der NS-Zeit*, v. 74–6.

[67] Quoted in ibid. 81.

justice system—whether this involved dismissal from employment, formal warnings, fines, court hearings, 'protective custody', or some other sort of confinement.[68] The Gestapo did not have to deal with more than 13 per cent of all the Socialists in order to provide a sufficiently efficacious demonstration and that was probably also the case elsewhere.

The major 'bourgeois' or non-working-class party in Bavaria was the Bavarian People's Party (the BVP). Its leading representatives in federal, state, and even local politics were all placed in 'protective custody'; those who had been conspicuous in their support for the party were included in the round-up.[69] The 'spiritual' opponents of Nazism also came in for attention, although it proved more difficult to dispatch the clergy, which continued to be something of a counter-authority throughout the course of the Third Reich.[70]

The Jews were targeted very early: they were to be fought as a group rather than as individuals who might escape the net.[71] Nation-wide orders were issued to the police on 12 May 1933 to respond to the 'oppositional attitude' of the Jews by searching the headquarters of all Jewish organizations for 'treasonous material'. This 'preventive' measure was carried out in Bavaria, coupled with arrests and interrogations (as in Nuremberg, where 200 individuals were brought in with the help of the local SA). While nothing turned up, records were seized,[72] and the action had the effect of intimidating and isolating the Jewish population. One historian says that at least in the early days of the regime the Bavarian Political Police were not the 'absolute master' when it came to dealing with the Jews—for any number of party and state organizations were interested in the persecution.[73]

By the beginning of August 1933 'protective custody' orders and internment for a time in a concentration camp were a frequently used weapon of the new dictatorship. By then some 4,152 persons were still interned in Bavaria (probably half of them were functionaries in the Bavarian People's Party).[74] The object of the exercise was to influence public opinion in Bavaria. In the absence of enthusiasm, silence, compliance, or apathetic accommodation was to be preferred to opposition or dissent. The arrests were orchestrated in such a way that 'in each village and each city at least several people were touched by them'. These 'disappeared' into custody and were usually 'depressed and terrified' upon their release; their reappearance con-

---

[68] Hartmut Mehringer, 'Die bayerische Sozialdemokratie bis zum Ende des NS-Regimes: Vorgeschichte, Verfolgung und Widerstand', in Broszat *et al.* (eds.), *Bayern in der NS-Zeit*, v. 348–9.
[69] Aronson, 117.
[70] For the early accommodation of the churches see Klaus Scholder, *Die Kirchen und das Dritte Reich*, i. (Frankfurt, 1977), 277ff.; Ernst Christian Helmreich, *The German Churches under Hitler: Background, Struggle, and Epilogue* (Detroit, 1979), 121ff.
[71] Aronson, 121–2.
[72] Report of the action in Bay HStA: MA106410.
[73] Aronson, 122.
[74] Ibid. 117; 2,000 BVP persons is the figure mentioned in a report from Heydrich.

tributed to the intimidation and climate of fear.[75]

It has been estimated for Germany as a whole that by the end of summer 1933 some 100,000 people, mainly party-political opponents, had been robbed of their freedom at one time or another, with between 500 and 600 killed.[76] The wave of 'arrests'—which at times can only be called simple kidnapping by unauthorized persons—led the victims to a police gaol or, even worse, to one of the thirty or so 'wild' concentration camps which sprang up across the country to deal with putative 'enemies'. The main proponents of these measures were local SA units, who were keen to place people in 'protective custody'. These camps were a characteristic feature of the Nazi 'revolution', and even though from early 1934 they gradually came under the control of Himmler and the SS, or were eliminated, their significance for the introduction of the terror needs to be recalled, all the more in a study of the relationship between German society and the police. These brutal institutions represented the enforcement powers of the new regime, and were a place-holder for the Gestapo and SS, which soon established command. Frequently these camps served as internment sites for those more or less systematically harassed by the police, SS, or SA.[77]

It is clear from official complaints across the country that by the end of 1933 and beginning of 1934 misuse of police authority, even given the new standards, was rampant. Diels himself said in a communication in mid-January 1934 to local officials that the days when 'quick measures' could be tolerated were over; henceforth, proper procedures should be followed. At about the same time Minister of the Interior Frick demanded that denunciations even by the Nazi Party itself should henceforth be checked more closely before making an arrest; only if someone were suspected of committing a crime should proceedings be instituted. The police should not employ 'protective custody' simply at the urging of some local Party type. That defence lawyers could be taken into custody merely for representing the interests of their clients could not continue.[78]

5. NATIONALIZATION OF THE GESTAPO

The 'Night of the Long Knives' is the name given to the events surrounding the murders on 30 June 1934 of the leaders of the SA, such as Ernst Röhm,

---

[75] Aronson, 118.

[76] Sauer, 871.

[77] See Lawrence D. Stokes, 'Zur Geschichte des "wilden" Konzentrationslagers Eutin', *VfZ* 27 (1979) 570–625.

[78] Communications of 15 Dec. 1933, 9 and 16 January 1934, cited in Broszat, 'Kozentrationslager', 29–31.

and other rivals.[79] That Himmler's SS was involved makes those events appear in retrospect as part of the inexorable rise of Himmler, the Gestapo, and eventually the SS state. The actions were carried out—including the execution of an indeterminate number of people (it is usually put in the hundreds)—by the SS with the knowledge of the Gestapo and the armed forces. Apart from settling old scores, this pre-emptive strike at the leadership of the SA paid dividends in terms of public opinion. Described as an attempted 'Röhm revolt', it offered the Nazi leadership an opportunity to present a new face to the German public.[80] The rowdiness and disorder associated with the SA, which had once been useful, was now declared out of fashion. The 'Night of the Long Knives' opened the door to the 'cooler' variety of Gestapo social control and appealed to Germans' sense of law and order.[81]

Although the SA was not dissolved, it had been reined in and was no longer a serious rival to Himmler, who thereafter moved towards further centralizing police power and the concentration-camp system. Throughout 1933 and 1934 he succeeded in having himself appointed to the position of head of the political police in some twelve other German states. The pattern was generally to incorporate already existing 'political' departments of local forces, more or less along the lines already seen in Prussia and Bavaria. Some of these new bodies carried the title 'Gestapo', as in Prussia, but others became police forces concerned with 'politics', as with the Bavarian Political Police. This series of conquests was crowned on 20 April 1934, when Himmler took charge of the Prussian Gestapo. By that date he held the leadership of all regional political police forces (still, each rested on local, not federal, law). There were efforts by the older established state authorities to retain some control over the political police, but once the ambition of the SA was curtailed it was only a matter of time before the decisions went completely in favour of Himmler and the Gestapo.

Hitler named Heinrich Himmler Chief of the German Police on 17 June 1936, and as Reichsführer at the head of the SS he also remained one of the most important of Germany's leaders. He had the ability to issue orders while wearing either hat, which among other things gave him an enormous advantage in dealing with rivals. Within a week of his promotion he was able to formalize his control as Germany's new police chief by creating national headquarters for the various branches of the police: the most important of these in the context of the present study was the creation under Heydrich of

---

[79] For an introduction and general account of the Röhm purge see Max Gallo, *The Night of the Long Knives*, trans. L. Emmet (New York, 1972), 11ff.; see the remarks on the older literature in Conan Fischer, *Stormtroopers: A Social, Economic and Ideological Analysis 1929–35* (London, 1983), 6ff.; Bessel, 130ff.

[80] Bessel, 139.

[81] Ibid. 140.

a unified Security Police (Sicherheitspolizei, or Sipo), which combined both the Political Police and the Criminal Police (the Kripo).[82]

Himmler's appointment inaugurated a new era, although it was also the culmination of developments that began in January 1933. The significance of the organizational changes beginning in 1936 was that for the first time in its history the German police, including the political branches, was centralized. As late as August 1936 there were seventeen different names for the Gestapo and/or political police forces across Germany, an apparent chaos which was ended when on 20 September all were formally brought under Gestapo headquarters in Berlin.[83] Continuing efforts to centralize the police (or *Verreichlichung*) ended most, though certainly not all, of the disarray.[84]

The Gestapo was not just another institution of the state; to a great extent it was able to act independently of the administrative set-up in Germany. It 'operated upon an entirely different principle from that of the civil administration', and (beginning in 1936) did not base its actions merely on 'regularly legalized rules' but also on 'special principles and requirements', which 'is tantamount to saying that it operated as the instrument of the Führer's authority' and 'had no need of further legitimation in law'.[85] Despite some appearance to the contrary, the Gestapo could very nearly decide for itself what the law was, act accordingly, and ignore objections.

A further reshuffling of the police took place on 27 September 1939, through the creation of a more systematic scheme setting out clearly the division of labour of all those concerned with 'security'. The establishment of the Reich Security Main Office (Reichssicherheitshauptamt, RSHA) had little impact on the powers of the Gestapo. Although the new apparatus had the advantage of being systematic, with its fourteen or so separate branches the RSHA was too compartmentalized, all the more since secrecy was the rule not only towards outsiders, but even within the organization. By no means were all jurisdictional disputes settled.[86]

---

[82] The place of the Kripo and other 'control organizations' in the police network receives extensive coverage in the next chapter.

[83] BAK: R58/236.

[84] For example, on 20 Sept. 1936 central control was extended with the appointment of Security Police Inspectors (Inspekteure der Sicherheitspolizei, IdS). These men were supposed to co-ordinate local political police and gradually to bypass the older administrative and police set-up, so that it has been suggested that they were 'the first planks in the new police organization Heydrich intended should supplant the old'. While this intention was only partially realized, and had the effect of constantly reducing the power of local Police Presidents—e.g. by making Gestapo officials *federal* civil servants (in Mar. 1937)—it was part of the trend towards the creation of the political police as an independent entity outside the control of the traditional state institutions: Buchheim, 93.

[85] Ibid. 54. Buchheim calls the process *Entstaatlichung* (p. 55).

[86] See e.g. Peter R. Black, *Ernst Kaltenbrunner: Ideological Soldier of the Third Reich* (Princeton, 1984), 176ff.

6. CONCLUSION

Any account of the introduction of the terror system must bear witness to the violent behaviour of the Party bullies, the SA, the use of 'protective custody', the chaotic first concentration camps and beatings, all of which quickly became public knowledge. They were designed in part to have a 'demonstration effect', which was not lost on the family, friends, and neighbours of victims. The Gestapo's work was not to be hindered by concerns about either personal freedoms or the rule of law. While terror and brutality were never far below the surface whenever anyone contemplated deviation from the letter or even spirit of the law, the use or threat of violence alone does not convey an adequate picture of the routine operation of the 'police state' and the Gestapo. At the same time as the Gestapo emerged to do old jobs 'better' than ever, there also developed a vast new body of law to be enforced, new spheres of behaviour which were to be supervised and regulated. There was in fact a veritable avalanche of laws, regulations, and edicts—in the area of race alone—of such scope that effective policing would never have been possible without also attaining some degree of co-operation from the general population. No police can be entirely dependent upon fear engendered by brutal methods, and certainly not the Gestapo, whose job it became to play a 'positive' role in the formation of the 'new order'.[87]

The Gestapo built upon the tradition of political police in Germany, but went well beyond it. Not only was it centralized as never before, but it claimed to stand outside the law, justice system, and traditional administrative and police discipline. Hans Buchheim insists that the 'perversion' of the Gestapo did not derive from the creation of a political police as such, but that factors external to the police were ultimately to blame. It is not clear what one is to make of such an effort to distinguish internal and external factors. In any event, it was relatively easy to transform the already existing political police, and many of its professional personnel, into the dictatorship's trusty enforcer. Young Hans Bernd Gisevius, a trained (non-Nazi) civil servant, was 'very glad' to be assigned to the Gestapo in the summer of 1933 because he 'hoped to contribute to the re-establishment of a proper executive organization which would provide for law, decency, and order'. His happiness 'was doomed to be short-lived', and the opposite of what he had hoped for resulted.[88]

[87] Buchheim, 117.
[88] Gisevius, in IMT xii. 167.

2

Local Organization of the Gestapo and Police Network

ACCORDING to the recollections of many who once lived in Nazi Germany, the effectiveness of the Gestapo and the surveillance system rested on the large 'army' of spies and paid informers at the disposal of local officials.[1] It is true that the citizen never felt far from the gaze of Nazis, whether in public, at work, or even at home. However, this sense of being watched could not have been due to the sheer physical presence of Gestapo officials. Membership in the Gestapo was in fact remarkably small.

By the end of 1944 there were approximately 32,000 in the force, of whom 3,000 were administrative officials, 15,500 or so executive officials, and 13,500 employed workmen, 9,000 of whom were draftees. Those in 'administration' had the same training as other civil servants, and dealt with issues such as personnel records, budget, and supplies, and legal problems such as those stemming from passport law. The 'executive officials', especially trained in the 'leader school' (Führerschule) were assigned tasks according to the various desks (Referate) into which the Secret Police was subdivided. These officials 'executed the real tasks of the Gestapo as laid down by law', although 'a number of these officials also were engaged in pure office work'.[2] The Gestapo also took over other organizations and some of their personnel, such as the customs frontier guard, and so on, but these had little to do with the day-to-day policing inside Germany, and can be left out of account here. Otto Ohlendorf, head of the SD, put the total membership in the Gestapo at 30,000, but included not only those stationed outside Germany proper, but also the assistants, workers, and office personnel; he estimated that most were in the administrative or support staff, with 'one specialist' or executive official 'to three or four persons' in the Gestapo.[3]

[1] A classic example of the emphasis on numbers is Eugen Kogon, *Der SS-Staat: Das System der deutschen Konzentrationslager* (1946; Munich, 1974), 28, who speaks of an 'army' of agents reaching as much as a quarter of a million in the war; Franz Dröge, *Der zerredete Widerstand: Zur Soziologie und Publizistik des Gerüchts im 2. Weltkrieg* (Düsseldorf, 1970), 54, suggests that for every 2,500 citizens there was one SD worker; had Dröge included the whole range of those in the police network the ratio of police to population would have been much lower again.
[2] See IMT xxi. 294ff. for affidavits. For the same points see the testimony of Werner Best, ibid. xx. 123ff. Note the national figures in StA M, Gestapo 23, RSHA, Feb. 1944: Gestapo total 31,374, Kripo, 12,792, and SD, 6,482, for a grand total of 50,648 as of 1 Jan. 1944 in the Sipo (security police).
[3] See IMT iv. 345.

Just how it happened that people in Nazi Germany could have come to feel that spies were just about everywhere will be taken up later. At this point it is worth while to look at the organizational forms taken by the Gestapo and the police network at the local level.

1. Organization of the local Gestapo

Given the small number of officials in the Gestapo, their distribution had to be thin on the ground. A survey in March 1937 of personnel for the entire area within the Düsseldorf Gestapo region showed a total of 291 persons, of whom 49 were concerned with administrative matters and 242 involved in police work (in 'Außendienst'). At that time 126 officials were stationed in Düsseldorf, a city with a population of approximately 500,000. Other cities within the overall jurisdiction of the Düsseldorf headquarters were assigned additional personnel: Essen had 43 officials to cover a population of about 650,000 while Wuppertal had 43 and Duisburg 28, for populations in excess of 400,000. Oberhausen had 14 officials, München-Gladbach 11, while Kleve and Kaldenkirchen, with 8 each, were the smallest two of the eight cities in the jurisdiction to have their own Gestapo posts; the many other cities of the area did not have such posts. In comparison with the rest of the country, numbers for Düsseldorf were relatively large, partly because of the 165-kilometre national border for which it was responsible.[4] Still, given the demands made by the regime, this was a small force to police the roughly 4 million inhabitants of the jurisdiction—known for its support of opposition parties such as the SPD and KPD, and for being a haven of 'political Catholicism', and with relatively large Polish and Jewish populations.

Information from various localities indicates that typically the few people in each local post were divided into officials, teletypists, assistants, clerks, typists, drivers, and so on. These were normally subdivided into various departments and separate subsections (Referate), more or less on the ever-changing patterns of Berlin. Thus, the Gestapo (Office IV of the RSHA) had separate subsections from A to F. Subsection IVa looked after 'opponents, sabotage, protective service'; IVb concerned itself with 'political churches, sects, and Jews'; IVc dealt with 'personnel files, protective custody, press, Party'; IVd worked on the 'greater German spheres of influence', and therefore dealt with foreign workers and the occupied territories. 'Counter-espionage' was handled by IVe, while IVf had jurisdiction over 'passes and border police' affairs. The subsections were divided in turn into ever more specialized desks.[5]

The range of political behaviour that came within the sphere of the Gestapo was large and constantly growing. The desk in the Düsseldorf Gestapo con-

---

[4] BAK: R 58/610, 55–6: Personalstatistik der Staatspolizei, 31 Mar. 1937.
[5] See the organization of the RSHA and the Gestapo in it in Black, 297ff. (app. D).

cerned with Polish and eastern workers as of 15 July 1943 had twelve separate subsections dealing with everything from 'refusal to work' and 'leaving the workplace without permission' to 'forbidden sexual relations'. The section on the 'Economy' was divided into eight subsections. While the regular police were in charge of enforcing economic regulations brought in for the duration of the war, the Gestapo was to be called in when, for example, the deed caused unrest in the population or when the perpetrator was a public figure.[6]

Outside the largest cities, such as Berlin, Hamburg, or Munich, the various desks (Referate) in any given local Gestapo might comprise only a single official, and in many places this person had to look after more than one desk.[7] At Koblenz, for example, it was recalled that the one man who was to deal with the Jews also looked after Freemasonry.[8] In Darmstadt the man in the Judenreferat was entirely on his own, and had difficulty even getting a secretary until after the regime began to step up its official anti-Semitism.[9] Even in large cities such as Düsseldorf it was claimed that there was one man in charge of the Jewish section (an Oberinspektor), with 'two or three assistants'.[10]

The number of officials registered in various surveys of the Gestapo may be inflated—at any rate, if the example of Eutin in Schleswig-Holstein is any guide. The survey of March 1937 mentioned above registered three Gestapo people in that town, when in fact this was not the case. Lawrence Stokes maintains that the leading local administrators (a Regierungspräsident, an Oberregierungsrat, and a Regierungsrat) were assigned the duty of looking after political police matters in addition to their other jobs. They had to take care of between fifteen and twenty-five other areas of administration (Referate), a number of which had nothing whatsoever to do with 'police' work. If this case is representative of circumstances in a small town, the survey in 1937 not only exaggerates the numbers in the secret police, but conveys a false impression of the extent of Gestapo professionalization.[11]

---

[6] HStA D: RW 36/3, 6ff., plan of Düsseldorf Gestapo.
[7] For Bavaria's Gestapo organization see BAK: R58/1112, 145–6, and R58/242, 101.
[8] Karl Heinz Hoffmann in IMT xx 160; cf. the few in Bielefeld, ibid. xxi. 293–4
[9] Klaus Moritz and Ernst Noam, *NS-Verbrechen vor Gericht 1945–1955: Dokumente aus hessischen Justizakten* (Wiesbaden, 1978), 272–3.
[10] Hoffmann, in IMT xx. 160.
[11] See Landesarchiv Schleswig-Holstein, Reg. Eutin, A II 2 (260/17 462), Geschäftsbehandlung bei der Regierung und der Verteilung der Geschäfte unter Mitgliedern: see also Lawrence D. Stokes, *Kleinstadt und Nationalsozialismus: Ausgewählte Dokumente zur Geschichte von Eutin, 1918–1945* (Neumünster, 1984), 504.

2. THE EVERYDAY OPERATION OF THE GESTAPO

The work of the late Reinhard Mann makes possible some general statements about Gestapo activities. Mann studied a random sample of 825 cases drawn from the 70,000 surviving files of the Düsseldorf Gestapo. Apart from Würzburg, whose files are dealt with in detail below (beginning in Chapter 5), these kinds of documents have not survived for any other Gestapo post.[12] A brief examination of Mann's random sample will give some idea of the routine operations of the Gestapo.

TABLE I. *Proceedings of the Düsseldorf Gestapo 1933–1945*

	No.	%
Continuation of forbidden organizations:		
Continuation of political parties and associations	204	
Continuation of forbidden religious associations and sects	15	
Continuation of dissolved associations and activity for the forbidden youth-groups	26	
TOTAL	245	30
Non-conforming behaviour in everyday life:		
Non-conforming verbal utterances	203	
Non-conforming work or leisure activities	38	
TOTAL	241	29
Other forms of non-conformity:		
Acquiring or spreading of forbidden printed matter	37	
Listening to foreign radio	20	
Political passivity	7	
Assorted others	75	
TOTAL	139	17
Conventional criminality	96	12
Administrative control measures	104	13
TOTAL	825	100

Source: R. Mann, *Protest und Kontrolle*, 180.

Table 1, which is taken from Mann's study, shows the preoccupations of the Düsseldorf Gestapo over the course of the Nazi dictatorship. From his sample, 245 (30 per cent of all cases) pertained to tracking prohibited, mostly

[12] More will be said about Mann's work and the strengths and weaknesses of Gestapo case-files as historical sources.

left-wing, organizations. Of the 204 cases of people involved in illegal political parties or organizations, 61 pertained to those suspected of links with the KPD and 44 with the SPD; in 69 cases it was not possible to establish specific political affiliation. When it came to organized political parties, the main opponents were clearly the Marxists. The pursuit of religious-oriented or youth organizations took a much smaller share of the Gestapo workload.[13]

The efforts to track illegal organizations show an increase from 1933 (when 14 of the 245 cases came to light); the highest number of such cases began in 1935, with 57 cases, up from 30 the year before. Then a more or less steady decline set in. In 1937 42 cases were opened, but next year the number fell to 18, with only 13 in the following year; after a brief flurry in 1940, the drop continued, with only 2 in 1941. There were 7 cases in 1942, 4 in 1943, and 1 in 1944.[14] The declining number of cases after 1935 reflects the success of the Gestapo in eliminating organized opposition.

The Düsseldorf Gestapo pursued nearly as many persons suspected of 'non-conforming everyday behaviour'—29 per cent of all its cases—as it did in its efforts to deal with outlawed organizations. Much energy was expended in controlling the spoken word in Nazi Germany, as most instances of non-conformity brought to Gestapo attention (203 cases out of 241) pertained to airing opinions in public. (More will be said about this matter later.) The Gestapo was also involved in regulating work and leisure activities. Many of the 241 cases in this category had to depend heavily on the co-operation of people beyond the ranks of the Secret Police who brought information; there were too few Gestapo members to accomplish this kind of policing on their own.

The Gestapo was keen to enforce policies with regard to obtaining and/or spreading information disallowed by the regime. Fifty-seven cases (7 per cent of the total) concerned such matters. Other forms of non-conformity— 'political passivity' and a wide variety of deviations lumped together as 'other kinds' of non-conformity—took up nearly 10 per cent of the Gestapo case-load. The last-named category, with 75 cases, is a catch-all which contains everything from the Hitler caricaturist, to the reluctant military recruit of 'mixed race', to the Catholic school rector denounced for insufficient Nazi zeal.[15] It is evident that the Gestapo was operating with a concept of opposition and security which went well beyond conventional definitions. There were 104 cases (13 per cent of the total) brought to the attention of the Gestapo upon suspicion that someone had broken 'administrative control measures'— bending or breaking rules concerning residency requirements, for example.

Because crime was to some extent politicized, the Gestapo spent much effort (12 per cent of all its cases) in dealing with what in Table 1 is called

---

[13] See Reinhard Mann, *Protest und Kontrolle*, 180, table 7, and 188, table 14.
[14] Ibid. 182, chart 1.
[15] Ibid. 266ff.: 'nearly 10 per cent' is reached by adding 7 plus 75 = 82/825.

'conventional criminality'. They investigated accusations involving 'morals charges' and falsifications to the authorities. Indeed, local Gestapo officials were at times utterly ruthless and single-minded when it came to prosecuting homosexuals, especially if they were Jews.[16] Of all the 'conventional' offences it investigated, however, the largest single category was 'economic' charges of various kinds. An examination of the Düsseldorf files themselves shows that before 1939 there were efforts to stop the smuggling of money over the border into Holland or Belgium, and when the war came there was great concern to enforce the special measures introduced to regulate the economy.[17]

Mann's quantitative analysis of Gestapo activities is useful, in that it suggests in broad outline something about the Gestapo workload and routine operation. This work—which his untimely death in 1981 prevented him from completing—has limitations for the present study on the enforcement of racial policy, however, since Mann excludes certain categories of Gestapo case-files, namely those which pertain to 'racially foreign' groups such as the Jews and foreign workers. These limitations are examined below in Chapter 5.

A preliminary comparison of Düsseldorf and Würzburg reveals a remarkable similarity in the organization and *modus operandi* of the Gestapo. This finding is to be expected, given the efforts that were made to achieve central control. But the preoccupations of the local Gestapo varied according to the local circumstances. One obvious and persistent concern of the Düsseldorf Gestapo, which emerges with especial clarity in contrast to the Würzburg post, is that the Gestapo in the Rhineland had to spend much effort in policing both the River Rhine and the border, with regard to the flow of people, goods, and money. The border is far away from Würzburg, and thus is hardly mentioned in the files. Nor were the illegal Communist and Socialist movements anything like as important in the largely agricultural and rural Würzburg area as they were in the Rhineland, and the Gestapo divided its resources accordingly. Würzburg officials had more time to deal with the pettiest infringements when it came to the Jews. Similar charges were laid and followed up in Düsseldorf, but for the most part they seem not to have been taken up with quite the same zeal as in Würzburg. Other local variations in the Gestapo routine undoubtedly existed—for example, in places which had neither Jews nor much of an illegal workers' movement. In Düsseldorf and Würzburg Catholicism and policing the pulpit were also of great importance, and countless priests were hauled in for minor infractions.

---

[16] See the case in Elke Fröhlich, 'Die Herausforderung des Einzelnen: Geschichten über Widerstand und Verfolgung', in Broszat *et al.* (eds.), *Bayern in der NS-Zeit*, vi. 76ff.

[17] See Reinhard Mann, *Protest und Kontrolle*, 252, table 31, for a detailed breakdown of the criminality.

3. GESTAPO PERSONNEL: WAS THERE A PURGE OF THE POLICE?

It has been claimed that following the Nazi 'seizure of power' the ranks of the police were 'cleaned out' and replaced with card-carrying Nazis. Members of the new Gestapo were allegedly drawn primarily from the SS, who were much preferred to those in the old political police forces inherited from the Weimar Republic.[18] In fact, considerable evidence exists that many officials were co-opted and continued to serve: the supposed purge was not nearly as wide-spread as is sometimes claimed.

In their autobiographical accounts and in post-war trials leading Gestapo figures have generally put forward the view that many (non-Nazi) career policemen merely stayed at their desks and simply continued their work, eventually becoming members of the Party and/or the SS. This is a striking theme in the testimony of those heard at the Nuremberg International Military Tribunal after 1945. Werner Best, one-time head of training, personnel, and organization at Gestapo headquarters in Berlin, a trained lawyer, and a man who played a vital part in building up the Gestapo, maintained that there were relatively few contacts between the NSDAP and the police before 1933, and believed that, far from there having been any significant purge of the political police across the country in the wake of the 'seizure of power' most people were kept on. As an example from his own experience he mentioned the Hessian police chief who was allowed to stay in office even though he was a known Freemason and democrat. Best said that the most spectacular example of all was that of another non-Nazi, Heinrich Müller, who later became head of the Gestapo itself under Himmler and Heydrich.[19] As the need arose, the Gestapo recruited new officials from various police branches but took 'only relatively few' from the SS, SA, or Nazi Party; belonging to 'police agencies was not highly paid and therefore was not very much sought after'.[20]

Cross-examined over an apparent contradiction between his testimony at Nuremberg and a famous book he had penned in 1941, Best insisted that while SS members who applied to join the Gestapo were duly considered, he

---

[18] For example, Liang, 165ff., speaks of a 'purge'; Tuchel and Schattenfroh, 63ff., deal with the *Säuberungen*; Bramstedt, 96, reports on the 'purification of the Political Police'. For an examination of the purge in the civil service as a whole see Jane Caplan, *Government without Administration: State and Civil Service in Weimar and Nazi Germany* (Oxford, 1988), 145–6, in which she notes that across Germany, at all levels of administration, 'altogether, the purge itself directly affected about 1 to 2 per cent of the professional civil service, though its indirect effects were certainly more widespread'. She shows that though standards varied considerably, 'Jewish officials, known Communists, social democrats, and Centre party members or sympathizers, were the most common victims.' One wonders if the concept of a purge sufficiently takes into account the relatively restricted kinds of 'opponents' who were dismissed or had been retired, and the fact that roughly 98% of the civil service remained at their desks.

[19] Best testimony, in IMT xx. 125–6. There is a great deal of information on Best in the BDC. Dr Ulrich Herbert of Essen is presently writing a biography of Best.

[20] Best, in IMT xx. 126.

had given no 'ratio of figures' in his book. It was true, he said, that in time more of the new members taken in were in the SS, but this was not initially the case. 'I can say again today that the number of the regular officials—those old officials previously taken over as well as the candidates from the protection police'—that is, the regular police—'was much higher than the number taken in from the SS.'[21] One former local Gestapo deputy chief had the impression that 'on the whole' the officials there 'had been detailed or transferred to the State Police' and 'had entered the police before 1933'.[22] Robert Koehl's recent study reinforces Best's account. In 1939, he maintains, 'only 3,000 Gestapo officials out of 20,000 had SS rank', and the proportion in the other two main police forces 'was even less, though sizeable in absolute terms'.[23]

Otto Ohlendorf, later head of the SD, shared these views. As he said at Nuremberg:

When I became acquainted with the State Police it was certainly true that the nucleus of expert personnel had been taken from the Criminal Police and the majority of the leading men in the State Police offices, that is, in the regional offices of the State Police, had risen from the ranks of the civil administration, possibly also from the Police administrations of the various Länder [*Länderpolizeiverwaltungen*], and that they had, in part, even been detailed from the civil administration. The same was true for the experts within Amt IV—the Gestapo.[24]

Ohlendorf believed that while career civil servants probably made up the majority of the Gestapo in the early years of the Third Reich, by the time the war came 'that probably was no longer the case', if only because members of the Gestapo included numerous clerks and assistants of various kinds. He felt, on the other hand, that as a rule the preponderance of civil servants continued 'insofar as the specialists were concerned'.[25]

Rudolf Diels, the first head of the Gestapa under Göring in Berlin, claimed that he had not been interested in a purge of the police. A man whom Diels recruited, who was later sacked and eventually became an opponent of Nazism, said that many of the higher officials assigned to the Gestapo 'were by no means all Nazis. For the most part they were young professional civil service officers who felt ashamed at having been placed in this den of thieves. If they had obtained any support from their chief—who knows whether they might not have reduced the chaotic stronghold into an asylum of public

---

[21] Ibid. 142.
[22] See the testimony of Karl Heinz Hoffmann in IMT xx. 158; he refers to Koblenz. He added that 'according to my recollection, there were at most 10 to 15 percent of them who had entered the organization voluntarily after 1933'.
[23] Robert Lewis Koehl, *The Black Corps: The Structure and Power Struggles of the Nazi SS* (Madison, Wisc., 1983), 159–60.
[24] IMT iv. 344–5.
[25] Ibid. 345.

order?'[26] Diels deliberately selected higher officials 'who were not good Nazis—none of his subordinates would then enjoy the full confidence of the Party'.[27] Diels's own account points to the 'insignificant changes' in the personnel of the Prussian Gestapo during its initial establishment under his hand in 1933; some new members brought in were simply ambitious, but others, such as the senior official Arthur Nebe, a highly respected detective who *was* (initially) a true believer in Nazism (but who later joined the conspiracy against Hitler), were inclined to think that more 'law and order' and tighter police administration would be a good thing.[28] Diels maintained in his memoirs that the people he recruited were not opportunists, remained moral, Christian, and in the main not Party members; 'Göring did not demand it. To be sure, in the course of time one had to dress oneself in brown or black'—that is, join the Party or the SS.[29] Diels blamed the problems of the later Gestapo on Himmler, so that there is some self-justification and apology in his remarks, and those in the know at the time saw Diels himself as one of the 'March casualties', one of those who converted to Nazism after the elections that month in order to reap the benefits.[30]

Do these and other similar accounts hold up under close scrutiny? Christoph Graf studies the development of the Gestapo in Prussia during the transition phase from the Weimar Republic to the Nazi dictatorship, and especially the part played by Diels. Graf argues that relatively few open and early sympathizers of Nazism show up in the biographies of later Gestapo officials because until 20 July 1932 all participation by officials in Nazism was forbidden and taboo, a fact of particular importance to anyone in the Political Police. Any such activity had to be kept secret. The same was generally true everywhere in Germany. Benno Martin, for example, Police President of Nuremberg from 1934, and in the upper echelons of the local force from as early as 1925, later admitted to having had contacts with the NSDAP before 1933, although these had been hushed up until after the 'seizure of power'.[31]

However, it is not so clear that Graf has fully refuted Diels, Best, Ohlendorf, and the others. It is true that the Berlin headquarters were hardly an 'apolitical' force, as Graf makes clear. Among these people there was a good deal of sympathy for Nazism (at least for right-wing politics); between one-fifth and two-fifths of them even held membership of Nazi vocational organizations (Fachschaften) before 1933. However, there was no wholesale purge, in the sense of simply replacing the older police across the board.

Graf himself shows that many officials within the Berlin headquarters of

---

[26] Gisevius, 56.

[27] Ibid.: 'In time they were all eliminated as "unreliable".'

[28] Diels, 167.

[29] Ibid. 167–8. For the portrait of Nebe see Gisevius, 56ff.

[30] Heinrich Orb, *Nationalsozialismus: 13 Jahre Machtrausch* (Olten, 1945), 124–5.

[31] Ruth Bettina Birn, *Die höheren SS- und Polizeiführer: Himmlers Vertreter im Reich und in den besetzten Gebieten* (Düsseldorf, 1986), 340.

the Gestapo stayed at their desks, just as Diels and others said they did. A major reason for their continuing in office, he suggests, was a lack of alternatives due to a clearing out of possible opponents in the summer of 1932, thanks to the efforts of Franz von Papen.[32] Of the officials who managed to survive this event and the Nazi 'co-ordination' period, more than half of the 'older custodians' (that is, those in service before 1933) did not leave and were still there into the war-years.[33] Far from being merely political appointees, half of them had been trained as 'full jurists', and, especially in the Criminal Police service, many held doctorates.[34] One account based on the study of 135 officials who served in the RSHA—therefore at the highest levels, where political convictions were important—a study otherwise sceptical of claims made by Diels and others, remarked that in the Gestapo under Diels's command 'the older career officials still dominated until 1934', and even afterwards there was a continuing 'need for specialists'.[35]

Graf has mixed up two questions, the one dealing with a supposed purge, the other with the political beliefs of Gestapo officials. He perhaps went astray when he generalized from an analysis restricted to the transition phase under Diels (roughly 1932–4). He identified 65 officials in the Berlin headquarters of the Gestapo under Diels, although for the country as a whole there were perhaps 3,000 of them at the beginning of 1933.[36] But, more importantly, his object of investigation was the capital city of Prussia and Germany, where political trustworthiness came in for especially close scrutiny. He failed to see that, as a body, this echelon combined a good deal of technical expertise *and* appropriate political beliefs, so that any purge would have been unnecessary, even if it had been desirable. What was it like elsewhere?

Outside Gestapo headquarters in Berlin most people who ended up in the Gestapo were not previously connected with Nazism. To be sure that would not officially have been allowed in the Weimar days, as already mentioned. Still, no case has yet come to light of a local purge of major proportions, although such a move was definitely within the realm of possibility. Keeping in mind the obvious intent of affidavits submitted by individual Gestapo members to the Nuremberg trials, it is worth noting that 665 of them mention

[32] Graf, 83ff., has important things to say about the 'Papen *putsch*'.
[33] Ibid. 394.
[34] Ibid.
[35] Friedrich Zipfel, 'Gestapo and SD: A Sociographic Profile of the Organizers of the Terror', in Stein Ugelvik Larsen *et al.* (eds.), *Who were the Fascists? Social Roots of European Fascism* (Bergen, 1980), 308–9. There were 66 professional graduates of various kinds among the 135 (46 of them lawyers); 12 additional non-graduates also had a profession, 23 others had had subordinate positions in the police or administration. 'As a group they were intelligent and proficient.' See also his 'Gestapo und SD in Berlin', *Jahrbuch für die Geschichte Mittel- und Ostdeutschlands*, 9–10 (1961), 284, where a table indicates that the local Stapostelle Berlin (responsible for the capital city only) recorded 391 male employees on 25 June 1935. Thirty-six of these were in the SS, 23 of whom were listed as 'clerks'.
[36] See the figures in Diels, 166.

the issue of membership, and state that 'when the Gestapo was created, the requirements for personnel were for the most part met out of the existing Political Police'.[37] A detailed examination of the personnel in the Würzburg Gestapo (below) reinforces that contention.

In cities as far apart as Bremen, Hamburg, and Munich, the men who made up the variously named 'political police' forces tended to be conservative, nationalist, and 'correct'—and, to say the least, more than reserved when it came to supporting any of the left-wing parties. In Bremen, according to two recent accounts, there was a considerable degree of personnel and institutional carry-over from the older political police (the Zentral-polizeistelle).[38] It is also true that an approach based on something like a spoils system was taken to appointments to the Gestapo, so that there was a gradual infiltration by members of the Party, SS, and SA. Those who did not have the necessary qualifications might be taken on as relatively unimportant 'employees' for a time.[39] Marssolek and Ott's point about Bremen would seem to fit the pattern across the country very well:

Finally, the great continuity is remarkable within the Bremen Gestapo at the level of the middle-rank officers. Herrlein, Ripke, Parchmann, and Hafemann remained from beginning to end, albeit not above the function of section-leaders [Referatsleitern]. This continuity required an intimacy of the persecutors with the resistance—at least with parts of it.[40]

When obvious political appointees from the Party, SA, or SS—such as Hamburg's Political Police chief from March to May 1933, Anatol Milewski-Schroeden—did not measure up to the 'professional' demands of the job, the reins were quickly returned to more qualified people, especially those in the older department in charge of fighting 'Marxism and Communism'.[41] Peter Kraus, for many years a leading light in the Hamburg Political Police (called in that city the 'Staatspolizei' since 1927), and active sympathizer with the Nazi Party since 1932, stayed in office (as did most of the fifty-six others from the old Political Police) and led the fight against the Communists.[42] While the Nazis in Hamburg, as elsewhere, did not want the political police in the

[37] IMT xxi. 299. Forced membership was mentioned in 127 affidavits. George C. Browder, 'Sipo and SD, 1931–1940: Formation of an Instrument of Power' (University of Wisconsin Ph.D. thesis; Madison, 1968), 77, does not believe there was a purge; for the same point see Alwin Ramme, Der Sicherheitsdienst der SS (Berlin, 1970), 50, and Delarue, 89ff.

[38] Inge Marssolek and René Ott, Bremen im Dritten Reich: Anpassung, Widerstand, Verfolgung (Bremen, 1986), 176; Herbert Schwarzwälder, Geschichte der freien Hansestadt Bremen, iv. Bremen in der NS-Zeit (1933–1945) (Hamburg, 1985), 110–11.

[39] Zipfel, 'Profile', 304.

[40] Marssolek and Ott, 183. Cf. Heinz Höhne, The Order of the Death's Head: The Story of Hitler's SS, trans. R. Barry (1966; London, 1972), 163ff.

[41] Helmut Fangmann, Udo Reifner, and Norbert Steinborn, Parteisoldaten: Die Hamburger Polizei im 'Dritten Reich' (Hamburg, 1987), 51–53; for an identical case in Nuremberg see Reiche, 180.

[42] Henning Timpke (ed.), Dokumente zur Gleichschaltung des Landes Hamburg 1933 (Frankfurt, 1964), 174.

hands of non-political experts, it is clear that political convictions were never sufficient. There were chaotic times in the changeover years of 1933 and 1934; the many policemen who stayed in the service in time came to forget or ignore the letter of the law, and, encouraged by their superiors to fulfil their duties in 'the interest of national security', gave full rein to hatred and brutality.[43]

In Munich Himmler set about establishing a reliable political police force from the moment he was given the position of Bavaria's Police Commander. With the able assistance of Heydrich he recruited initially some 152 'well-trained' persons from various levels of service and branches of the Munich police.[44] As elsewhere, some were in the Nazi Party, but most were not. The new police (BPP) grew rapidly; a number of SS were taken on but appear mainly as assistants (Hilfskräfte).[45] Several of the new recruits in Bavaria are worth a brief mention because the individuals involved seem representative of the ways in which the new political police co-opted long-serving (non-Nazi) experts and tempted them to stay on.

One of the most able officials was Heinrich Müller, a man who later (1939) became head of the Gestapo under Himmler and held the position throughout the war-years. One Nazi insider and opponent of Müller, Walter Schellenberg (one of the heads of SD), recalled his first meeting with the boorish Müller. Apart from his appearance, about which Schellenberg had some unflattering things to say, it was noted that

although he had worked his way up to the top, he could never forget his origin. He once said to me in his crude Bavarian accent, 'One really ought to drive all the intellectuals into a coal mine and then blow it up.' Any form of real conversation with him was almost impossible; it consisted on his part almost entirely of coldly phrased questions and was largely an interrogation.[46]

Heinrich Müller was born in Munich on 28 April 1900, the son of Catholic parents, his father a minor rural police official. Heinrich participated in the First World War from 1917 and, as a flyer, earned decorations, among them the Iron Cross (1st class). After the war he entered the Munich Metropolitan Police, in which, thanks to great energy, he rose quickly. He was involved in the political police department, where he specialized in left-wing parties and groups. A compliment of sorts was paid to Müller in a political evaluation made in early 1937:

It must be acknowledged that he proceeded against these movements with great severity, in fact partially even ignoring the legal regulations and norms. It is no less clear, however, that Müller, had it been his task, would have proceeded just the same

---

[43] Ibid. 179.
[44] Aronson, 100–1.
[45] Ibid. 101.
[46] Walter Schellenberg, *The Labyrinth: The Memoirs of Walter Schellenberg*, trans. L. Hagan (New York, 1956), 8.

against the Right. With his vast ambition and relentless drive, he would have done everything to win the appreciation of whoever might happen to be his boss in a given system.[47]

Like Diels in Prussia, incidentally, he was said to prefer the appointment of men under him who had either served less than he or were dependent upon him, or just less competent. 'When it came to the selection of these officials, he took no political considerations into account, because he had merely his own egoistic aims in mind.'[48]

Müller had not been a member of the NSDAP before 1933—nor was he at the time of his political evaluation—and was not active in any of its affiliated organizations. The local Party district headquarters recommended that Müller should not get the promotion for which he was in line in 1937, because he had done nothing of merit for the Nazi cause. He had risen to the top without Party approval, in part because his chief Heydrich thought it an advantage not to have connections to the Party. Heydrich wanted to curtail the influence of the NSDAP almost from the day Hitler was appointed Chancellor.[49]

When Heydrich and the Nazis decided to take over the Munich Metropolitan Police building on 9 March 1933, Müller and Franz Josef Huber (among others), another prominent official who was to have a successful career in the Gestapo, offered some resistance. Local Police President Julius Koch was promptly deposed, but, rather than dropping Müller, Heydrich decided to take advantage of his knowledge of the Communists and his expertise in police business. On both counts Müller was worth keeping, all the more as he changed his attitude to Nazism, or at least served his new bosses as though he did.

Franz Josef Huber, who had been in charge of looking after the Nazis in the Munich police before 1933, was also permitted to stay. Like Müller, he was young (born in 1902), and the son of a Catholic policeman. In Huber's file there is a very negative political evaluation (also from 1937, on the occasion of a promotion inside the Gestapo), even more critical than the one on Müller. Huber was branded an informer who went around denouncing colleagues just before the 'seizure of power' for using the greeting 'Heil Hitler!' It was 'completely out of the question that he had changed his political views'. If he acted as though he had given up his 'ultramontane views', then this was purely to survive in his job. The evaluator reported that Huber feared being dismissed because of his well-known hatred of National Socialism prior to 1933, but thought that dismissal seemed more 'appropriate' than a

---

[47] See doc. 13, 4 Jan. 1937, in Aronson, 321.
[48] Ibid.
[49] After Müller became head of the Gestapo in Sept. 1939 the position he left as head of the Reich Centre for Jewish Emigration was inherited by Eichmann: Hannah Arendt, *Eichmann in Jerusalem: A Report on the Banality of Evil*, rev. edn. (New York, 1965), 67.

promotion![50] Huber too was nevertheless given this promotion (and many more), eventually ending up as Gestapo chief in Vienna in the same year (1939) that Müller was made Gestapo chief in the RSHA.

Only a systematic analysis of a broader sample of the Gestapo across Germany would establish just how representative the above examples are. At the very highest levels of the police, to be sure, expertise was important, but political (Nazi) background and personal relationships with Himmler or Heydrich were crucial.[51] Robert Koehl maintains that while the sixteen Inspectors of the Security Police and SD, whose very titles implied 'a firmer union of SS and Police, and included several old and convinced SS officers from 1931–1932 days, the bulk of the Security Police were professional police officials who had risen through co-operation with Heydrich. They exemplified the traits of conscientious bureaucrats willing to serve the Nazi cause rather than of devoted SS men.'[52]

4. GESTAPO OFFICIALS IN WÜRZBURG

According to Himmler's decree of 15 July 1937, the Gestapo in Bavaria was in future to be organized as follows. There was one Leading Gestapo post (Staatspolizeileitstelle), responsible for the district of Munich-Upper Bavaria, with four ordinary posts (Staatspolizeistellen) in the administrative centres of the four remaining government districts. In Würzburg, Duty Station (Dienststelle) 9, the political police of the 1920s was changed in 1929 into the 'state police administration'. As of 1 April 1933, as indicated above, all such sections through Bavaria came under Himmler as Bavaria's Police Commander. The law of 1937 confirmed the changes in Munich's Metropolitan Police and gave the Munich Gestapo the right to issue orders to the other posts in Bavaria, obtain records from them, and so on. It also changed the earlier political sections of all police directories into 'independent authorities'. Thus, four (central) Gestapo posts appeared in Augsburg, Nuremberg-Fürth, Regensburg, and Würzburg. All local Gestapo posts were at once directly responsible to Berlin headquarters (the Gestapa) although in theory they were also to inform the relevant local administrative heads (Regierungspräsidenten). In addition, as shown below, the local Gestapo could

---

[50] Doc. 14, 12 Feb. 1937, in Aronson, 322–3.

[51] See the biographies in Birn, 330ff., and Graf, 330ff.

[52] Koehl, The Black Corps, 160. On the gradual merger of police and SS, it should be noted that those who attained the 'SS recruiting standards' could be accepted into the SS and, in a second distinct step, might be promoted 'to an SS rank equivalent to their police rank', in what was called 'rank parity' (Dienstrangangleichung), which therefore involved much more than merely being co-opted into the SS. See Buchheim, 118ff. Gerald Reitlinger, The SS: Alibi of a Nation 1922–1945 (1956; Englewood Cliffs, NJ, 1981), 39, in emphasizing how many police stayed at their desks, said the myth was demolished 'that the inquisitors of the Gestapo were a new race of men, a scum brought to the surface by revolution'.

call on the ordinary police, mayors, magistrates, and so on as auxiliaries (Hilfsorgane). Matters relevant to the Gestapo which came to the attention of these latter groups were to be forwarded.[53]

Co-operation between the Gestapo and the incumbent state authorities seems by and large to have worked well, as in the persecution of the Jews, for example, and even in the organization and execution of the deportations.[54] There were to be further changes in the organization of the political police in Bavaria and in other states, as Himmler, Heydrich, Best, and others sought to create a genuinely national police (Reichspolizei), but the Gestapo in Bavaria persisted in the pattern established in 1937.

The information which would be required to give a detailed and exact plan of work of the Gestapo in Würzburg did not survive, but there was a considerable degree of centralization and standardization across the country: what has already been said about the organization of local Gestapo posts also applied there. When it comes to the personnel, it is possible to reconstruct some of the story on the basis of materials now located in the Berlin Document Centre. The 1937 survey mentioned earlier placed twenty-two Gestapo officials in Würzburg, of whom only eleven were on active duty (Außendienst), that is, not preoccupied with administration; in Aschaffenburg there was an outpost (Außendienststelle), with six additional officials. Together, these people were responsible for all of Lower Franconia's population of 840,663.[55] The number of officials there and everywhere else increased with the coming of war and with the assignment of new duties related to war measures, including keeping watch on prisoners of war and foreign workers.

It is possible to identify many, but not all, of the men who at one time or another were part of the Würzburg Gestapo. Career patterns there seem consistent with those already mentioned, and there was no purge of the police. Links with the Nazi Party, SS, or SA developed slowly. Only two Gestapo members—Josef Gerum and Ernst Gramowski—joined the Party before 1933, and, significantly, both rose to the top in the Third Reich, at one time or another becoming leaders of the local Gestapo. Several other men moved to the NSDAP in 1933, and some joined various Nazi formations. These early joiners (Heisig, Vogel, Völkl, and Wittmann) also had successful careers. Virtually all the others stayed out of the NSDAP itself until the 'loosening' (*Lockerung*) of Party membership in 1937. In fact, because nearly all those in the Würzburg Gestapo joined as of 1 May 1937, they were probably advised to get on the Party books. Those who came to the Gestapo

[53] BAK: R58/241, 101ff.

[54] H. G. Adler, *Der verwaltete Mensch: Studien zur Deportation der Juden aus Deutschland* (Tübingen, 1974), 372ff.

[55] BAK: R 58/610, 91: Personalstatistik der Staatspolizei, 31 Mar. 1937. The population figure is for 1939.

later, and who were not in the Party, joined the Party almost at the same time as they moved into the political police.

It was certainly possible for people to join the NSDAP in the years between 1933 and May 1937; in fact, the membership increased more or less steadily. After May 1937 there was a dramatic increase, when whole groups of civil servants, like the Gestapo, made the move.[56] Reich Minister of Justice Gürtner indicated in letters to officials in his jurisdiction in February 1937 that he 'expected' them to join the Nazi Party; this suggestion was very likely also made to the police, including the Gestapo.[57] A Bamberg judge later explained that there were also positive inducements to join when in May 1937 admission to the NSDAP became easier. Many joined because 'it was obvious to the servants of justice that a non-Party member could expect neither promotion nor advancement'.[58]

Those who served in the Würzburg Gestapo seem virtually without exception—at least so far as it has been possible to determine—to have been career policemen, or had been specifically trained (however briefly) for the police before 1933. There were blatant political appointees, especially at the top, when, for example, 'deserving' Party member and 'old fighter' Josef Gerum was handed the leadership of the Würzburg post in April 1934. Though his political credentials were impeccable—in the Party since 1920, participant in the abortive Hitler *putsch* in 1923, jailed (for four months) with the Führer himself in Landsberg prison—Gerum was also a trained policeman, and was in the Bavarian police (if at the lowliest rank) already in 1917. Gerum and those like him in the senior ranks, who had the appropriate political views, were selected at least in part because of their technical training. The non-political types who stayed at their desks implicitly accepted the legitimacy of the regime and the definitions of the tasks of the police. They may not have been card-carrying members of the Party, but they were hardly opponents of the system.

The appendix to this chapter (p. 76) lists all those who served at one time or another in Würzburg. Not included are the clerical staff (mainly women) or the officials from Nuremberg, who became closely involved in the Würzburg post's activities when, in the summer of 1941, the Würzburg Gestapo post lost its independence and became a branch of the Nuremberg operation.[59]

Ascribing motives to those who joined the Gestapo is problematical. Hannah Arendt characterized Adolf Eichmann, a man in many ways representative of the policeman in the Third Reich, with the label 'banality of evil'. Most of them were neither crazed, demented, nor superhuman, but

[56] Kater, *The Nazi Party*, 263ff., figs. 1–4.
[57] The letter is printed in Dr [Hans] Schütz, *Justiz im 'Dritten Reich'. Dokumentation aus dem Bezirk des Oberlandesgerichts Bamberg* (Bamberg 1984), annex 4.
[58] Ibid. 81.
[59] Thereafter it had the cumbersome title 'Geheime Staatspolizei—Staatspolizeistelle Nürnberg-Fürth, Außendienststelle Würzburg'.

terribly ordinary. According to his own testimony in Jerusalem, Eichmann, a man at one stage in charge of sending countless thousands to Auschwitz, was not an anti-Semite.[60] He was a perfect example of the 'compartmental' thinker, one who insisted that he had never taken a decision on his own, but could point to either a 'relevant Reich law' or 'implementation orders' or 'police regulations, the decrees, orders, and instructions of Himmler and the head of Security Police as legislative basis'.[61]

The historian Shlomo Aronson and others offer some speculation as to why some stayed in their jobs. These conjectures are worth recalling because they probably apply to many other officials beyond the more important central characters such as Müller and Huber. For most it was preferable to stay rather than to give up their cherished careers, after long years of apprenticeship and, with few other prospects in view, especially because of the massive unemployment throughout the country. From 30 January 1933 it was obvious that the police in general (and the political police particularly) were going to become much more important than before, so that if one could hang on in the transition phase career prospects were almost certainly going to improve. Besides these kinds of self-aggrandizing motives, other factors came into play, some of which have already been mentioned, such as the desire for 'law and order'.

Aronson's portrayal of Müller suggests a somewhat uncritical adoption of the 'apolitical German civil servant', a man who felt good only in his office.[62] Similarly, Friedrich Panzinger, a colleague of Müller in Munich before 1933, who rose with him later in Berlin (also a non-Party member until 1937), said that Müller never acted out of 'fanatical devotion to the Führer', as the saying went, but from a sense of 'traditional duty to the profession in which he found himself'; 'it would have appeared to him as cowardice and treason to leave it'.[63] An alternative view of Müller is offered by Walter Schellenberg, a man who got to know and dislike him. Though Müller may or may not have been a dyed-in-the-wool Nazi, he was certainly not against some form of authoritarian state with a secret police. He shocked Schellenberg during a conversation in the spring of 1943 by lauding the Stalinist system, in which a 'unified and really uncompromising spiritual and biological force' was developing. Müller said that the problem with Nazism was that it made 'too many compromises', whereas the Communists had 'a consistent attitude to life' which was 'lacking among most of our Western intellectuals, excepting perhaps some of the SS'. Müller said he was forced to conclude that in all

[60] Jochen von Lang (ed.), *Das Eichmann Protokoll* (Berlin, 1982) 41.

[61] Ibid. 113. See especially Hans Mommsen, 'The Realization of the Unthinkable: The "Final Solution of the Jewish Question" in the Third Reich', in Gerhard Hirschfeld (ed.), *The Policies of Genocide: Jews and Soviet Prisoners of War in Nazi Germany* (London, 1986), 93ff.

[62] Aronson, 229–30. This view of Müller is widely shared, e.g. by Crankshaw, 68: 'He was the arch-type of the non-political functionary, in love with personal power.'

[63] Panzinger joined the SA in July 1933; he is quoted in Aronson, 230; cf. Höhne, 164ff.

important respects, when the Soviet leader was compared to Hitler 'Stalin does...things better'.[64] Müller had definite ideas about how the country should be run, and these are poorly described by the term 'apolitical'. The new regime and its leading policemen, such as Himmler and Heydrich, held out positive inducements to such people. The absence of unity and lack of central control of the political police from the days of Weimar were over, and a new sense of legitimacy was conferred upon the police not enjoyed since the days of Imperial Germany.The country was 'co-ordinated', and so were efforts to fight crime. In his efforts against Communism before 1933, Müller and people like him had been frustrated by the ways Weimar offered a modicum of protection for the accused. He had then threatened to overstep legal boundaries; now he was given official sanction and encouragement.

5. THE GESTAPO SPY NETWORK

Little information has survived on the Gestapo spy network, one thought by contemporaries to be so extensive that escape from surveillance was all but impossible. This group was in fact much smaller than believed, but Werner Best was going too far when he nearly denied its existence altogether. At the Nuremberg trials he said that it was not true 'that the Gestapo had a net of spies and information agencies which kept track of the entire people'.[65] But a group of informers was linked to the Gestapo on a regular basis—although one should not inflate its size and the number of undercover agents.

Some people were various kinds of confidential informers. The most important of these were the 'V'-persons (agents): often paid, but not always, they were recruited by the various 'desks' or specialists in the local Gestapo branches; there were also 'G'-persons (contacts), in general, occasional tellers of tales; finally came 'I'-persons (reporters), who were not really part of the network proper but kept track of the public mood and reported to the police.[66]

Very little is known about such people, about their number, the rate of their turnover, their occupations, and the contribution they made to policing Nazi Germany. One Bavarian locality where some information has come to light is Nuremberg, the immediate superior headquarters for the Würzburg Gestapo. As of 1 September 1941 there was a total of 150 Gestapo officials centred in the Middle Franconian city, responsible for a population which totalled 2,771,720, distributed over 14,115 square kilometres.[67] Elke Fröhlich discovered that in the years 1943–4 there were six officials in charge

---

[64] Schellenberg, 319–20.
[65] IMT xx. 128.
[66] Gertrud Meyer, *Nacht über Hamburg: Berichte und Dokumente* (Frankfurt, 1971), 81. These were *Vertrauens-/Verbindungs-Leute, Gewährs-Leute,* and *Informations-Leute.*
[67] BAK: R 58/856, 116 ff.: 1 Sept. 1941, 'Schlüsselmäßige Stellenverteilung auf die Staatspolizei(leit)stellen'.

of the informers' department—section IVn—and that there were some 80–
100 people regularly informing the Gestapo but not formally members of it.[68]
The figures for Nuremberg were probably not all that exceptional, since the
numbers of informers and areas of specialization that any given Gestapo post
could support, as well as the size of their remuneration and even their
reliability tests, were regulated nationally, as were most other political police
matters. The ratio of informers to full-time officials in Nuremberg was at the
outside one paid informer for every official. Normally these people conveyed
information on an area of specific concern to the regime, while continuing
to pursue their regular full-time jobs and professions. In Bremen a few who
worked on the docks and in factories were paid to report on what they saw,
and apparently some foreign workers provided useful information.[69] However,
the relatively small numbers of Gestapo members were far from being at the
head of an 'army' of agents.

The Gestapo's confidential informants have recently been the subject of a
publication by Walter Weyrauch.[70] In 1945, under the auspices of the United
States military government, Weyrauch had analysed a collection of the
Frankfurt Gestapo card-files on informers. His updated summary deals only
with the 1,200 or so cards of people who at one time or another were paid
to inform. He deliberately excludes other kinds of collaborators, such as those
he calls 'spite informers', even though, as Chapter 5 will show, they were of
far greater significance in generating cases than those who were paid and/or
who worked regularly for the Gestapo and SD on an honorary basis. The
contribution of confidential informers, in so far as Reinhard Mann detected
their efforts in initiating cases in Düsseldorf, seems to have been small, for
the category of cases he labelled 'observations of the Stapo-Düsseldorf and V-
Persons' comprised only 15 per cent of all cases, although what proportion
of these can be traced to the activities of the Gestapo itself and what proportion
to informers is not clear.[71]

Weyrauch sees the 'typical Nazi informant' in the Frankfurt data as 'uncon-
nected with the Nazi party or the official German government structure';
such a person might often be known as 'unsympathetic' to Nazism and
'sometimes seemed suited for a leadership position after the war'.[72] The
informers of the Frankfurt Gestapo included a disproportionately large
number of Swiss citizens (who seem to have been permanent German residents), though no specific figures are given; 'enemy citizens' living in the

[68] Fröhlich, 212.

[69] Cf. Marssolek and Ott, 183, and Schwarzwälder, 407–8.

[70] Walter Otto Weyrauch, 'Gestapo Informants: Facts and Theory of Undercover Operations',
Columbia Journal of Transnational Law, 24 (1986), 554ff. An expanded German account is due to
be published by Vittorio Klostermann (Frankfurt).

[71] Most V-persons were paid, but some offered information on a more or less regular basis for
no fee.

[72] Weyrauch, 560.

country were also recruited to inform.[73] Informants were drawn from people who had a record of known opposition to the regime and some individuals whom the regime considered 'tainted' for 'ethnic or religious reasons'. It is a grim fact that some Jews as well as some Catholic priests acted as Gestapo informers; these assertions are supported by evidence from other parts of the country.[74]

Weyrauch remarks that some priests misused the confessional to gain confidential information, then turned it over to the secret police. He adds that 'personal knowledge about one such case makes me hesitate to pass judgment. This particular priest was revered as a saint among his parishioners for his unselfish devotion to his tasks, sometimes under circumstances that seemed to require extreme personal commitment and courage. Yet he appeared as a confidential informant in the Gestapo files.'[75]

Weyrauch suggests that 'circumstantial coercion' was probably the over-riding factor behind the confidential informers' activity. However, he admits that 'the index-cards were silent about specific threats', that the extent to which these putative threats 'amounted to duress as a legal defense is a matter of speculation', and that 'significantly the vast majority of suspect persons seem to have been able to avoid becoming confidential informants after having been interrogated and detained by Gestapo officials'.[76] In the end, a leap of faith is required to accept the notion of circumstantial coercion as the overriding factor. It may be suggested instead that positive motives might have been behind collaboration, as, for example, has been established for collaborators elsewhere in Europe.[77]

Material on several Gestapo agents that survives from Aachen suggests that coercion was not invariably used. The Gestapo and its regular informers were evidently always on the look-out for recruits. An Aachen report to the Cologne Gestapo of 24 August 1942 stated that an agent who was on holiday chanced to meet a certain priest whom he had known for some time. The priest was characterized as 'suitable' for the job of informant because of his positive opinions and disposition towards the regime. From agents' files in the Düsseldorf archive one gets the distinct impression that many saw working

---

[73] Ibid.

[74] Ibid. 577ff. Cf. BAK: 58/610. There the case of a priest was dealt with in accordance with a decree of 1 Feb. 1937, which indicates that the matters were regulated nationally. As for the information contained in his résumé, his 'fee' of 'RM 60 monthly' is noted, his area of expertise—naturally enough political Catholicism—his reliability, and so forth. More on this topic is given in ch. 5.

[75] Weyrauch, 579.

[76] Ibid. 565, 567, 569.

[77] Recruiting a social spy network involved asking some people to do things they might not feel good about. One young woman, a good National Socialist, who was unwilling to co-operate by informing simply said so, and nothing further occurred. See Melita Maschmann, *Fazit: Mein Weg in der Hitler-Jugend* (Munich, 1981), 43ff. Other examples of Gestapo pressure are in Christoph Klessmann and Falk Pingel (eds.), *Gegner des Nationalsozialismus* (Frankfurt, 1980), 195ff.

for the Gestapo in similar terms. Agents who wished to discontinue, or who failed to show the requisite enthusiasm, were simply dropped. One agent, it was reported, simply lost interest, another was let go because of a nervous disorder, while yet another had to be taken off the roll when he was drafted into the armed forces.[78]

Detlev Peukert believes that the information passed on to the Gestapo from planted spies was not as useful as the denunciations from the population at large or the reports of 'the smaller agents on the periphery of the Communist milieu'.[79] Still, there is evidence in the Gestapo materials that specially planted agents at times played an important role. The Aachen Gestapo, for example, wrote in October 1944 that one of them was working under cover on the Communist Party; he is described as 'very gifted' in making contacts with 'enemy circles', 'intelligent, cautious, but nevertheless unerring'. He could be regarded as 'reliable . . . his reports were flawless and led to the greatest success'. 'His active and gifted collaboration' is mentioned in a letter to Cologne headquarters. On the basis of one of his reports it was possible to destroy a very large 'terror organization of mixed character'.[80]

Gertrud Meyer's account of Gestapo methods of tracking the workers' movement in Hamburg shows that in a number of instances undercover agents were crucial in the arrest of Communist functionaries, who were subsequently killed.[81] In the autumn of 1934 a Gestapo spy in Würzburg, acting as an *agent provocateur*, went so far as to initiate and organize an underground KPD group, even getting the illegal literature from the police, only to turn in those who could be recruited.[82] A number of other works also show that the Gestapo had to make greater efforts in planting spies in the working-class movement than was usually the case when it came to dealing with 'opponents'. While some collaborators may have had to be intimidated into working with the police, as Meyer and others show, this was not invariably the case.[83] More will be said about the role of agents and political denunciations in the working-class milieu below; here it should be noted that even a few spectacular 'successes' led to an overestimation of the strength of the Gestapo, especially within the underground opposition movement.[84]

[78] See HStA D: RW 34, Nr. 33, Staatspolizeistelle Cologne.
[79] Detlev Peukert, *Die KPD im Widerstand: Verfolgung und Untergrundarbeit an Rhein und Ruhr 1933 bis 1945* (Wuppertal, 1980), 123.
[80] HStA D: RW 34, Nr. 33.
[81] Meyer, 77ff.
[82] Mehringer, 'Die KPD', 228–9.
[83] Marssolek and Ott, 183, also speak of KPD members being forced to spy; Peukert, *Die KPD*, 125ff., also hints at the pressure applied.
[84] Peukert, *Die KPD*, 121. See also Allan Merson, *Communist Resistance in Nazi Germany* (London, 1985), 50ff.

6. OTHER INFORMERS: THE 'SECURITY SERVICE' (SD)

The SD also played a part in the enforcement process. Some confusion has arisen on this point because Reinhard Heydrich, eventually 'Chief of the Security Police and of the SD' within the national umbrella body, the RSHA, was (under Himmler) technically the head of *all* police.[85] In 1932, a year after the SD was created as a separate branch of the SS, Heydrich was made its chief. Before Hitler's appointment the SD served as watch-dog of both SS and the Nazi Party, but from 1933 it developed various missions that would make possible a distinctive contribution. One account emphasizes the role that members of the SD played in consolidating the political police in the hands of Himmler and Heydrich.[86] Notwithstanding 'increasingly close personnel and institutional connections' between Gestapo and SD after 1933, however, 'attempts to delineate their respective areas of responsibility testified [to a rivalry]... without removing it'.[87]

Walter Schellenberg, subsequently a leader of the SD, recalls in his memoirs the aims of the organization as told to him when he moved to Frankfurt in 1934, when the rivalries were in full swing:

An SS Oberfuehrer whom I had already met... explained to me the mission of the SD and its aims. The SD was the chief organ of the information service of the Party. Its task was to inform the top Party leaders of all opposition movements and forces at home and abroad. It covered the administration, the Party, industry, the theatre, journalism, the police—in fact there was no sphere that was not under the watchful eye of the SD, no place where it did not seek out the first signs of opposition among movements or individuals 'hostile to the state'.[88]

Not only was this mission in actual or potential conflict with any number of other organizations, especially the Gestapo, but, according to Schellenberg, how it was to be accomplished posed a 'tremendous administrative problem'. The SD was a Nazi Party institution, and its relatively few full-time members were paid by it. It was organized across the country in a set-up broadly similar and parallel to that of the Gestapo. In time, at least on paper, there was a neat-looking division of tasks, a 'steel net' of Gestapo, SD, and Criminal Police through which no 'opponents' should be able to pass.[89]

---

[85] The RSHA included the SD 'Domestic' (under Ohlendorf) and SD 'Foreign' (led by Schellenberg).

[86] Lawrence D. Stokes, 'The *Sicherheitsdienst* (SD) of the *Reichsführer* SS and German Public Opinion, September 1939–June 1941' (John Hopkins University PH.D. thesis; Baltimore, 1972), 51 ff. For a recent interpretative essay see Michael Geyer, 'National Socialist Germany: The Politics of Information', in Ernest R. May (ed.), *Knowing One's Enemies* (Princeton, 1986), 310 ff.

[87] Stokes, *Sicherheitsdienst*, 86.

[88] Schellenberg, 9.

[89] Regional heads were the 'inspectors of Security Police and SD'; these men were supposed simultaneously to be in charge of Gestapo Offices (Stapoleitstellen) and the SD Main Sectors

The SD emerged on the domestic front as 'a national intelligence service based not on police spies and informers, but on every citizen who would feel a patriotic duty to give information'.[90] It relied for much of its information on well-placed volunteers or 'honorary members' in order, not only to fight 'opposition', but to provide Nazi leaders with accurate accounts of public opinion. SD informers were to keep in touch with the ebb and flow of German life, and constituted 'a most comprehensive secret Gallup Poll rather than a police force or spy network'.[91]

The secretiveness of the SD, however, gave rise to all kinds of rumours and even complaints from the Nazi Party. In the summer of 1933 some Gauleiters charged that the SD was undermining authority, but even less powerful Party types, such as its 'old fighters', on occasions bemoaned its existence, saying it was 'not National Socialist' for such snooping to take place.[92] Hans Buchheim believes that the main reason why the SD was not simply disbanded in the years leading up to the war was probably that through it 'Himmler could be sure of retaining his monopoly' as watchdog 'within the National Socialist movement'.[93] The role of the SD was so complicated and confused that many members themselves were uncertain about their tasks and their place in the Nazi police system. One historian says that by the late 1930s 'SD membership had become so complex', its self-images so incompatible, that it was torn between 'terroristic police work', 'illegal "dirty work"', and the demands of its 'idealistic functionaries'.[94]

Heydrich's decree of 1 July 1937 on the 'division of labour between Gestapo and SD' attempted to put an end to the worst territorial disputes. The two organizations were said to comprise a 'unity' in which all duplication of effort and competition was to be avoided; one 'supplemented' the other, but was neither superior nor inferior. The ṢD was to deal 'exclusively' with the areas of 'learning' (*Wissenschaft*), art, Party and state, constitution and admin-

---

(Leitabschnitte), as well as the Criminal Police Offices (Kripoleitstellen); beneath the regional level the net spread to the larger centres or strategically important ones, such as border-crossing points. See Black, 300, app. E. The SD came under the Reich (state) budget in 1940–1, according to Browder, 'Sipo', 366ff.

[90] George C. Browder, 'The SD: The Significance of Organization and Image', in Mosse (ed.), *Police Forces*, 207.

[91] Ibid. 220.

[92] George C. Browder, 'Die Anfänge des SD: Dokumente aus der Organisationsgeschichte des Sicherheitsdienstes des Reichführers SS', *VfZ* 27 (1979), 506. There were complaints that the SD's 'secretive surveillance' opened the door to denunciations. See Berchtesgaden Ortsgruppe, 23 Jan. 1935, to Kreisleitung, in StA M: NSDAP 357; the file contains other such concerns. That the Party continued to be touchy about the SD is evident from Hess's directive of 14 Dec. 1938, in which he tried to set out how the two should work together; he reiterated that 'the task of the SD was not to keep watch on the Party, but the enemies of the Party': BAK: R58/275, 191 (a).

[93] Buchheim, 71.

[94] Browder, 'The SD', 221.

istration, foreign lands, Freemasonry and associations, while the Gestapo's jurisdiction was Marxism, treason, and emigrants. In addition, the SD was to handle 'all general questions and matters of principle' in the areas of 'churches and sects', pacifism, the Jews, right-wing movements of various kinds, the economy, and the Press—but, and this is the vital point, it was to avoid all matters which touched 'state police executive powers [*staatspolizeiliche Vollzugsmaßnahmen*]', since these belonged to the Gestapo, as did all 'individual cases'.[95]

Estimates of membership in the SD have ranged widely. By the summer of 1941 there was a total of 57 SD Branches and/or Main Branches (SD Abschnitte/Leitabschnitte) for all of the 'new Germany'.[96] Though the figures cannot be established, those given by Otto Ohlendorf put them at 3,000 salaried and 30,000 part-time or 'honorary' members.[97] When evidence of political 'criminality' was discovered, the SD, which had no police powers, had to hand the case over to the Gestapo or other police for executive treatment (*exekutivmäßig*).[98] As will be shown later, when it came to enforcing the law, or the spirit of National Socialism, the SD was not as active as is often supposed.

In July 1944 a list of some forty-three informers (V-persons) was sent to the Würzburg SD headquarters from the Aschaffenburg subsection. The individuals, who were to continue in their normal line of work, were to report on specific areas of social life according to their speciality, vocation, or everyday experiences. The list of ten men who were to provide information on administrative matters contains numerous local notables, including three mayors, two magistrates, a tax inspector, three other kinds of higher administrative inspectors, and several other city officials; those in the 'education and religious life' section were two senior educational administrators, a senior teacher, and three additional teachers, as well as two businessmen; the person dealing with 'financial matters' was the assistant manager of a local savings bank; and so on. The people who were to report on the 'general life of the people' included mainly women, housewives as well as those employed outside the home. For the most part skilled workers and managers were to inform on 'industry and energy'. The evidence suggests that SD informers were

---

[95] A copy of the law is in Rürup (ed.), 64ff. Karl Heinz Höppner said that when it came to supporting the Gestapo's efforts, such as in the 'destruction and neutralization of the opposition', the SD was of little help because 'it was the task of the Security Service to investigate failures in all spheres of life. Individual cases were examples. It was not its task to institute proceedings with any other offices against individuals': IMT xx. 193, 196–7; cf. Eichmann, in Lang (ed.), 30.

[96] Werner Best, *Die deutsche Polizei* (Darmstadt, 1941), 65.

[97] Ohlendorf, in IMT xx. 329.

[98] See the memoranda in LHA Ko: 662,6/383, esp. SD-Abschnitt Koblenz to Außenstelle Trier, 3 Dec. 1941 and 22 July 1943.

overwhelmingly volunteers.[99] Walter Schellenberg recalled that these informants 'were usually men of wide experience in their own fields and were thus in a position to furnish very valuable information, giving special attention to reports on public opinion and reactions to legislation, decrees and other measures taken by the government'.[100]

Werner Best, not only a leading Gestapo official but in the SD as well, helped compose a decree of 11 November 1938 which mentioned that an important duty of the SD was to act in 'support of the Security Police'. He said later that little came of that intention. As Best put it, 'in those years there were experiments constantly going on with the SD' and

the chief of both the Security Police and the SD, Heydrich, was interested in having the SD gain an insight into the activity of the offices and agencies of the State. The exact wording of this decree was chosen in order to justify the aim sufficiently. In truth the scope of tasks to be put to the SD whose model was to be the great foreign intelligence service...developed in such a manner that the SD was not to be an auxiliary branch of the Police but rather a purely political information organ of the State leadership, for the latter's own control of its political activities.[101]

At the Nuremberg trials the historian Gerhard Ritter testified about the activities of the SD at the University of Freiburg, where he was a professor. According to Ritter the organization kept itself informed about the research activities as well as the attitudes of the university population, including criticism of leaders and the public measures they took. However, he was aware of no case where the SD actually turned over someone or even reported a faculty member to the Gestapo. He had felt it necessary to be cautious about what he said in his lectures, and was on one occasion reprimanded by the Gestapo, but this was 'a result of a denunciation' which 'did not originate with the SD'.[102]

7. POLICE BEYOND THE GESTAPO

Karl Heinz Hoffmann, a senior local Gestapo official who served in Koblenz and Düsseldorf, testified at Nuremberg about the importance of the Gestapo's links to the older state apparatus, the so-called 'inner administration'. Like Best and others, Hoffmann portrayed the Gestapo as a group of higher officials who were not 'everywhere', as contemporaries often feared. 'In towns and districts in which there were no offices of the Stapo, its lower levels were

[99] Sta W: NSDAP GL Mainfranken, IV/Nr. 8. For more on the SD in Mainfranken see Broszat *et al.* (eds.), *Bayern in der NS-Zeit*, i. 592ff.

[100] Schellenberg, 9. For comment on the collaboration between the two kinds of spies see Browder, '*Sipo*', 187.

[101] IMT xx. 140–1. Cf. Wilhelm Hoettl, in PS 2614, ibid. xxxi. 37–8.

[102] See Affidavit SD-65, ibid. xlii. 465–8.

represented by the district and local police officials, and the gendarmerie. Approximately 80 per cent of all matters came from these police offices.'[103] Best said that with so few officials actually in the Gestapo it was necessary to call upon district and local police authorities—the chief magistrates of the district, the gendarmerie, and the municipal police—who acted either on the basis of information which came to their desks or on instructions from state police authorities.[104] Best maintained that 'as far as the volume is concerned the district and local police authorities handled the major part of the individual state police cases as the state police offices only sent out their officials for their own information in special cases, above all, in cases of treason and high treason'.[105]

There was a close relationship between the traditional criminal police, the detectives (Kripo), and the Gestapo, 'at least on paper', as it was put by a man who served in the Kripo, and this derived from the obvious fact that 'to National Socialist Germany it went without saying that the battle against the political enemy of state and against the anti-social criminal should be conducted by one hand'.[106] The Kripo retained an identity separate from the Gestapo, although in time there was a convergence as the former became more and more like the latter, complete with powers of 'preventive arrest', at least concerning the criminality of groups such as the gypsies, the work-shy, or so-called asocial elements.[107]

The organizational charts and historical sketches for use inside the police itself made a great deal of the ways in which the Kripo was to be distinguished from the Gestapo. The Kripo was supposedly that 'branch of the police which concerned itself with the surveillance and laying hold of common (non-political)' criminals; its tasks were mainly the 'prevention and investigation of (non-political) culpable actions'. Unlike the Gestapo it could work more openly and had the complete backing of virtually all law-abiding citizens.[108] Institutionally, the Kripo was centralized under Himmler in 1936 so that the leadership of both the Kripo and Gestapo was in his hands. With the creation of Kripo posts across Germany more or less on the Gestapo (and SD) model, the criminal police was centralized for the first time in its history and the country was covered in a 'steel net' through which, supposedly, no criminal could pass.[109] Kripo and Gestapo grew closer when both became part of the new body called the Security Police (Sipo) in June 1936 (under Himmler), and in 1939 both—along with the rest of Germany's police—were centralized

---

[103] Ibid. xx. 157.
[104] Ibid. 127.
[105] Ibid.
[106] Bernd Wehner, *Dem Täter auf der Spur: Die Geschichte der deutschen Kriminalpolizei* (Bergisch Gladbach, 1983), 161.
[107] Buchheim, 113.
[108] All in BAK: R58/275 13 ff., Organisation der Polizei, 1935.
[109] Wehner, 162.

in the RSHA, where the Kripo chief was Arthur Nebe in Office V, while the Gestapo was under Müller in Office VI.

But quite apart from such institutional developments, there was bound to be a blurring of the distinctions between the Gestapo and the Kripo in that certain conventional crimes came within the jurisdiction of the former, if they were allegedly committed by Jews or foreign workers; in addition, on occasion Kripo officers were handed 'political' tasks. Criminality was gradually turned into a political and even a racial category, so that increasingly the Kripo came to be involved in 'political' matters. The notion of 'prevention of crime' already contained in the 'law against dangerous repeat offenders and for regulation of their security and improvement' (24 November 1933), was capable of indefinite expansion, and eventually more and more categories of offenders were added to the list of people whose crimes were to be 'prevented' before they could act: beggars, vagabonds, prostitutes, pimps, pushers, black-marketeers, hard-nosed traffic offenders, the work-shy, gypsies, and others were included.[110] The treatment to be accorded to these and other social outsiders—as embodied, for example in the 1937 decree on 'preventive police measures to combat crime', which consigned 'asocials' to concentration camps—was similar to that meted out to political 'criminals' or to race 'enemies'.[111]

Pursuit of deviations from the letter and even the spirit of the law was stepped up with the coming of war, and Kripo and Gestapo, directed from the RSHA by their common Senior Chief, Heydrich (himself under Himmler), set about tightening the 'steel net' over the country. Apart from the convergence of goals, there was something of a personnel link as well; local Gestapo officials, particularly at the middle and lower ranks, had previously been members of the criminal police, and in fact a large number of Gestapo members were detailed from the Kripo into the secret police.[112] Kripo and Gestapo continued to use traditional kinds of executive authority, such as arrest, interrogation, and confiscation of property. This ability set both apart from the SD, which as a Party organization was not permitted these methods of operation.[113] In spite of these and other shared experiences, there is no question that the Gestapo played by far the greater role in the Nazi system of terror, not least because it expressly concerned itself with the regime's attempts to modify political attitudes and behaviour of all kinds—well beyond dealing with deviations from criminal law.

Notwithstanding its relations to the Gestapo, at the top leadership level

---

[110] Wehner, 201.

[111] Peukert, *Volksgenossen*, 253 ff.

[112] Such a development is also confirmed by Ohlendorf (IMT iv. 345), Gisevius (ibid. xii. 167 ff.), and Kaltenbrunner (ibid. xi. 309).

[113] Koehl, *The Black Corps*, 162, says that the SD lost its powers of investigation and arrest by 1937, and that 'put it in the shade as a truly important service'.

and in its everyday operations the Kripo remained a distinct organization. In a newspaper article of 17 February 1941 Heydrich noted that, in marked contrast to the Gestapo, the public image of the Kripo, which went back well beyond 1933, was as a 'friend and helper' against all kinds of criminality; an 'ethical' dimension had been added to its work, such as the effort to watch prices, protect youth, struggle against dangers to 'positive population development' ('abortion and homosexuality'); where necessary it could use 'preventive' measures. The Kripo could turn up information relevant to the secret police, and vice versa, and the closest co-operation was sought. The aims of the Gestapo, 'only a tiny percentage' of which could be spoken of publicly, according to Heydrich, pertained to work against the enemies of the people and the state, spies, saboteurs, and traitors; it also had the duty to enforce laws and ordinances resulting from war measures, and those stemming from 'handling the Jewish question', such as 'emigration of the Jews'.[114]

The regular uniformed police, divided before 1933 into seventeen or so different provincial (land) forces, was centralized at last on 28 March 1940, when it was brought under the federal budget, but even earlier, under Kurt Daluege, the police had been unified to a large extent with the new title of 'order police' or Orpo (Ordungspolizei).[115] That change followed Himmler's appointment as Chief of all German police in June 1936. One of Daluege's tasks after 1933 had been to 'clean out' the police in Prussia, but the extent of the cleaning was limited, at least if the uniformed city police in Prussia, the Schupo (Schutzpolizei), can be taken as a guide. As it was a subsection of the Orpo, the Schupo's 'cleansing' probably reflected the trend in the rest of the Orpo. Of 50,000 or so patrol-men, 2.7 per cent (or a total of 1,370) were dismissed; a higher percentage of officers, who were in the public eye, met this fate—but still, only 294 out of 2,400 were sacked.[116] The gradual infiltration of Nazis into the police seems to have begun later, and was a process which was never taken to its full conclusion. Robert Koehl believes that the proportion of SS members in the Kripo and Orpo was smaller than in the Gestapo, and, moreover, that when the numbers of SS in the upper echelons of the former increased, most continued to be drawn, not from the ranks of the SS, but from the police, who were asked to don SS garb; at least some police directors or police presidents who joined the SD did so less out of political or ideological conviction than simply 'in self-defense' to hold their own against ambitious junior officers. Even later, when the sixteen Inspectors

---

[114] The article is in HStA D: RW 36, Nr. 7, 5–7.
[115] H.-J. Neufeldt, J. Huck, and G. Tessin, *Zur Geschichte der Ordnungspolizei* (Koblenz, 1957), 7ff.
[116] Eric D. Kohler, 'The Crisis of the Prussian Schutzpolizei 1930–32', in Mosse (ed.) *Police Forces*, 149. Daluege claimed in a letter to Hitler (3 Feb. 1934) that he had cleared out on average 7.7% of the eleven categories of officials in the Prussian police administration; see Caplan, *Government without Administration*, 145.

of the Order Police joined the SS, the 'long police careers' behind them rendered their 'high SS ranks secondary'.[117]

The ordinary police stations (the Polizeirevier of the Schupo) in cities such as Berlin continued to work as before the days of the dictatorship, and to play their part in enforcing even specific Nazi policies, such as those pertaining to racial matters. They received denunciations and complaints of all kinds from the population, and these were dutifully checked, whether or not they amounted to breaches of the traditional criminal code or of specific Nazi measures—such as giving refuge to Jews who went underground after 1941 to avoid deportation. Some idea of how enforcement operated can be deduced from the remarks of the Schupo man to a group of Jews hiding in Berlin— which subsequently, thanks to fake documents, managed to elude his grasp. After checking all their identification papers, the policeman remarked:

So, then, I want to explain to you the basis of my coming here. I am happy to say that I have been able to convince myself that everything here is in the best conceivable order. But we received a denunciation that Mr R supposedly regularly hides illegally quartered Jews in his apartment! You're shocked, right? But you have no idea how many denunciations we must cope with at headquarters! And it is our duty to check each and every one of them, even if most turn out to be malicious suspicions or backbiting.[118]

Although there were remarkably few Gestapo people on the ground, there were many professional and amateur helpers on whom they could rely.

8. THE NAZI PARTY'S POLICE FUNCTION

After Hitler's appointment, the Nazi Party, which had once been geared for ceaseless electioneering and, through the SA, had fought it out in the streets with political opponents, went through a transformation in its character and operation. As might be expected, it came to play a role in the police network. A detailed study of the Nazi Party's place in policing Germany and the activities of its numerous ancillary organizations, from the German Labour Front (Deutsche Arbeitsfront, DAF) to the local branches of the Hitler Youth, and so on, remains to be written. But it is possible to gain some idea of what such a study might show.

There was a general increase in membership from 849,009 in early 1933 to 2,493,890 in mid-1935; after a short respite, those on the Party roll increased again from May 1937, and at about the time of the outbreak of the Second World War membership stood at 4,985,400.[119] But beyond this

---

[117] Koehl The Black Corps, 160.
[118] Else R. Behrend-Rosenfeld, Ich stand nicht allein: Leben einer Jüdin in Deutschland 1933–1944 (1945; Munich, 1988), 227–8.
[119] Kater, The Nazi Party, 263, fig. 1.

number the many more uniform-wearing citizens in the various Party formations and affiliated organizations created a 'demonstration effect' emphasizing the omnipresence of the 'brown masses', who were difficult to avoid,
especially since numerous public displays and parades were called for.[120]
They were also expected to play a role through 'word-of-mouth propaganda'
(*Mundpropaganda*); this technique could amplify the official line or, through
rumours, demean opponents or foreign enemies, and so on.[121]

Those associated with the NSDAP in one way or another were also to
reinforce the regime's teachings by noting dissent and opposition and passing
the information on directly to the Gestapo or, rather more likely to their own
leaders, who would tell the police. Just how important a factor this semi-
official co-operation was in the policing of Nazi Germany is difficult to say,
although if Reinhard Mann's figures concerning the causes of initiating cases
with the Gestapo were to be taken in isolation, one could simply conclude
that the role of the NSDAP in the policing of the country has been wildly
exaggerated. Mann found that only 6 per cent of all cases began with a tip-
off from one of the many Nazi Party organizations. However, several points
need to be made in order to put these figures into perspective.[122]

Systematic surveillance of the population was called for by the Nazi 'block'-
leaders (Blockleiter), and cell-leaders (Zellenleiter). The numbers in these
positions, created in 1933, respectively reached 204,359 and 54,976 in
1934–5; by January 1939 there were 463,048 block- and 89,378 cell-
leaders.[123] Both before and even after 1933, the vast majority performed tasks
which involved considerable expenditure of time, on an unpaid basis.[124] It
has been suggested that their everyday activities—which included drawing
up a 'household card-index' of all the people in their area, collecting for Nazi
charities, and later, in the war, passing out ration-books, and so on—did
more for 'the strengthening of the regime than did the Gestapo'.[125] These
numerous 'little men' were most receptive to neighbourhood or apartment
snoopers.[126]

At the Nuremberg trials Party officials at the lowest end of the scale were
accused both of being 'little Caesars' who lorded it over households in their
realm, and of being police informers, though both charges were emphatically
denied.[127] On 5 October 1936 Rudolf Hess, deputy Party leader, warned these
functionaries that they were 'never' to get involved in the 'snooping' or

---

[120] Unger, 86–9.
[121] Ibid. 90ff.
[122] These figures are discussed in ch. 5.
[123] Kater, *The Nazi Party*, 190.
[124] See Gauleiter Karl Kaufmann, in IMT xx. 66.
[125] Erich Kordt, *Wahn und Wirklichkeit* (Stuttgart, 1948), 46.
[126] Ibid. 46–7; for a contrary view see the defence summary at Nuremberg, IMT xxi. 481ff.
[127] For a summary see IMT xlii. 22ff.

'spying' on those in their care.[128] Yet some of the tasks entrusted to them made that difficult to avoid. They were often asked to investigate the political background of someone from their area who applied for a position in the civil service or who came up for some kind of promotion. Even senior members of the Gestapo, such as Heinrich Müller, were not immune from being checked out for a 'political evaluation' (*politische Beurteilung*). Such reports, which dealt with twenty-three specific questions, could only be drawn up by calling upon the lowliest cogs in the Party machine, for they alone knew how generous a citizen was in giving to Nazi collections, and, importantly, his or her 'reputation'.[129]

Some Nazi Gauleiters asked local leaders to list every citizen's political habits on the card-index file (including matters such as whether the family had possessed a 'national' flag before the swastika-flag law of 1935), subscribed to the Party paper, and so on. A check was supposed to be made on the political reliability of every citizen, but such far-reaching measures were probably not implemented.[130] On the other hand, there is evidence from elsewhere that any kind of political deviation was recorded.[131]

More specific inquiries might take place as the occasion demanded such as when Minister of the Interior Frick asked local Party offices to check whether civil servants complied with their duty to vote in the elections of March 1936. The SD wanted to know who might vote No in the elections of April 1938.[132] Local Party leaders handled countless matters, such as complaints of one neighbour against another, grumblings about provisioning of a local restaurant, treatment of wounded soldiers on the home front, personal disputes—especially about rents and living conditions in the apartment buildings.

On 14 December 1938, and not for the first time, Hess issued orders which specifically denied the Party the right 'to institute investigations and interrogations in the jurisdiction of the Gestapo'. Apprised of an operation of a 'political-police character', the NSDAP was to inform the nearest Gestapo post.[133] A reminder issued by Bormann in August 1943 about restricting the role of the Party as information-gatherer—a job said to belong to the SD—suggests that earlier efforts to delineate lines of competence between the Party

---

[128] See document PL 34, ibid. 327.
[129] Dieter Rebentisch, 'Die "politische Beurteilung" als Herrschaftsinstrument der NSDAP', in Detlev Peukert and Jürgen Reulecke (eds.), *Die Reihen fast geschlossen: Beiträge zur Geschichte des Alltags unterm Nationalsozialismus* (Wuppertal, 1981), 107ff.
[130] The order is from Gau Cologne-Aachen, 31 Jan. 1941, in IMT xx. 105; Hans Wegschneider, mayor and Ortsgruppenleiter in Hirschdorf, said that that instruction, as many others, was never received: ibid. 89ff.
[131] Friedrich Percyval Reck-Malleczewen, *Diary of a Man in Despair*, trans. P. Rubens (1966; New York, 1970), 200, wrote that the block-leader made a special note of anyone who used the traditional greeting 'Gruß Gott!' ('God be praised') instead of 'Heil Hitler!'
[132] IMT xxxv. 5; and ibid. 652–3.
[133] See HStA D: RW 36, Nr. 17, 39.

and SD did not put a stop to the Party's ambitions.[134]

The war opened greater possibilities for the Party to broaden its control over the population and to undertake new tasks in the administration of welfare, made necessary by the war.[135] Given the inflated authority which resulted, Michael Kater points out that 'some local party leaders went so far as to exercise their prerogative by proxy, like a Zellenleiter near Würzburg who entrusted his 14-year-old daughter with the task of snooping on the neighbours'.[136] It may be an exaggeration to suggest that the Party in the provinces constituted 'the real control of the population', but there is no doubt that at the neighbourhood and village level it participated in the enforcement process.[137]

9. CONCLUSION

This chapter concludes the discussion of the emergence of the Gestapo and its local operations. The emphasis has been placed on the history of the institution, its tasks and personnel, and its relationship to the police network and Nazi Party. Members of the Gestapo were not merely fanatical Nazis, men put in place after a thorough purge of the older political police. Most were not initially members of the Nazi Party, but were trained policemen, and many were carry-overs from the Weimar days. It was a much smaller force than is sometimes suggested, a kind of high-level group of 'experts', though certainly not 'apolitical' ones. It did not possess the omnipotence often attributed to it, but relied upon the collaboration of a whole host of organizations and institutions. Once moved into action, it pursued the accused in a relentless fashion, and at times organized wholesale round-ups of suspects. However, it did not have sufficient personnel in its local branches to do much more, in the first instance, than the work of sifting through the massive numbers of accusations which came to light. Nor did it have sufficient resources to generate its own cases, but relied on information supplied from elsewhere. As will become clearer in the chapters that follow, all control organizations of Party and state relied to a greater or lesser extent upon the provision of information by the population, although the degree of co-operation varied over time, and according to the issue and the locality.

---

[134] Ibid., pp. 25–7. For numerous illustrations see the Eisenach Kreisleitung files in Ann Arbor, Michigan.

[135] Dietrich Orlow, *History of the Nazi Party: 1933–1945* (Pittsburgh, 1973), 264.

[136] Kater, *The Nazi Party*, 222; cf. the testimony of Blockleiter (and judge) Dr Ernst Hirt from Nuremberg, IMT xx. 99 ff.

[137] Zdenek Zofka, *Die Ausbreitung des Nationalsozialismus auf dem Lande* (Munich, 1979), 300. Cf. the testimony of Kreisleiter Willi Meyer-Wendeborn of Cloppenburg, Oldenburg, in IMT xx. 66 ff., and Gauleiter Karl Kaufmann of Hamburg, ibid. 24 ff.

APPENDIX: PERSONNEL IN THE WÜRZBURG GESTAPO

The order of entries is: name, date of birth, highest rank, and date of joining NSDAP, where information is available.

Bauer, Karl (19.9.1893), Krim. Sek.: in NSDAP, 1 May 1937, in SS (1.4.33).

Baumann, Georg (n.d.), Krim. Ob. Sek.: in NSDAP, 1 May 1937.

'B.L.' (1901): in NSDAP, end 1939.

Gerum, Josef (22.9.1888), Krim. Rat: in NSDAP, 1 Jan. 1920; in SS (15.9.32) (later 'was one of the most feared, brutal, and ruthless Gestapo-Chefs in Würzburg').

Göss, Stefan (6.2.1903), Krim. Sek.: in NSDAP, 1 May 1937.

Gramowski, Ernst (2.4.1903), Krim. Komm.: in NSDAP, 1 Dec. 1931; in SS (6.11.41) date of entry unknown (later a head of the Gestapo in Würzburg).

Gundelach, Oswald (18.2.1904), Krim. Ob. Ass. in SA (date unclear, probably post-1933): in NSDAP, 1 May 1937.

Heisig, Helmut (1.8.1902), Krim. Rat.: in NSDAP, 1 May 1933; in SS (21.12.38) (head of Würzburg Gestapo for a time).

Keil, Franz (2.4.1898), Krim. Sek.: in NSDAP, 1 May 1937.

Krapp, Georg (24.2.1887), Krim. Sek.

Krauß, Friedrich (17.2.1902), Krim. Sek.: in NSDAP, 1 May 1937 (joined Gestapo in 1939).

Laub, Hans (24.12.1899), Krim. Sek.: in NSDAP, 1 May 1939.

Lutz, Balthasar (2.11.1895), Krim. Sek.: in NSDAP, 1 May 1937.

Pössinger, August (14.11.1897), Krim. Sek.: in NSDAP, 1 May 1937.

Schäfer, Franz, (22.8.1898), Krim. Sek.: in NSDAP, 1 May 1937.

Schilling, Hans (31.7.1904), Krim. Ob. Sek.: in NSDAP, 1 May 1937.

Stolz, Georg (30.9.1899), Krim. Sek.: in NSDAP, 1 May 1937.

Vogel, Georg (27.9.1895), Krim. Insp.: in NSDAP, 1 May 1933.

Völkl, Michael (13.7.1892), Krim. Insp.: in NSDAP, 1 May 1933; in SA, 1 Dec. 1933.

Wittmann, Franz (27.11.1895), Krim. Insp.: in NSDAP, 1 May 1933.

Zwingmann, Josef (20.2.1902), Krim. Sek.: in NSDAP, 1 May 1937.

Source: BDC. For Gerum see also Fröhlich. 76ff. For a guide to the ranks see Black, 293–4.

II
German Society

3

Würzburg and Lower Franconia before 1933

THE operation of the Gestapo had to adjust to social circumstances. Though the country was centralized and controlled as never before, local diversity persisted in dialect, customs, religion, and political views. Some districts were notorious for their support of Nazism, while some Catholic and rural areas, and the red working-class neighbourhoods in the biggest cities, were slow to convert or remained downright hostile. There was considerable variation in responses to government racial policies, such as those designed to isolate the Jews or to keep the army of foreign workers separated from the population. Even two small Protestant towns in rural settings, Northeim and Marburg, responded differently to Nazi racial doctrine.[1] It is important to note that the patterns of Jewish settlement were not identical; some Jews stayed on in the scattered small communities in rural parts, most moved to the metropolitan centres, but many areas had never had any Jews to begin with. Any discussion of how the Gestapo went about enforcing racial policy must take into account the peculiarities of the locality under study. This chapter looks at the history, religion, and politics, of the people who lived in Lower Franconia. It places particular emphasis on their experiences with the Jews. The next chapter gives an overview of the area in the Third Reich.

1. LOWER FRANCONIA

Franconia, or 'Franken', was one of the five tribal or 'stem' duchies that comprised 'Germany' on the day of its birth in the year 911, when a German king was elected successor to the monarchy created by Charlemagne. The district lies on either side of the Main river which flows westwards until it meets the Rhine at Frankfurt. Over the centuries, the long-settled area was continually disrupted by intruders, but an identifiable folklore, culture, and dialect(s) persisted, and it is still possible to distinguish its inhabitants from those to the south, the Bavarians, as well as the Swabians to the south and west and the Hessians to the north. Divisions based in dialect and culture were reinforced by religious differences, even within Franconia.

'Protestant Franconia' refers to the two districts of Upper and Middle

---

[1] For contrasting responses to anti-Semitism see Allen, *The Nazi Seizure of Power*, 84ff., and Milton Mayer, *They Thought they were Free* (Chicago, 1955), 125ff.

Franconia. Like Lower Franconia, they were given those names as part of the rationalization scheme introduced in 1837 by King Ludwig I of Bavaria. By the end of the Weimar Republic the similarity between Upper and Middle Franconia was reflected in the decision of the Bavarian government to link them under a single administrative capital in Ansbach. Protestantism was the religion of 64.83 per cent of the inhabitants of the two districts in 1933, almost the exact reversal of the overall Bavarian figures (with 69.9 per cent Catholic).[2] Not surprisingly, Upper and Middle Franconia did not vote as uniformly for the Catholic Centre Party as elsewhere in Bavaria: in thirteen federal elections before 1914 some districts never returned a Centre deputy to the Reichstag (Hof, Bayreuth, Nuremberg, Erlangen-Fürth, Dinkelsbühl).[3] In the Weimar Republic this was the part of Bavaria from which the NSDAP received its greatest support; in the elections of July 1932 the Party obtained from Upper and Middle Franconia, respectively, 44.4 and 47.7 per cent of the votes cast, and in November 1932 41.3 and 42.3 per cent, well above the Bavarian figures of 32.9 and 30.5 per cent.[4]

Lower Franconia can be distinguished from the rest of Franconia by religion. Predominantly Catholic, the area supported the Catholic political parties and, at the end of Weimar, was far more reluctant to vote Nazi than the other two districts of Franconia. It also retains a distinct dialect, Ostfränkisch, which contrasts greatly with the Bavarian tongue found to the south (Bayerisch), beginning in the Middle Franconian city of Nuremberg.[5]

The social and economic structure of Lower Franconia is predominantly rural and agricultural. The district is dotted with numerous small town communities, only one 'large' city, Würzburg, and only two others even close to half that size—Aschaffenburg, and Schweinfurt. In 1933 Würzburg had a population of 101,003, while Aschaffenburg and Schweinfurt had 36,260 and 40,176 respectively.[6] All three are located in the valley of the River Main. One account estimates that no more than 70,000 people out of a total district population of 796,043 worked in any sort of industry in 1933; only six of the twenty-two administrative subprefectures could be described as 'relatively prosperous industrial areas', so industry was confined to a few isolated clusters.[7] Bavaria was less developed in industrial employment than the country as a whole, but even within Bavaria Lower Franconia was slow to

---

[2] Helmut Witetschek, KLB ii. Ober- und Mittelfranken (1967), p. xxvi.

[3] Dietrich Thränhardt, Wahlen und politische Strukturen in Bayern 1848–1953 (Düsseldorf, 1973), 105.

[4] Pridham, 322.

[5] Max Spindler, Bayerische Geschichte im 19. und 20. Jahrhundert, 1800–1970 (Munich, 1978), ii. 708ff.

[6] Baruch Z. Ophir and Falk Wiesemann (eds.), Die jüdischen Gemeinden in Bayern 1918–1945 (Munich, 1979), 255, 398, 433.

[7] Rolf B. Memming, 'The Bavarian Governmental District Unterfranken and the City Burgstadt 1922–1939: A Study of the National Socialist Movement and Party–State Affairs' (University of Nebraska Ph.D. thesis; Lincoln, 1974), 11.

develop and remained largely 'pre-industrial'. Whereas 46.4 per cent of Bavaria's employed population worked in agriculture and forestry, the figure was 54 per cent in Lower Franconia; 24.2 per cent of Lower Franconians worked in industry and crafts lagged a little compared with 27.8 per cent for all of Bavaria.[8]

In the Lower Franconian countryside there were major pockets of rural poverty with few social amenities, such as the romantic and 'mysterious' region of the Spessart, linked to the main highway system by unpaved road. After 1933 Nazi Gauleiter Otto Hellmuth sought to improve the Rhoen hills in the northern part of the district through road construction and clearing of forest lands, but the attempt to modernize misfired when it turned out that the land was virtually useless for farming or even rearing sheep. Deforestation and road projects, along with the activities of newly created military camps, drove deer and wild boars from the hills into otherwise productive farmland, and to rescue the crops these had then to be hunted down by foresters.[9] The most sumptuous of the agricultural products of Lower Franconia was, and remains, the famous Franconian wine. The vineyards, reduced in their extent along the River Main over the centuries, gradually became concentrated in the so-called Main triangle formed by abrupt changes in the course of the river, with Würzburg at the centre.

Christianization of the district was begun by the Irish Bishop Kilian in the late seventh century, and in 742 Würzburg became the seat of the bishop because of its central location. It was fortified by 1030, became a kind of city-state, the location for many of the Church's monasteries and hospitals, and in 1582 a university was built. In Napoleonic times it lost its remaining independence and, at the end of the era, became part of the new kingdom of Bavaria.

2. THE JEWISH COMMUNITY IN LOWER FRANCONIA

The earliest recorded presence of Jews in Lower Franconia is 1147, when, in an attempt to find refuge from persecutions at the hands of crusading armies in the Rhineland, some Jews settled in Würzburg, while others moved to neighbouring Aschaffenburg and Nuremberg. There may have been some Jews in Würzburg shortly after 1096 and the first crusade.[10] The reception accorded Jewish refugees, settlers, and traders varied enormously, and could change abruptly with the introduction of a new temporal or religious ruler, new teachings, or with the sudden glow of old fears and new phobias.

---

[8] Kershaw, *Popular Opinion*, 13–15.
[9] Memming, 71–3.
[10] Roland Flade, *Die Würzburger Juden. Ihre Geschichte vom Mittelalter bis zur Gegenwart* (Wüzburg, 1987), 2 ff.; Arnd Müller, *Geschichte der Juden in Nürnberg 1146–1945* (Nuremberg, 1968), 14ff.

Besides the occasional persecutions in Würzburg, some of the bishops, who were the temporal as well as spiritual leaders of the city, from time to time thought of banning all the Jews. In 1562 Bishop Friedrich von Wirsberg, who had been disappointed in his hopes to have them converted, finally forced them out. Eleven years later Bishop Julius Echter broadened the ban to forbid Jews even temporary entry into his territory. Though a handful managed to hang on in the city until 1642, just before the end of the Thirty Years War (1648), the right to live in the city was denied for a further 150 years.[11]

Some Jews were permitted to trade in the city, but were not allowed to remain overnight; they paid special tolls and body taxes, and had to wear a yellow ringlet on their clothing.[12] In time the city tolerated a few petty traders in wares they carried with them each day (*Sackjuden*), and eventually some were allowed to rent storage space. Various stipulations were devised to assure that these 'house-Jews' (*Kammerjuden*) did not compete directly with the citizens of the city.[13] For the most part Lower Franconia's Jews, down to the beginning of the nineteenth century, continued to live in medieval conditions with restrictions on their every move.

The right of Jews to live in Würzburg for the first time since 1642, as well as the beginnings of their emancipation, began with the disintegration of the *ancien régime* that collapsed under the sword of Revolutionary and Napoleonic France. Würzburg itself was removed from the rule of its bishops, secularized, and for a brief period given to the 'enlightened' Grand Duke Ferdinand of Toscana (1806–14), who made it possible for Jews, at least 'those who could demonstrate their integrity, cleverness and substantial wealth', to dwell in the city.[14] Such measures kept out poor rural Jews from the numerous small communities near by, but at least the city gates were opened a little. After Ferdinand's brief rule, Würzburg, along with the rest of Lower Franconia and other territories, became part of the Bavarian monarchy. The 'Edict concerning the relations of the Jews in Bavaria', which had already been promulgated in 1813, was introduced to the new parts of the realm in 1816. Old Jewish corporations and institutions were ended and Jews attained a degree of equality before the law hitherto unheard of.[15]

Full emancipation was not granted, however, and in Bavaria, as in many other German states, Jews would have to 'earn' legal equality through 'assimilation' into society.[16] Those who could not assimilate had to pay the old

---

[11] In 1422 and 1453 thought was given to banishing the Jews. See Flade, *Würzburger Juden*, 42–5, 53–4.
[12] Ibid. 56; discussion of markings or hat went back to 1329 in Würzburg (p. 35).
[13] Ursula Gehring-Münzel, 'Emanzipation', ibid. 61–4.
[14] The Grand Duke is quoted ibid. 67.
[15] Stefan Schwarz, *Die Juden in Bayern im Wandel der Zeiten* (Munich, 1963), 121ff.
[16] See Reinhard Rürup, *Emanzipation und Antisemitismus. Studien zur 'Judenfrage' der bürgerlichen Gesellschaft* (Göttingen, 1975), 37ff.

special taxes, were forbidden to vote, could not be elected, and could not serve in the civil service. There was a limit to the possibilities for integration, however, since the edict's 'register section' (*Matrikelparagraphen*) stipulated that the total number of Jewish families permitted to be resident in any locality was to be restricted to the number officially registered there on the date of the edict. This legislation (which among other things also insisted that Jews adopt family names) was more restrictive in Bavaria than in most other German states, and contributed to the numerical stagnation of the Bavarian Jewish community. Once the number of permitted Jews was fixed on the 'register lists' (*Matrikellisten*) in any given village or town, it could not be changed.[17] The city of Würzburg, for example, officially had twenty-nine families for nearly fifty years after the edict had come into effect. A place among the select twenty-nine could only be acquired through death or when a father retired for the benefit of a son. A few exceptions to the normal number allowed a given community could be made for academics and those involved in large trading establishments.[18]

The edict stipulated that Jews could enjoy full resident rights 'above the normal number' if they became farmers, artisans, or opened a factory. The intention was to encourage Jews to leave their occupations in trade and to take up more 'useful' work, thus contributing towards their assimilation. These were the aims espoused by proponents of Jewish emancipation in the German Enlightenment.[19] A few others were tolerated ('second-class Jews'), but they could be told to leave at a moment's notice. By the mid-nineteenth century there were fifty Jewish 'citizen families' in Würzburg, and an additional sixty-three 'second-class' families.[20] Only in 1861 were the onerous requirements finally dropped in Bavaria.

Across Bavaria there were variations in the receptivity to Jewish migrants over the centuries, as can be deduced from the 1818 census data, when only five Jews lived in the rather large and well-endowed territory of Lower Bavaria—located to the east of Munich—and proportionately there were hardly many more (a total of just 489) in all of Upper Bavaria, a district which included the fairly large city of Munich. By contrast, Lower Franconia was the Bavarian district with the largest number of Jewish inhabitants, and offered residence to 16,637, or 38.9 per cent of the monarchy's total.[21]

Together, the three Franconian districts contained a Jewish population of 34,739 in 1818, 71.3 per cent of the Bavarian Jews, and while the figures in 1900 had declined across all of Franconia (in part reflecting a movement

---

[17] Schwarz, 181–209.
[18] Gehring-Münzel, 98.
[19] Ibid. 98–100. Cf. Klaus Epstein, *The Genesis of German Conservatism* (Princeton, 1966), 176ff., and Jacob Katz, *Out of the Ghetto: The Social Background of Jewish Emancipation 1770–1870* (Cambridge, Mass., 1973), 176ff.
[20] Gehring-Münzel, 100.
[21] Ophir and Wiesemann (eds.), 13.

to Munich), at that time they still had 30,074, or 67.1 per cent of the total.[22] Jewish settlement in Lower Franconia itself tended to be in small pockets scattered across the district. On the death of Chief Rabbi Abraham Bing in 1841, for example, the 17,000 Jews in his flock lived in 216 villages and towns.[23]

Jewish urban communities in Lower Franconia were affected by the processes which accompanied the transformation of Germany from a rural-agrarian to an urban-industrial society, especially after 1890. Bavaria's economic backwardness relative to other German states saw it lose a large number of its Jewish population to more 'advanced' districts, particularly to the big German cities with 100,000 or more inhabitants, or else to emigration overseas. Würzburg attracted some of those who left the countryside, with the result that its Jewish population gradually increased from 1,099 in 1867 (2.6 per cent of the city's inhabitants), to 1,518 in 1871; at the turn of the century the number rose to 2,567, but then the percentage of Jews in Würzburg went into decline. By 1925 only 2,261 Jews lived there; not only had the percentage fallen as the city's population rose with the general movement from the countryside, but it had declined absolutely from its all-time high in 1900[24] The scope of the loss can be gathered from the three census-years 1910, 1925, and 1933, in which the number of Jews in Bavaria declined from 55,100 to 49,100, then to 42,000.[25]

The implications of similar developments across the country were obvious to the Jewish author Felix Theilhaber in 1911. In the book he published that year on *The Decline of the German Jews* he said that, unless such trends could be reversed, the end of centuries of life in Germany would come to a close. Germany's Jewish population declined as a percentage of the total population every census year from 1880, when the figure stood at 1.09 per cent, to 0.76 per cent in 1933.[26] Bavaria's Jews already experienced natural population decline, with just one birth for every three deaths in 1933; the process was reinforced by conversions to other religions or renunciation of Judaism.[27]

[22] Ophir and Wiesemann (eds.), 13.
[23] Gehring-Münzel, 94.
[24] Ophir and Wiesemann (eds.), 433; Flade, *Würzburger Juden*, 145. The highest percentage (4.5%) was reached in 1880.
[25] Esra Brennathan, 'Demographische und wirtschaftliche Struktur der Juden', in Werner E. Mosse (ed.), *Entscheidungsjahr 1932: Zur Judenfrage in der Endphase der Weimarer Republik* (Tübingen, 1966), 90.
[26] Ibid. 94.
[27] Flade, *Würzburger Juden*, 146–8.

3 THE SOCIAL-ECONOMIC POSITION OF THE JEWS

By 1933 46 per cent of the Jews in Germany belonged to the 'independents', in comparison with a figure of only 16 per cent for the population as a whole; and, while 18.4 per cent of all employed persons were occupied in 'trade and commerce', 61.3 per cent of the Jews came into this category, so that the occupational structure of the Jews was distinct.[28] A similar structure existed for Bavaria. In 1925, for example, 12.6 per cent of its employed population was in trade and commerce, but 66.8 per cent of all Bavarian Jews were so occupied (in the cities the percentage was lower, on the land higher). In Würzburg a relatively small number of the city's Jews (32.6 per cent) were occupied in trade and commerce, but they were especially visible in businesses such as department stores (six of ten in the city were Jewish, none of them representatives of the national chains), and well over half of all the wholesalers and roughly a third of all retailers in textiles were Jews; they dominated the wholesale trade in agricultural products (owning about a quarter). In 1931, 89 of 138 firms in the wine and spirits trade were owned by Jews, and they had a monopolistic position in the wholesale trade in wine that year, as they owned 71 out of 90 establishments.[29]

Roland Flade insists that not all Jewish wine-dealers in the city were wealthy, for 'about a third' of them could be classified as belonging to the petty bourgeoisie or even the lower class. This observation, while important, is rather beside the point in a consideration of the question of visibility of the Jews. Helen Fein sees the disproportion of Jews in certain occupations as representing a 'middleman minority'; Jews were over-represented in Würzburg as doctors, chemists, and lawyers—comprising at the end of Weimar 11, 27, and 26 per cent of each group.[30] Fein notes that such minorities 'are more liable to be ousted because they are from the start excluded from the universe of obligation and because the role they play motivates competitors to improve their own condition by getting rid of them'.[31]

The Würzburg and Lower Franconian Jewish community belonged overwhelmingly to the middle class. In the city, at least to judge by the amount of taxes paid to the Jewish religious community, there was a distinct upper class of industrialists, better-off merchants, and department-store owners; in 1920 they made up 4 per cent of all Jewish citizens. An 'upper middle class' of prospering merchants, smaller industrialists, and the most prominent representatives of the free professions made up just over the next 20 per cent.

---

[28] Monika Richarz (ed.), *Jüdisches Leben in Deutschland: Selbstzeugnisse zur Sozialgeschichte 1918–1945*, iii (Stuttgart, 1982), 19.

[29] Roland Flade, *Juden in Würzburg 1918–1933* (Würzburg, 1985), 57–64.

[30] Helen Fein, *Accounting for Genocide: Victims—and Survivors—of the Holocaust* (New York, 1976), 49.

[31] Ibid. 89.

After that, another 18 per cent were employed in the free professions and/or owned middle-sized businesses. These figures indicate that 43.5 per cent of the Jews in town could be classified as belonging to the middle and upper middle class. Next down the social scale, the largest single group (46.5 per cent) was made up of the lower middle class of clerks, white-collar workers, small retailers, simple civil servants, bookkeepers, and artisans.[32] The remaining 10 per cent of all Jews, who either paid no church taxes at all or gave the minimum, were the only ones not in the middle class. Ten per cent of all Jews in town were from Eastern Europe ('Ostjuden') well received neither by the population in general nor by their co-religionists.[33] While all Jews were not doing as well as the owner of the large department store in town, and many small traders barely scraped by, Jews constituted a visible 'merchant minority' in Würzburg, just as they did in the surrounding rural areas.

The Jews were also set apart from their neighbours in the villages of Lower Franconia. Julius Frank, born in 1889 in Steinach a.d. Saale (near Bad Kissingen), and the son of a cattle-dealer, writes of what everyday life was like for a Jewish family in the countryside. The Jews of Steinach made up about 10 per cent of the village population at the turn of the century, but, Frank says, they constituted the village 'middle class'. They spoke a different language—closer to High German with numerous Hebrew words mixed in—they habitually dressed better, ate different food, and frequently went to their own school, at least in the early grades, if the community was large enough to support one. According to Frank the Jews were conscious of their socially superior status and participated infrequently in the social life of the village, preferring, for example, to have their beer delivered rather than drink it at the local pub.[34] He speaks of the lack of a 'genuine feeling of community' between the Jews and the other villagers, and sees a connection with 'a latent anti-Semitism'. Werner Cahnmann, who had experiences similar to Frank's in a comparable rural district to the west, thought that the Jews 'became the leaders in modernity' in rural areas. 'The village Jews were not peasants of a different ethnicity. They were urbanites transmuted into rural fold.'[35] According to a recent account, the social reception of the Jews, especially in the provinces, 'lagged in general far behind the degree to which they had been integrated into the national and economic life of Germany'.[36]

[32] The figures are from Flade, *Würzburger Juden*, 212.

[33] Ibid. 209. There were 231 Eastern Jews in Würzburg in 1920: see S. Adler-Rudel, *Ostjuden in Deutschland 1880–1940* (Tübingen, 1959), 23ff.

[34] Julius Frank, in Richarz, ii (1979), 190ff. For a parallel case see Liselotte Stern from Weikersheim, in Richarz, iii. 168ff.

[35] Werner Cahnmann, 'Village and Small-Town Jews in Germany: A Typological Study', *YLBI* 19 (1974), 126–7. See also Francis Henry, *Victims and Neighbors: A Small Town in Nazi Germany Remembered* (South Hadley, Mass., 1984), 15ff., and John K. Dickinson, *German and Jew: The Life and Death of Sigmund Stein* (Chicago, 1967), 12ff.

[36] H.I. Bach, *The German Jew: A Synthesis of Judaism and Western Civilization, 1730–1930* (Oxford, 1984), 137.

4. ANTI-SEMITISM

Anti-Semitism was not unknown in the cities of Lower Franconia, but, as in the countryside, much of it remained politically latent, since for one reason or another organizations did not openly embrace it. Alongside the traditional hostility towards Jews based on religious teachings, especially in areas where Jews were resident, there developed in the course of the late nineteenth century a racial and political variety; both types 'existed side by side and provided mutual support for each other'.[37] In Würzburg the outbursts against the Jews were rare in the modern era, although one of the most infamous anti-Jewish riots broke out in the city in early August 1819, before sparking off similar events in Bamberg, Bayreuth (in Franconia), and some thirty additional cities. The riots of 1819 that began in Würzburg were not, as is often claimed, a protest movement directed at the harsh regime and with a heavy student involvement. In fact, students did not participate, and, according to a recent study, the stimulus to the riots may have come 'from those who saw themselves harmed by the entry of Jews into their occupations, namely, merchants who had previously enjoyed a monopolist position within the civic commerce. A brooding apprehension, perhaps even fear and terror, over infiltration of society by residents of the ghetto, who were held to be a dangerous element, was aroused in the population even when there was no actual, direct competition.'[38]

Perhaps because many citizens were outraged at the so-called 'Hep! Hep!' riots in 1819, in which two people were killed, Würzburg never developed a tradition of anti-Semitism. Only in the aftermath of the First World War, when a deep social crisis affected Germany as a whole, did anti-Semitism spread as never before.[39] One of the most vitriolic of the national organizations was the German People's Protection and Defiance League (Deutschvölkischer Schutz- und Trutz-Bund), whose branch in Würzburg demanded on its foundation in late 1918 the 'total destruction of the domination by national and racial foreign elements'.[40] An impression of the kinds of messages it sought to convey locally over the course of its rather brief existence (it was outlawed by the government after the assassination of Walther Rathenau in 1922) is conveyed by a statement of 'advice' printed in its weekly for 26 October 1923. It was demanded that the Bavarian government take the following steps to 'solve the Jewish question':

[37] Kershaw, *Popular Opinion*, 230.

[38] Jacob Katz, *From Prejudice to Destruction: Anti-Semitism, 1700–1933* (Cambridge, Mass., 1980), 102; cf. Gehring-Münzel, 78–9.

[39] See Werner Jochmann, 'Die Ausbreitung des Antisemitismus', in Werner E. Mosse (ed.), *Deutsches Judentum in Krieg und Revolution 1916–1923* (Tübingen, 1971), 500.

[40] Quoted in Flade, *Juden in Würzburg*, 236. On the organization in Franconia see Uwe Lohalm, *Völkischer Radikalismus: Die Geschichte des Deutschvölkischen Schutz- und Trutz-Bundes* (Hamburg, 1970), 307ff.

1. It is absolutely necessary to kill the Jews . . . ! Otherwise, the efforts of Christianity will be for nothing . . . 3. It is absolutely necessary to nullify the law on the emancipation of the Jews. 4. It is absolutely necessary to burn down the synagogues and Jewish schools, and what remains of the walls after the burnings ought to be buried, so that no stone remains visible. 5. It is absolutely necessary to take away from the Jews all prayer-books and Talmuds because they learn from them the curses and lies.[41]

The overall effect of such organizations and of the affiliated student organization is difficult to assess, although the constant hate-mongering, exaggerating, and lying could not easily have been ignored, precisely because the organization was so active in exposing its doctrine in countless small ways—for example, by posting anti-Semitic graffiti in conspicuous places throughout the city. One of its leaders, the notorious Dr Otto Hellmuth, subsequently became the Nazi Gauleiter of Lower Franconia.

In the period of Weimar's 'stable' years Würzburg's political parties, at least those of the centre and right of centre, for the most part did not regard opposition to anti-Semitism as part of their work. The Catholic Bavarian People's Party (Bayerische Volkspartei, BVP) openly flirted with the racist movement at least until Hitler's attempted *putsch* in November 1923. Local conservative parties, the DNVP and DVP, displayed some anti-Semitism and put up candidates for federal elections known to be anti-Semitic. The left-wing SPD and KPD, along with the trade-union movement and the liberals (DDP), did what they could to fight the contagion of anti-Semitism.[42]

5. Response to Nazism

In the last days of Weimar, Lower Franconia, in contrast to other parts of Germany, was in a relatively stable economic condition. That is not to say that the area was not affected by the depression that hit Germany in 1929. In fact, there was an economic crisis in the countryside even during the years of stability (1924–9), a result of increased farm indebtedness, the flight of labour to the cities, and rural 'over-population' caused by an ancient Frankish law of inheritance, according to which land was distributed equally to all the sons. The net effect was to make rural poverty difficult to avoid.[43] Still, of the three Franconian subdistricts, this area's peasants were on average the least in debt, but their holdings were the smallest (suggesting the need to supplement income by hiring themselves out as labourers elsewhere). Not surprisingly, Lower Franconia had the lowest unemployment quota of the three, but that

[41] Quoted in Flade, *Juden in Würzburg*, 251.
[42] Ibid. 267–72.
[43] Memming, 25–6.

was a result of the absence of industry.[44]

Lower Franconia's overwhelming Catholicism was consistently reflected in the politics of the district, and before 1914 the tradition of voting for a candidate of the Catholic Centre was well established.[45] The pronounced district-wide party identification with the Catholic Centre Party continued into the Weimar era, although the more democratic voting procedures, coupled with the crises resulting from the lost war, inflation, economic rationalization, and depression, produced some movement. Nevertheless, though there was some decline in support for the Centre's offshoot, the BVP, over the course of the Weimar Republic's federal elections it remained at approximately 50 per cent throughout, so that it is clear that this party had a firm hold on its 'political space' and that any others entering the arena of Lower Franconian politics would very likely be competing for what remained.[46] Apart from the Catholics, the two left-wing parties made up a second block of votes. They consistently rallied a smaller, but no less loyal, clientele and largely held on to it during the crisis that came with the depression.[47] There was little space open to the Nazis in the third block of voters, the so-called 'bourgeois Protestant' group, so the scope for eliciting support for the NSDAP was limited.[48]

Lower Franconia gave the NSDAP the smallest percentage of support in all of Bavaria. One obvious factor is Catholicism, which in 1933 was the religion of 76.8 per cent of the population of Würzburg (the figure was 82.5 per cent in the district as a whole).[49] However, not only the religious factor was at work in dampening enthusiasm for the Nazis, since Lower Franconia gave less support to the NSDAP than parts of Bavaria with a higher percentage of Catholics. By tradition Würzburg and district are an area considered to be 'resistant to politically extreme points of view'.[50] The NSDAP was also poorly organized and badly led, with few branches and sparse finances. Only 17.7 per cent of Würzburg's vote went to the Nazis in the federal election of 1930;

[44] Jürgen W. Falter, 'Der Aufstieg der NSDAP in Franken bei den Reichstagswahlen 1924–1933: Ein Vergleich mit dem Reich unter besonderer Berücksichtigung landwirtschaftlicher Einflußfaktoren', *German Studies Review*, 9 (1986), 344.

[45] Thränhardt, 105.

[46] Ibid. 164. For the latest literature see Thomas Childers, *The Nazi Voter: The Social Foundations of Fascism in Germany* (Chapel Hill, 1983), 119ff.; Richard Hamilton, *Who Voted for Hitler?* (Princeton, 1982), 420ff. See also Juan J. Linz, 'Some Notes toward a Comparative Study of Fascism in Sociological Historical Perspective', in Walter Laqueur (ed.), *Fascism: A Reader's Guide* (Berkeley, 1976), 3ff.

[46] For all of Franconia the percentage of votes cast for the Left in 1930, the two elections of 1932, and that of March 1933, were 24.6%, 24.0%, 23.7%, 22.1%: Falter, 350. In Würzburg, the SPD and KPD gained between them some 26.3% of the vote in 1930, and 29.1% and 27.8% in the two elections of 1932. The latter figures are from Herbert Schultheis, *Juden in Mainfranken 1933–1945* (Bad Neustadt a.d. Saale, 1980), 34.

[48] For details of the Left see Mehringer, 'Die bayerische SPD', and 'Die KPD in Bayern'.

[49] Klaus Wittstadt, *KLB* vi. *Unterfranken* (1981), p. xxviii; Ophir and Wiesemann (eds.), 434.

[50] Peter Spitznagel, *Wähler und Wahlen in Unterfranken 1919–1969* (Würzburg, 1979), 1.

that was just about the same as the overall figure for Bavaria (17.9 per cent), but ahead of Lower Franconia as a whole (12.3 per cent). In the election of July 1932 the percentage in Würzburg rose, but only to 22.8 per cent (in Bavaria it was 32.9 per cent, in Germany as a whole 37.3 per cent); the second election that year saw it fall to 19.9 per cent in Würzburg (30.5 per cent in Bavaria; 33.1 per cent in Germany as a whole).[51]

As of 1 January 1933, Lower Franconia had the lowest proportion of its population enlisted as Nazi Party members, not only in Bavaria, but out of all thirty-two districts across Germany.[52] It is all the more surprising, therefore, that Lower Franconians flocked to become members after Hitler assumed power. In fact, from 1933 the district led all Nazi Gaue in Bavaria in the proportion of its population that joined the Party (the so-called March converts), and ranked third nationally. Some of the shift can be accounted for by the abnormally low percentage previously on the books.[53] A recent study claims that the massive expansion of Party cells and blocks reported for the city of Würzburg, which began again when the freeze on membership was lifted in 1937, 'was an exercise in fantasy and wishful thinking for the NSDAP could hardly claim to have rallied the entire population of Würzburg to its cause', as would have been the case had it (as announced to Munich headquarters) established '34 Ortsgruppen, 159 cells and 831 blocks', so that in effect the network embraced '36,668 households or 132,444 inhabitants', virtually the entire population.[54] But there is good reason to maintain that the figures were probably not too far off the mark. It is very doubtful that Munich headquarters could be duped so easily, for the new officials would be expected to provide regular reports, and new joiners would not only be assigned individual membership numbers but would also be expected to pay dues.

Obstacles to Party membership to some extent had been removed on 28 March 1933, when German Catholic bishops suspended the ban on Catholic membership. Initially, too, the Church took a positive attitude to the new regime and signed a concordat on 20 July 1933. In rural, devout areas such a reversal of opinion could give the impression that the Church was leading its flock to the Nazi ranks. Even after the leaders of the Church, especially Bishop Ehrenfried of Würzburg, switched to courageous opposition, the Church, once having apparently given its blessing to the Nazis, could not easily revert to a position of disapproval.

At any rate, by the early years of the Third Reich the political behaviour, social attitudes, and cultural traditions which seemed to set Lower Franconia apart from the national and even Bavarian norms were being eroded, with

---

[51] For the Würzburg data see Schultheis, 34; for the rest see Pridham, 322.
[52] Kershaw, *Popular Opinion*, 27–8.
[53] Ibid.
[54] Memming, 79–80.

many people adjusting to the new circumstances. Full-blooded enthusiasm of all the people was not necessary to the functioning of the new order. One writer claims that in the small city of Bad Kissingen, which provided a good deal of support for the NSDAP before 1933, 'after the initial euphoria and fear . . . the rural population assumed a massive indifference toward party–state policies, remained stubbornly loyal to the Catholic Church, and benign toward its Jewish citizens'.[55] Another characterizes the struggle of the Catholic Church with the Nazi regime as a kind of 'war of attrition', which developed as the previously enthusiastic hierarchy in the Church began to have second thoughts, reaching 'a period of high tension between 1935 and 1938 and a final flare up to dramatic confrontation in 1941'.[56]

The role of anti-Semitism in the 'success' of the Nazis in Lower Franconia is difficult to determine. William Allen's oft-cited conclusion about the small town of Nordheim is suggestive, but in the end hard to prove. He insists that local people 'were drawn to anti-Semitism because they were drawn to Nazism, not the other way around', and that 'many who voted Nazi simply ignored or rationalized the anti-Semitism of the party, just as they ignored other unpleasant aspects of the Nazi movement'.[57] In Würzburg anyone who voted for the NSDAP could hardly have been unaware that anti-Semitism occupied a prominent place in the Party's programme, a fact given abundant reinforcement by visits of Gauleiter Julius Streicher from neighbouring Middle Franconia. There had also been tasteless propaganda campaigns—for example, against the Jewish method of slaughtering livestock in accordance with ancient religious teachings, a campaign which was actually crowned by success when Bavaria introduced a prohibition in 1930.

Scandal-mongering against the Jews turned ugly in March 1929, when a murdered child was found in Manau, a small village in the area. Immediately the Nazis resuscitated the medieval superstition that the murder of a young child was somehow required by Jewish religious practice. Such nonsensical claims led to a spectacular court-case, played out for all it was worth by the two men formally charged with libel (Julius Streicher, and the *Stürmer*'s editor, Karl Holz). Though they were found guilty and sent to gaol for several months, the affair was cleverly exploited and, in the words of one account, 'it really was rather a victory for the NSDAP', who gained invaluable publicity from it.[58]

Counter-demonstrations in Würzburg by Jews and others, though successful in expressing disgust, amplified the importance of the charges and

---

[55] Ibid. 189.
[56] Kershaw, *Popular Opinion*, 192.
[57] Allen, *The Nazi Seizure of Power*, 84. For a discussion of the question see Hermann Greive, *Geschichte des modernen Antisemitismus in Deutschland* (Darmstadt, 1983), 138ff.; Kershaw, *The 'Hitler Myth'*, 229ff.
[58] Arnold Paucker, quoted in Flade, *Juden in Würzburg*, 334. For earlier charges see Stefan Lehr, *Antisemitismus: Religiöse Motive im sozialen Vorurteil* (Munich, 1974), 52ff.

added to the publicity. At one meeting 1,500 people gathered in protest, most of whom were outraged at the right-wing radicals, although the 300–400 Nazis who infiltrated the meeting caused an uproar. Holz and Gauleiter Hellmuth, who were present, charged prominent local officials with being 'slaves to the Jews [Judenknechte]. Mayor Hans Löffler, accused of being the 'Jews' Mayor', asked the assembled to recall that just as Würzburg had been the scene of the last burning of witches during Europe's witch-craze in the early modern era, it should 'also be the last city in which one became inflamed over ritual murder'.[59]

Hitler's visit to Würzburg in early August 1930, as part of the election campaign, was prepared for by two weeks of fevered propagandizing. Some 5,000 people turned out on the evening of 5 August, and, even though tickets went for one mark (50 pfennigs for standing room), there was a sell-out days in advance. According to a police report, those at the event came from 'all groups in the population', and many loyal members were trucked in from the surrounding countryside. Hitler's entry at dusk was heralded by a band, and he spoke for a good two and a half hours. Attacking the Weimar system, and playing upon the nationalist theme, he spread the word of *Mein Kampf* on issues such as space in the east, bread, emigration, birth control, raising exports, pacificism, and so forth. For Germany, the crowd was told, there were three ways out of the morass: (1) the people had to be made conscious of their blood-bonds; (2) the best heads had to be placed in government; and (3) the will to live and to battle had to be acknowleged. After some thoughts on German history, he devoted special attention to portraying the Jews as 'parasites on the body politic [Schädlinge am Volkskörper]'. His speech was greeted with a 'loud applause' and there followed a robust singing of the *Deutschlandlied*, after which the meeting broke up without incident.[60] Hitler made no bones about his view of the Jews and his racism. Leaflets distributed by the Party in Würzburg subsequently made it clear what it had in mind for the Jews if and when it became the governing party.

The most spectacular local anti-Semitic action before 1933 was occasioned by a visit to the city on 19 November 1930 of a Hebrew-speaking theatre-group Habima, from Moscow. Local Nazis, led by Hellmuth, could not resist the temptation to call for a public protest against what was termed the 'cultural Bolshevism' represented by Habima. On the evening of the performance a large number of young people, many of them Nazi Party members, gathered before the City Theatre to prevent the audience from entering. A small contingent of police could not prevent the demonstrators from beating on the doors and walls of the theatre with fists and sticks, and screaming repeatedly, 'Down with the Jews, out with the Hebrews! Knock them dead!'

[59] Quoted in Flade, *Juden in Würzburg*, 334. See C.V. [*Centralverein-Zeitung*], 5 and 12 Apr., 10 May 1929.
[60] BayHStA: MInn 73818: Polizeidirektion Würzburg, 6 Aug. 1930.

By the time more police arrived, the crowd had grown to an estimated 1,000, and was moved from the theatre only with difficulty. Many who had attended the performance were later accosted and accused of having sympathy for the Jews; some were assaulted and chased through the streets in fear for their lives. As one Jewish eyewitness put it, 'How I got home, I cannot really say, only that it was around one or two in the morning and the fear did not leave me for days.'[61]

A few people were apprehended as having been responsible for the incidents, but their trial, which began in early February 1931, was quite a farce. Some of the accused turned up in dinner-jackets, and spectators arrived in court under the direction of Gauleiter Hellmuth. 'Laughably small punishments' were predictable when the offenders 'came up against a state attorney and a judge who made no bones about their anti-Semitic attitude'.[62]

The anti-Semitism of the local Nazi Party in this area was made abundantly clear also in its press. Local scandal-sheets comparable in many ways to Streicher's *Der Stürmer* (which also circulated in the city) spread racial views tinged with pornography. Women who were accused of having sexual relations with Jews were named in the Nazi rag, and such accusations led to libel cases which simply fuelled the sensationalism and small-town gossip. The local Nazi paper, *Die Freiheit* (Freedom), reported the 'sinning women' to the local citizens in its edition of 21 August 1931:

The young women of Würzburg feel and think German. They have, even if for the most part unconsciously, their racial pride. And therefore it is no wonder if shabby exceptions are found all the more disgraceful. This is the new German era of 'freedom, beauty and honour', of moral degeneracy and shame. We know these Löwenstein, Rosenbusch, Stern, Oppenheimer, Strauss, and a good many more. We also know the names of the shameful women [*Schandmädchen*] who have no qualms about having relations with Jews. We warn Rita D., Grete M., Tilly Sch., Ilse, etc. Beginning with the next edition we shall publish the full names of these women and expose them to general condemnation.[63]

As threatened, the paper gave out the names the very next week, a practice which was to become a commonplace in the Third Reich's smuttier papers.

Nazis were also active at Würzburg's university. There was an anti-Semitic tradition among students in Germany, and before 1914 various forms of that prejudice 'conquered the majority' of them across the country, and this certainly spread during the Weimar years.[64] After the First World War students bitterly fought elections to the national umbrella-organization, the

---

[61] Quoted in Flade, *Juden in Würzburg*, 344.
[62] Dieter W. Rockenmaier, *Das Dritte Reich und Würzburg: Versuch einer Bestandsaufnahme* (Würzburg, 1983), 34; cf. Flade, *Juden in Würzburg*, 341–9.
[63] Quoted in Flade, *Juden in Würzburg*, 350.
[64] Konrad H. Jarausch, *Students, Society, and Politics in Imperial Germany: The Rise of Academic Illiberalism* (Princeton, 1982), 355.

German Students' Union. By 1931 the National Socialist Students' Association had a majority in the Union, and one of its members was president.[65] The tenor of student debates on the Würzburg campus is indicated in their discussion of a motion of February 1929, moved by the Nazis on the local student council. It demanded the introduction of a *numerus clausus*, that is, a restriction on the number of Jewish students permitted to study, so that their presence at the university would not rise above their percentage in the population. As 6.4 per cent (in 1928) of Würzburg's registered students were Jews, such a demand entailed that many would have to be forced out.[66] The motion was passed, supported not only by Nazi representatives, but also by those from various fraternities, including a Catholic organization. Though the student council voted for the measure, it could not be implemented because the university Senate declared it a violation of the Weimar constitution. The proposal was made once again with great fanfare in December 1931, and, while it too came to nothing, it was a prelude to the complete exclusion of the Jews from universities in the Third Reich.[67] Such campaigns attracted the educated élite and spilled over into the town as well. The 'public declaration' of thirty-six local professors in the autumn of 1932, that Germany should be 'liberated' from 'the domination of the parliaments' indicates that the students were not the only ones at the university in Würzburg moving to the right.[68]

6. The 'seizure of power' in Würzburg

In what was to be the last remotely free election, in March 1933, the vote for the NSDAP rose slightly in Würzburg, where it reached 31.5 per cent of the total; in the district as a whole the figure stood at 33.9 per cent. Both were well below the figures for Bavaria (43.1 per cent) and Germany as a whole (43.9 per cent). In Würzburg the BVP was ahead of the Nazis, with 36.1 per cent of the vote, and the SPD/KPD block received 22.3 per cent; both blocks were down only slightly from the previous election.[69] People remained relatively cool towards Nazism. The Party's efforts to get elected to Würzburg's city council were also rebuffed. At the turn of the year 1932/3

---

[65] Geoffrey J. Giles, *Students and National Socialism in Germany* (Princeton, 1985), 67–72. For student politics and anti-Semitism see esp. Michael H. Kater, *Studentenschaft und Rechtsradikalismus in Deutschland 1918–1933* (Frankfurt, 1975), 145ff.

[66] Birgitt Grieb-Lohwasser, 'Jüdische Studenten und Antisemitismus an der Universität Würzburg in der Weimarer Republik', in Herbert Schultheis (ed.), *Ein Streifzug durch Frankens Vergangenheit* (Bad Neustadt a.d. Saale, 1982), 262.

[67] Ibid. 324ff.

[68] Roland Flade, *'Es kann sein daß wir eine Diktatur brauchen': Rechtsradikalismus und Demokratiefeindschaft in der Weimarer Republik am Beispiel Würzburg* (Würzburg, 1983), 117.

[69] Schultheis, 34; Pridham, 322.

the BVP and SPD controlled a majority between them (twenty-six out of forty seats), while the NSDAP had only four representatives.[70]

In spite of the limited results, the NSDAP was a presence in the city during the last years of Weimar, and not infrequently carried protests and demonstrations to the point of violence. Particularly visible and vulnerable targets of hostility in the late Weimar days were Jews and Jewish department stores in town. Since their appearance in the days of Bismarck's Germany, these establishments had borne the brunt of anti-Semitic attack, and the Nazis merely accelerated the tradition.

After Hitler's appointment, and especially after the Reichstag fire, systematic police actions were undertaken against Communist functionaries. After the March election the net was widened to include other opponents, such as the leaders of the Socialists' paramilitary organization, the Reichsbanner. By the middle of March, fifty-one of them from Würzburg were in 'protective custody', from a total of 261 for all of Lower Franconia. In Würzburg alone 108 house-searches were conducted, and arms of all kinds confiscated.[71] Efforts of local leaders of the SPD and KPD to join forces to resist the Nazis came to nothing because no agreement could be worked out at the national level.[72] Some leading Socialists were dreaming. For example, SPD executive member Hans Vogel, who came from Berlin to address a meeting in Würzburg just before the elections, could think of nothing better to say than to remind the faithful that 'the spirit has always triumphed over the sword. And because we are a spiritual movement, we are permitted to have the certainty: we will come after Hitler'.[73]

The Nazi leadership in Würzburg waited until the results of the last 'free' elections (5 March 1933) before 'seizing' power there. Not only could the Storm-troopers and SS intimidate their opponents as never before, in their capacity as members of the new auxiliary police, but they could now present themselves as the Chancellor's Party and set up loudspeakers in the main city squares to broadcast Hitler's messages. The Party was far from winning a majority in Würzburg, but its 31.5 per cent of the vote showed that it was backed by as many as 19,237 citizens there. The Catholic Party managed to hold on to 22,046 and the SPD 10,184 votes.[74]

The leaders of Würzburg's Nazis decided to treat the results as a victory. Hannsheinz Bauer, a young Socialist at the time, remembered how word got around on the evening of 9 March that something was going to happen at the city hall. Shortly after Bauer got there Storm-troopers arrived, most of them students. Michael Meisner, a man from the town establishment,

---

[70] Rockenmaier, 33.

[71] Situation report, 22 Mar. 1933: *KLB* vi. 3.

[72] Helmut Raab, *Der Arbeiter im Reich des Hakenkreuzes: Widerstand und Verfolgung in Würzburg* (Würzburg, [1983]).

[73] Quoted in Rockenmaier, 36.

[74] Werner Dettelbacher, *Damals in Würzburg* (1971; Würzburg, 1982), 115.

remembered the response of a policeman whom he had asked what was up: 'It's a bunch of real young lads . . . it's unbelievable, they're raising the swastika flag over our city hall!'[75] It mattered not the least that mayor Hans Löffler was far from favouring the act. A table was brought out, on which Kreisleiter Theo Memmel stood to address the crowd, and at the end of the speech everyone sang the national anthem and the Party song, the Horst Wessel Lied. Bauer recalled that for him what was really symbolic about these theatrics happened during the singing. 'An old-age pensioner, who stood at the edge of the street, had neglected to remove his hat. All at once a strapping SA man jumped at him, clobbered him with a punch to the ground, so that blood ran from his nose, and then hurried back immediately to his troop.'[76]

The removal of unsympathetic mayor Löffler took a few days, but in the mean time, in line with the standard operating procedures of other Nazi 'seizures of power', political opponents were dealt with. On 10 March the headquarters of the trade unions was stormed, confiscated, and renamed after Nazi Gauleiter Otto Hellmuth. The offices of the two major opposition newspapers were also raided: the socialist *Volksfreund* was banned; while the moderate bourgeois organ, the *Fränkisches Volksblatt*, though gagged, was allowed to appear again. At 7.30 in the evening a first burning of confiscated socialist books, placards, and such took place in front of the distinguished Residenz palace near the centre of town, with Weimar's black–red–gold flag thrown in on top.[77] According to the SPD's Hannsheinz Bauer, there was never really a question of stopping the local 'seizure' by force of arms because the paramilitary branch of the SPD, even if combined with that of the KPD and with trade-unionists, would simply have been no match for the better-organized and more numerous Nazi groups.[78]

In the meeting of the city council on 23 March Nazi councillor Wolz proposed that the street named after the first president of the Weimar Republic, the socialist Friedrich Ebert, be returned to its original name. Thirty-one councillors voted against the motion, while only five from the 'bourgeois coalition' went along with the four Nazi representatives.[79] Because mayor Löffler added his weight to the majority decision, pressure was soon brought to bear on him to resign. An SA delegation successfully appealed to the district's chief administration officer, and he was removed from office. A short while later his deputy, Julius Zahn, followed. The new mayor was the young Nazi Party Kreisleiter Theo Memmel, who, among other things, now saw to it that numerous streets were renamed.[80]

[75] Michael Meisner, *Bekenntnisse eines Außenseiters* (Würzburg, 1985), 158, puts the date at 6 Mar.
[76] Quoted in Rockenmaier, 37.
[77] Dettelbacher, 115; Rockenmaier, 38.
[78] Rockenmaier, 40, quotes Bauer and another Socialist, Gerda Laufer.
[79] Dettelbacher, 115.
[80] Rockenmaier, 42; Schultheis, 39; Dettelbacher, 115.

Würzburgers offered a final show of defiance when municipal elections were held on 12 April. Out of a total of twenty-eight seats (reduced from the usual forty), the NSDAP wrested but ten; the Catholic BVP, with eleven, outdid the Nazis by one, and the SPD, against the odds, managed to get five. Assorted 'others' picked up the remainder. Curiously enough, this city council went along with a unanimous vote for Memmel as mayor, but even so it was only a matter of time before the Nazis forced their opponents out of the council; the SPD went on 20 June (nationally the Party was banned shortly after), and the BVP's turn came at the end of the month. To make the loss of power abundantly clear, many of the local representatives of both parties in Würzburg (and elsewhere in the district) got a taste of 'protective custody'. By July the Nazis were the only ones left on the city council.[81]

According to long-time socialist Gerda Laufer, as well as the young lawyer Michael Meisner, notwithstanding the defiance shown in the council elections, things changed quickly. Laufer said she 'was deeply shaken that people whom one regarded as friends, who were known for a long time, from one hour to the next transformed themselves'.[82] Meisner recalled that while there was a certain air of normality about town, trusted parts of the bourgeois social world were disappearing.[83] Word got out that the SA was carrying out brutal beatings in the old fortress above town, and Laufer remembered that too. By the summer of 1933 Dachau, barely in operation, was already a byword in Würzburg for brutality and torture. Workers did not openly resist, but they were slow to embrace Nazism. The Nazis transformed 1 May, the day for workers in Europe to demonstrate their socialist leanings, into a general holiday and a day to celebrate work. The first of these occasions went off without a snag in 1933, when, in front of the Residenz, Gauleiter Hellmuth reviewed a two-and-a-half-hour parade of nearly 32,000 men.[84]

The people in Würzburg were probably impressed with the Nazis' success in curing unemployment. According to the official statistics, unemployment fell by 50 per cent in Bavaria in the first two years of the new regime.[85] Even if the figures were exaggerated, and many people were forced into unsuitable labour or compelled to cease registering for unemployment benefits, the aimless drift of the last days of the Weimar Republic was clearly over.[86]

One person who lived through the times believed that Würzburg in general went over to the support of Nazism, or at least of Hitler:

---

[81] Rockenmaier, 43.

[82] Quoted ibid. 40.

[83] Meisner, 158–9.

[84] Dettelbacher, 115 ff.

[85] Kershaw, *Popular Opinion*, 77.

[86] For remarks on the 'cures' of unemployment see Timothy W. Mason, *Arbeiterklasse und Volksgemeinschaft: Dokumente und Materialien zur deutschen Arbeiterpolitik 1936–1939* (Gütersloh, 1975), 46 ff.

The city on the Main willingly offered a home to the Hitler cult. Already on his birthday, on 20 April, almost all of Würzburg hung out the flag, and in the evening there was an elaborate musical celebration in the public hall. At the beginning of May Hitler and the old Reich President Hindenburg were named honorary citizens of the city.[87]

Hitler was honoured in other ways, and on 21 August, during a brief stop-over in town, the 'cult' was given a shot in the arm. One local paper (the *General Anzeiger*) wrote in hushed tones as follows:

No one knew it, but it was heard: 'The Chancellor is in Würzburg!' And, because on an occasion earlier this week the same rumour went from mouth to mouth, no one at first wanted to believe it. But the cry grew louder: 'The Führer is in Würzburg!' And ever greater grew the circle, which heard the call, until a desire for certainty arose. And so, quietly, in the high summer sun, people moved off to see the Führer, to greet him, to cheer him. So it was around 5.00 in the afternoon that the Julius promenade and the Place in front of the 'Würzburg Hof' grew black with people who all wanted to see and greet the Führer. It did not take long before the Chancellor of the German people showed himself at the window of the hotel, and the jubilation broke all bounds. For minutes at a time, there resounded tumultuous calls of 'Heil' up to the Führer, who smilingly appreciated the greeting spontaneously brought to him by the enchanted mob of people. Already by 5.30, after a short pause for a rest (the Chancellor was *en route* from Bad Godesberg to Munich), the Führer had left Würzburg once again, accompanied by a 'Heil' greeting of many thousands of voices from the grateful Würzburgers, who were happy to be able to greet Adolf Hitler once more within the walls of their city. Even if it was only for a few minutes.[88]

His next visit to the city, in July 1937, was organized in detail, and he reviewed the troops before the Residenz, standing in the front seat of a Mercedes. The throngs which gathered overflowed Würzburg's largest square.

Religious issues continued to be important. It would take some time before Catholics could adjust to the dissolution of their organizations, and many were disgusted that BVP's representatives were not only expelled from office, but frequently taken into 'protective custody' and beaten.[89] Nor did Catholics appreciate being under the thumb of Nazi Gauleiter Otto Helmuth, a man known as a 'Catholic-gobbler' (*Katholikenfresser*). That reputation was fuelled by onslaughts against the Catholic Party, the editor of the Catholic Sunday newspaper, the *Fränkisches Volksblatt*, and local priests who caused the slightest irritation. In small ways Hellmuth deliberately provoked Catholics, such as by naming his daughter Gailana after the Franconian duchess who, legend had it, was the person responsible for murdering the Irish missionaries Kilian,

---

[87] Rockenmaier, 44.
[88] Quoted ibid. 45–7; cf. Bruno Fries *et al.*, *Würzburg im III. Reich* (Würzburg, 1983), 33.
[89] Walter Ziegler, *KLB* iv. *Niederbayern und Oberpfalz* (1973), 8, report for 16–30 June 1933.

Kolonat, and Totnan. The height of it, though, was that he named his dog after Kilian, patron saint of the city![90]

However, the concordat of late July 1933 between the Papacy and Hitler's Reich helped ease acceptance of the regime by Catholics. Though Würzburg's distinguished Bishop Matthias Ehrenfried had little time for Nazism, the local Church, here as elsewhere, did little to discourage Catholics from participating in the public life of the regime. Gauleiter Hellmuth did his part in establishing a *modus vivendi* by not arresting Ehrenfried, despite his hatred of him; he did not want to create a martyr. Nevertheless, individual Catholic priests, if they stepped out of line, had the full weight of the regime descend upon them. Ehrenfried himself, who was no defender of Weimar and is usually regarded as a staunch monarchist, was protected up to a point by his office, but he was in trouble throughout the regime. On at least three separate occasions his palace was stormed by 'spontaneous demonstrations of the public'.

Bishop Ehrenfried had warned, in a message to his flock back in June 1931, of the dubious religious and moral teachings of Nazism, and insisted that clerics could not participate in any form of National Socialism; nor, for that matter, were Party members as a group, and with flags, permitted to attend church. On 6 July 1933 Ehrenfried said that the Church and its followers had, and would continue, to obey legal authority; in the 'new circumstances' it was not the job of individual priests to make condemnations. Where appropriate, he said, the higher authorities of the Church would become involved. What this last statement signifies is a mystery, but it shows that, privately as well as in public, priests were advised to be circumspect and to avoid provocations.[91]

While the hierarchy of the Church and the Papacy generally refrained from challenging the regime, individual members of the clergy were not entirely docile. In the bishopric of Würzburg, over the course of the twelve-year Reich, some 425 Catholic clerics of all ranks—for any number of different reasons, some very small, others more serious—had a brush with Nazi authorities. Some were simply kept under surveillance, some were fined, while others were barred from religious instruction or prevented from speaking from the pulpit. A priest could be sent to a concentration camp,and two from Lower Franconia died in Dachau.[92]

---

[90] Meisner, 160.
[91] Rockenmaier, 67–8.
[92] For the full account see Ulrich von Hehl (ed.), *Priester unter Hitlers Terror: Eine biographische und statistische Erhebung*, 2nd edn. (Mainz, 1985), 1415ff. See also Joachim Maier, 'Die katholische Kirche und die Machtergreifung', in Wolfgang Michalka (ed.), *Die nationalsozialistische Marchtergreifung* (Paderborn, 1984), 152 ff.

German Society

7. Conclusion

Würzburg was a 'university and civil-servant city (*Universität- und Beamten-Stadt*) which identified with cultured, civilized, middle-class values, and with the poets' and thinkers' Germany. The district as a whole, and the city in particular, gave Nazism a cooler reception than in many other places. From the Nazi standpoint, both Würzburg and Lower Franconia left much to be desired. Gauleiter Hellmuth called it the 'blackest district in all of Germany', by which he meant that, unfortunately, it clung to its religious faith and practices. And yet there were currents of opinion here which favoured National Socialism; in the elections of March 1933, which admittedly made it difficult for some on the Left to vote, nearly one third of all the voting adults in the city (31.5 per cent) voted Nazi. There was no landslide victory in this city or in Lower Franconia, but there was a significant degree of support.

Lower Franconians were generally unenthusiastic about the Nazi cause before 1933, and the district contrasts with the predominantly protestant Middle Franconia, centred around Nuremberg, which was more 'on side', especially when it came to anti-Semitism. Lower Franconia should not be identified—as it is sometimes—with *Franken* (Franconia), the latter almost a byword for Protestant, rural support for the NSDAP and for Nuremberg Gauleiter Julius Streicher's rabid anti-Semitism.[93] Lower Franconians' political attitudes and responses to Nazi policies and teachings diverged sharply from the norm associated with *Franken*. It is therefore particularly important to study their behaviour after 1933 because a surprisingly abrupt transformation occurs, whereby a sizeable number of people came to be prepared to accept the regime, its laws and teachings, and to co-operate with the Gestapo. Evidence in the Gestapo case-files indicates a not insignificant degree of willingness to co-operate, accommodate, adjust, collaborate, or merely comply. There were probably many parts of Germany which were more co-operative or collaborated to a greater extent than was the case in Lower Franconia.

[93] For an examination of the rise of the NSDAP in the rest of Franconia, see especially Rainer Hambrecht, *Der Aufstieg der NSDAP in Mittel- und Oberfranken (1925–1933)* (Nuremberg, 1976), 85 ff.

4

Anti-Jewish Actions in Lower Franconia after 1933

IN a letter written after the war Paula Eppstein, a young Jewish Gymnasium student in Würzburg in 1933, wrote as follows:

My family and I had no doubt that anti-Semitism, once legal, would have catastrophic consequences for the Jews in Germany, that, utterly regardless of how long Hitler would be in power, the fanaticism of his followers would not dissipate so fast, that also the property, the existence, and the life of many Jews, particularly in smaller areas, were deeply threatened. We really had tremendous anxiety, but we did not know offhand whether we could do anything in order to protect or rescue ourselves.[1]

This statement may be taken as a general indication of the experiences of Jews in Würzburg and Lower Franconia. Having settled in tiny communities in the countryside around Würzburg, they stood out because of the public nature of their occupations and were hence more vulnerable to attack than those who lived in big cities like Berlin or Frankfurt, where a degree of anonymity provided a modicum of protection. Jews residing in the sleepy villages that dotted the rural landscape became immediately aware of their defencelessness against the assaults of local Nazis who regarded Hitler's appointment as the beginning of a revolution, one that gave them a free hand to deal with opponents, especially the Jews. While the first months after the 'seizure of power' were devoted primarily to the pursuit of political opponents on the Left (SPD and KPD), Nazi leaders out in the provinces exercised sufficient authority to persecute the Jews in their area even before orders came from above. Periodic beatings, confiscation of property, especially of motor-vehicles owned by Jews, took place in many areas across the country, including Würzburg, after the last 'free' election on 5 March 1933.

Reconstruction of the information available to 'ordinary' citizens concerning the anti-Semitic actions in Lower Franconia down to the outbreak of the war shows that actions against the Jews in Lower Franconia were widely publicized, and therefore unmistakably coloured the context in which the Gestapo operated. All in all, it was virtually impossible to live in the district and avoid bearing witness. It is clear that there, as elsewhere, not everyone simply gave in to the 'teachings of contempt' and complied with the letter and spirit of Nazi anti-Semitic laws and regulations, although there was

---

[1] Quoted in Flade, *Juden in Würzburg*, 354. Cf. Klaus Kirschner, '"Da brennt's in Ermreuth!" Juden und Nazis in einem fränkischen Dorf', *Frankfurter Hefte*, 10 (1979), 37ff.

remarkably little criticism. The Gestapo was well aware that 'one is every-where "informed", has his "opinion", but one does not show it and is practised in being silent', especially in public.[2] Against the background of silence, 'indifference'[3], or 'passive complicity',[4] a minority, but not an insignificant one, took anti-Semitism as seriously as did some of the Nazi leaders.

I. EARLY ANTI-SEMITIC ACTS

Within a week of the election of 5 March 1933, boycotts of Jewish businesses, especially the hated department stores, were in evidence in at least a dozen German cities.[5] In response to pleas for assistance against the confiscations and boycotts, the police said nothing could be done. The slightest criticism, or even a question regarding the legality of what was happening, was met with arrest under the 'protective custody' orders. It did not make much difference that on 14 March a specific instruction came from the Reich Minister of the Interior Frick that such excesses must cease, nor that there was another to the same effect, ten days later, from the Party.[6]

By 26 March Hitler had decided to institute an officially inspired boycott. Called for 1 April 1933, the nation-wide boycott of Jewish firms, including not only retail outlets but lawyers and doctors as well, met with mixed responses across Germany. The organizing committee had planned for two SA men to be stationed at the entrance of each Jewish business to dissuade customers from entering. In Berlin there was something of a carnival atmos-phere, although in Frankfurt and elsewhere excesses were committed.[7] According to one Nazi insider, the crowds gathered in Berlin around the stores, many of which were closed for the day, more out of curiosity than to demonstrate their disdain.[8] From working-class districts in particular came word that some people had made a point of shopping in Jewish firms that day. But in distant Würzburg apparently no one dared such gestures, and

---

[2] GSA: HA/Rep. 90P: Gestapo Aachen, LB, 5 Sept. 1935; Gestapo Düsseldorf, LB, 5 May 1935.
[3] Kershaw, *Popular Opinion*, 277.
[4] Kulka and Rodrique, 'The German Population', 426. See also Otto Dov Kulka, '"Public Opinion" in National Socialist Germany and the "Jewish Question"', *Zion*, 40 (1975), p. xliii.
[5] Heinrich Uhlig, *Die Warenhäuser im Dritten Reich* (Cologne, 1956), 209. See also Heinrich August Winkler, *Mittelstand, Demokratie und Nationalsozialismus* (Cologne, 1972), 183ff.
[6] See Helmut Genschel, *Die Verdrängung der Juden aus der Wirtschaft im Dritten Riech* (Göttingen, 1966), 45ff.
[7] Karl A. Schleunes, *The Twisted Road to Auschwitz: Nazi Policy toward German Jews 1933–39* (Urbana, Ill., 1970), 84ff.; Genschel, 51ff.
[8] He is quoted in Schleunes, 88. Goebbels, in self-delusion or otherwise, records the 'success' of the boycott in his diary and the direct role Hitler played in the whole affair: see Goebbels, *My Part in Germany's Fight*, 236ff. For a sample of the publicity leading up to the boycott see *Das Schwarzbuch: Tatsachen und Dokumente. Die Lage der Juden in Deutschland 1933*, ed. Comité des Délégations Juives (Paris, 1934; repr. Frankfurt, 1983), 292ff.

the boycott, announced with great fanfare at a mass rally the night before in the central market-place, was observed.[9]

On the Monday following the boycott (3 April) business returned to normal in Würzburg, but many Jews remained deeply shocked and disappointed at the turn of events. In a number of ways pressure continued to be exerted against them. By late 1933, in several villages across Lower Franconia mayor and council formally denied Jews not merely permission to live and work, but even to travel through on their way to another place. Eight separate places were mentioned in a letter of complaint from the Bavarian Jewish self-help association to the Bavarian Ministry of Economics in October 1933. The letter stated that some mayors were being requested by the Nazi Party to post signs that prohibited entry to all but locally resident Jews. It is worth noting that the association did not feel that it was in a position to object to the blatant prejudice and racial discrimination, and hoped to move the authorities by pointing out how the signs were hurting the economy and ran contrary to the 'law for the protection of retail trade' of 15 September 1933.[10]

Such harassment of the Jews was meant to force them out of the economy, to alienate them from their neighbours, to push them out of the villages and towns, and ultimately out of Germany. Between 1933 and 1939, as a kind of mirror of the persecution of the Jews, the number of Jews living in Bavaria declined by more than 50 per cent (from 35,452 to 14,684); in Lower Franconia the decline was 59.4 per cent (from 8,520 to 3,461).[11] The worst-affected areas in all of Bavaria were the Protestant rural areas of Middle Franconia, which had a stronger anti-Semitic tradition; there the Jewish population dropped from 11,631 to 3,523 between 1933 and 1939.

Official records show that a more or less unrelenting campaign of har-assment was allowed to continue, and was, moreover, encouraged by the Party, notwithstanding the occasional pious statements of leaders that such 'individual actions' should cease. Jews were made to feel that they could expect little help from their neighbours and that anti-Jewish policies would increase in number and be enforced down to the smallest detail. Any sym-pathy that might be shown for their plight or reserve about the efficacy of anti-Semitic policies could be treated by anyone who wished as cause for a report to the authorities. The ways in which barriers were drawn between the Jews and everyone else in Germany are treated in the remainder of this book, but here it is important to recall that they left the country, especially the rural areas, primarily out of a fear of violence to their persons or property. News of a beating, arrest, or damage to property travels fast in the rural and small-town milieu.

In the early years of the dictatorship, when eliminating high unemployment

---

[9] Schleunes, 89; Flade, *Würzburger Juden*, 264–6; Schultheis, 46–7.
[10] StA W: NSDAP/GL/XII/2, 13 Oct. 1933.
[11] Ophir and Wiesemann (eds.), 24.

and getting the economy going again were the priorities, the new leadership in Berlin gave no priority to anti-Semitic policies. The Reich Ministry of Economics even thought it ill-advised to draw up lists of Jewish and non-Jewish businesses with the aim of some sort of indirect boycott, because the effort was bound to cause economic disruptions.[12] While the efforts of local hotheads could be appreciated, it might be surmised, their actions had to be kept within certain bounds, lest the economy collapse. For the most part the instigators of the actions against the Jews belonged to one or another of the Nazi Party organizations, SA or SS. The Hitler Youth was also frequently involved, especially as local nuisances.

However, there was a kind of limited semi-official quarantine placed on the Jews' economic activities. Nazis or their relatives who frequented Jewish businesses—or were attended to by Jewish doctors, dentists, or other professionals—were taken to task whenever such behaviour was brought to light. In April 1935 the authorities in Würzburg reported that there had recently been a concerted effort to boycott Jewish department stores, doctors, and lawyers; on 20 April 200 people gathered in front of the Jewish department store Ruschkewitz in order to identify any members of the NSDAP who might be shopping in the store. While the police moved them away without incident, members of the Nazi Party, SA, and SS were involved in an attempt to enforce their own form of 'silent boycott'.[13] Before the end of the year, however, Ruschkewitz sold out to Joseph Neckermann, who thereby founded what became after 1945 a department-store empire. Many others took advantage of these 'Aryanization' procedures; such actions could be seen elsewhere, not just in Würzburg.[14]

Local records give the distinct impression that the SA and Party were determined to boycott the Jews, but more than one source suggests that, in spite of it all, Catholics in Bavaria, as well as in the country as a whole, were slower to respond. A selection of Gestapo reports for all of Prussia, which survives for the first years of the dictatorship, makes this clear. Of the Catholic population, the Gestapo reported in mid-1935 that those in Recklinghausen, Westphalia, had 'no proper understanding for the fact that in the last while the Jewish question has been placed in the foreground and, because of its religious views', the population of the area did 'not accept the nature of the struggle against the Jews'. However, the view which predominated within the 'movement' and the SA was that the time had come to 'solve the Jewish question radically'. The idea 'was to wind up the Jewish problem from below', to take hold of it in such a way that, eventually, 'the government must follow'.[15]

---

[12] See e.g. letter of 5 Oct. 1933 in StA W: LRA/3261: Bad Brückenau.
[13] Bay HStA: MA 106680: RP report, 7 May 1935, repr. in Broszat et al. (eds.), *Bayern in der NS-Zeit*, i. 442; cf. LHA Ko: 441/28264: RP report, 5 Dec. 1935.
[14] Flade, *Würzburger Juden*, 276–7.
[15] GSA: HA/Rep. 90P: Gestapo Recklinghausen, 6 June 1935; cf. Gestapo Aachen, 8 May 1935.

Once the unemployment was reduced and power consolidated, the early official brakes on Nazi anti-Semitism which was aimed at the economic activities of the Jews were gradually released, and at all levels the effort was focused on getting rid of Jewish entrepreneurs, whether bankers or newspaper-owners or the lowliest cattle-dealers in Bavaria. Where necessary, intimidation was applied—for example, against peasants, to put a stop to their ingrained and persistent habit of dealing with Jewish traders. Even late in 1935, when such acts were officially taboo, hop-growers from communities around Hersbruck (Middle Franconia) who dared sell to Jewish traders were branded as traitors and marched through the villages with signs round their necks.[16] Such measures hardly met with instant success, for as late as mid-1937 long lists of those who kept on dealing with the Jews were drawn up and direct pressure applied.[17] The situation was the same across Bavaria; districts with a tradition of Jewish cattle-dealers (which included even anti-Semitic areas such as in Middle Franconia) had to be forced to give them up, and when, by 1938, Jews were finally driven from the trade altogether, the mutterings of the peasants indicated that they were missed.[18]

In addition to efforts to drive the Jews out of the villages and towns of the area, there was a campaign led by local hotheads in the Nazi movement to put up anti-Jewish signs as a social reinforcement. At the entrances of many villages, as well as in certain establishments like restaurants and hotels, signs appeared that features slogans such as 'Jews not wanted here' or 'Entry forbidden to Jews'. Dr Rosenthal from Würzburg wrote to the 'Association of Bavarian-Israelite Communities' in October 1934 (as he had done at roughly the same time in 1933) to complain again that across Lower Franconia there was an increasing number of such signs posted at the entrance to villages. Each village could decide for itself whether to allow such signs, he maintained, and the regional authorities had no jurisdiction in the matter. Rosenthal wanted some lobbying done by the Bavarian association with the Bavarian Ministry of Economics to change things, because every day the signs caused 'public defamation of rural Jews'.[19] Although this was mainly the work of people in the Nazi movement, there were times when a placard was displayed on the initiative of a pub- or restaurant-owner, either to curry favour with such people or to protect himself from the charge of being a friend to the Jews after he had been denounced to the Party for letting them in.

There was no law or regulation which denied Jews service in restaurants

---

[16] Bay HStA: MA 106694: RP report 10 Oct. 1935, repr. in Broszat *et al.* (eds.), *Bayern in der NS-Zeit*, i. 456.

[17] StA W: NSDAP/GL/XII/6: Hundsfeld, 18 June 1937. For nearby Hesse see HHStA: Abt 483/6741: letter to Gestapo Kassel from Landrat Gelnhausen, 30 Nov. 1937.

[18] StA W: LRA Bad Neustadt 125/5, GS Bischofsheim, 28 Jan. 1938, also cited in Kershaw, *Popular Opinion*, 243. In the same village, however, violence against the Jews was occasionally reported: see Bay HStA: MA 106 681: report of RP, 10 Nov. 1938.

[19] StA W: NSDAP/GL/XII/1, 9 Oct. 1934. Thirteen towns and villages are mentioned.

and pubs, but where owners were 'soft' on the issue local hacks were quick
to organize mini-boycotts.[20] People involved in tourism or business in the
numerous spa centres in Bavaria worried about the impact on trade, and
many of these concerns were expressed to the authorities. While the legality
of the signs remained unclear, no one seemed to know how to handle the
situation. The people who put them up in Middle Franconia (Streicher territory) were not prosecuted, and this response in that area left the authorities
in Lower Franconia in a quandary about what should be done. While the
police in Würzburg itself officially banned such placards on 27 April 1934,
they not only continued to appear but actually spread, with the result that
on 29 January 1936 Rudolf Hess wrote to all local Party branches instructing
them to avoid placards which incited violence, such as 'Jews enter this village
at their own risk'; he saw nothing wrong with those that declared 'Jews are
not wanted here'.[21]

These official and semi-official actions had a considerable impact in re-
inforcing negative attitudes towards the Jews, even when the violence, and
especially the requirement to cut useful economic ties with Jews, were far
from being approved. In some parts of Lower Franconia, including areas
which were reticent in supporting the Nazis before 1933, people began to
turn their backs on the persecuted, and more than anything else wanted to
see them leave.[22]

2. THE NUREMBERG LAWS

The Nuremberg Laws of September 1935 provided legislative support for
harassment of the Jews, which was already well under way. Over the preceding spring and summer a wave of anti-Jewish excesses had swept the
country, though one leader after another officially 'regretted' them and gave
notice that they should stop, particularly as they were having an adverse
effect on the economy.[23] Reich Bank President Hjalmar Schacht, disturbed at
the economic repercussions, called a meeting of the relevant ministers for 20
August 1935, but no binding decision was taken.[24] Yet another call went
out to end the 'spontaneous actions', and Schacht met Hitler for conversations
on 5 September, just ten days before the Party rally. There is insufficient
evidence to settle the long-standing debate as to whether there was a direct

---

[20] See chs. 5 and 6.
[21] StAW: NSDAP/GL/XII/1: GS Geiselbach, 6 Apr. 1935. For similar complaints that anti-
Semitic signs would backfire see GSA:HA/Rep. 90P: Gestapo Koblenz, 5 July 1935. See StA W:
NSDAP/GL/XII/1 for the Würzburg ban. For Hess see BAK: Sammlung Schumacher, 240, II.
[22] See StA W: LRA Bad Neustadt, 125/4. 1 Dec. 1936, also in Kershaw, *Popular Opinion*, 240.
[23] Genschel, 105ff.; Uwe Dietrich Adam, *Judenpolitik im Dritten Reich* (Düsseldorf, 1972), 122–
4.
[24] See Genschel, 112–13; Adam, *Judenpolitik*, 123–4.

connection between calling off the radicals and offering a 'legal' resolution of the problem. Hitler's speech to the Nuremberg Party rally suggests such a link. On this occasion he declared that it was necessary to adopt a 'legal regulation of the problem', which was justified in order to head off spontaneous 'defensive actions of the enraged population'.[25]

The Nuremberg Laws declared illegal all further marriages and sexual relations outside marriage 'between Jews and citizens of German or kindred blood'. Jews could no longer employ 'German' women as domestic servants, nor were they permitted to raise the national flag.[26] *The Times* of London waited until its edition of 8 November to deliver its 'interim report' on the impact of these laws. Under the heading 'Persecution in a new pitch, a cold pogrom' it spoke of the 'irreparable injustice and harm' being perpetrated because of the laws, and added that 'perhaps the most pertinent comment, which can be heard expressed with understandable bitterness and disgust in circles by no means fully "non-Aryan", is that the new laws are making Nazi Germany more than ever into a paradise for blackmailers'. Especially troublesome were the confusion in the regulations and the question of enforcement:

Nobody can yet say to what extent, if any, they will check the pioneer process by which individual fanatics and—still worse—subordinate authorities, with subtle guidance from higher quarters, endeavour to blaze the trail. The law still lags far behind realities, and every day that passes enables its amateur interpreters to win fresh ground from which it will not be easy to dislodge them. No regulations are likely to bring dismissed Jews back to their posts, and none can bring suicides back to life.

The author of *The Times* article remarked that the laws were bound to be more devastating for the Jews than the 'individual actions'.

But the Nuremberg Laws, in the absence of interpretative regulations, are being used to justify every sort of indignity and persecution, not only by individuals, but by the established authorities. The intimidation system of the Nazi revolution, with its indefinite 'protective' or 'preventive' custody, its concentration camps, its pillorying, and other social and economic pressure, led from the first to the rapid growth of the loathsome practice of denunciation, which has not yet been stamped out despite many pious declarations by public authorities. The opportunities offered by the new laws are unlimited, as any lawyer can bear witness who has tried to look after the interests of 'non-Aryans' or political suspects. Any individual can report his Jewish enemy or competitor as having been seen in the company of an 'Aryan' woman, or trump up alleged business obligations from the past.

The article concluded that the Jews in Germany were without hope. 'Unless some attempt is made in high quarters to check the ferocity of the anti-Semitic fanatics', the Jews 'will be condemned, as it were, to run round blindly in

[25] Quoted in Kershaw, *The 'Hitler Myth'*, 236.
[26] The law is reprinted in Hirsch, Majer, and Meinck (eds.), 350–1.

circles until they die. This is the process to which the term "cold pogrom" has been applied.'[27]

German Jews, hitherto reluctant to join the Zionist cause for a homeland in the Near East, were undoubtedly shocked. *The Times* referred to the legislation as the 'ghetto laws', and it was not a pleasant prospect to be subject to them. The majority, those in the non-Zionist camp, especially the assimilationists, saw the laws as a bitter set-back; these were Jews who were almost 'more German than the Germans'.[28] One of the major national Jewish organizations said the laws 'constituted a severe blow for German Jewry', not least because overnight the hundred-year-long struggle for their emancipation was reversed, and they were turned into second-class citizens. The numerically smaller Zionist groups hoped to make the best of a bad situation.[29]

The message in the Gestapo records and elsewhere for the period after September–October 1935 is summarized tersely by one, which states that 'because of the Nuremberg Laws, the Jews have been much reserved of late'.[30] The Gestapo in Bavaria said that 'many Jews appear, finally, to have come to the understanding that it is good and proper to behave cautiously as guests in a host land'.[31] The underground Socialists' reports correctly saw that the laws had the effect of declaring the Jews 'outside the nation and legally unequal. It is an act of oppression and spiritual sadism.' In so far as it pertained to sexual relations, the Jews were declared 'inferior to all other peoples and races; they are ascribed a position, so to speak, outside humanity'.[32] The Government President of Lower Franconia reported for December–January 1935–6 that 'since the decreeing of the Nuremberg Laws the Jews have become very modest in their public appearances. The observation can be made that the Jews are making the switch, are selling off their businesses and preparing themselves for emigration.'[33]

Ordinary Germans' reactions to the Nuremberg Laws are difficult to reconstruct—the few recorded statements in various kinds of contemporary documents are not particularly revealing. One set of sources that has survived consists of reports of the Gestapo, although for the most part the material pertains to the Prussian areas of Germany, from the Rhineland all the way to eastern Germany.[34] There are also scattered accounts from Bavaria. Since

---

[27] *The Times* (London), 8 Nov. 1935.

[28] See e.g. BAK: R58/604: Gestapo Hanover, 4 Mar. 1936.

[29] See Abraham Margaliot, 'The Reaction of the Jewish Public in Germany to the Nuremberg Laws', *Yad Vashem Studies*, 12 (1977), 75ff.

[30] LHA Ko: 441/28267, Gestapo Koblenz report, 4 Oct. 1935.

[31] Bay HStA: MA 106687, 1 May 1936, also in Broszat *et al.* (eds.), *Bayern in der NS-Zeit*, i. 460–1.

[32] Sopade, ii. (Aug. 1935), 996–7.

[33] *KLB* vi. 84.

[34] Otto Dov Kulka is preparing an edition of these records. For a critique of the material see his 'Die Nürnberger Rassengesetze und die deutsche Bevölkerung im Lichte Geheimer NS-Lage- und Stimmungsberichte', *VfZ* 32 (1984), 582ff.

some of the Gestapo material derives from Catholic and/or rural areas not unlike Lower Franconia and other parts of Bavaria, it can convey some impression of the range of probable responses to the Nuremberg Laws in Lower Franconia.

The Gestapo accounts that survive for the months leading up to the Nuremberg Laws are strewn with stories of the massive numbers of 'spontaneous excesses' which took place throughout the country, including Bavaria. Some idea of the scope they attained in some areas may be gathered, for example, from a report from Osnabrück in August 1935. In that city and surrounding area there were 'massive demonstrations' against Jewish businesses, which were publicly branded and surrounded by mobs; people who frequented Jewish businesses were photographed and the pictures were displayed in public. The streets were alive with action—parades and so on. In the countryside peasants found to be dealing with Jewish cattle-dealers were denounced by name to the Nazi rag, the *Stürmer*. The 'high point of the struggle against the Jews', as the report went, was a meeting on 20 August, which brought together 25,000 people to hear Kreisleiter Münzer on the theme of 'Osnabrück and the Jewish Question'. The situation was so inflamed, however, that the Gestapo and other state officials had to call on Münzer to put a stop to the 'individual actions', and he did so by publishing a warning in all the local newspapers; these actions were officially outlawed on 27 August.[35]

The vandalism and terroristic acts aimed at Jews cooled off after September 1935. As one Gestapo report from Catholic Münster put it, 'after the promulgation of the Jewish laws at the Party meetings in Nuremberg, a certain tranquillity set in with regard to the Jewish question. Excesses against Jews, as well as individual actions against Jewish businesses, have not taken place again in the past month.'[36] The 'tranquillity' following the promulgation of the Nuremberg Laws, noted the report, suggests a kind of accommodation to the new circumstances and is in marked contrast to the repeated complaints in the Gestapo reports about the attitude of Catholics to the Jewish question. For example, the Aachen Gestapo regretted on 5 September that the 'mentality of the Catholic population judged the Jews in the first instance as human beings' and only secondarily 'from the racial-political point of view'.[37] While this complaint finds an echo in several reports from the summer (but also into September), the Gestapo was beginning to note signs of adjustment, especially after the middle of September. A report for October from Münster noted the population's 'satisfaction', and that the actions against the Jews had 'settled down'; the word from nearby Dortmund said that 'almost all' non-Jewish citizens gave the laws their 'fullest recognition'; Magdeburg in

---

[35] GSA:HA/Rep. 90P: Gestapo Osnabrück, 4 Sept. 1935.
[36] Ibid.: Gestapo Münster, 6 Nov. 1935.
[37] Ibid.: Gestapo Aachen, 5 Sept. 1935; cf. ibid.: Gestapo Recklinghausen, 6 June 1935.

the east said in its November report that 'the population regards the regulation of the relationships of the Jews as an emancipatory act, which brings clarity and simultaneously greater firmness in the protection of the racial interests of the German people'; the people in Kassel were said to have an understanding for the legislation concerning the Jews, though part of the middle-class population felt that it was too radical.[38]

For Bavaria the reports are equally terse. Thus, one from Augsburg, written early in 1936, said that the population 'fully understood this clean-up effort', though it regarded the laws themselves as 'one-sided' in that they only punished the male. 'According to the general view, both parties ought to be taken to task.'[39] In the Nuremberg area the laws were received with 'great enthusiasm'. Lower Franconia's government President said that the measures 'were approved of by the nationalistically inclined population, while the Jews were hit by consternation, expressed in an increasing desire to emigrate'. All in all, the celebrations at the Party meeting, he continued, 'raised the trust in the Reich government, gave heart and confidence to the doubters, and made the job of the grumblers and agitators' more difficult.[40] In Munich the Gestapo reported that 'little is said' about the new legislation, 'although there was general agreement with it'.[41]

The Gestapo in Kassel—in Protestant Hesse, just to the north of Bavaria—observed in its report of December 1935 that

although the understanding for the Jewish question has grown among the people since the Jewish legislation, a part of the bourgeois population considers the Jewish policy of the government too radical. The usual phrases keep turning up about 'decent Jews' and the like. It is also believed that a moderation in Jewish policy would radically relieve our foreign-exchange situation.[42]

The report from Potsdam for November drew a distinction between those who were 'educable' and those who were not; the latter 'did not understand ...racial thought, in particular as it has been actualized in the racial laws'. This 'misunderstanding' was 'in part deliberate'.[43] It was said that the non-Nazis in Aachen remained 'untouched' by the Nuremberg events; given the 'well-known mentality of the Catholic population [of the area] nothing more was to be expected'. To be sure, the legislation was greeted to the extent that it would put a stop to the excesses.[44] 'The non-National Socialist part of the

---

[38] See ibid.: Gestapo Münster (Oct. report); Dortmund (Sept. report); and Nov. reports from Magdeburg and Kassel.
[39] Bay HStA: MA 106697, 3 Apr. 1936; also in Broszat et al. (eds.), Bayern in der NS-Zeit, i. 460.
[40] Bay HStA: MA 106680, 8 Oct. 1935.
[41] BAK: R58/671, Gestapo Munich, 3 Oct. 1935.
[42] BAK: R58/529.
[43] GSA: HA/Rep. 90P: Gestapo Potsdam, report for Nov. 1935.
[44] BAK: R58/531: Gestapo Aachen, 7 Oct. 1935. This was a reaction very similar to that in Cologne and Düsseldorf.

population' in nearby Trier 'remained as before under the influence of clerical and reactionary circles', so that opinion was divided on the latest turn of events.[45] Even so, by early in the new year the report from Trier was that people only rarely retained economic relations with the Jews, many of whom were emigrating.[46]

Regardless of whether the laws found an approving, disapproving, or indifferent audience, once in existence they became part of the structure of everyday life for all Jews or those who had anything to do with them, whether in business or in more personal matters. The laws also codified existing practice: avoid Jews socially, and in particular have no sexual relations with them. Even actions which might be construed as merely sympathetic to their plight were now given a new, more dangerous twist, because anyone friendly to the Jews could be denounced on suspicion of having illicit relationships. The promulgation of these measures marked an important point in the persecution of the Jews in Nazi Germany, and they certainly made it much easier for radicals to take up the struggle on a 'legal' basis. More will be said in later chapters about popular responses to these laws and other anti-Semitic policies as they were reflected in the Gestapo case-files.

The Nuremberg Laws facilitated the petty victimization that had been going on well before September 1935. One of the earliest denunciations of social relations between Jewish and non-Jewish persons recorded by the Gestapo in Würzburg concerns a case in which a Dr Karl Wesen and his student Jürgen Ernst reported directly to the police that on the evening of 28 May 1933 two people in the Cafe Kies had behaved in an openly 'provocative' fashion. One of these people was Jewish—a certain Alfons Golom—the other a young typist-clerk by the name of Helena Valentin (born 1912). On the May evening in 1933 she was 'done up' in such a way, and was flirting with Golom so openly, that Wesen and Ernst took it upon themselves to follow them when they left the restaurant and to 'tell her off' because of the un-German way she acted. When she answered that it was none of their business, and that in any case, she would be ashamed to call herself German, she was slapped and the couple chased through the streets. The case is interesting because Wesen and Ernst may not have been Nazi Party members. (Valentin had been friends with Golom since November 1932, as it turned out from the story they gave later, when the Gestapo got hold of them.) The case also shows that more than two years before the first laws on 'race defilement' were passed in September 1935, relationships between Jews and non-Jews were already policed.[47]

---

[45] Ibid. 534: Gestapo Trier, 5 Oct. 1935.

[46] Ibid. 656: Gestapo Trier, 5 Mar. 1936.

[47] StA W: Gestapo 9073; in Gestapo 10210 an arrest for 'race defilement' was made on 30 Aug. 1935. For an example from elsewhere see GSA: HA/Rep. 90P: Gestapo Düsseldorf, July 1935.

Nazi Party radicals could take advantage of the new laws to settle old scores, and they denounced Jews even for actions which had occurred before 1933. The Jewish merchant Max Oppenheim (born in Würzburg in 1898) was reported by the NSDAP on 5 September 1935 for having had sexual relations with 'German' women up to the period in 1930. The grounds for his arrest were that his behaviour, 'which had only recently come to light', had caused a public outcry; 'wide circles of the population and especially the NSDAP have been set into such vehemence and upset that the worst is to be feared for his personal security'. For his 'own safety' he was placed in protective custody. He was released when he assured the local Gestapo that he was about to emigrate.[48]

Cases were initiated by members of the NSDAP against Jewish neighbours who did not show sufficient 'respect'. Thus, 'Party comrade' Wolfgang Kreuzer sent a five-page typed letter to the local Party headquarters (whence it was forwarded to the Gestapo), in which he denounced Isay Ostrach (Jewish and a Polish citizen) on a large number of counts, including, in passing, the possibility that he might be involved in 'race defilement'. The police were asked to investigate 'the conditions in the house', and turned up virtually nothing except that Ostrach was not liked by his neighbours.[49] The new laws constituted an important weapon for anyone who wished to take advantage of them, and precisely because they pertained to a matter of extreme importance to Nazism allegations easily found their way on to the Gestapo's desk.

3. 'Reichskristallnacht', 9–10 November 1938

All the official, semi-official, and personal hostility aimed at the Jews paled in comparison with the events of the 'night of broken glass' (Kristallnacht), the pogrom of November 1938 which hit the Jews and their property across Germany. As is well known by now, the pogrom began when a Polish Jew, 17-year-old Herschel Grynszpan, shot Ernst Vom Rath, third secretary of the German Embassy in Paris. His parents, once resident in Germany, had just been deported to Poland, and on 7 November young Grynszpan decided to take his revenge. Vom Rath died of his wounds on 9 November at 4.30 p.m. His death could not have come at a worse time, for 9 November was already a day of special significance in Nazi lore: it was the anniversary of Hitler's attempt in 1923 to seize power in the abortive *putsch* in Munich. Customarily, out of remembrance for the few Nazis who died in the attempted coup, Hitler met with his old cronies and, among other things, passed out Party promotions. At the 1938 gathering in the old Munich city hall, word came

[48] StA W: Gestapo 8989.
[49] Ibid.: Gestapo 9100, letter of 25 Feb. 1936. There are even more examples from areas with a tradition of anti-Semitism, e.g. around Marburg, Hesse (StA Marburg: LRA/180/4829).

at 8.30 p.m., just as the evening meal was being served, that Vom Rath had died. Joseph Goebbels, the Propaganda Minister, apparently regarded the assassination as a chance to regain a position of influence by putting back some dynamism into the struggle against the Jews, and leading it himself.[50] Following a brief meeting alone with Hitler, the Führer retired and Goebbels gave the assembled Party members what was by all accounts a masterful speech, in which he conveyed the general idea that direct actions against the Jews ought to begin at once. Telephone orders went out across Germany, in a more or less *ad hoc* fashion, to commence the 'spontaneous actions' against Jews and their property.[51]

On 9 November, at 11.55 p.m., a telegram was sent from Berlin (which had been notified in the meantime) to all Gestapo posts, announcing that 'at any moment in all of Germany actions will be taken against Jews, and particularly against their synagogues. These [demonstrations] are not to be disturbed, although, in agreement with the ordinary police, it is to be ensured that plundering and other particular excesses are to be prevented.' Important materials which turned up were to be confiscated, and the preliminary steps taken to arrest a total of between 20,000 and 30,000 Jews; those chosen should be of the wealthier class. It added that further orders would be sent later in the night. At 1.20 a.m. Berlin ordered the Gestapo to arrange meetings with the local NSDAP to work out details for carrying out the demonstration. The Gestapo was to make clear that it was under orders to keep matters in bounds; 'German' lives and property could not be endangered; Jewish businesses and homes could be destroyed, but plunderers would be arrested; the businesses of 'Germans' had to be protected from potential damage; and foreigners, even when they were Jews, were to be left alone. Better-off (and healthy male) Jews were to be arrested in numbers which could be handled in local facilities; they were not to be mishandled, and would be sent to concentration camps as soon as possible. The orders were not followed to the letter, for, as one of the many telegrams from Berlin in the subsequent weeks complained, some Jews sent to concentration camps were 'nearly 80 years old, obviously sick and mentally weak'.[52]

These behind-the-scenes machinations are reconstructed on the basis of the materials from Würzburg, so that there is little doubt that the instructions reached Lower Franconia, but there was much more chaos on the ground than might be deduced from such records. Most Lower Franconians would have had no idea about the plotting that went on at local Gestapo and Party

---

[50] See Adam, *Judenpolitik*, 204 ff. For additional background see Rita Thalmann and Emmanuel Feinermann, *Crystal Night 9–10 November 1938* (New York, 1974), 11 ff.; Hermann Graml, *Der 9 November 1938: 'Reichskristallnacht'*, 4th edn. (Bonn, 1956), 4 ff.

[51] Adam, *Judenpolitik*, 207; Schleunes, 236 ff.

[52] For all of the above see BAK: R58/276, 124 ff. See also Uwe Dietrich Adam, 'Wie spontan war der Pogrom?', in Walter H. Pehle (ed.), *Der Judenpogrom 1938* (Frankfurt, 1938), 74 ff.

headquarters, but, once the pogrom began to unfold, they would have learnt about the events from local press coverage and by word of mouth. Though many Jews had already moved away from the district, tiny pockets continued to exist throughout Lower Franconia, unlike other areas in Bavaria and Germany, so that 'the population in this area was to a far greater extent witness to the devastation and many experienced at first hand the merciless fate of the Jews'.[53]

It was virtually impossible to avoid bearing witness in villages like Frankenwinheim in Lower Franconia. Just after the turn of the century the Jews had made up 10 per cent of the population of 588, and, as throughout the district, these numbers declined thereafter. On the morning of 10 November this village was the site of a forced public gathering of Jews from Frankenwinheim and neighbouring Lülsfeld. The SA stationed in Gerolzhofen and Volkach, who engineered this event, ordered Jewish women to dress in religious garb and carry all the furniture and holy materials into the street, set fire to them, and watch. Something like 200 other villagers looked on as well; the police, like the firemen, stood by, and at its conclusion put every Jewish man, woman, and child in gaol in Gerolzhofen. In their absence, property was plundered.[54]

Almost overnight, many small Jewish communities came to an end, and, in the words of the leading administrative officer for Lower Franconia, the villages and small towns became 'free of Jews [judenrein]'.[55] Ophir and Wiesemann's chronology of events in the small communities makes the scope of the catastrophe clear. The sixteen Jews who lived in Adelsberg (total population about 370) until the pogrom left the village within a month, never to return. Back in 1910 Jews made up just over 11 per cent of the population there, had their own synagogue, butcher, teacher, and ritual bath. During the pogrom uniformed Nazi Party members from outside the village itself showed up and broke the windows of the synagogue and Jewish homes; the next day the SA arrived from nearby Gemünden and, in small groups, broke into Jewish homes and destroyed the synagogue's interior. These events 'were played out in the presence of numerous village inhabitants'.[56] Burgpreppach counted a Jewish community of 126 in 1910 (just over 22 per cent of the village population); by 1933 the figures were already reduced to 78, and at the beginning of 1938 54 still hung on. During the pogrom the SA came from nearby Bamberg, apparently making the rounds of small Jewish com-

[53] Kershaw, *Popular Opinion*, 261–2. The same pattern, in fact, was to be seen in the Palatinate, the district just across the River Rhine to the west of Lower Franconia. See Karl Heinz Debus, 'Die Reichskristallnacht in der Pfalz: Schuldbewußtsein und Ermittlung', *Zeitschrift für die Geschichte des Oberrheins*, 129 (1981), 445ff., and Kurt Düwell, *Die Rheingebiete in der Judenpolitik des Nationalsozialismus vor 1942* (Bonn, 1968), 175ff.

[54] Ophir and Wiesemann (eds.), 291–3.

[55] Bay HStA: MA 106681: report, 10 Jan. 1939.

[56] Ophir and Wiesemann (eds.), 247–8.

munities in the area, along with some of the local Nazi zealots, broke into the main building of the Jewish community (containing synagogue, school, and teacher's residence), and at high noon set fire to it, including all its furniture and the sacred books and scrolls. By 1 January 1940 only seven Jews remained in the village.[57] In Schöllkrippen near Alzenau the forty-four Jews resident in the town on the day of the pogrom left for ever within the week.[58]

Numerous other small communities in Lower Franconia experienced a similar exodus. Worth mentioning are the places where the numbers dropped off virtually to zero by the end of 1939, as in Burgsinn; Ebelsbach; Eschau; Fechenbach; Geldersheim; Gemünden; Geroldshausen; Gnodstadt; Goßmannsdorf a.M.; Großlangheim; Großostheim; Hammelburg; Heßdorf; Höchberg; Hofheim i.UFr.; Hörstein; Hösbach; Hüttenheim i.Bay.; Karlstadt; Kleinbardorf; Kleinheubach; Kleinlangheim; Kleinwallstadt; Klingenberg a.M.; Lendershausen; Lülsfeld; Mainbernheim; Marktheidenfeld; Marktsteft; Memmelsdorf i.UFr.; Mittelstreu; Oberaltertheim; Reckendorf; Rimpar; Schonungen; Sommerau; Sommerhausen; Tauberretttersheim; Veitshöchheim; Wasserlos; Westheim; Willmars.[59] Jews either emigrated or sought refuge in the anonymity of bigger cities.

Even when a Jewish community was not wiped out, the events of the pogrom were dramatic and horrendous. In Oberthulba (population 821 in 1933) the number of Jews had declined by 1937 to just 31. The detailed police report of the pogrom there indicates that it began only late, on 10 November. 'Civilians' smashed in the windows of Jewish homes, broke into some, and demolished or plundered virtually everything in them. According to the police report, when on the morning of 11 November the pogrom of the night before was discussed in the village 'the population to an extent agreed that for once the teeth should be shown to the Jews and their property, in part, destroyed'. Some people were 'opposed, however, to some shady elements who used the action for their own advantage and who stole furniture and such from Jewish houses'. Two men were subsequently arrested and later released. Both were considered by the local policeman to be 'unreliable' because of their association with the Communist Party before 1933.[60] The pogrom was not so brutal and destructive everywhere, but virtually every community in which Jews still resided by November 1938 experienced it. Thus, there is evidence of the action directed at Jews, their property, or that of the Jewish community in villages such as Acholshausen, which had but two, as did Allersheim and Arnstein; Bütthart had five; Eschau two; Euerbach four; Fechenbach two; Geldersheim three; Gochsheim seven; Goßmannsdorf five; Hessdorf six; Hösbach five; Lülsfeld nine; Marktsteft three; and Rödelsee

[57] Ibid. 275–8.
[58] Ibid. 394–5.
[59] See ibid. 247ff.
[60] Full account in StA W: NSDAP/GL/XII/6: report of GS 11 Nov. 1938.

had six.[61] A large percentage of these people had stayed on because of their advanced years, and because they could imagine few alternatives.

Where larger numbers of Nazi Party, SA, and SS members could be gathered together and directed, as in the bigger urban centres, the brutalities and destruction of property were that much more extensive. The events in Aschaffenburg, according to a detailed local police report, took a particularly nasty turn. The city's population (which stood at 36,260 in 1933, 591 of them Jewish—reduced to 339 in the period up to the pogrom) witnessed the complete destruction of the synagogue through a fire that began early in the night of 10 November. Events there seem to have been inspired, as everywhere else, by orders to the local Party from Munich. The message must have been sent very late on 9 November or early the next morning, because the Würzburg Gestapo telephoned at 2.30 a.m. to tell local police (the ordinary police as well as the Gestapo and SD branches) what to do during the 'action'. Wanton destruction was perpetrated on at least four Jewish businesses, including a department store and restaurant, and the windows of apartments were broken; someone threw two fire-bombs into one residence. These acts were carried out by large groups of roving bands (no figures are mentioned) moving through the city. Four people were brought in by police when caught plundering. By noon on 10 November more police had to be assigned to watch the many people gathered on several streets in the inner city.

In the course of events in Aschaffenburg two Jewish men were beaten and shot by the SA. One of the Jews; a 61-year-old man, was led through town, beaten, and shot three times in the stomach; he died five days later. One account says that the subsequent trial of the SA men who were responsible was eventually dropped on the intervention of the Würzburg Gestapo.[62] Besides the open violence, an estimated thirty Jewish men were arrested and eventually sent to Dachau. The events spilled over into the nearby village of Goldbach (population 3,569 in 1933, of which 38 were Jews); it took until 7.00 p.m. on 10 November for the pogrom to reach there. By then an estimated 400–500 'citizens' went on a rampage that lasted until early the next morning. Once again, the synagogue was demolished, windows in the homes of Jews smashed, and the interiors wrecked. Similar events, involving 'about 1,000' persons, took place an hour later in neighbouring Großostheim (population 3,840 in 1933, 28 of them Jews). In Hösbach (population 3,376 in 1933, of whom 15 were Jews) the actions aimed at the few Jews who remained in town began late on 9 November, and were stopped with difficulty, but not before some plundering had taken place. The uproar dragged on until

---

[61] See Ophir and Wiesemann (eds.), 247ff. There is no information on several of the very smallest communities.
[62] Ibid. 259.

11 November, when the community's four gendarmes finally restored order at 3.00 a.m.[63]

In the city of Bad Kissingen (population 8,579 in 1933, of whom 344 were Jews) and surrounding area a torrent of brutality and destruction overwhelmed the Jewish population. The numbers of Jews in the city had already been reduced by two-thirds, and stood at only 103 on the day of the pogrom; many of these were elderly people. At 2.00 a.m. the 'action' began with the burning of the synagogue and the building of the Jewish motor-car dealer; both fires were put out an hour later, but not before massive destruction. The store windows of Jewish businesses were all smashed, as were those of their apartments and homes. Altogether, some fourteen businesses were destroyed or heavily damaged; besides the synagogue, two other buildings owned by the Jewish community were affected. At 7.30 a.m. on 10 November the order police in Bad Kissingen were notified by the Würzburg police of the 'spontaneous demonstrations' which were taking place in all of Germany. They were advised to check with the Gestapo and NSDAP leaders to ascertain exactly when and where the local 'actions' would break out. Only a small contingent of police, in civilian clothes, was to accompany the 'demonstrators' in order to prevent plundering, to put seals on the destroyed property of the Jews, and so forth. Because of anxiety that fires might get out of hand, the fire department was to be informed. Arson was to be prevented, even of Jewish buildings. Besides the destruction of property, twenty-eight Jews were placed in 'protective custody' on the orders of City Commissioner Dr Conrath, 'in order to prevent excesses from the aroused mass'.[64]

The pattern that was repeated in towns and villages where Jews could still be found throughout the district around Bad Kissingen (as elsewhere) seems to have involved the arrival of a large group of non-resident demonstrators, who promptly set upon local Jews and their property. This was precisely the case, for example, in Maßbach (population 1,307 in 1933, of whom 34 were Jews). According to the gendarme, a 'large group' arrived on motor bikes after midnight on the night of 10–11 November; the windows of eight Jewish buildings were broken and the synagogue demolished. Four apartments were totally gutted and destroyed in renewed demonstrations on the evening of 10 November. In Poppenlauer (population 1,616 in 1933, of whom 45 were Jews) a group of sixty demonstrators showed up from out of town, destroyed the synagogue's interior, and attacked the property of local Jews. In Steinach a.d. Saale (population 811 in 1933, of whom 39 were Jews) the 'action' commenced only at midnight on 10–11 November (the reason for the delay is not known). Upon the arrival of a more radical local Nazi who worked in Schweinfurt, however, the Nazis in town resolved to take the necessary

---

[63] For the reports see StA W: LRA 2260 IV: Aschaffenburg.
[64] See ibid.: LRA 1121: Bad Kissingen.

action, all the more so as they were worried about being out of step with events elsewhere. After attacking Jewish residences and the synagogue, according to the police report, the 'demonstrators quietly retired at about 1.30 a.m.'. He added that the events were 'received with satisfaction' by the local population.[65]

The events in Würzburg itself were massive in scope, well organized, and destructive. Around midnight on 9 November word came to NSDAP Kreisleiter Knaup (probably from Gauleiter Hellmuth, who was in Munich for the Party's festivities) concerning the 'spontaneous' actions that would be breaking out against the Jews. In accordance with instructions from Berlin, a meeting was held at Gestapo headquarters to work out the details of the responsibilities of Party, Gestapo, Kripo, and ordinary police. Knaup began assembling his local Party bosses (Ortsgruppenleiter), in so far as he could get hold of them in the middle of the night. He managed to collect six of them and gave instructions by telephone to one more, but three or four others could not be reached. The 81st SS Standard in Würzburg was apparently given the order already at 3.10 a.m. to burn the synagogue in the Domerschulstrasse, but did not do so for fear of damage to surrounding buildings. The interior of the building was ransacked. The synagogue in neighbouring Heidingsfeld was not spared the torch. Word reached the ordinary police in Würzburg at 7.30 a.m. from Kurt Daleuge, its chief in Berlin, who said that the police should accompany the demonstrations in civilian garb, but that the Gestapo would take care of arrests.[66]

As ordered, the Ortsgruppe of the NSDAP from Würzburg south appeared at 7.00 a.m. in strength at the local football field. Its leader, Martin Neef, divided the 800–1,000 men into large squads, assigned specific targets, and set them to work. Evidently not all of those assembled agreed with the 'tasks', or perhaps they were just not in the mood for such vigorous activity at such an early hour, and baulked at following orders. But hesitation was overcome and the mobs set out in the early morning. Whether all the other NSDAP groups managed this show of numbers cannot be ascertained, but if the participation of the SA and SS is also assumed, there can be little doubt that several thousand men were running amok in Würzburg at a time when most citizens would have been able to see and hear them in action. Aschaffenburg, a city about one-third the size of Würzburg, managed to mobilize a thousand, and, as already indicated, even small outlying villages were visited by mobs several hundred strong.

Among the fatalities in Würzburg was a man who died after jumping through the window of his home to avoid the mob. An old man who was hauled from his bed and beaten died of his injuries the next day. One account

---

[65] Ibid. See also Schultheis, 359ff.
[66] BAK: R58/276, 136.

suggests that three women committed suicide as a direct result of the pogrom.[67] Approximately 290 Jews from Würzburg and the surrounding area were sent either to Buchenwald or Dachau.[68] In Germany as a whole some 91 Jews were murdered in the course of the pogrom, while several hundred died after about 30,000 Jews were shipped to various concentration camps; an estimated 36 people were seriously injured or committed suicide; 267 synagogues were burnt or destroyed; 7,500 businesses were wrecked and/or plundered; all Jewish cemeteries were also damaged; total property damage was in the range of 25 million marks.[69]

Anyone relying for information on the local newspapers would hardly guess just how dramatic the pogrom had been in Würzburg. One, the *General Anzeiger*, reported on 10 November that the Würzburg population had become so outraged at the assassination in Paris that 'spontaneous actions' took place in revenge; the next day it added information on the fates of the synagogues and other property damage. 'Thousands of persons', it said, 'wandered through the streets to reach the synagogue in order to see the work of destruction.' The *Mainfränkische Zeitung*, the local organ of the NSDAP, used the same bland phrases about the 'deep anger' of the German people. The *Fränkisches Volksblatt* virtually repeated that account word for word. The monthly report sent to Munich by Lower Franconia's leading administrative official calmly remarked that the 'atonement', and especially the imposition of a fine on the Jews of Germany, 'was generally approved'.[70]

In the days and weeks that followed, official measures aimed at the Jews were issued with greater zeal than ever. These flowed from a gathering of top Reich ministers on 12 November, which Göring had called to deal with the matter. Not only were the Jews collectively fined one billion marks to pay for the damages, but conference participants tried to outdo each other in suggesting ways to restrict the freedom of movement of the Jews. Special efforts were undertaken to remove Jews from the economy. The 'Aryanization' process was greatly accelerated, and led in some instances to a scramble for the spoils. For example, when the 3,700 or so Jewish-owned retail firms of all sizes in Berlin were confiscated, a report from the City President's office recorded that 'on the whole the impression created by Aryanization is *not* pleasing': there were at least three or four applicants for each business.[71]

Numerous additional decrees drastically narrowed any rights Jews still enjoyed. On 12 November the Reich Cultural Chamber prohibited Jews from attending the theatre, cinema, and concerts; on 15 November the Ministry

---

[67] Schultheis, p. 79.
[68] Ophir and Wiesemann (eds.), 446.
[69] Heinz Lauber, *Judenpogrom 'Reichskristallnacht' November 1938 in Großdeutschland* (Gerlingen, 1981), 123–4.
[70] The articles are reprinted in Schultheis, 71ff.; Bay HStA: MA 106681, also in Broszat *et al.* (eds.), *Bayern in der NS-Zeit*, i. 475.
[71] BAK: R7/2170, 10.

of Education banned Jewish students from the school system (on 8 December this was expanded to include the universities): a police order following the Reich Minister of the Interior's decree of 14 November gave a kind of 'ghettoization' power to local authorities, who could restrict Jews' appearance in public (in both time and place); the Reichsführer SS Himmler decreed on 3 December that Jews' driving-licences were invalid, and they were in future to be denied the right to visit the sports facilities, ice-skating rinks, and public and private swimming pools of all kinds, and were not allowed in certain parts of the capital city. By early 1939 what was left of Jewish doctors, dentists, veterinarians, chemists, and so on—in so far as their careers endured until then—were one after another forbidden to practise, except with respect to other Jews.[72] The SD concluded its report of the events across the country by stating that the Jews 'have finally been shut out of German social life, so that only emigration remains as a means of securing their existence'.[73]

During the 'night of broken glass' the Gestapo emerged as head of local tactical operations, acting in the literal sense as an executive in charge of underlings. In Würzburg it took a leading hand in storming Jews' apartments and in carrying out arrests.[74] The power-relationships within the police network—SD, SS, Kripo, ordinary police—also came into sharp relief at that time. The SD, for example, was relegated to the role of sorting out the materials of an 'intellectual' kind—archives, documents, writings, and so on—which turned up during the wrecking of Jewish buildings such as the synagogues. Local SS bands were called in to reinforce the mobs and, in the event, to help keep order. The Kripo was responsible for dealing with criminal transgressions, although its role was more 'political' than was usually the case. Finally, the ordinary uniformed police were to make sure that plundering was kept to a minimum.

The Nazi Party leaders and some of its local members, just like Goebbels, attempted to use the pogrom to reassert dwindled power and prestige at the expense of the Jews. This had been one of the few opportunities since 1933 or so to rediscover its 'revolutionary' ethos, and to become more than a mere practitioner of rituals, collector of charity funds, and overseer of the daily lives of citizens. Typical of what happened in many places were the events in Munich. There, in direct response to Goebbels, the Party had already set fire to buildings and smashed windows of businesses by 10.00 or 11.00 p.m. on 9 November. Friedrich Karl von Eberstein, Police President of the city and Chief of the SS in the area, first heard of what was going on when he received a call from the chief magistrate to tell him that the Planegg Castle, owned by the Jewish Baron Hirsch, was on fire. Von Eberstein was summoned immedi-

---

[72] For the decrees see Bruno Blau, *Das Ausnahmerecht für die Juden in Deutschland* 1933–1945 (Düsseldorf, 1954), 55ff.; for the record of the meeting see IMT xxviii. 499ff., doc. PS-1816.

[73] BAK: R58/1094: SD annual report (1938), 35.

[74] See Flade, *Würzburger Juden*, 312ff.

ately to a meeting with Himmler and higher SS and Gestapo officers at which it was decided what was and was not 'acceptable'. Following this meeting, word went to Berlin and orders were issued to the Gestapo for all of Germany.[75] Where the local party Gauleiter was not keen on carrying out the pogrom, as was the case in Hamburg and several other areas, the events did not prove as disastrous.[76]

The 'night of broken glass' was the last large-scale public assault on the Jews inside Germany. The SA, like the Party, had been given a degree of autonomy, but both were quickly brought to heel. At the local level, in Würzburg as elsewhere, from now on the Gestapo was not going to tolerate anything more than 'cold pogroms', that is, persecution through administrative channels. If for a moment on the night of 9–10 November there appeared any question that the Gestapo was not in charge, by the time of the meeting at Gestapo headquarters early in the morning of the 10th the situation had returned to normal. In the last year or so of the war the Party once again came into prominence at the local level, but it was never a challenge to Gestapo dominance.[77]

4. POPULAR REACTIONS TO NAZI ANTI-SEMITISM

Marlis Steinert, whose study of Nazi Germany touched briefly on the pogrom, suggested that the 'violence was almost unanimously rejected, although often because of the unnecessary destruction of goods'.[78] The Israeli historian Otto Dov Kulka is in general agreement with that interpretation, but puts it in unambiguous terms by saying that 'the outstandingly characteristic aspect of most of these reactions... is not so much denunciation of the anti-Jewish acts on moral grounds as criticism based on essentially pragmatic considerations. This comes out in the repeated statements denouncing the destruction of property and the economic damage being done to the German people and to the state's plans for the economy.' He suggests that it is against this background that there was 'a "gradual improvement" in the popular mood, especially after a fine of one billion marks was imposed on Jewish property'.[79] Although Kershaw and Kulka differ on a number of points, Kulka would accept Kershaw's conclusions that 'a strong motive for the

---

[75] IMT xx. 292–3.

[76] See the testimony of Karl Kaufmann of Hamburg, ibid. 38ff. See also Donald McKale. *The Nazi Party Courts* (Lawrence, Kans., 1974), 163ff.

[77] See Earl R. Beck, *Under the Bombs: The German Home Front 1942–1945* (Lexington, 1986), 151ff.

[78] Steinert, 37.Cf. Anselm Faust, *Die Kristallnacht im Rhineland: Dokumente zum Judenpogrom im November 1938* (Düsseldorf, 1987), 41ff.

[79] Otto Dov Kulka, '"Public Opinion" in Nazi Germany and the "Jewish Question"', *Jerusalem Quarterly* 25 (1982), 138.

condemnation of the pogrom in the eyes of many people was the futile destruction of property'; that such objections 'were wholly compatible with unreserved approval of the draconian but "legal" form of "punishment" which the State itself decreed in the immediate aftermath of the pogrom'; and that on the whole the picture that emerges 'seems for the most part, therefore, a rather dismal one in which material self-interest and legal rectitude prevailed over humanitarian considerations'.[80]

Even a number of leading Nazis who were known to be anything but sympathetic to the Jews were appalled at the course of the pogrom, especially the plundering, 'but not the action as such'.[81] A recently published autobiography of Michael Meisner, a non-Jewish lawyer from a renowned Würzburg family, described the 'unimaginable cruelties' of the events in Würzburg. What stuck in his mind, however, as he wrote about his experiences nearly fifty years after the event, was the destruction of property.[82] In November 1938 he represented the legal interests of one of the Jewish department-store owners in town. Although Herr and Frau Zapff had managed to get out of town before the pogrom, their property was not spared. Meisner's task was to survey 'the barbarism' along with the architect Gerhard Saalfrank.

I had never before seen such vandalism with my own eyes. That all the windows were destroyed was self-evident in the term 'night of broken glass'. But the upholstered furniture was cut up, the Persian rugs shredded, the valuable pictures torn from their frames, tables and chairs hacked into small pieces, and, in the basement, all the bottles smashed and all the provisions, such as preserves, marmalade, and so on, thrown in on top, so that the mass of destroyed food in the basement stood a good quarter of a metre deep. My friend Gerhard Saalfrank, who had not remained entirely untouched by Nazism, marched away, infuriated, from this crudity.[83]

Individuals from all over the country, as well as some foreign observers, have left records of the pogrom.[84] The impressions registered in some of these

---

[80] Kershaw, *Popular Opinion*, 268–9.

[81] For a local example see StA Marburg: LRA 180: Gestapo Kassel to Landrat in Marburg, 13 Jan. 1939. See also McKale, 163ff.

[82] See also William S. Allen, 'Die deutsche Öffentlichkeit und die "Reichskristallnacht": Konflikte zwischen Werthierarchie und Propaganda im Dritten Reich', in Peukert and Reulecke (eds.), 397ff., who remarks that many who disliked the pogrom approach held private property in great esteem, others put economizing and thriftiness first, and many put a premium on the sanctity of religion, while still others set great store by 'law and order', and so on. Von Eberstein said that in so far as the SS did not participate in the pogrom, it was not because of any philo-Semitism: 'I can only say that the SS, just like the Party, was anti-Semitic, but quite apart from any material loss [which undoubtedly resulted from the pogrom] . . . we considered this indecent and the SS did not participate in it' (IMT xx. 294).

[83] Meisner, 169.

[84] See the oft-cited remarks of the United States Consul-General in Stuttgart reprinted in Paul Sauer (ed.), *Dokumente über die Verfolgung der jüdischen Bürger in Baden-Württemberg durch das nationalsozialistische Regime 1933–1945* (Stuttgart, 1966), ii. 33ff.; he simplifies the categories of response into those who were in favour of the pogrom (20%) and those against it (80%), whereas more differentiation is required.

accounts indicate that, though outraged at the destruction of property, they tolerated it even as they witnessed it at first hand. Ruth Andreas-Friedrich, a Berlin journalist, was appalled when, upon hearing a distant noise, she and her friend tracked it down until they came upon five men in civilian clothes who, in a very workmanlike fashion, were beating out the windows of a Jewish shop. A mob gathered, and stood silently by, nearly 'hypnotized', as one store after another was destroyed. Andreas-Friedrich desperately wanted to do something, and whispered to her friend that they should be ashamed of themselves for just standing there. Later on, she would do a good deal to help the Jews in Berlin. But on this day she followed the advice of her friend, who counselled silence and discretion: what good would martyrdom do anyone? Andreas-Friedrich reflected that there was too much obedience and too little civil courage.[85] Not everyone in the capital was disgusted, and some expressed their delight (*Schadenfreude*) to a Jewish family on the morning following the pogrom there.[86]

Also in Berlin, author Jochen Klepper, himself living in a mixed marriage with a Jew, was somewhat encouraged because the population in the city was appalled at the pogrom, and believed that nearly everyone except the young rejected it, even those known to be good Nazis. Klepper was led to feel that the German people 'could be counted on', and yet he was disquieted; 'the people were a comfort, their moral powerlessness a terrible worry'.[87] (He and his wife and child committed suicide in 1942.) The worker Karl Dürkefälden in Celle noted in his diary that 'for the most part' the German people did not agree with the pogrom but did nothing against it. On the morning following the destruction in that town, it was said, the police arrested a pedestrian who dared ask: 'What should the poor people do now?[88] The underground Socialist movement, in its ceaseless effort to find support for its belief that the Nazis' hold on the country was about to slip, emphasized the extent to which some parts of the country rejected the pogrom. Their report of events in Bavaria, however, suggested that it was the *method* that many people found disquieting.[89] No doubt many local villagers in rural areas, such as Lower Franconia, were outraged that the trouble-makers who arrived to wreck homes and burn buildings were frequently strangers and city people who had no business in their village in the first place.

While the Churches as institutions remained silent, a handful of individual

---

[85] Ruth Andreas-Friedrich, *Der Schattenmann: Tagebuchaufzeichnungen, 1938–1945* (1947; Berlin, 1983), 32–3. Cf. Reck-Malleczewen, 70.

[86] Inge Deutschkron. *Ich trug den gelben Stern* (1978; Cologne, 1983), 35.

[87] Quoted in Gerhard Hay, 'Das Jahr 1938 im Spiegel der NS-Literatur', in Franz Knipping and Klaus-Jürgen Müller (eds.), *Machtbewußtsein in Deutschland am Vorabend des Zweiten Weltkrieges* (Paderborn, 1984), 326.

[88] Herbert and Sibylle Obenaus (eds.), *'Schreiben wie es wirklich war!' Aufzeichnungen Karl Dürkefäldens aus den Jahren 1933–1945* (Hanover, 1985), 85.

[89] Sopade, v (Nov. 1938), 1206.

clerics of Catholic and Protestant denominations in Bavaria, as elsewhere, dared to condemn the event from the pulpit. For all of Bavaria only rare examples of such dissent have been recorded. In the six-volume collection of documents on the 'church situation', the records sometimes convey ambiguous messages. In Upper Franconian Wunsiedel, for example, two Evangelical and four Catholic clerics, known locally as slaves of the Jews [*Judenknechte*], were attacked in the course of the action in November by 'the outraged mob'; they were brought to police headquarters, and some of their house windows were broken. There is nothing in the report to indicate whether these attacks resulted from any stand taken by the clerics concerning the pogrom, or whether local activists were merely taking advantage of the situation to settle old scores; only one Evangelical pastor from Mistelgau, near Bayreuth, was actually charged by the Gestapo for negative comments on the pogrom.[90] Yet on the same page that mentions how the six clerics got into trouble for not being anti-Semitic enough, it is noted that 'numerous teachers' of the area, in reaction to 'the brazen challenge of world Jewry through the cowardly murder in Paris', refused to teach religion any further, presumably because they were dissatisfied with the less than enthusiastic response of the Churches to anti-Jewish actions.

The situation report for Lower Franconia does not mention clerics, but speaks instead of the 'great general reservation' in evidence in the weeks that followed.[91] The reports from the rest of Bavaria are similar, although one magistrate said that in his area of the Palatinate (Frankenthal) 'the largest part of the population regarded the action against the Jews as a just and necessary consequence of their provocative behaviour'; those who had no sympathy for the pogrom pointed to the destruction of property and food that would have been better given to the poor. One priest in the Palatinate thought that those who smashed windows were little better than Bolsheviks, and in Nuremberg on the Sunday after the events another priest apparently expressed similarly negative views.[92]

An opinion on the stance of the organized religions was offered in an SD report for neighbouring Württemberg (none survives for Bavaria). The SD said that the Catholics were worried that the terror aimed at the Jews might come their way next. Old liberals and democrats were especially sympathetic to the Jews, while one-time 'reactionaries' such as members of the Pan-German League agreed with the measures.[93] In an effort to explain the absence of the Catholic hierarchy's condemnation, some historians have pointed out that some Catholics were themselves attacked as part of the

---

[90] *KLB* ii. 300, 309.
[91] Ibid. vi. 146ff.
[92] See LA Speyer: H33/1270, 2 Dec. 1938 (from Neumarkt i.d. Oberpfalz, *KLB* iv. 224). Cf. Müller, 245.
[93] StAL: K110/44: SD report for the last quarter of 1938.

events.[94] However, Gordon Zahn maintains that 'the position taken by the Catholic Church... was one of mixed support and opposition'; all in all, 'a historical balance might well reveal that the support actually outweighed (in a purely quantitative sense...) the opposition represented by the famous leaders of the German Catholic resistance and the hundreds of priests and laymen who suffered and died in Dachau' and other such places.[95] Protestantism was more positively disposed to the regime, and its leaders had 'welcomed the Third Reich'; while not everything after 1933 worked out as they would have wished, they found it possible to make adjustments.[96]

5. CONCLUSION

A recent characterization of popular opinion concerning anti-Semitism in Nazi Germany, by Kulka and Rodrique, states that the 'devout' Christian population, along with the Marxist Left, the liberal intelligentsia, and some in business, were 'openly' critical of Nazi anti-Semitic actions 'on ideological, religious, social or economic grounds'. The term 'open' is too strong in this context; the people in these groups said very little openly one way or the other. Perhaps the authors wanted to convey the impression that the people in this category had strong reservations, while a few of them were outspoken in their criticism. In any event, according to their analysis, a second group accepted the main thrust of Nazi teachings on race, while a third, mainly the Nazi radicals, criticized the policy as 'too moderate'. The largest segment of the population fell into a fourth division of opinion, marked by a 'lack of reaction on the issue usually going hand in hand with general ideological and political indifference'.[97]

Such a division of opinion is consistent with Ian Kershaw's main conclusion, that in spite of the efforts since 1933 German popular opinion remained 'largely indifferent and infused with a latent anti-Jewish feeling', but that, 'further bolstered by propaganda, [it] provided the climate within which spiralling Nazi aggression towards Jews could take place unchallenged'.[98] One SD informant from Bad Kissingen in Lower Franconia reported that word about the possible removal of Polish, Czech, and Austrian Jews to the east after the successful Polish campaign in late 1939 was 'welcomed by

[94] Burkhard van Schewick, 'Katholische Kirche und nationalsozialistische Rassenpolitik', in Klaus Gotto and Konrad Repgen (eds.). *Kirche, Katholiken und Nationalsozialismus* (Mainz, 1980), 91.

[95] Gordon C. Zahn, *German Catholics and Hitler's Wars* (New York, 1969), 72.

[96] J. R. C. Wright, *'Above Parties': The Political Attitudes of the German Protestant Church Leadership 1918–1933* (Oxford, 1974), 145. See the critical remarks in Richard Gutteridge, *Open thy Mouth for the Dumb: The German Evangelical Church and the Jews 1870–1950* (Oxford, 1976), 186ff.

[97] Kulka and Rodrique, 426.

[98] Kershaw, *Popular Opinion*, 277.

Party comrades and by a great proportion of the national comrades, and suggestions were heard that the Jews who still live in Germany should also set out on their march into this territory'.[99] Even before the war broke out, as Kershaw remarked recently, 'attitudes towards the Jews had hardened even among the broad apathetic sector of the population'; by then there existed a broad 'feeling that there *was* a "Jewish Question", that the Jews *were* another race, and that they deserved whatever measures had been taken to counter their undue influence, and should be excluded from Germany altogether'.[100]

The remainder of the book looks at the process by which racial policies were enforced. As will become clear, the regime was less dependent than might be expected upon an enthusiastic reception by all, or even most, citizens.

[99] Ibid. 361; the quotation is from an SD report of 27 Nov. 1939.

[100] Kershaw, 'German Popular Opinion', 370. Cf. the important contemporary opinion survey of Michael Müller-Claudius, *Der Antisemitismus und das deutsche Verhängnis* (Frankfurt, 1948), 155ff.

III

Enforcing Racial Policy

5

The Gestapo and Social Co-operation
The Example of Political Denunciation

I F autobiographies of survivors and eyewitness reports are to be believed, inside Nazi Germany hardly anyone felt entirely safe, whether at work, play, during leisure activities, at school, or even in the privacy of the home.[1] It can also be ascertained that the work of the Gestapo was deliberately shrouded in secrecy. The uncertainty, therefore, about the sources that moved it to act would have helped convey an impression of omnipotence.[2] As Friedrich Zipfel remarked, secretiveness about the Gestapo was deliberately fostered in order to intensify the isolation of the individual citizen. 'One can evade a danger that one recognizes, but a police working in the dark becomes uncanny. Nowhere does one feel safe from it. While not omnipresent, it *could* appear, search, arrest. The worried citizen no longer knows whom he ought to trust.'[3]

It would be foolish to question the existence of such worries and exaggerations in Nazi Germany, and this study proceeds from the assumption that fear was indeed prevalent among the German people. The Gestapo had a reputation for brutality, and terror would seize individuals instructed by postcard to report to local Gestapo headquarters 'for the purpose of answering some questions'.[4] Rumours about what went on in Gestapo cellars served to intensify the fear of being informed on or of being turned in on suspicion of the least deviation. However, it is also true that the Gestapo lacked the physical resources to execute surveillance of the vast majority of the population. How was it structurally possible, then, that the population could become terrorized? No doubt many other officials were also concerned with monitoring behaviour, and this too was well known to most Germans. But to suggest that the function of surveillance and control was performed almost exclusively by institutions that formed part of the so-called police state tends to place undue emphasis on coercion, force, or even open violence, and to regard the populace

---

[1] The theme is a recurrent one in the creative literature on the Nazi era; for an analysis see Frederick J. Harris, *Encounters with Darkness: French and German Writers on World War II* (Oxford, 1983), 97ff.

[2] Barrington Moore, jun., *Terror and Progress USSR* (Cambridge, Mass., 1954), 159, noted in his book on the Soviet system that 'the population undoubtedly exaggerates the number of informers and is encouraged in this exaggeration' by the regime.

[3] Friedrich Zipfel, *Gestapo und Sicherheitsdienst* (Berlin, 1960), 5.

[4] Allen, *The Nazi Seizure of Power*, 189, suggests that 'the Gestapo became extraordinarily efficient by reason of rumours and fears'.

as essentially passive, apathetic, or just not involved. At least some degree of active participation of 'ordinary' citizens was required for the function of most policing or control organizations in Nazi Germany. This part of the book examines that participation. As will be seen, the key relationship between the Gestapo, German society, and the enforcement of policy was constituted by what can be termed political denunciations, the volunteered provision of information by the population at large about instances of disapproved behaviour. The present chapter moves beyond an investigation of the formal institutional development of the police to study as well what has been termed the process of 'informal social reinforcement of the terror system'.[5]

I. GESTAPO FILES AS HISTORICAL SOURCES

The Gestapo case-files are rare sources: they were destroyed nearly everywhere. Even in Würzburg officials managed to burn all the files of persons whose names began with the letters A to G; all those between H and Z, except names beginning with V, seem to have survived intact.[6] Each file was originally created by the police when for some reason or other an individual was brought to its attention. The dossiers are extremely heterogeneous: some contain only a tiny scrap of paper, while others run to many pages, complete with the transcript of interrogations, so-called confrontations between the accused and witnesses, an account of the trial and punishment meted out, and even at times correspondence from the concentration camp. Although the files do not appear to have been tampered with, it is clear that many potentially valuable kinds of information were never entered in the first place. For example, there is no mention of torture or even of the officially condoned 'intensified interrogation', a procedure described perhaps more accurately at the Nuremberg trials as 'the third degree'. The often brutal nature of the interrogation or the zeal of officials cannot be deduced from the written record; that side of the story can only be told through proceedings of post-war trials or the accounts of survivors.

Gestapo sources predominantly involve those at the lower end of the social scale. The extent to which people from the upper reaches of the officer corps, the upper bourgeoisie, or the nobility participated in the regularities of the Nazi dictatorship will have to be studied from other sources. Members of the nobility were certainly denounced by those of the same social standing, but not usually to the police, largely because they had other ways of seeking redress and of exercising social power. Furthermore, the police showed some respect for members of the nobility, and tended to hold any charges against

---

[5] Allen, *The Nazi Seizure of Power*, 157.
[6] For a description of the material see Mehringer, 'Die bayerische SPD', 328–9.

them in abeyance, or even in certain circumstances, to dismiss them.[7] A noble from southern Germany, Friedrich Reck-Malleczewen, on visiting Gestapo headquarters found 'quiet, dignified offices, courteous subordinates and as responsible officer . . . a polite and tactful young man who asked leave to finish his cigar, and was, generally, the very model of a man of breeding and poise'.[8] Reck was a man who got away with a great deal, though he went too far by refusing in 1944 to serve in the civilian home defence (the Volkssturm); he was shot in Dachau in October 1944 for 'undermining the morale of the armed forces'.

Charges in Gestapo files, even signed confessions, cannot be taken at face value, as evidence that a 'crime' was committed. One recent study of the persecution of the Jews, based on selective use of the Düsseldorf Gestapo files, insists that when people slipped through the fingers of the Secret Police it was because they had 'managed to cover their tracks'—they had fooled the Gestapo.[9] As explained below, however, they might just as easily have been falsely charged. In fact, the incidence of false charges was so great in Nazi Germany that they constituted a real problem for the regime, one it never solved.[10]

The Gestapo also used dirty methods such as intimidation, extortion, and blackmail to force victims to sign 'confessions'.[11] The extent to which these methods were used is impossible to judge, so the evidence in the files has to be treated with caution. Some officials acted with such brutality and applied such overwhelming pressure that some people saw no way out but to sign. The reality of Gestapo interrogation could be exhausting for the victims, with days and weeks filled with terror and anxiety; once temporarily released, some attempted suicide to escape the relentless cross-examination by the tireless officials.[12] The agony could begin with an innocent visit to the Secret Police to report a lost passport; an official who was unwilling to accept that the item had been misplaced could turn the process into a nightmare of

---

[7] See e.g. Marie Vassiltchikov, *Berlin Diaries, 1940–1945* (New York, 1987), 83, for the denunciation of her mother, a White Russian Princess; for another occasion see Tatiana Metternich, *Purgatory of Fools* (New York, 1976), 99. Peter Hoffmann, *German Resistance to Hitler* (Cambridge, Mass., 1988), 72–3, remarks: 'The Army and its officer corps, however, were largely immune to Gestapo surveillance and penetration and to the influence of the Nazi Party. The social fabric of the Army officer corps and its code of ethics left little room for informers.'

[8] Reck-Malleczewen, 202.

[9] Sarah Gordon, *Hitler, Germans, and the 'Jewish Question'* (Princeton, 1984), 213.

[10] Reinhard Mann, *Protest und Kontrolle*, 300

[11] Cf. Allen, *The Nazi Seizure of Power*, 195, or the story of Gestapo man Heinrich Baab in Kay Boyle, *The Smoking Mountain: Stories of Germany During the Occupation* (New York, 1963), 3ff.

[12] Hans Robinsohn, *Justiz als politische Verfolgung: Die Rechtsprechung in 'Rassenschandefällen' beim Landgercht Hamburg 1936–1943* (Stuttgart, 1977), 81ff. Cf. Günther Weisenborn, 'Reich Secret', in Eric H. Boehm (ed.), *We Survived: Fourteen Histories of the Hidden and Hunted of Nazi Germany* (Santa Barbara, 1985), 197, and *id., Der lautlose Aufstand: Bericht über die Widerstandsbewegung des deutschen Volkes 1933–1945*, 4th edn. (Frankfurt, 1974), 43ff.

outlandish allegations, beatings, and confinement overnight in a holding-cell where the mistreatment of others could be overheard.[13]

The police employed both *agents provocateurs* and entrapment, and when all else failed they were not above simply planting evidence. Such methods were used especially when it came to dealing with 'opponents' such as the Communists and the Jews. This issue is explored in detail in the next chapters, but is mentioned here in order to clarify the limitations of case-files as sources. Nor did the Gestapo simply follow the exact letter of the law when it came to dealing with opponents. For example, it would not only enforce the countless hundreds of laws explicitly formulated to deal with the Jews, but would also use every other kind of law to harass them. Such a practice says a great deal about their *modus operandi*, and also entails that some of the files must be regarded as incomplete sources. At the same time it has to be recognized that even though the files are far from uniform, leave details unstated, and contain distortions, they nevertheless constitute an invaluable source for the social history of Nazi Germany.

2. DENUNCIATIONS, GESTAPO CASES, AND THE REGIME

Political denunciation, as a particular variety of ordinary citizens' participation in the functioning of the 'police state' in Nazi Germany, has received some general attention in a short essay by Martin Broszat, which grew out of research for the Munich Institut für Zeitgeschichte's massive research project on 'resistance and persecution'.[14] Using local Party and administrative materials, he makes it clear that denunciation represented an integral part of the social constitution of Nazi Germany and that it played an important role in the terror system. Reinhard Mann treats denunciations as one of the mechanisms that caused the Gestapo to move into action on any particular case.[15] His findings derive from a study of materials drawn from the 70,000 surviving Düsseldorf Gestapo case-files, but the operations of the police were sufficiently centralized and standardized, as indicated above, to justify combining them, with some qualifications, into an analysis based on materials from the 19,000 case-files in Würzburg.

Mann focused on a specific sub-group of the 70,000 Gestapo dossiers, namely those classified by the Gestapo as 'local card-file Düsseldorf' (Ortskartei Düsseldorf). These cards were for internal office use by the Gestapo, and were (and still are) the reference keys to the large collection of Gestapo case-

---

[13] Moritz and Noam, *NS-Verbrechen vor Gericht*, 238 ff

[14] Broszat, 'Politische Denunziationen', 221 ff. For the post-war legal problem of dealing with the matter see Hans Carl Nipperdey, 'Die Haftung für politische Denunziationen in der Nazizeit', in H. C. Nipperdey (ed.), *Das deutsche Privatrecht in der Mitte des 20. Jahrhunderts: Festschrift für Heinrich Lehmann zum 80. Geburtstag*, i (Berlin, 1956), 285–307.

[15] See his essay in Reinhard Mann, *Protest und Kontrolle*, 287 ff.

files. Under 'local card-file Düsseldorf' there are approximately 5,000 cards, referring to specific case-files by number, divided into fifty-two subdivisions. Each division corresponds to an aspect of the Gestapo's daily workload and routine preoccupations. The largest single group of case-files pertains to the Communist Party (with 1,050 cards), with small numbers of cards on virtually every other political party (including the Nazi Party) and 'associations' of all kinds; there are also cards on the paramilitary organizations once prominent in the Weimar Republic—the police, the youth movement, pacifists, Freemasons, and monarchists; there are many more on all the religious denominations, and a large number deal with various 'sects', with others covering topics ranging from the press, radio, art and music, to the economy and trade unionism, to the resistance movement, 'opposition', 'malicious gossip', treason, and sabotage. Mann's analysis deals with forty-one of the fifty-two categories, or 3,770 of the 5,000 case-files. His decision to exclude from the analysis approximately 1,230 cards, and hence case-files, is discussed presently. From the 3,770 cards he selected 825 case-files by random sampling techniques for close analysis. Additional files, some of which might have come from the 1,230 formally excluded, were drawn into the investigation through the procedure of a 'snowball selection' designed to trace social nets to which an individual might have belonged. For example, according to this procedure, once a file was selected in the main sample, other persons mentioned in that dossier would eventually be included in the study. An unknown number of cases would have been analysed through the adoption of this 'snowball' procedure. In the tables constructed by Mann only the 825 cases from the main sample are cited. His quantitative analysis is important especially because it removes much of the mystery about what the Gestapo did on a routine basis.

Criticism of Mann's work must be tempered, of course, by the fact that it remained incomplete at his death in 1981. Moreover, his pioneering effort represents an extremely important contribution to the study of the routine operation of the Gestapo, and it is most fortunate that his manuscripts and sketches have recently been published. It is still the case that readers need to be made aware of a limitation of his analysis, a consequence of his decision to eliminate those eleven categories of cards mentioned above. At issue is not so much that he decided not to deal with 1,230 cards, but the *kind* of card, and hence the case-files, that were thereby excluded from his analysis. The following specific categories of cards were left out: 'Germans returning from abroad, foreigners, Jews, emigrants, foreign workers, prisoners of war, military espionage, economic sabotage, separatism, foreign legionnaires, and racially foreign minorities'. Mann's explanation for excluding these groups is given in a footnote. He observed that these cards pertained primarily to foreigners, who, like 'Jewish fellow citizens were subject to different legal norms', and he claimed that inclusion of such persons 'would have complicated the investigation further'.[16] These comments seem evasive; they are hardly convincing arguments to support the decision to exclude these groups in a study devoted to everyday life in Nazi Germany. Had Mann lived longer, he might have reorientated his investigation to include these groups as well. However, the fact remains that their exclusion may have had important consequences for the results of his study. Because his quantitative analysis of the Gestapo's operations excludes explicit consideration of most case-files in which the police were faced with enforcing policy on 'racially foreign' groups in Germany, there is a high probability that it underestimates the extent of popular participation—through the provision of information—in the functioning of the Gestapo. To arrive at conclusive findings, of course, one would have to examine in detail those files excluded by Mann, but until that is done one may make an initial judgement on the basis of an examination of Gestapo dossiers from Würzburg, specifically of the kind excluded in Mann's investigation. One is bound to conclude from such an examination that, had Mann taken his sample from all of the 5,000 Gestapo files (rather than the 3,770) in the 'local card-file Düsseldorf', then the percentage of cases which began with a denunciation would in all probability have been higher than indicated in Table 2.

In spite of this limitation in Mann's study, however, a sense of how denunciations fitted into the routine operation of the Gestapo can certainly be gained by examining figures drawn from his analysis of the Gestapo Düsseldorf files. Table 2, which is taken from his study, shows that of the 825 randomly sampled files the largest single number (213, or 26 per cent) consisted of files initiated when private citizens voluntarily informed the police. Another 24 cases (or 3 per cent) were opened when businesses of one kind or another reported to the authorities; these cases might well be added to those tip-offs 'from the population'. There were additional cases that could not easily be identified as originating with information 'from the population', but according to Mann there was a strong probability that they did. He believed that, were these to be included, the cases initiated by private citizens would be registered as 33 per cent 'at the least'. Such figures need to be treated with caution, for very often the original source of the complaint is not specified, or at least not always clear. In as many as 103 cases (13 per cent) no information whatsoever is given about why a proceeding was initiated. At other times a dossier might begin with a cryptic note, such as 'It has been possible for us to ascertain here', and so on. Mann decided to place files like this in the category he labels 'observations of the Stapo-Düsseldorf or "V-persons"'.[17]

---

[16] Mann, *Protest und Kontrolle*, 105 n.27. Cf. Reinhard Mann (ed.), *Die Nationalsozialisten: Analysen faschistischer Bewegungen* (Stuttgart, 1980), 9 ff.

[17] Reinhard Mann, *Protest und Kontrolle*, 293. *V-Mann/-Leute* is the short form for Vertrauensmann/-leute or 'confidential agent(s)'.

TABLE 2.—Causes of the Initiation of a Proceeding with the Düsseldorf Gestapo (1933–1944)

	No.	%
1. Reports from the population	213	26
2. Information from other control organizations	139	17
3. Own observations of Düsseldorf Gestapo, V-persons	127	15
4. Information via communal or state authorities	57	7
5. Statements at interrogations	110	13
6. Information from businesses	24	3
7. Informaton via NS organizations	52	6
8. No information	103	13
TOTAL	825	100

Source: R. Mann, Protest und Kontrolle, 292.

Evidence in Würzburg and elsewhere suggests that in all likelihood most of his categories contain instances of denunciations, though not all the accusations were lodged directly with the Gestapo. A case could commence when an individual merely dropped a hint sure to be overheard by some official or even a tell-tale neighbour. A classic example of the latter is offered in the story by Rolf Hochhuth, since turned into a film, Eine Liebe in Deutschland.[18] Beyond that, once in the grasp of the Gestapo, victims could easily incriminate themselves or others in the course of interrogation: and it is clear that on occasion chance played a role in the Gestapo's being made aware of some 'criminal' behaviour or other.

Though care must be taken with quantitative analysis of materials such as Gestapo case-files, especially regarding the sources that led to the opening of a case, it is clear that denunciations from the population were crucial to the functioning of the Gestapo. We know that 26 per cent of all cases began with an *identifiable* denunciation, and this must be taken as a minimum figure. Many of the other categories in Table 2—such as cases that began with information 'from Nazi organizations', 'other control organizations', 'communal and state authorities'—were also to a large degree dependent upon tips from citizens. With all due caution, it seems justified to suggest that denunciations from the population constituted the single most important cause for the initiation of proceedings of all kinds.

Put another way, these figures indicate that the regime's dreaded enforcer would have been seriously hampered without a considerable degree of public

[18] Rolf Hochhuth, Eine Liebe in Deutschland (Reinbek bei Hamburg, 1980) esp. pp. 115 ff.

co-operation. This behaviour has hitherto been largely ignored or not fully understood. To ask whether this is evidence that the public was converted to Nazism, or that the Nazi message had actually become widely accepted— as Mann would have it—is rather misconceived, because co-operation or collaboration was motivated by a whole range of considerations. The question of motives aside, denunciations from the population were the key link in the three-way interaction between the police, people, and policy in Nazi Germany. Popular participation by provision of information was one of the most important factors in making the terror system work. That conclusion suggests rethinking the notion of the Gestapo as an 'instrument of domination': if it was an instrument it was one which was constructed within German society and whose functioning was structurally dependent on the continuing co-operation of German citizens.[19] In support of Mann's quantitative analysis, it should be added, there is abundant corroborating evidence in the eyewitness accounts and in other fragmentary police reports of various kinds from localities elsewhere in Germany.[20] For reasons just mentioned, it is clear that his analysis probably underestimates the extent of denunciations precisely because he excluded the kinds of cases where informing from the general population was required—and attained—by the Gestapo.

That the Gestapo was to a large extent a reactive organization, at least when it came to generating cases, may be deduced from Table 2. Its own observations or those of its agents initiated only 15 per cent of all proceedings of the Düsseldorf Gestapo. Information obtained through interrogations, which set in motion 13 per cent of the cases, indicates a more active role in these instances (on which more below), though such undertakings may have been stimulated from a source external to the Gestapo. An important part was also played by the numerous other 'control organizations', including the regular uniformed police, the Kripo, SD, and SS; collectively they were responsible for the initiation of 17 per cent of all cases.

It is possible that some cases were sparked off by a tip from official sources, as when a Gestapo official merely wrote in the file that 'according to a confidentially disclosed report made to me today, it is alleged that the butcher Hans Drat remarked as follows', and so on.[21] Still, there would seem no reason

---

[19] See Peukert, *Die KPD*, 116ff. I discuss the use of such words as 'instruments' to refer to the terror in my 'Terror System'.

[20] Cf. Jörg Kammler, 'Nationalsozialistische Machtergreifung und Gestapo—am Beispiel der Staatspolizeistelle für den Regierungsbezirk Kassel', in Eike Hennig (ed.), *Hessen unterm Hakenkreuz: Studien zur Durchsetzung der NSDAP in Hessen*, 2nd edn. (Frankfurt, 1984), 506ff.; Gerhard Hoch, *Zwölf wiedergefundene Jahre: Kaltenkirchen unter dem Hakenkreuz* (Bad Bramstedt, [1980]), 231; Dieter Rebentisch and Angelika Raab, *Neu-Isenburg zwischen Anpassung und Widerstand* (Neu-Isenburg, 1978), 104ff. See the eyewitness accounts of Peter Brückner, *Das Abseits als sicherer Ort* (Coburg, 1980) 145; Reck-Malleczewen, 69ff.; and Dietrich Güstrow, *Tödlicher Alltag: Strafverteidiger im Dritten Reich* (Berlin, 1981), 148ff. Note also Bernt Engelmann, *Im Gleichschritt marsch* (Cologne, 1981), ch. 4.

[21] HStA D: Gestapo 17, 922. (Düsseldorf. Sept. 1939).

for the dossier to be silent if the tip came from an official or even semi-official body. In all likelihood the source was 'from the population', but the full details of this side of the story remain hidden.[22]

The legal façade surrounding the 'seizure of power' no doubt paid dividends in that many law-abiding citizens, out of respect for the legal norms, simply complied and co-operated with the new regime. Because the take-over was not patently illegal, many could choose to ignore its revolutionary character, especially after the radicals were subdued following the purge in June 1934. The stoic acceptance, however, seems to have yielded to more positive attitudes. Hans Bernd Gisevius, a member of the Gestapo in 1933, later recalled that there was a new mood and a widespread (though far from unanimous) positive disposition towards the regime, especially in the efforts to put down the supposed Communist threat.[23] What struck him most forcefully was what he called 'individual *Gleichschaltung*', by which he meant a kind of willing self-integration into the new system.[24]

The terror system had both a formal side—embracing the whole range of institutional arrangements—and an informal side that worked in tandem with those arrangements. Much less has been written about the 'informal' politics in the Nazi dictatorship, but there is much evidence to suggest that existing informal power-structures underwent adjustments as many people began to bring their attitudes on all kinds of issues into line. People may have experienced anxieties, but there were other positive factors at work. Golo Mann remarked that even the massive force and brutality of the Nazi 'seizure of power' were to a considerable extent overlooked: 'it was the feeling that Hitler was historically right which made a large part of the nation ignore the horrors of the Nazi take-over . . . People were ready for it.'[25] As self-imposed conformity spread, a new social attitude emerged, and at least in some cases transformation took place in a matter of hours, days, or weeks of Hitler's appointment.[26] People out of the country for a brief sojourn were astonished on their return.[27]

Some thought it advisable to make known, without having been asked, that they had no sympathy for the newly proclaimed enemies of the system.[28] In October 1933, for example, Agnes Meyer, a cashier in a Würzburg grocery, turned in a customer who had insisted on getting the 3 pfennigs owed to her in change. She was accused of having said that she was fed up paying

---

[22] See StA W: Gestapo 753 for one of the rare denunciations from the SD. The denouncer was married, Protestant, and not a Party member.

[23] Gisevius, 101–2.

[24] Ibid. 105.

[25] Golo Mann, *Deutsche Geschichte des 19. und 20. Jahrhunderts* (Frankfurt, 1967), 811.

[26] See Stern, *Dreams and Delusions*, 169–70.

[27] See e.g. Thomas Mann's daughter, Erika Mann, *School for Barbarians: Education under the Nazis* (London, 1939), 18ff.

[28] Allen, *The Nazi Seizure of Power*, 157.

taxes, and especially with laying out money for family allowances. Under questioning by the Gestapo the woman conceded that she might have implied that some people who got such allowances might not have to quibble over small change. Meyer was adamant that an insult to the Führer was intended.[29] Similarly, in late 1943, during an air-raid attack in Kitzingen, Johann Müller, a Catholic with two children, overheard Hugo Engelhardt make the following remark: 'Yes, families with many children should be supported, but with the truncheon. And anyone who had more than three children should be castrated!'[30] Engelhardt was reported and brought to trial. Again, this kind of petty tale-telling went beyond any specific injunction of the regime, and, in both these cases, helped reinforce the system's teachings on population policy.

No specific law was ever passed, that required citizens to inform on one another, though there was a stipulation in the already existing German criminal code (paragraph 139) that made it a duty to report certain offences one suspected were about to be committed; the law on high treason made a crime out of the failure to communicate to the authorities knowledge of a possible attempt at treason, including threats to Germany's allies, and so on.[31] The presidential decree of 21 March 1933 against malicious attacks on the government, and the law of 20 December 1934 against malicious attacks on the state and Party, were both designed to stop gossiping in public places, but also pertained to private remarks which might be repeated later in public. Neither made denunciation a formal duty, or even mentioned the matter, though both seem to have presupposed that the good citizen would inform upon hearing such gossip.[32] Clauses in the law were so broadly formulated that the most innocuous criticism of the Party, state, its leading personalities or enactments, could conceivably be a basis for denunciation.[33]

Generally speaking, all authorities of party and state reacted positively to those who brought accusations, regardless of how insignificant the allegation, dubious the source, mixed the motives—even if it concerned an act (an anti-Hitler statement, for example) perpetrated prior to 1933, when such behaviour was not even illegal. Although the flood of denunciations at times inclined various institutions to consider insisting upon signed complaints, verbal and even anonymous tips were usually followed up, and, significantly enough, whether the name of the accuser would (if available) be made public was left to the police. In other words, the extent to which an individual had

---

[29] StA W: Gestapo 5217.
[30] Ibid. 5168.
[31] Best, 42.
[32] For the laws see Hirsch, Majer, and Meinck (eds.), 90–1, 453–4.
[33] See the discussion in Peter Hüttenberger, 'Heimtückefälle vor dem Sondergericht München 1933–1939', in Broszat *et al.* (eds.), *Bayern in der NS-Zeit* iv (1981), 435ff.

recourse to legal defence, even when the charges were false or carelessly laid, was determined by the Gestapo.[34]

In discussions with Minister of Justice Gürtner in early May 1933, Hitler complained that 'we are living at present in a sea of denunciations and human meanness', when it was not infrequent for one person to condemn another, especially out of economic motives, merely to make capital out of the situation; the resulting worry that one could be turned in for deeds which went back many years was most unfortunate, in that it 'brought monstrous uneasiness in the entire economy'. He added that 'it was not the task of the Third Reich to atone for all the sins' of the Second, so that, especially in the area of economic and tax crime, a line had to be drawn.[35] It was clear to local state officials in Bavaria that, by mid-summer 1933, 'many people feared denunciations and their consequences',—a fear, incidentally, that made it very difficult to gauge public attitudes towards the new National Socialist system.[36] Needless to say, Nazi Party types took advantage of the novel situation to settle accounts with old enemies, and 'ordinary' citizens were not above capitalizing on the opportunity to get rid of business competitors through allegations that led to arrest and internment.[37]

The many false charges from across the country that were evident in the first months of the new regime reached altogether unacceptable proportions by April 1934, when the Reich Minister of the Interior demanded that local authorities take steps to curb the rapid expansion of all denunciations, too many of which were based merely on conflicts with neighbours. He wanted the authorities to prosecute those who made 'thoughtless, invalid complaints' to the police.[38] But at almost the same time (18 April) Rudolf Hess announced in a statement that 'every Party and folk comrade impelled by honest concern for the movement and the nation shall have access to the Führer or to me without the risk of being taken to task', a statement openly encouraging even anonymous informers to come forward.[39] During the peacetime years the flood of reports continued without apparent respite, against the hopes of anxious contemporary observers.[40]

At the beginning of 1939 Minister of the Interior Frick passed on to local officials the concerns of Hermann Göring about denunciation and the 'Jewish question'. Göring, who was, among other things, in charge of the 'four-year

---

[34] Broszat, 'Politische Denunziationen', 223–4.
[35] The quotation is from Lothar Gruchmann, *Justiz im Dritten Reich: Anpassung und Unterwerfung in der Ära Gürtner* (Munich 1988), 835.
[36] See e.g. Bay HStA: MA 106682: RP report, Schwabia/Neuburg, Augsburg, 6 July 1933; GSA: HA/Rep. 90P: Gestapo Düsseldorf, 5 May 1935.
[37] Bay HStA: MA 106677: RP report, Upper and Middle Franconia, 6 October 1933.
[38] Broszat, 'Politische Denunziationen', 223; the date of the decree was 28 Apr. 1934.
[39] Richard Grunberger, *A Social History of the Third Reich* (Harmondsworth, 1974), 146.
[40] *Sopade*, iv (Nov. 1937), 1555ff., suggests that the regime could no longer rely on voluntary denunciations as in the early years.

plan', expressed satisfaction at the orderly implementation of the 'planned measures for the effective removal of the Jews from the German economy and the use of Jewish wealth for the aims of the four-year plan'. However, he was far from happy with the recent phenomenon of '*German* fellow citizens' being informed upon 'because they once bought something in a Jewish store, lived in the same house as Jews, or otherwise had had business relations with the Jews'. The importance of explaining to the people why the Jews had to be removed from the German economy should not lead to the 'spying out and denunciation of such long past events'. As far as possible, all (unspecified) 'necessary measures' should be used to stop such denunciations in the future, since the economic plans were to a considerable degree dependent upon the 'requisite rhythmical and smooth exertion on the part of all German people'.[41]

The coming of war in 1939 brought with it many radical measures for the control of the population, its opinions, attitudes, and welfare. In fact, according to the 'special war law' of 17 August 1938, even a statement that might injure or destroy 'the will of the German people or an allied people to assert themselves stalwartly against their enemies' was declared criminal.[42] There were literally hundreds of regulations of various kinds that could only be enforced if the 'loyal citizen' would inform. Great attention was to be paid to the home front in this war because of the widespread paranoia among leading Nazis, and especially Hitler, as to the causes of Germany's defeat in 1918. In some instances, the population went beyond exposing those acts or attitudes formally or even informally forbidden; there were many cases, as will be seen below, where the people were well in advance of what the regime actually expected.

In a memorandum to the Gestapo just after the outbreak of war in 1939, Heydrich insisted that the police should pay particular attention to maintaining popular morale by ruthlessly dealing with all kinds of potentially defeatist statements made in public; the full co-operation of the citizenry, and of influential opinion-formers and monitors such as pub-owners and employees in public transport, should be sought. On the home front, for the duration of the conflict 'personally motivated baseless or exaggerated denunciations' should be handled on the spot with a harsh warning, and in the most serious cases the false accuser should be sent to a concentration camp.[43]

In the meantime, however, the Propaganda Ministry brought out a decree that opened the way for a new wave of denunciations. Joseph Goebbels's 'exceptional radio measures', issued on 1 September 1939, forbade listening to all foreign radio broadcasts; appeals were then made to the public to report

---

[41] BAK: R58/264; 192: Frick to Reichsstatthalter, 10 Jan. 1939.
[42] See Hirsch, Majer, and Meinck (eds.), 456–8.
[43] BAK: R58/275, 202–4, 3 Sept. 1939; Chef Sipo to Stapo(leit)stellen.

anyone who defied the ban.[44] The measures taken by Heydrich and Goebbels on the very same day, almost pulling in opposite directions, is a good example of what Martin Broszat calls 'polycracy', the many-centred nature of power in Nazi Germany.[45] Goebbels justified his action on the basis that the home front had to be protected from the 'lies' and 'weapon of poison' represented by foreign radio. Paranoia about repeating the mistakes allegedly made in the First World War affected not only Hitler but many others in the government hierarchy.[46] Drastic deterrents were proposed; in the most serious cases the punishment was to be death. The minister made the point that Germany, in the heart of Europe, could hardly be shielded in any other way than by introducing such draconian measures.[47]

Within hours Minister of Justice Gürtner registered severe reservations concerning these measures. His experts who reviewed the decree immediately pointed out that the outside world might assume a lack of trust and confidence between government and people, but an even more important objection pertained to the effect it would have at home. 'I fear in addition', Gürtner wrote to Goebbels at noon on 1 September, 'that the decree of such an ordinance would open the floodgates of denunciation and all national comrades would stand more or less helpless *vis-à-vis* such denunciations.'[48] The plan went into effect with minor modifications.

The ban on listening to 'enemy broadcasts', once legally binding, was energetically enforced by the Gestapo and associated police networks. Even government officials at the ministerial level had to apply for permission to listen in—strictly in the line of duty.[49] Citizens defying the ban did so with the greatest care. With luck, they already had a set of earphones they could use, and dared not forget to change the station before switching off, lest they leave a tell-tale clue.[50]

The atmosphere of suspicion and despair thus created is illustrated by examples drawn from the diary of William L. Shirer, a newspaper man and broadcaster who experienced Nazi Germany at first hand from 1934 to late 1940. On the train from Munich to Lausanne on 4 February 1940, Shirer, an inveterate diarist, committed several stories to paper.

---

[44] For the public appeals see Deutschkron, 59.

[45] Broszat, *Der Staat Hitlers*, 363ff. For a critique see Jane Caplan, 'Politics and Polyocracy: Notes on a Debate', in Charles S. Maier *et al.* (eds.), *The Rise of the Nazi Regime: Historical Reassessments* (Boulder, Colo., 1986), 51ff.

[46] See Mason, *Arbeiterklasse*, 1ff.

[47] For the decree see Hirsch, Majer, and Meinck (eds.), 458–9, and Joseph Wulf, *Presse und Funk im Dritten Reich: Ein Dokumentation* (Frankfurt, 1983), 378–9.

[48] The letter is in C. F. Latour, 'Goebbels' "Außerordentliche Rundfunkmaßnahmen" 1939–1942', *VfZ* 11 (1963), 419–20.

[49] See the correspondence from Gürtner, Lammers, Schlegelberger, Schacht, Rosenberg, Rust, and Muhs, ibid. 430ff.

[50] See Deutschkron, 60.

1. In Germany it is a serious penal offence to listen to a foreign radio station. The other day the mother of a German airman received word from the Luftwaffe that her son was missing and must be presumed dead. A couple of days later the BBC in London, which broadcasts weekly a list of German prisoners, announced that her son had been captured. Next day she received *eight* letters from friends and acquaintances telling her they had heard her son was safe as a prisoner in England. Then the story takes a nasty turn. The mother denounced all eight to the police for listening to an English broadcast, and they were arrested.

(When I tried to recount this story on the radio, the Nazi censor cut it out on the ground that American listeners would not understand the heroism of the woman in denouncing her eight friends!)

2. The parents of a U-boat officer were officially informed of their son's death. The boat was overdue and had been given up by the German Admiralty as lost. The parents arranged a church funeral. On the morning of the service the butcher called and wanted a few words with the head of the house in private. Next came the grocer. Finally friends started swarming in. They had all heard the BBC announce that the son was among those taken prisoner from a U-boat. But how to call off the funeral without letting the authorities know that someone in the confidence of the family listened to a foreign station? If the parents wouldn't tell, perhaps they themselves would be arrested. A family council was held. It was decided to go through with the funeral. After it was over, the mourners gathered in the parents' home, were told the truth if they didn't already know it, and everyone celebrated with champagne.[51]

Shirer does not speculate on the motives of the woman who turned in her eight friends, and it may well be that she was moved out of fear that, if she did not do so, someone would have charged her with having 'criminal' knowledge. More than one person offered information after reflecting on such a possibility.[52]

If the official attitude towards denunciations was in general ambivalent, and changed according to the exigencies of the moment, dealing with false charges or those laid with a reckless regard for truth was even more perplexing. Simple mistakes in judgement were not solely to blame, since frequently blatant personal motives, such as resentment, revenge, or jealousy, were at work. The problem of false charges plagued the regime in the years of peace, but created more havoc once war broke out and social life came increasingly under police jurisdiction. As a letter of 1 August 1943 from the Minister of Justice to judges across Germany put it, 'the denouncer is—according to an old saying—the biggest scoundrel in the whole country. That is true in the first instance of those who, in spite of knowing better, falsely report a fellow citizen to the authorities in order to cause him some unpleasantness.'[53] The minister noted, however, that caution was required when dealing with those

---

[51] William L. Shirer, *Berlin Diary* (New York, 1941), 214–15 (emphasis original).
[52] See Engelmann, *Im Gleichschritt*, ch. 4.
[53] Heinz Boberach (ed.), *Richterbriefe: Dokumente zur Beeinflussung der deutschen Rechtsprechung 1942–1944* (Boppard, 1975), 171.

who informed recklessly. While the regime did 'not want to turn the people into denouncers and snoopers' so that everyone was continuously spying on everyone else, no regime could overlook the utility of the informer. Therefore, in sentencing even the thoughtless and the careless accusers, too strict a standard ought not to be applied, lest 'the often useful sources in the discovery of criminal activities might also dry up'.[54]

The files of the Würzburg Gestapo and those in Düsseldorf indicate that these guidelines and others offered at different times did not stop the flow of false accusations. In the months following the outbreak of war, in an effort to put a stop to the blatant falsities, local Gestapo officials began advising some of the falsely accused to institute proceedings against those who had turned them in.[55] If a false accusation had particularly serious results, such as death through suicide, the Gestapo itself laid charges, as it had done in Düsseldorf in late 1935, when a man anxious to get rid of his wife accused her of having illegal sexual relations with a Jew.[56] Reinhard Mann's figures demonstrate that denunciations from ordinary citizens grew with the coming of war, reached their highest point in 1941, and then declined slowly at first, nearly to disappear altogether after 1943.[57]

Some of the problems stemmed from confusion about the nature and mission of the organizations charged with 'security' in the Third Reich. Local Gestapo officials occasionally published reminders in the press that the Gestapo was not the 'complaint bureau for personal spitefulness or even of base denunciations'.[58] Heydrich felt it necessary to issue a public statement in mid-February 1941 to clarify some of the issues. Gestapo and SD, he was well aware, were 'wrapped in the rumoured and whispered secretiveness of the political criminal novel', regarded with 'a mixture of fear and foreboding', and people wanted 'relatively little' to do with either. Nevertheless, he pointed out that some people believed that there was nothing, 'down to the tiniest egotistical wish', that the Gestapo could not make happen. The Gestapo had become something between a 'maid for all occasions and rubbish-bin of the Reich'.[59] Another memorandum sent to all local Gestapo headquarters from Berlin on 24 February 1941, concerning denunciations among relatives, particularly husbands and wives, suggests that the mechanism of denunciation was being used for private ends completely unanticipated by the regime.[60]

---

[54] Ibid. 171–2.
[55] See e.g. StA W Gestapo 5988, case Oct. 1939.
[56] HStA D: Gestapo 65053. This case is discussed in ch. 6.
[57] See Reinhard Mann, *Protest und Kontrolle*, 294, chart 4; and see ch. 7 below.
[58] See Jörg Schadt (ed.), *Verfolgung und Widerstand unter dem Nationalsozialismus in Baden* (Stuttgart, 1976), 303ff., for an interview with the head of the Karlsruhe Gestapo on 20 June 1934, carried in the *Neue Mannheimer Zeitung*.
[59] HStA D: RW 36/7, 5.
[60] Cf. Moore, *Terror*, 159, on the USSR under Stalin: 'There is enough evidence from persons

3. DENOUNCERS AND THEIR MOTIVES

A brief word needs to be said about the denouncers themselves and their motives. Richard Grunberger suggests that in Nazi Germany denunciation offered the 'humbly stationed in life' an 'equality of opportunity for laying information' against their 'social superiors', and that 'this harnessed a vast reservoir of personal resentment and spite to the purposes of the state'.[61] Grunberger has a point, but it is surprising that he emphasizes the resentment directed against 'social superiors'. It would appear, even from the examples he gives, that people usually informed on others in their own social class.

Peter Hüttenberger's conclusion from his study of cases of malicious gossip before the Munich Special Court, that the 'denouncers belonged to the same milieu as the denounced', fits the cases handled by the Gestapo in Würzburg and Düsseldorf and is confirmed by evidence from elsewhere—as, for example, in the massive collection of the post-1945 trials of those whose tip-offs led to Gestapo proceedings eventually resulting in death.[62] Hüttenberger discovered a massive number of denunciations in his work on the Special Court trials, and his analysis led him to maintain that denunciations 'arose as a rule from personal arguments, enmities and aversions of all kinds, and naturally also out of dislike between National Socialists and non-National Socialists'.[63] Hüttenberger's analysis of the 5,422 persons accused of malicious gossip reveals that, by his definition, the 'upper class' and the 'educated bourgeoisie' were 'nearly totally absent'.[64] He concludes that this was not because they made no such comments, but that they uttered them 'in a closed, private milieu which was not so susceptible to denunciation' as they would have been had they been uttered in public places such as a pub or store, or at the work-place.[65]

It is also true that people in positions of social authority were, on some occasions at least, accorded a degree of licence in their language. Incautious or even 'criminal' statements could sometimes be overlooked if made by a village doctor or the boss. Peter Bielenberg, senior person in a factory, drove

---

who have been associated with the secret police, either as victims or officers, to indicate clearly the reliance on quantity.'

[61] Grunberger, 145.

[62] Hüttenberger, 517. See the collection in *Justiz und NS-Verbrechen: Sammlung deutscher Strafurteile wegen ns. Tötungsverbrechen 1945–1966*, 24 vols. (Amsterdam, 1968).

[63] Hüttenberger, 517–18. Early in 1939, from exile in Zurich, Erika Mann interviewed a woman married to a Munich medical doctor, who complained that they lived 'in constant danger—of arrest at any moment, denounced by anyone who finds it worth his while, for some unfortunate remark he may or may not have made. If my husband has to press a Nazi patient for his bill we live in fear of his saying we've made fun of the Führer or joked about the Minister of Propaganda. And if that happens we'll both be arrested with no one to ask why—and our son would have to manage for himself' (E. Mann, 4).

[64] Hüttenberger, 518.

[65] Ibid. 469–70.

his office clerk's wife to hospital when she was ill. Upon picking her up at home, he observed a framed slogan on the living-room wall which said 'Der Führer hat immer Recht' ('The Führer is always right'). Bielenberg was astonished at the behaviour of his clerk, who was not even a member of the Party, and asked: 'However could you frame and hang up such rubbish?' The clerk said nothing until much later, when his boss was arrested and incriminated in the plot of July 1944 to assassinate Hitler; only after this arrest did the clerk inform the Gestapo of the incautious remark.[66] Such an incident appears to confirm the view that informants told on those in their own class, and that there was a certain reluctance to report on one's 'betters'.

Hüttenberger's quantitative analysis of the Munich special Court led him to conclude that once the absence of the upper class and the educated bourgeoisie is accounted for, the gossipers and those who turned them in ranged across the remainder of the social spectrum. He believes that a good number of those charged in these years had supported the Nazis at the polls before 1933, so that an 'attitude of disappointment' may have played a role in loosening their tongues.[67] While not all such gossip was reported and prosecuted, in so far as it *was* picked up the regime relied upon denunciations.

Martin Broszat writes of three specific cases in Bavaria in which statements made in public led to charges of 'injury to the state'; one, made by a highly respected local doctor, was more or less overlooked, while those from two members of the rural lower class were followed up.[68] Some people in such positions got a 'slap on the wrist' for 'crimes' for which others were sent to concentration camps. Certainly, a denunciation of someone in a vulnerable group, such as the Jews or other social outcasts, was taken by local officials as an opportunity to 'discipline and punish', regardless of the social class of the victim. When it came to the reporting and handling of complaints, the relevant factor was often 'the social prejudices of the denouncers, the police, the public prosecutors and the judges'.[69] Reck's diary, referred to above, noted how an old lady lived in 'seclusion in her two-room apartment on Munich's Maximilianstrasse. A well-known actor who had managed to win great popularity with the Nazis decided that he wanted these two rooms. He found it unheard of for an old Jewish woman to be inhabiting them and denounced the old lady to get the apartment.' Coming in late 1938, this was as good as a death sentence, and, too weak to face the 'bitter path' that lay ahead, she committed suicide.[70]

Martin Broszat, on the other hand, was struck by the above-average degree

[66] Christabel Bielenberg, *Ride Out the Dark: The Experiences of an Englishwoman in Wartime Germany* (1968; Boston, 1984), 237.

[67] Hüttenberger, 471.

[68] Broszat, 'Politische Denunziationen', 232.

[69] Ibid.

[70] Reck-Malleczewen, 70–1.

of willingness to denounce within the ranks of the 'Mittelstand', which he believed had arisen in good part because older concepts of honour and class had disintegrated during the crises of the Weimar Republic. Where these concepts tended to persist—in the nobility, certain professions, the civil service, the organized working class, and within religious bodies, there were relatively few denouncers.[71] There is some point to what Broszat says, but it needs to be recalled that even the legendary solidarity of the organized working class was no protection. The Left itself seems to have consistently exaggerated the degree to which infiltration of its ranks was dependent on agents planted by the Gestapo. Although there were spectacular examples of agents working for the Gestapo who contributed to the destruction of underground activities, the Left underestimated the number of denunciations made by comrades in the movement.[72] The trade-unionist Franz Vogt was correct to claim that the denouncers represented 'the most serious impediment to systematic illegal activity', but his figures for planted Gestapo spies are almost certainly too high.[73]

Detlev Peukert's study of the Gestapo Düsseldorf's actions against the KPD confirms that estimates of the numbers of Gestapo operatives were excessively high. He suggests that the Communists (not unlike the Socialists) regarded National Socialism primarily as an instrument of large capitalist interests, and only secondarily as a popular mass movement. They thus 'underestimated in their conception of resistance the role of spontaneous, massive denunciation out of agreement with Nazism or from personal vindictiveness'.[74] Perhaps they found it difficult to admit that some workers had made their peace with the new regime. Though working-class areas were relatively resistant to Nazification, denunciations were not rare. 'Neighbours who for years were inconspicuous and apolitical now revealed themselves as fanatical Nazis, while others, through particularly keen engagement, sought to have their late conversion to the NSDAP—as so-called "March converts"—forgotten.'[75]

One should not be over-hasty in assuming that voluntary and occasional informers were motivated by 'higher' (though misguided) concerns.[76] Reinhard Mann concluded that out of the total of 213 denunciations 'from the population' a remarkable 37 per cent were used to resolve private conflicts, no motive could be discovered in a further 39 per cent of the cases, while only 24 per cent were motivated by loyalty to the regime as such.[77] Once

[71] Broszat, 'Politische Denunziationen', 225ff.
[72] Cf. Meyer, 77ff. Fröhlich, 172ff.; Mehringer, 'Die KPD', 226ff.; Merson, 50ff.
[73] Vogt, in Peukert and Bajohr, 140. Cf. *Sopade*, ii (Sept. 1935), 1057ff., for similar views.
[74] Peukert, *Die KPD*, 121.
[75] Ibid. 121–2.
[76] But for an example of such 'idealism' see Güstrow, *Tödlicher Alltag*, 145ff. A nanny reported the medical doctor she had taken care of 'to win him back again for the Führer'.
[77] Reinhard Mann, *Protest und Kontrolle*, 295, table 37.

again, these statistics suggest that the important ingredient in the terror system—denunciation—was usually determined by private interests and employed for instrumental reasons never intended by the regime. The more important point is that all denunciations functioned in a 'system-loyal' fashion, in so far as they gave practical effect to the regime's intentions to monitor and modify social behaviour.

Everyday life became politicized in Nazi Germany, and, given the racial policy that was a paramount concern, the sphere of sexual and friendly relations came under special scrutiny. The regime deliberately politicized these relations, especially between Jews and non-Jews, and later between Poles and non-Poles. Medical and other authorities, in the course of physical examinations, were instructed to be on guard for possible transgressions of these and other laws and regulations. The importance of doctors for the regime's efforts to police intimate spheres of life was recognized very early. Within months a law was passed (July 1933) on the prevention of hereditary diseases, which declared that all doctors 'without regard to professional confidentiality' had a duty to report pertinent discoveries.[78]

Some people saw opportunities for personal gain in the new laws and regulations. A few unscrupulous characters even thought of planning careers around them. A letter of early September 1938 from the Gestapo headquarters in Berlin instructed all its posts in the western parts of Germany to be on the look-out for a certain Herbert Neesemann, who was falsely claiming in Amsterdam to be in the employ of the Gestapo and the German military.[79] However, for the most part ordinary citizens seized on the situation in specific circumstances and for specific purposes related to their private lives. This was a pattern that developed especially in cases involving the increasingly powerless Jews. Leonard Gross tells of the story of a young Berlin Jew, known as 'a ladies' man', who chanced to meet a Gentile woman, a former intimate friend, 'who had not taken their parting lightly'; she got her revenge in 1939 by turning him in to the nearest policeman.[80] A simple quarrel between long-time friends in Würzburg reached such a pitch in August 1938 that a certain Arthur Winkler charged his friend Josef Weigand's wife with libel—the exact basis of which is not clear in the file—whereupon in retaliation Weigand denounced Winkler on the serious charge of 'malicious gossip', for having said that a local Nazi Party leader had associated with Jews before 1933. Even though the personal motive behind that allegation was obvious (and admitted under cross-examination), it was investigated; eventually it was Weigand who was charged for uttering malicious gossip.[81]

The willingness to accuse a spouse alarmed both the Gestapo and the Reich

[78] *Reichsgesetzblatt*, I (25 July 1933), para. 7.
[79] HStA D: RW34: Cologne Gestapo.
[80] Leonard Gross, *The Last Jews in Berlin* (Toronto, 1983), 60.
[81] StA W: Gestapo 10937.

Justice Ministry. In the war years, when the strain of separation and general conditions placed an increased burden on marriages, steps had to be taken. On 24 February 1941 Gestapo headquarters in Berlin sent a letter to all local Gestapo posts concerning the matter of relatives—particularly married couples. As a representative example, the letter cited the case of a man who had denounced his wife on suspicion of espionage and for other acts deemed injurious to the Reich. She had been arrested and gaoled while the charges were investigated, all of which 'took some time', but it turned out that the accusations were utterly without foundation. The local police concluded that the man, who had not been living with his wife since 1929, had laid the charges in order to obtain a favourable divorce settlement. In response to Heydrich's warning about misuse of the system, orders were issued to the police to be more thorough in their investigation of the motives behind a denunciation, especially in the case of relatives. A married man should answer under oath whether divorce proceedings had already commenced or were contemplated.[82]

Yet denunciation of one spouse by another, and on dubious grounds, continued—as testified, for example, by a case in Würzburg that began in April 1941, after Heydrich had issued stern warnings. An ex-policeman (born in 1898) went to Gestapo headquarters to charge that his wife was ill-disposed towards National Socialism, and had been even before 1933. He accused her of having said, among other things, that she had no intention of raising her children 'for the brown mob' and that it would have been better had Hitler been shot during the *putsch* attempt of 1923. The ex-policeman also incriminated a number of other family members, but all complaints were shown to have no foundation. Such a result should not have surprised the police, who knew that the informant had been dismissed from the police for misbehaviour (among other things, he had earlier been a member of both the Communist Party and the SS at the same time). The police backed up his wife's testimony that he was schizophrenic, and noted in their report that he had been twice committed for psychiatric investigation.[83] In another case, a man from Würzburg, back from the front in 1942, had a quarrel with his wife and told her to leave, whereupon she went to the Gestapo with a charge. The Gestapo concluded that she sought revenge by attributing to him the 'treasonous' statement, 'I'm not going to raise any children to be shot dead for the Third Reich!'[84]

Such cases were not isolated ones, as is made clear by the circular letters sent to local judges by the Minister of Justice. Thierack wrote to the judges on 1 November 1944 about how they should react in five separate kinds of cases where either husband or wife denounced the spouse. The examples he

---

[82] BAK: R58/243, 317–18; Berlin, 24 Feb. 1941, Chef Sipo to Stapo(leit)stellen.
[83] StA W: Gestapo 1936.
[84] Ibid. 12049.

gave show how denunciation was used by one or other for personal purposes, although in passing the informants might put the police on the trail of criminal deeds. One example drawn from his letter is indicative, and incidentally, suggests that to some extent the 'better' social classes were not entirely immune from denunciations. Two medical doctors were married, with one child; when the man passed on to his wife a venereal disease he had contracted during an illicit affair, she was angry but forgave him until she discovered that he was continuing the affair. In a moment of rage she telephoned the criminal police and alleged that her husband had conducted illegal abortions. This information eventually led to a trial at which her husband was found guilty and sent to gaol for eight months; his career was also ruined. Subsequently, he instituted divorce proceedings on the grounds that his wife's complaint to the police about her suspicions amounted to breaking her marriage vows of trust. The judge in the case granted the divorce and found the woman at fault. Such a verdict would probably have given her no grounds for claiming financial damages, and might have denied her custody of their child, although there is no mention of these matters.

For the Minister of Justice this case, and similar ones he addressed in his discussion, entailed several important legal issues. He pointed out that there was no generalized duty to denounce whenever there was a suspicion of a crime and that the state did not demand breaches of the marriage trust as a matter of routine. On some occasions, such as in the event of milder crimes, the community had a 'fundamentally greater interest' in the 'continued maintenance of the mutual trust of the married couple'. While the citizen's duty to the community had to take precedence over marriage vows in cases of serious offences (such as high treason, undermining the morale of the military, murder, providing abortions), the minister explained, every denunciation of a spouse which eventually resulted in the discovery of a serious crime did not automatically provide grounds for winning in a divorce court. Nor were judges to conclude that the denunciation of one spouse by the other in itself constituted grounds for divorce. Pointing to the case of the physicians, Thierack emphasized the importance of having the right kind of motives. Both he and the divorce judge were of the view that the wife had informed on her husband 'merely out of hatred and revenge'. She was driven to act only when angered; she was not certain about the deeds in question, but brought the charges 'to make her husband's life miserable and to ruin his way of life'. For the minister, the correct decision had been reached in the divorce case, even though the investigation had shown the man to be guilty of the crime originally suspected by his wife.[85]

Thierack reflected the deep concern of many Nazi leaders about the spread of denunciations and their implications for social life. For these leaders, the

---

[85] Boberach (ed.), *Richterbriefe*, 363ff.

motives of the informer were extremely important, just as they were to the
local judge if and when conflict between husband and wife reached court.
Although some of the second thoughts of the Minister of Justice and the
judges were shared by the Gestapo, or at least the men who ran it in Berlin,
nevertheless in daily practice, as in the case of the two physicians, once an
accusation was brought to police attention it was relentlessly followed up.

The Würzburg and Düsseldorf Gestapo case-files reveal that charges were
investigated if there was a remote possibility that there might be something
in them; the question of motives was taken into account only as a secondary
matter. Thus, a case where both husband and wife laid dubious charges and
counter-charges was investigated at great length because of a possible link
to a Jewish person.[86] A further indication of the extent to which denunciations
infiltrated marriage relationships can be gathered from a case that has
attained a degree of notoriety because the trial that arose from it after 1945
was widely discussed in legal circles. On leave in 1944, a German soldier
privately made derogatory remarks about Hitler and other leaders to his wife.
Upon his return to the front the wife, 'who had turned to other men',
denounced him and subsequently testified against him. He was sentenced to
death under the law concerning malicious gossip, although in fact, after
spending some time in gaol, he was sent back to the front. After 1945 the
wife and the judge who had tried the case were brought to court under the
law concerning unlawful deprivation of a person's freedom. While the judge
was acquitted, she was found guilty (and the verdict was upheld on appeal)
because, while she had acted on the basis of Nazi 'law', her deed was contrary
'to the sound conscience and sense of justice of all decent human beings'.[87]
The decision formed an important topic in the post-war debate between the
legal positivists (who objected to it) and the advocates of pragmatic natural
law.

This case also illustrates another aspect of political denunciations. By the
standards of evaluating motives outlined by the Minister of Justice Thierack
mentioned above, the woman had acted for 'all the wrong reasons'. For the
police, however, a serious 'crime' had been alleged, and for their investigation
of the charge the accuser's motives necessarily became secondary. Whether
or not a serious crime had been committed was a matter separate from the
question of the source of the information. No doubt it would have been
comforting to someone like Thierack if the woman had acted out of 'proper'
National Socialist motives, if she had felt duty-bound as a good citizen or
convinced Nazi to report a 'serious' crime, even though the accused person
happened to be her husband. The police in their daily practice, however, had
little choice but to follow up all and any allegations, especially ones pertaining

---

[86] StA W: Gestapo 18089: case in spring 1940.
[87] See *Harvard Law Review*, 64 (1951), 1006–7.

to an 'important' crime such as providing abortions. In fact there were extremely few charges that were laid clearly for the 'right' reasons—and to deal only with these would have left the police virtually unable to function. In any event even a mischievous charge might have some valid basis or lead to the detection of a 'serious' crime—which was, with hindsight at least, sufficient justification to have proceed with the investigation. This was a logic that could not be escaped. In spite of Thierack's wishes, motives were not important to the functioning of the Gestapo. To understand how the Nazi police system operated, as opposed to how Thierack and some top Nazis might have wished that it would operate, the historian has to resist undue preoccupation with the motives of informers, and deny them the prominence they have often been given. The Gestapo knew how to do this.

4. ANONYMOUS DENUNCIATIONS

Reinhard Mann concluded that about 3 per cent of all denunciations from the population were from anonymous sources. It is not certain that the figure was really that low, since the files do not always make clear whether the tip-off came from a known individual or was from a source unknown or anonymous. Such tips were particularly used in charges against Nazi functionaries. For understandable reasons, even if there were firm grounds for suspecting that a 'crime' had been committed by such persons, it was hardly wise to come forward because, among other things, counter-charges could be laid for defamation of the Party name, uniform, symbols, leaders, and so on. Such complaints seem by and large to have been sent directly to Gestapo headquarters, more or less out of reach of the Party figure involved. The latter might be charged with taking too large a meat ration (such a case occurred in 1942) or benefiting materially from the confiscation of Jewish businesses.[88] An actual name could be introduced in a charge laid against a disliked functionary by suggesting that a third party had said that so-and-so had said something.[89] Even more threatening to Party members, especially if they had any social, or even business, contacts with Jews, was the charge that they were 'soft' on the 'Jewish question'.[90] If Communists were suspected of being at work, the police took infinite pains to investigate. In tiny Miltenberg, near Würzburg, an anonymous letter arrived at the local SA headquarters early in 1937, denouncing five specified individuals on suspicion of Communist activities. All were questioned at great length by the Gestapo. There was nothing to the story save the personal hatred of the SA leader—who wrote the note himself—and at the conclusion of the case the Gestapo eventually

[88] Cf. StA W: Gestapo 1927; 9873; 16714.
[89] Ibid. 11294.
[90] See chs. 6, 7.

charged him. The SA man contradicted himself from the beginning: the case should have been seen for what it was much sooner.[91]

Given the increasingly radical measures taken by the regime in the war years, anonymous denunciations, even of senior Party functionaries, were taken seriously. In August 1943 a charge was made by letter that Kreisleiter Ingebrand of Bad Neustadt had taken advantage of his position to obtain a safe place during the fighting in France. He managed subsequently, it was claimed, to get himself recalled to Germany, where he was enjoying too much food and leisure activity—including hunting expeditions. Though the police felt that the letter was probably an attempt to get revenge and that it originated from someone near the Kreisleiter, the charges were investigated.[92]

An anonymous charge could arise out of economic motives, as suggested in a letter by a 'German competitor' (in the wine business) to the Würzburg Gestapo in May 1938. While it indeed turned out that the denounced business had been purchased from its former Jewish owner, the transaction had in fact been conducted according to the letter of the law.[93] Nevertheless, much worry was expressed that Nazi Party members had managed personal pay-offs or 'spoils' of one kind or another.[94]

A final case of an anonymous accusation suggests that people had come to be quite scrupulous in their view of what constituted 'criminality'. In January 1942 the Catholic village priest in Laufach received a note defaming the Nazi leadership, but instead of destroying it the priest turned it over to local police, and at least one man was subsequently brought in for interrogation and to check whether his handwriting matched that of the note. Perhaps the priest considered the letter a provocation by enemies unknown. Even an unwilling recipient of such a 'criminal' document felt compelled to pass it on once it was in his possession. A case like this indicates how widespread the sense of fear and distrust was at this time, even in the idyllic countryside of northern Bavaria.[95]

5. 'Social misfits' and the use of denunciations

A common assumption about denouncers is that for the most part they are social misfits whose character weaknesses come to light under certain social conditions. Richard Cobb's statement is representative. In his book on the police in Revolutionary France he claims that such people 'are, unfortunately, an international phenomenon; any period of war or civil disturbance or acute

---

[91] StA W: Gestapo 3596.
[92] Ibid. 2555.
[93] Ibid. 9529.
[94] Ibid. 10181; 9873.
[95] Ibid. 8279. For additional cases of anonymous tips and the Gestapo in Würzburg see Fröhlich, 138ff.

shortage is likely to stimulate that vocation'.[96] Such an interpretation offers a timeless, ahistorical view. It would be a mistake to think that in Nazi Germany denouncers were only or even primarily drawn from the margins of society.

It also needs to be said that, just as almost all aspects of social life in the Third Reich were politicized, so too were the tales told by the chronic complainers, the grumblers, and the petty gossipers. The Würzburg authorities no longer dismissed their charges as trivial or obvious nonsense. These people, with a degree of social power they never had before, now saw how they might win arguments, settle scores, pay off debts, get rid of bothersome people, all with the help of the Gestapo. It was expeditious to come up with a politically relevant charge, but even the suggestion to the police that something 'suspicious' was in the air would work for a time. Even when the police were confronted with unsavoury characters they generally proceeded as though there might be something in the allegations. From Würzburg in early 1935 comes a case where a family reported their neighbour, Hans Fichtel, for allegedly having said 'to hell with' the Swastika flag! The charge was taken up by the Gestapo even though the family who made it were known to the police—to the whole city, for that matter—for their false accusations. 'The entire family, because of its many previous convictions, had been ostracized in Würzburg and must now be supported by the welfare office.' This reputation did not prevent their charges against Fichtel from being followed up.[97]

Reinhard Mann's quantitative analysis of Gestapo cases shows up the alarming consequences that such denunciations could have for the victim. He found that of all those people reported to the police out of personal motives, one quarter were provisionally arrested and spent an average of three days in custody until the baselessness of the charges could be established. Even in those instances where nothing quite so drastic took place, Mann correctly points out that merely being cross-examined by the Gestapo, especially if it took place at headquarters, was already a dreadful experience. One need only reflect on the sinister reputation of the police, the uncertainty of the outcome, the incalculability of the procedure, and the admissibility of evidence about statements made before 1933.[98]

Werner Best said at Nuremberg that the Gestapo was deluged by petty denunciations, especially involving the loosely defined crime of malicious gossip. These 'came to the police from outside, and were not sought for, for 90 per cent of these cases were not worth dealing with'.[99] Though they grew

---

[96] Richard Cobb, *The Police and the People: French Popular Protest 1789–1820* (Oxford, 1970), 80. See the differentiated remarks of Elton, 374–5.

[97] StA W: Gestapo 18039; cf. 16835.

[98] Reinhard Mann, *Protest und Kontrolle*. 300–1.

[99] IMT xx. 128.

so great as nearly to overload the system, care should be taken in considering them dysfunctional, for, like all tips, they reinforced the social controls of the Gestapo and other authorities. Ironically, on occasion official campaigns against those who laid personally motivated charges had the consequence of increasing them. According to Martin Broszat, the attempt in early 1934 to stop the 'grumblers' (Nörgler) and 'alarmists' (Miesmacher) only added to their number, since asking for public co-operation to enforce the ban opened the door to a further wave.[100]

Social misfits of all kinds continued to hound their neighbours. In numerous cases some citizens repeatedly denounced others, and these were taken seriously though the police noted in the files that the informant was somewhat limited mentally.[101] A woman known to be suffering from venereal disease whose husband left her for another dropped a hint to the Labour Front (the DAF) that the new woman might be Jewish. This charge, clearly made from dubious motives, was checked and found to be without any foundation.[102]

Under the influence of alcohol, or armed with the most far-fetched reasons, a person could feel, none the less, confident that the Gestapo or one of the many other authorities would listen. In October 1933 SA man (and barber) Heinrich Sachs turned in a man he met in the street who was drunk, 'because possibly the man might know something'. The drunk had a photograph with him, and said that one of the people in it owned a printing-press. There was nothing to the case.[103] In December 1937 allegations were made about the behaviour of Mayor Hofmann of Leidersbach, near Würzburg. Not for the first time, the accuser was a disenchanted Party member, a drunk with a police record, and rarely in regular employment. The problem probably started, according to the dossier, when some years earlier Hofmann had disciplined the denouncer for appearing drunk in SA uniform; since then the man had sought revenge, and pursued the mayor with a series of denunciations. Hofmann, himself a Party member, decided to take his Party comrade before the Party court.[104] Writing from Würzburg's city gaol in mid-1940, Thomas Kuchenmeister, an unskilled worker with a reputation as a drunk, and himself charged with theft (later also with being a vagrant), alleged that in the cafe Werner in Trappstadt 'treasonous' behaviour was afoot. After placing the establishment under surveillance 'in an appropriate manner'— and Kuchenmeister under observation by a psychiatrist—the authorities found the charge to be baseless.[105]

In the war years the range of activities which could be denounced increased

[100] Broszat, 'Politische Denunziationen', 223.
[101] StA W: Gestapo 3391.
[102] Ibid. 13060.
[103] Ibid. 5457.
[104] Ibid. 7949.
[105] Ibid. 13574.

dramatically. Failing to darken the windows at night, forgetting to change the radio dial away from the 'enemy' channels after listening to forbidden broadcasts, and infringement of the numerous regulations on food, clothing, and shelter—all could have dramatic consequences if noticed. All these charges, and many similar ones, from the dubious sources mentioned above were not merely registered by the police but actively investigated, with numerous interrogations and so on. The examples chosen here pertain to one group of citizens informing on one another, and they show that denunciations were not employed only by certain 'in-groups', such as Party members, against 'out-groups', such as Jews and others.

Another instance when a denunciation appears to have been launched 'for all the wrong reasons' began when the SD in Würzburg was informed in early 1941 by Nurse Maria Markler of the NSV that Paster Bach, who lived in Zeil, near Würzburg, had offered criminal advice to the mechanic apprentice Karl Hof (born 1923), also living in that village. In its short note to the Gestapo the SD said that Bach (born 1882) had been a 'venomous and dangerous enemy of National Socialism', a judgement confirmed by Nurse Markler. Hof had, to be sure, been known to police before as a 'show-off', who had left school in 1937 at the age of 13 and who had been reported for sexually assaulting a 6- or 7-year-old girl. Even his own father and grandfather, who were brought in for questioning, described Hof as 'rude', 'lying', and 'insolent'. Hof reported that when he told Bach that he wanted to join the pioneers—the army's under-age organization—the priest had said that it 'would be suicidal for such a young person now, in wartime, to report voluntarily to the pioneers'.

Had this charge been sustained, the priest would almost certainly have paid with his life. It turned out that Hof had fabricated the story as an act of revenge for the hatred he had developed as a schoolboy. Hof said that long ago

I planned that I would take revenge on this man at the first and best opportunity... Several weeks ago I was speaking with the NSV nurse Markler, who is the wife of my boss, about Pastor Bach. Markler mentioned to me that she had already had arguments with Pastor Bach over matters concerned with the BDM [Bund deutscher Mädel: Hitler Youth girls' organization]. Further, she said to me that she would be making a report about the activities of the BDM and mentioned also in this regard Pastor Bach. I considered that the time had come for me to avenge myself on Pastor Bach, which is why I made the statements already known to you. In answer to why I put things together in this way, I can only say that it just popped into my head, that is, I had not thought it over beforehand.

Curiously nothing further happened to Hof; he had enlisted on 5 May 1940, and this might have helped. It seems also that the regime did not really want to be hard on even admitted false denouncers when the person denounced was declared an 'opponent'. Beyond that, the case also shows that charges of even such a reprehensible type as Hof's would be dutifully investigated.[106]

Hof was not the only frustrated person to seek revenge on former teachers in this way. Students were among the first to bring information to the Würzburg Gestapo. In April 1933 a group of high-school students charged that their teacher, Dr Georg Kepner, who was then living in Nuremberg, had forbidden them to wear their Nazi emblems in school. Kepner admitted having said—*before* Hitler's appointment—that wearing the emblems might be taken as insulting to the Jewish students in class.[107] In fact, the propensity of schoolchildren to denounce teachers who had disciplined them threatened to get out of hand on some occasions, if the complaints in Bavaria can be taken as representative. A circular from the Ministry of Education of 16 June 1936 noted with alarm that 'students, without the knowledge of their parents, are reporting to the police, or at another convenient place known to them, that their teachers have displayed political unreliability or even a treasonous attitude. The reporters are often students who have had to be disciplined during instruction.'[108] Though many of the charges turned out to be without foundation, they were damaging to the schools' reputation. The ministry wanted such complaints to be handled internally, in the first instance at least, by the local school administration. Needless to say, enforcing such a policy was difficult, if not impossible—not least because of the many ways a determined student could find to lodge a complaint. Not only unruly students reported on their teachers; some diligent pupils also informed. According to many accounts, members of the various branches of the Hitler Youth, down to the lowest levels, were particularly keen to denounce teachers, religious instructors, and, on occasions, even their parents.[109]

In due course some of the heterogeneous group described above as the 'social misfits' were themselves termed 'enemies of the community' (*Gemeinschaftsfremde*). Had the regime lasted longer, this loosely defined category of people would surely have been subjected to treatment much like the kind administered to the Jews and others.[110]

One final point concerning the relationship of these characters and the regime's police system needs to be mentioned. Local police officials could always exercise their prerogative to follow up denunciations. However, the Gestapo acted far more rigorously in cases of accusations against 'opponents'. As will be seen in the next chapters, the police's level of tolerance was at its lowest when it came to any hint of 'race crimes'. Jews and other racial 'outgroups', such as the Poles, Eastern workers, and prisoners of war, were held

[106] StA W: Gestapo 2038.

[107] Ibid. 11991.

[108] Quoted in Broszat, 'Politische Denunziationen', 228.

[109] See e.g. Ernst Schmidt, *Lichter in der Finsternis: Widerstand und Verfolgung in Essen 1933–1945*, 2nd edn. (Frankfurt, 1980), 213ff.

[110] See Peukert, *Volksgenossen*, 246ff.; for an outline of the law see Hirsch, Majer, and Meinck (eds.), 252ff.

in particular contempt. Before too long the Gestapo was paying attention to the town drunk, the work-shy person, the man always at loggerheads with his neighbours, who wanted to complain about a Pole who was riding a bicycle or drinking at the local pub. But one should avoid concluding that denunciations were chiefly the work of the misfits one might expect to find in any society. For one thing, in Nazi Germany there were an awful lot of 'social misfits': it is safe to say that in this period their numbers swelled to include people who would normally not be so labelled. However, solid citizens, such as teachers, priests, and medical doctors, also denounced 'crimes' that came to their attention. During a visit to their family doctor in Schweinfurt in August 1941, the father of a 15-year-old young girl told the doctor that a Polish foreign worker had made her pregnant. 'In order to protect the remaining youth in the area' the doctor reported the matter to the magistrate, who passed it on to the Gestapo. After 'hard-nosed lying', the deed was admitted under questioning, and not one but two Polish workers were sent to a concentration camp, where they died from 'special handling'.[111] The above-mentioned cases cited by Minister of Justice Thierack as examples of the dubious use of denunciation include no marginal social types. There were (1) a 46-year-old technical school teacher and his wife; (2) a husband and wife in their thirties, both medical doctors; (3) a merchant (*Kaufmann*) and his wife; (4) a lawyer and his wife; and (5) a Nazi Party official, listed simply as a 'camp-leader' (*Lagerführer*), and spouse. If anything linked these people, it was not an inferior social status.[112]

6. CONCLUSION

The Nazi regime criminalized any behaviour that might have an oppositional aspect to it. Apart from helping the regime to enforce policies of all kinds, this practice, as Peter Hüttenberger explains, permitted the regime to pick up 'dissatisfaction of the population in areas where social assistance was not effective'; thereby, the regime 'strengthened its domination down to the lowest levels of society, in that it picked up non-conforming types of behaviour that were already developing and, by isolating the individual concerned, destroyed them. The denunciation constituted an important precondition for this.'[113]

One might have expected more attention to popular forms of denunciation in the many books recently devoted to the 'history of everyday life' (*Alltags-geschichte*) and those that focus upon 'resistance and persecution'. However, for the most part, such studies tend to touch on the police only in passing.

---

[111] StA W: Gestapo 6962.
[112] Boberach (ed.), *Richterbriefe*, 363ff. In case 3 the wife of the merchant had turned him in earlier for listening to foreign radio when she felt he was about to beat her.
[113] Hüttenberger, 518.

This chapter has suggested that an adequate assessment of the terror system is essential to any consideration of social behaviour and that establishing the degree of ordinary citizens' participation in the police state is relevant to any local or regional case-study that, which has to be concerned at least in part with evaluating the extent and bases of popular consensus.

The motives for offering information to the authorities ranged across the spectrum from base, selfish, personal, to lofty and 'idealistic'. The records project an image of the denouncers—who, not surprisingly, tended to come from the same milieu as those on whom they informed—as drawn largely from groups at the lower end of the social scale. This image is probably correct, but must be qualified lest these groups be judged too harshly. It needs to be borne in mind that upper-income groups and the nobility for the most part did not need to utilize the police, since they had other and more effective avenues through which to exercise social power. Moreover, the police, themselves largely drawn from the lower social orders, were more deferential in cases involving the nobility and the upper bourgeoisie, and pursued individuals from the lower end of the social hierarchy with greater alacrity. Even so, individuals from all social classes offered information to the police. The regime was bound to have second thoughts about this participation when, at times, it was inundated with charges, too many of which were careless or just plain false. But, despite some misgivings, it was felt better to have too much information and co-operation than too little.

6

Racial Policy and Varieties of Non-Compliance

NAZI racial policy was codified in a series of laws, ordinances, and decrees which began in 1933 and grew in scope with the increasingly radical approach adopted by the regime. A recent collection of official measures applied to the Jews has many hundreds of separate entries, and even then makes no claim to being complete.[1] Police regulations designed to establish the racial segregation of foreign workers, who were brought to Germany with the onset of war in 1939, are recorded in a volume that exceeds 200 pages in length.[2] In addition, there was a vast array of racially inspired measures, of many kinds with respect to the German people themselves, quite apart from the other steps that were undertaken to monitor, control, and modify their thoughts, words, and deeds.[3]

The final chapters of this book focus on the enforcement process—how the regime went about implementing this vast racist repertoire. As suggested in the last chapter, an essential ingredient for enforcement was the provision of information, which was volunteered, solicited, coerced, or collected by agencies of Party and state. Moreover, information was required of such a nature and in such quantities that it could be produced only with the help of 'ordinary' citizens. With such co-operation, the regime found it possible to infiltrate all kinds of social spaces, eventually overriding conventions so as to breach the private spheres of family, personal, and sexual life.[4]

Given the countless forms racial policy assumed, it is necessary to restrict the focus of the examination. This chapter and the one following deal with certain limited aspects of the anti-Jewish policies, while the last chapter examines cases involving Polish workers. An attempt is made to assess the effort to separate these ethnic groups from the population at large. The examination is based primarily on Gestapo case-files from Würzburg, and is supplemented by selective use of those in Düsseldorf.

The Gestapo, as already indicated, was the local body ultimately responsible

---

[1] See Joseph Walk (ed.), *Das Sonderrecht für die Juden im NS-Staat* (Heidelberg, 1981), xi.

[2] *Allgemeine Erlaßsammlung*, pt. 2, ed. RHSA (1944) in IfZ.

[3] See e.g. Peukert, *Volksgenossen*, 246ff.; Gisela Bock, *Zwangssterilisation im Nationalsozialismus: Studien zur Rassenpolitik und Frauenpolitik* (Opladen, 1986), 178ff.; Hans-Walter Schmuhl, *Rassenhygiene, Nationalsozialismus, Euthanasie: Von der Verhütung zur Vernichtung 'lebensunwerten Lebens'* (Göttingen, 1987), 151ff.; Angelika Ebbinghaus *et al.*, *Heilen und Vernichten im Mustergau Hamburg* (Hamburg, 1984).

[4] For earlier enforcement problems see Michael Kunze, *Highroad to the Stake: A Tale of Witchcraft*, trans. W. E. Yuill (Chicago, 1987), p. xii.

for the fate of the Jews, up to and including their deportation to the death camps in the east. Particularly illustrative of the enforcement practice are the large number of files pertaining to those accused of (vaguely defined) 'friendship' with Jews, as well as those charged with 'race defilement'. As is rightly pointed out by Sarah Gordon in her study of Düsseldorf, one way to evaluate this behaviour is to look at what happened to social and personal ties that crossed the ethnic boundary. The regime gradually made such trangressions subject to ever harsher punishments.[5]

In spite of the threat of sanctions, some people refused to comply, and kept up or even established new social contacts with the Jews when such behaviour was criminalized and exceedingly dangerous. Those known to have been picked up by the Gestapo are studied in this chapter. The next one will show how the Gestapo applied pressure in order to obtain compliance. Of course, as the examination will make clear, such a division is somewhat arbitrary, because any evaluation of the courage and commitment of the dissenters must take into consideration the nature of the situation they faced and the size of the odds against them.

1. Persecution of the Jews in Gestapo files

'Race defilement' (*Rassenschande*), forbidden (extramarital) sexual intercourse between Jews and 'non-Jews', was declared a crime according to the Nuremberg Laws of 1935.[6] Even 'friendly' or social relations with Jews constituted an area of potential 'criminality', but not officially a specific crime as such. 'Behaviour friendly to the Jews' (*judenfreundliches Verhalten*) was a term of abuse and a catch-all accusation that could be levelled at persons who had uttered a mild disagreement with some aspect of the racial policies, or had otherwise given reason for suspicion that they did not accept the letter or spirit of Nazi anti-Semitism. Such people were also termed 'friends of the Jews' (*Judenfreunde*) or 'slaves of the Jews' (*Judenknechte*), although they might simply have retained purely economic, instrumental contacts with them.[7] The Gestapo was exceptionally sensitive, and ready to act on any information that helped to enforce racial/sexual segregation.

The absence of a single anti-Semitic 'law' did not hinder denunciations, but in a sense encouraged them, since the vaguely defined policies and

---

[5] Gordon, 213.

[6] See Ernst Noam and Wolf-Arno Kropat, *Juden vor Gericht 1933–1945: Dokumente aus hessischen Justizakten* (Wiesbaden, 1975), 109ff., and Wilhelm Stuckart and Hans Globke, *Kommentare zur deutschen Rassengesetzgebung* i (Munich, 1936), 40ff.

[7] For some of the ways the charges were used see Fred Hahn, *Lieber Stürmer! Leserbriefe an das NS-Kampfblatt 1924 bis 1945* (Stuttgart, 1978), 229ff. For reflections on the effects on the language see Victor Klemperer, *LTI: Lingua Tertii Imperii. Die Sprache des Dritten Reichs* (Frankfurt, 1982), 183ff.

prohibitions allowed for virtually unlimited areas of potentially 'criminal' behaviour. Some Gestapo dossiers begin with the cryptic remark 'suspicious behaviour'; others state, without another word in the dossier, that a citizen brought to police attention for unstated reasons was also 'known to be a friend of the Jews', or another file begins simply with the cryptic remark 'according to a reliable report' the accused person 'continues to maintain contacts with Jews'.[8] The doctrine might be reduced to the imperative, 'avoid Jews everywhere', but even in Nazi Germany the general accusation of being friendly with Jews had to be fitted into some specific law or other, such as that against malicious gossip, or the many flowing from the emergency laws of 1933, or the Nuremberg Laws of 1935. But these kinds of 'political' charges were taken very seriously because they might indicate that the individual concerned was rejecting the Nazi regime's doctrines on race.[9]

As shown above, from the time of the Nazi 'seizure of power', sexual and social relations between Jews and non-Jews had to be kept as inconspicuous as possible. Even before such imperatives were codified into law, Nazi radicals, as well as some 'ordinary' citizens, occasionally took it upon themselves to confront people who seemed unconvinced by the teachings on race. As the racial doctrine received more publicity and what was expected was made abundantly clear, the social and sexual contacts between Jews and non-Jews became more discreet. Not content with that, the regime sharpened its efforts.

Although the intensification of official pressure was important, the Gestapo on its own could not enforce racial policies designed to isolate the Jews. Table 3 suggests that more public co-operation through the provision of information was required in order to enforce racial policy, and more co-operation of this kind was attained than might be gathered from Mann's figures (as suggested in the last chapter, Table 2). Thus, for example, of the 175 cases pertaining to the separation of Jews and non-Jews in the Würzburg files in the specific area of sexual and social relations, 57 per cent began with a denunciation from a citizen. Mann's study of the Gestapo case-files in Düsseldorf, on the other hand, indicated that information from the population initiated about one-third of all cases. However, part of the explanation for the different figures can be traced to Mann's sample, which specifically excluded the files of the Jews (indeed, it left out 11 categories of case-files which pertained not only to the Jews, but several others defined by the regime as foreigners or as 'racially foreign'). Some of the sympathizers with the Jews, and many who voiced doubts in public about the regime's anti-Semitic policies or actions, to mention but two examples, would almost certainly have been covered by

---

[8] See StA W: Gestapo 3705; 4953; 4202. For additional information on the fates of the Jews and the Würzburg Gestapo, including false charges of 'race defilement', see Adler, 692ff.

[9] StA W: Gestapo 8135. In this case from Unsleben in late 1938 it was alleged (among other things) that a neighbour said that (at some point) Hitler went with Jewish women, in the course of counter-accusations in a libel action.

TABLE 3. *Causes of Initiating Cases of 'Race Defilement' and 'Friendship to Jews'*
in the Würzburg Gestapo (1933–1945)

Source of information	'Race defilement'		'Friendship to Jews'		Total	
	No.	%	No.	%	No.	%
1. Reports from the population	45	54	54	59	99	57
2. Information from other control organizations	2	2	6	7	8	5
3. Observatons by Würzburg Gestapo, V-persons	0	0	1	1	1	0
4. Information via communal or state authorities	0	0	0	0	0	0
5. Statements at interrogations	20	24	6	7	26	15
6. Information from businesses	0	0	0	0	0	0
7. Information via NS organizations	4	5	11	12	15	9
8. 'Political evaluations'	2	2	4	4	6	3
9. Not known	11	13	9	10	20	11
TOTAL	84	100	91	100	175	100

Source: Würzburg Gestapo case-files in StA W.

Mann's study if they had been accused of the more general 'crime' of 'malicious gossip', or if the Gestapo had put their case into one of the other categories covered by Mann's study, such as 'resistance' or 'opposition'. All that can be suggested here is that had Mann's sample been drawn from the full range of Gestapo activities, especially if it had included the Jews, then in all likelihood the overall percentage of cases which began with denunciations would have been higher. Some of the justification for that suggestion can be seen in Table 3, which is based on a study of Gestapo case-files in Würzburg.

Besides pointing to a high degree of public co-operation with the Gestapo in enforcing racial/sexual policy, Table 3 also shows that the Gestapo's 'own observations', at least when it came to enforcing racial/sexual segregation, were responsible for initiating less than 1 per cent of such cases, a figure which contrasts sharply with the general figure of 15 per cent pointed to by Mann in Table 2, and underlines the importance of the Gestapo's reliance on information from external sources. That an additional 15 per cent of all such cases began with information gathered at interrogations, as indicated in Table 3, leads one to suspect that once someone was brought in for interrogation, incriminating information could be wrested from that person. Table 3 shows that various other 'control organizations', such as the SD and Kripo, participated less in enforcing racial policy than in the overall work of the Gestapo. While they helped initiate some 17 per cent of all cases (see Table 2), they contributed to tracking only 5 per cent of all the more specific cases of race transgression. From the Würzburg files it looks as though the SD and the Kripo were not nearly as active as is sometimes supposed.

On the other hand, as Table 3 indicates, the role of the Nazi Party and affiliates was greater in enforcing racial policies than in the general functioning of the Gestapo. While they initiated 6 per cent of all cases of the Gestapo, the Party and affiliates initiated 9 per cent of the cases in the Würzburg files concerning enforcement of racial regulations. The Party was also responsible for an additional 3 per cent which began when it turned up incriminating evidence after being asked to conduct 'political evaluations'. Moreover, on the evidence of local Nazi Party files from several different areas, it would appear that many complaints were handled by the Party on its own and that it passed on only a portion to the Gestapo for 'executive' attention— arrest, interrogation, or imprisonment. Thus, for example, a letter of June 1936 from the Ochsenfurt propaganda office to Würzburg Party headquarters reported that a hotel- and restaurant-owner dared to put up Jewish persons and to serve them food, even though local Nazis frequented the inn. Since technically nothing illegal had taken place, headquarters was asked what could be done, beyond recommending that the Nazi Party boycott that business.[10] Apart from such internal complaints, however, countless private citizens went to local Party headquarters across the country to seek redress. The files from Eisenach in East Germany, for example, reveal a constant flow of complaints. Such documents reveal the NSDAP not merely as a source of information for the Gestapo but, up to a point, as an enforcer on its own. The scattered evidence also suggests that it was as prone to abuse for selfish ends as were the other authorities in Germany[11]

Paid informers or agents are conspicuous by their absence in Table 3. Perhaps there was enough volunteered information to make the use of agents superfluous. Rarely can it be shown that paid agents offered information about transgressions of racial policy. It may be that the Gestapo had to reserve planted informers of various kinds for the task of cracking the more tightly organized pockets of political resistance, such as those formed by the Com-

---

[10] StA W: NSDAP/GL/I/3.
[11] The files are in the Myers Collection at the University of Michigan, Ann Arbor, CF. StA M: NSDAP 318, letter of 5 Feb. 1936, which suggests how denunciations were also used to settle issues within the Party.

Enforcing Racial Policy

munist and Socialist parties. The absence of documents does not mean that agents were not more involved, but to attempt to say anything further would involve an intolerable amount of guesswork.

As might be expected, charges alleging 'race defilement' increased dramatically after the passage of the Nuremberg Laws, which specified the crime for the first time (although a number of charges of this type had been laid before those laws were in force: see Table 4). The table also indicates that the greatest number came in 1936; after that there was a gradual decline. The slack was more than taken up, however, by increases in the number of allegations for being 'friendly', sociable, or sympathetic to the Jews, as shown in the table. Indirectly, both sets of figures suggest that such relations were steadily broken off as they were uncovered, or soon disintegrated because of fear of being further denounced.

TABLE 4. *Accusations of 'Race Defilement' and 'Friendship to Jews' in the Würzburg Gestapo Case-Files (1933–1945)*

	'Race defilement'		'Friendship to Jews'	
	Total No.	Found to be false or baseless	Total No.	Found to be false or baseless
1933	2	1	1	1
1934	1	0	2	2
1935	5	1	2	1
1936	19	7	12	4
1937	14	5	7	3
1938	14	6	14	3
1939	8	3	17	7
1940	6	2	14	8
1941	4	2	9	4
1942	3	0	3	1
1943	1	0	1	0
1944	0	0	0	0
1945	0	0	0	0
Undated	7	3	9	7
TOTAL	84	30	91	41

Source: Würzburg Gestapo case-files in StA W.

2. OPPONENTS OF NAZI ANTI-SEMITISM AND THE FALSELY ACCUSED

Gestapo case-files are records of named individual persons who came to the attention of the Gestapo. Some of these dossiers were created, for example, when the Gestapo had reason to suspect that a person had defied the regime's position on the 'Jewish question'. Not all of these suspicions led to arrests, although some did; others eventually found their way into court, but more were evidently not considered worth pursuing after an initial inquiry. A precise analysis of the percentage of Gestapo investigations which led to arrest, trial, and conviction, like several other important aspects of the history of police practice, is not yet available. Reading through the two collections of case-files which survive, one observes that some of the 'dossiers' are little more than a scrap of information which, after having been brought to police attention, was merely noted without any follow-up, because it was too inconsequential or vague. In every instance, as far as is known, a personal case-file on the suspect was established, alphabetized, and cross-referenced for internal police purposes. The Gestapo (not unlike the rest of the Nazified police) was receptive to all tip-offs, and this was especially so when it came to important 'opponents', such as the Jews, and the policies which were hard to enforce, such as 'race defilement'. On these occasions in particular the Gestapo was anything but fastidious about verifying accusations. An anonymous tip, for example, could lead not only to a demand that a suspect appear at police headquarters, but to an arrest, an extorted confession, and prolonged detention. By virtue of the power to impose 'protective custody' no more than a hint was needed to take someone into custody if a high-profile 'crime' was suspected—and violations of the Nuremberg Laws were of paramount concern. Given all these considerations, it is difficult to accept Sarah Gordon's decision to treat each of the 452 cases of 'race defilement' and 'friendship to Jews' in the Düsseldorf files as evidence of an actual rather than merely alleged 'offence'. If she is unable to defend this decision, it would also be impossible for her to sustain a claim based on this decision, namely that all 452 people were 'opponents' of Nazi anti-Semitism.[12] Her subsequent

---

[12] Gordon, 213, maintains that all were 'guilty', and that those who got off had managed 'to cover their tracks'. This explanation is too speculative. She also claims that 'in all cases' the accused 'were denounced by one (and frequently two) "witness(es)", but unless three "witnesses" corroborated the charges, the Gestapo dismissed the accused with the usual stern warning'. This claim is not accompanied by supporting documentation. Gordon seeks correlational support for her assertion that even those who got off lightly were guilty by drawing up 'statistical profiles' of the accused and comparing these to the sociological structure of the area. Gestapo practices make this procedure even more problematical than it might be otherwise. For example, a case-file held by a Gestapo post might pertain to 'criminal' deeds committed elsewhere, and copies of a case could be sent to one's home area as a matter of record after the entire case had run its course elsewhere. Some of Gordon's 'illustrative cases' of opponents (pp. 233ff.), for example, pertain to non-resident persons who were by chance picked up by a branch of the Düsseldorf

categorization of these 'opponents' (as 'high', 'middle', or 'low') would then be invalid as well.[13]

Even in those cases where there are reasonable grounds for concluding that a 'crime' was committed, the 'guilt' in itself cannot always be taken as evidence of opposition to Nazi anti-Semitism. Moreover, the level or intensity of opposition cannot simply be deduced from the harshness of the regime's response, as Gordon would have it. For example, a newspaper vendor mentioned by Gordon who was imprisoned in 1934 got into trouble, not for selling newspapers to Jews as she suggests (such activities were not illegal at the time), but because by chance one edition of the Warsaw paper he distributed weekly carried a story, subsequently brought to the attention of the authorities, that claimed Hitler had Jewish grandparents. In another case mentioned by Gordon, astonishingly stringent punishments were imposed in 1936 on a 'Catholic civil servant' who was 'imprisoned for a year and a half and fined 10,000 Reichmark for having sexual relations with a Jewess and aiding Jews in financial matters'. The punishment was in fact meted out to this person and he indeed had had such an affair. However, the Gestapo was interested in his activity principally in his capacity as a customs official, and the crime for which he was charged and punished was aiding and abetting the smuggling of very large sums of money into Holland.[14] These cases suggest that the 'friendships' between Jews and non-Jews cannot simply be construed as evidence of opposition to Nazi anti-Semitism.

The files of the Düsseldorf Gestapo are not qualitatively different from those in Würzburg; thus, a careful reading of the dossiers in Würzburg should shed some light on what one might reasonably expect to find in the Düsseldorf files. In the Würzburg dossiers there are 91 cases in which there was some suspicion of 'behaviour friendly to the Jews'; 41 of these must be considered

---

Gestapo. See HStA D: Gestapo 37661: the 'Catholic salesman' (mentioned in Gordon, p. 235) was born in Bielefeld and lived in Berlin, but was caught helping a Jew, also from Berlin, at the border-crossing in Kleve. See also HStA D: Gestapo 46,339 for another example (Gordon, p. 236 n. 83). For initial sceptical responses to this treatment of the sources see the review by Jill Stephenson in *History*, 71 (1986), 338–9; also George Steiner, 'Enormities beyond Measure', *Times Literary Supplement* (13 July 1984), 793.

[13] Gordon, 212–13, says that 15% of all the accused (67 persons: p. 244) ended up in prison or in a concentration camp, and she labels them as 'high-level' opponents; the remaining 85% are termed either 'middle-' or 'low-level'. The last category (82 persons) had a brush with the Gestapo but virtually nothing happened to them. Many of these people may simply have been accused without much basis, and some were probably accused falsely. In view of how readily one could be denounced when the accusation involved race issues, and how widespread were the excesses routinely committed by the Gestapo, it is reasonable to conclude that in all likelihood many had also been charged without foundation in that group termed by Gordon 'middle-level' opponents, the 303 people 'who were arrested but not necessarily sentenced for concretely aiding Jews or having sexual relations with them'. (See also below, ch. 7, on 'Compliance through Pressure'.)

[14] For the 'illustrative cases' see Gordon, pp. 234, 236. The cases mentioned are in HStA D: Gestapo 21,810 and 36,150, respectively. In the latter case the Jewish woman was fined 150,000 Reichsmark.

either as patently false or without any foundation (Table 4). With regard to the 84 'race defilement' cases, 30 of the accused individuals must also be regarded as having been charged baselessly. Table 4 also illustrates the dramatic reduction in opportunities for laying charges (false and otherwise) in this area of social life after the emigration and/or deportation of the Jews. Even so, some false accusations continued after there were hardly any Jews left to be very 'friendly' with. (It was still possible, of course, to get into trouble by making an incautious remark about official policy.) The point is that on many occasions opposition to Nazi anti-Semitism was not involved.

Examples of cases from the Würzburg area involving false charges are worth exploring in order to convey a sense both of how the Gestapo operated and how ordinary people managed to adapt to the new facts of life. Walther Schuler, an ex-KPD member and worker from Ochsenfurt (born 1905), who had been in and out of Dachau since 1933, was denounced in March 1939 because of suspicion that he was visiting and discussing public affairs with some Jews in his building. After investigation the Gestapo concluded that there was nothing to the charges and that the motive for the denunciation was probably personal hatred. While Schuler got off, his Communist past had put him on the regime's list of enemies.[15]

Elise Pfister, a waitress in Würzburg, reported her employer in October 1938 because he allegedly said that Jews were welcome in his establishment so long as the other guests were not bothered. This turned out to be a false accusation—Pfister simply wanted to leave the firm—and the Gestapo concluded the case by saying that information from the woman 'should be treated with caution in the future'.[16] Leaving a position with a firm to better oneself without having to pay a penalty could be facilitated in this way, as other cases at the time also make clear.[17]

In October 1939 a forty-one-year-old Würzburg landlady, Amalie Zettel, was denounced as a 'friend to the Jews' by one of her tenants. While Zettel had purchased her house from an earlier Jewish owner, the transaction had been conducted according to the 'Aryanization' procedures, as investigation revealed. It was just such a denunciation that Göring had said should be stopped, and the Gestapo concluded its report on the matter as follows: 'The denouncer, Franzl Stock, is, according to reliable information, a tenant who, because of his anti-social behaviour in relation to the inhabitants of the house, has repeatedly given cause for complaints. After he had to be asked repeatedly for his monthly rent, he himself decided to lodge the allegation

---

[15] StA W: Gestapo 13701.
[16] Ibid. 17369.
[17] Cf. ibid. 11875. A dissatisfied woman clerk who was dismissed denounced her employer in 1939 for favouring Jewish customers; he was a Party member.

about the house-owner.' There was no basis whatsoever to Stock's charges, and Zettel in turn opened proceedings against him. [18]

On 29 June 1939 a Schweinfurt woman, Eva Trabold, considered to be of doubtful moral habits, was denounced to the gendarmerie station in König because one day, while 'taking the cure', she let it be known that she had had relations with two Jews, one old and one young, who kept her in money. After a good deal of secretive surveillance she was brought in for interrogation. It then appeared that Trabold had once said, 'I live from the capital of my Jewish ex-friends!' She insisted that this was meant as a joke; the police concluded that the charge could not be proved. [19]

In March 1936 another woman, suspected of being a prostitute, was accused of receiving too many men and of damaging the Nazi movement, since some of them were members of the SA and SS. The troubled denouncer went with the information via the Blockleiter and Ortsgruppe Würzburg South to the Party. The word was that members of the SS were in the apartment of a woman who as a prostitute was probably not particular as to the ethnic identity of her clients. When the neighbours and the woman were interrogated, the only connection with Jews turned out to be a rumour to the effect that before 1933 she had slept with some, but nothing turned up for the period after 1933. [20]

Tips from official or semi-official bodies of Party and state passed on to the Gestapo were hardly less flawed than those volunteered by ordinary citizens. The SD post in Schweinfurt asked the Würzburg Gestapo in September 1940 to investigate a charge that a Jewish man, Heinrich Kahn, was making a large number of purchases in town, and there was a rumour that he was in the company of a non-Jewish female. As it happened, Kahn had been given special permission to do the shopping, and the woman in question was blonde but, it happened, Jewish. [21] In November 1941 the same office wanted another rumour checked, this one pertaining to Jews in nearby Theilheim. That case was dropped after the mayor there said he was getting fed up checking out such complaints when nothing of a criminal nature ever turned up. [22] The DAF in Würzburg 'was informed' that there might be 'race defilement' involving one Julius Frank, and on 29 May 1936 asked the Gestapo to investigate. Some of those living in the neighbourhood of the elderly and crippled Herr Frank's business who had a view into his flat were interrogated, but none thought there could possibly be anything more to the charge than that someone was seeking revenge; it was also possible that someone had seen various women being entertained in the sublet apartment next door to

---

[18] StA W: Gestapo 5988.
[19] Ibid. 1488.
[20] Ibid. 2040.
[21] Ibid. 11079.
[22] Ibid. 11189.

Frank's. Young Lorenz Fredl, a non-Jew, had lived there for a time. (Friedl had been named in the original complaint as under suspicion of being accessory to 'race defilement'.) The police concluded that nothing further should be done concerning the matter.[23]

Erna Schmeltzer, aged 27, 'appeared voluntarily' at Würzburg's Gestapo post on 14 May 1941 to report that on a works outing in the rural area near the forest-house Gutenberg she noticed a man of 'Jewish appearance' of about 45 to 50 years of age in the company of a younger woman (20 to 25) with medium-blonde hair, non-Jewish in appearance. She did not know either of them, but said she would be able to identify them; she provided a detailed description of the couple, especially what they were wearing. The denouncer worked as a seamstress in the Franz Kreisel uniform factory, and perhaps some of the patriotism had rubbed off. In any case, she managed to identify the man from police pictures. Brought to Gestapo headquarters he turned out to be Jewish, but so was the woman in his company that day.[24]

Schmeltzer's act *might* have had something to do with 'idealism', but, as the preceding chapter has shown, numerous denunciations took place to gain satisfaction in some personal matter, and some were able to connect their intended victims with suspicions about social or sexual relations with Jews. Denouncers were well advised to protect themselves from the wrath of the police by ensuring that there was some plausibility to the charge. Just after the outbreak of hostilities, on 9 September 1939, the Gestapo in Würzburg was alerted by neighbours that 17-year-old Anna Reising, of Würzburg, was having visits from a 'suspicious man'. The Reising house was thereupon placed under surveillance. The family and neighbours were subsequently brought in, although it turned out that the man was neither particularly suspicious nor Jewish, but Anna's boyfriend. She explained that the whole uproar was really about a toilet:

As I have already mentioned, with those people [the denouncers] there is always an argument, and in fact only because of the matter of the toilet. Fourteen of us had to use one toilet, while only two of them used another. We finally managed to get it established that their toilet was to be used by us and other parties in the house, and since that time hatred has existed. We have not spoken to these people for 10 years.[25]

Correspondence from the Gestapo elsewhere in Germany makes it clear that laying false charges, even concerning the serious crime of 'race defilement', was not uncommon. A letter of 12 July 1937 from the Gestapo in Neustadt a.d. Weinstrasse to all police authorities of the Palatinate indicates that the police were sometimes too quick to act. The letter explained that

---

[23] Ibid. 8841. The letter begins: 'As we are informed' ('Wie mitgeteilt wird').

[24] Ibid. 14893.

[25] Ibid. 14940. Within months the family was again baselessly denounced for 'friendship to the Jews' by the same family, and the charge was investigated.

because the charge of 'race defilement' was itself so serious it could have 'lifelong' consequences for the persons involved; under the circumstances, especially as baseless accusations were being filed on occasion, it was important for local officers to be very conscious 'of the weight of their responsibility in the investigation of these latter cases'; they should keep firmly in view the 'extreme responsibility they held in their hands in regard to the happiness and future of German women and girls'.[26] A report of the Karlsruhe Gestapo for April/May 1938 noted that of the two charges of 'race defilement' it had just handled, one was false and the other a 'baseless suspicion of a sick and jealous married woman'.[27]

There were also false and frivolous charges in those files of the Düsseldorf Gestapo treated by Gordon as pertaining to 'opponents'. One instance is a case from mid-1935, a tragic example of a false charge of 'race defilement', included in Gordon's sample of 452 cases. A 36-year-old Catholic man from Odenkirchen, who was already separated from his wife, in the summer of 1935, apparently wanted to be free of her for good. He described himself as a 'merchant' (*Kaufmann*), but the Gestapo remarked in the file that he 'had a bad reputation and 'was generally considered a swindler'. The man accused his estranged wife and a Jewish man of having a sexual relationship; though this was not actually a crime until later (after the Party rally in September), it was a serious accusation well before. The Jew was taken into custody, whereupon he committed suicide. An investigation of the affair established 'no basis [for the allegation] since the national rising', that is, since Hitler's appointment in 1933, and the Gestapo released the woman from 'protective custody'. Her husband, however, was promptly placed under arrest (on 17 August 1935) 'for having caused the arrest of his wife and the Jew ... by way of false accusations'.[28]

Gordon is well aware that tip-offs to the police were occasioned by numerous motives; denouncers took advantage of anti-Semitism to advance their careers, and 'could run the entire gamut from real Jew-haters to revenge-seekers, opportunists, and even rejected lovers'.[29] If these were the kinds of people who denounced suspects in Düsseldorf because of possible acts of 'race defilement' or for 'friendship to the Jews', it is unlikely that they would restrict themselves only to bona-fide charges. Revenge-seekers and opportunists, let alone rejected lovers or vindictive spouses, are rarely quite so level-headed or scrupulous. Nor does Gordon deny that some people used the most outlandish charges 'to take their rivals out of circulation'.[30] It is clear that there were

[26] LA Speyer: Polizeibehörden/H77, 10.

[27] Schadt, 270. Frequently there were 'preventative denunciations': that is, people sought to exculpate themselves from a complaint they believed would soon be laid against them by laying charges of their own. See e.g. StA W: Gestapo 11294.

[28] HStA D: Gestapo 65053.

[29] Gordon, 241.

[30] Ibid.

some people who, in order to take advantage of the novel situation after 1933, were not above 'establishing a rival's guilt by referring to Jewish association in the past'.[31]

At any rate, not everyone in a Gestapo dossier, nor even everyone brought to court because of alleged 'political' criminality of some kind or another, was guilty, a fact attested by a number of sources, especially the post-war trials, where some of the more serious false denouncers were brought to justice. One study of 'race defilement' charges that managed to reach the courts in Hamburg, Cologne, and Frankfurt shows that while 522 were found guilty, 58 were declared innocent of the charges—slightly over 10 per cent.[32] The high percentages of false and baseless charges in the files—most of which did not come to court—is not surprising in view of the large number of amateur 'helpers' on the trail of 'crime', the susceptibility of the laws to misuse, and the willingness of the Gestapo and other authorities to follow up the tips.

3. NON-COMPLIANCE WITH NAZI ANTI-SEMITISM IN THE WÜRZBURG CASE-FILES

As a result of the vigilance of volunteer denouncers, official and semi-official snoopers, the extensive information-gathering and police network, the many Party operatives, and so on, it is clear that in Nazi Germany the 'more or less protected enclaves' that are the 'one prerequisite' for expressions of disobedience were gradually eliminated.[33] In spite of the odds, some non-compliance with Nazi anti-Semitism shows up in muted form in the Gestapo documents. In fact, the Gestapo files may well underestimate the degree of rejection of Nazi anti-Semitism for the obvious reason that a person would be foolhardy to speak openly about reservations he or she might have on that score when brought in for interrogation. All Jews and non-Jews did not simply give in to the inevitable and conform to official anti-Semitism.

The Jews had been a part of German social, cultural, economic, and political life for many centuries, and all social relations could hardly be eliminated overnight. In Lower Franconia and elsewhere, workers employed in Jewish firms or peasants enjoying established economic ties with the Jews only reluctantly dissolved those links, despite official and semi-official pressure; restraining customers from shopping in Jewish retail stores was not as simple or uncomplicated as had been thought.[34]

---

[31] Grunberger, 149.

[32] Robinsohn, 78. As many as 15.6% of all those brought to trial in Frankfurt were acquitted.

[33] Moore, *Disobedience*, 482.

[34] StA W: NSDAP/GL XII/1. The workers in the 29 cigar factories in Kahlgrund (employing 2,206 women and 242 men) were drawn from a 'poor and over-populated' area where the Jewish-owned factories played an important economic role. A local gendarme reported in Oct. 1935 that they 'appreciated their employer' and could not care less whether he was 'Aryan or Jew'.

But personal or sexual relationships across the ethnic boundary were immediately placed under the greatest pressure, since it represented the vital area in which the dreaded 'racial mixing' occurred, claimed by Hitler's *Mein Kampf* to be the single most important cause for the fall of civilizations. Jewish men caught violating the Nuremberg Laws were to be tried for 'an attack on German blood', while 'German' men were brought to court for 'treason against their own blood'. Though Hitler himself insisted initially that women (Jewish or not) were not subject to prosecution, Heydrich issued a secret order to the Gestapo on 12 June 1937 to take Jewish women involved in such relationships into custody, as also similarly involved non-Jewish women who had Jewish relatives or otherwise undesirable political views.[35]

'Race defilement' was suspected in the relationship between Oskar Spahn, a distinguished Jewish medical doctor in Würzburg, and Elisabeth Speiss, a non-Jewish woman who had begun to work for him as secretary-receptionist in 1924, aged 21. Dr Spahn's wife had died three years earlier. He was (it seems) much older than Speiss, but in time he became attached to her and admitted later to the Gestapo that he had wanted to marry her before the 'seizure of power' in 1933, but had not done so because of the strenuous objections of her relatives. She continued, however, to work for him even beyond 1933, when their behaviour turned from being merely undesirable in the eyes of her relatives into being potentially 'criminal'.

In time the regime's anti-Semitism, which was applied to one group or branch of Jewish professionals after another, also hit the medical doctors. On 30 September 1938 Dr Spahn was forced to close his practice, but his secretary, Speiss, stayed on to administer his property. Her brother was by then the (first) state attorney at the Bamberg Special Court, probably also a Party member, and was concerned about the persistence of the relationship between his sister and the doctor. He would have been the man who actually pressed the charges of race defilement against people in just such a 'criminal' union as existed between his sister and Dr Spahn. In response to his written request for Gestapo 'support', secret police headquarters in Würzburg put pressure on his sister to leave Dr Spahn's service, and began investigation of the relationship in search of evidence of 'race defilement'. This was a harassment tactic as much as an effort to uncover a 'crime'. The pressure of family and state proved more than Speiss could take, and on 8 March 1940 she finally resigned her job.

Little is said about Dr Spahn in the file—not even his age is given—nor what eventually happened to him or to Speiss. Nothing ever turned up to substantiate the suspicion of 'race defilement'. It is reasonably clear that a close relationship had existed. The Gestapo report comments that Speiss 'had

[35] See Hermann Graml, 'Die Behandlung der Anfällen von sogenanter Rassenschande Beteiligten "Deutschblütigen" Personen', *Gutachten des Instituts für Zeitgeschichte*, i (Stuttgart, 1958), 72ff.; Robert H. Proctor, *Racial Hygiene: Medicine under the Nazis* (Cambridge, Mass., 1988), 133–4.

been so much under the influence' of Dr Spahn, 'that she suffered an attack of hysteria on the occasion of the forced separation'. She certainly showed a good deal of civil courage and non-conformity with Nazi teachings. At the same time, given that they were in the public eye—he a known Jewish doctor, she his receptionist—they also had to watch their every move lest they fell victim to a denouncer, who might simply be a passer-by in the street, a patient in the office, the cleaning person, or the caretaker. That they were never denounced may reflect the scrupulousness with which they controlled their relationship.[36]

Non-conformity with Nazi anti-Semitism could be witnessed in other social spheres, such as the workplace. Employers have taken advantage of their employees for centuries in order to obtain sexual favours. That did not stop with the Nazi 'seizure of power'. However, as the next chapter makes clear, when there was even a hint that a Jewish employer was acting in this way, the Gestapo was quick to pounce. Trouble was also in store for non-Jewish German employers who developed emotional attachments to a (female) Jewish worker. On 26 April 1937 the Nazi Welfare Association (NSV) in Grombühl reported that Heinrich Schelling (born 1899) was having an affair with Luzie Weigert (born 1896, divorced, with a grown daughter), a Jewish woman who worked as a clerk in his radio retail business. The complaint made its way to the Kreisleitung of the NSDAP in Würzburg, which asked the Gestapo to investigate. (Here, incidentally, was yet another example of the role of the NSDAP and affiliated organizations in the police network.) The tip-off ultimately brought to light the testimony of factory-owner Albert Böttling (born 1875), a neighbour, who over many years had observed (and 'often heard, through the wall') the couple arguing and even hitting one another. He was convinced that they were intimate. Böttling also spoke of the help Weigert had given Schelling when the man was down on his luck in the years between 1928 and 1932. He suggested that the Gestapo also call on the ordinary policeman ('Hauptwachtmeister') Leimeister, who happened to be a neighbour of Luzie Weigert and could see into her bedroom.

Ordered to Gestapo headquarters in mid-1937, Schelling insisted that he had had no 'race defilement' relations with Weigert. In fact, he said that a bladder infection made sexual intercourse impossible for him. The infection was attested to by a doctor, 'race defilement' charges were dropped, and in the short run Weigert continued in Schelling's employ. For her part, Weigert maintained that she was not Jewish, and in due course appealed to the authority of last resort, the Reich Hereditary Office (Reichssippenamt).[37] That plea was rejected, but in view of the labour shortages of the time she was allowed to carry on, under condition that she stay out of the showroom of

---

[36] StA W: Gestapo 14779.
[37] See Horst Seidler and Andreas Rett, *Das Reichssippenamt entscheidet: Rassenbiologie im Nationalsozialismus* (Vienna, 1982), 59ff.

the business. Not surprisingly, Weigert's restricted movement in the small firm proved impossible, and, when spotted by a vigilant observer, the two were once again reported to the Gestapo. This cost Weigert two weeks in police custody and the removal of permission to work for Schelling. He escaped punishment when called up to the army. Schelling wrote letters on Weigert's behalf to Würzburg's police director, but these were received as indicative of the man's 'wrong-headed' attitude. One letter closes with the remark that 'while I formally did not behave entirely properly, that cannot be a justification for the innocent to suffer'. In April 1942 Weigert was 'evacuated' to the east to a fate unknown. These were two people whose relationship went back more than fifteen years, beginning well before 1933. Enforcing racial policy in such cases would have been impossible without the information brought forward by sources outside the Gestapo, including that offered by next-door neighbours.[38]

Some less glaring non-compliance with the letter of the law was of a symbolic kind. In mid-September 1939 Wilhelm Roth, a soldier leaving Theinfeld for the army, was denounced because he shook the hand of a Jewish man known to him. As the coded language of the day put it, 'the behaviour of Roth raised general anger in Theinfeld' and the matter was reported to the gendarme in nearby Kleinwenkheim. Passed on to the Gestapo, the matter was not pursued because Roth's troop was leaving for action.[39] An old kapellmeister from Nuremberg, Markus Sprattler, turned up in the files for having played a composition by Mendelssohn, using a false name for the composer. It was forbidden to play such 'Jewish music'. The performance was denounced in a letter of 19 September 1940 to the *Stürmer*, and passed on to the police for investigation. The 66-year-old Sprattler could not be brought in for questioning as he had joined an artist troup with the army.[40] Other cases also suggest that the Gestapo dutifully read the *Stürmer* and followed up letters to the editor, signed or not, as bona-fide denunciations.

Retired train-engineer Ernst Schmidt moved from Berlin to rural Bavaria, where he lived in Kleinlangheim; he was reported to the *Stürmer* in October 1937 because he had had social contacts with a Jewish woman and dined with her in a restaurant. Asked by the local mayor, a police official, about the report, Schmidt allegedly said, 'They can't take my pension away from me!' The police report also noted that Herr Schmidt continued to greet everyone with 'God be praised!' instead of 'Heil Hitler!'—his political views 'could well be imagined already from that'. Schmidt replied, 'I learnt in school how to greet people, and that's why I do it.'[41]

A sister (born 1878) of the distinguished Würzburg Bishop Matthias Ehren-

---

[38] StA W: Gestapo 12345.
[39] Ibid. 4139.
[40] Ibid. 11455.
[41] Ibid. 12675.

fried had learnt in November 1940 that an elderly Jewish woman, a former neighbour from Eichstätt, was sick, and therefore paid a visit, bringing some eggs as a present. To the Gestapo, informed by persons unknown, this was a serious matter, and a warning was issued.[42] That the anti-Semitism of the regime would be enforced with such scrupulousness was already well known by this date, but in the case of such 'distinguished' people knowledge of the incident would obviously spread in a Catholic city like Würzburg; the police action must have underlined their determination to enforce the rules. Other political opponents of Nazism, such as members of the SPD, were especially easy to keep track of with the help of co-operation from the population at large, and if they had anything to do with the Jews—some of whom were old acquaintances in the SPD—they were particularly vulnerable. In spite of the peril, however, at least some contacts seem to have been maintained.[43]

Georg Kron, a fanatically anti-Semitic Nazi in Bad Neustadt, tried, in the course of the 'action' in that town during the 'night of broken glass', to square matters with Jolana Krause (born 1879), a woman known locally as a 'friend to the Jews'. His search of Krause's apartment for hidden Jews was unsuccessful. She subsequently had him charged with breaking and entering.[44] That was a symbolic gesture, though a courageous one. The dentist Dr Friedrich Ilbert, from Urspringen, got into very serious trouble in May 1941 when he and a Jewish friend he had known since 1924 were denounced by an unknown person; apparently some 'suspicious' pictures were being taken. Dr Ilbert said he had merely greeted his old friend in the street, and that their friendship was reduced to such formalities. However, a camera was confiscated, and when pictures were developed which showed there was a 'crime' involved (perhaps homosexuality) he was sent to Dachau, initially for four months.[45]

When the transports began rolling to the east, civilians could not at first be sure of the destinations or fate of those on them. But while even people directly affected, Jews and those close to them, did not know the details, most people could hardly be unaware that the Jews sent east had a very uncertain future. Much of the collecting and shipping of Jews took place in the public view. Even if 'ordinary' citizens ignored what, in any case, they could do little about, some went the other way and continued to offer information and unsolicited co-operation to the Gestapo, which had the effect of delivering some defenceless Jews over to what they knew was a thoroughly anti-Semitic regime. At the very moment when the deportations were under way from Lower Franconia, the following case was brought to light.

It was reported to the ordinary police under the authority of the Mayor of

[42] Ibid. 6146.
[43] See e.g. ibid. 7457.
[44] Ibid. 2839.
[45] Ibid. 2159.

Miltenberg on 23 November 1941 that Elizabeth Mannheimer, a Jewish woman (born 1875), had bought schnapps in the store of the merchant Ludwig Hell (born 1878); these two people had known each other for nearly fifty years. Frau Helene Pfaff, 63-year-old mother of Maria Pfaff, had purchased schnapps in the same store in the morning, but in the afternoon wanted more—it was claimed that the additional drink was going to be sent to a son who was in the east fighting Soviet armies. Merchant Hell told Frau Pfaff's daughter, who went to pick up the schnapps, that he could sell her no more at the moment because her family had already made one purchase of 'goods in short supply' that day; at that point he turned to his old Jewish customer and sold her some schnapps. (Because there were so few Jews left in town—a mere twelve in all—there were no specific times set aside for their shopping, as happened elsewhere.) At a preliminary hearing by Ober-wachtmeister Flick, Hell denied that he was a 'friend to the Jews'. He (rightly) claimed that it was not forbidden to sell these goods to Jews, and furthermore, given the shortages, he had merely wanted to distribute what was available as fairly as possible. After Hell angrily left the police station, Flick wrote a damning report, in which, among other things, he observed that 'while on all fronts our brave soldiers are protecting the home from the greatest dangers, and many of these brave ones are being cut down in the cruellest ways by bloodthirsty Jewish creatures', merchant Hell, branded by the policeman as a 'slave of the Jews' (*Judenknecht*), dared to refuse to sell a drop of warming schnapps to the mother of a German soldier, but gave it instead to Frau Mannheimer, whose son 'sits in London and defames the Fatherland'. That report was sent to the magistrate in Miltenberg, who forwarded it to the Gestapo in Würzburg. On 19 December 1941 they brought in merchant Hell for questioning. His line of defence was that he was not informed that the second purchase of schnapps was to be sent to a soldier in the field. He was warned by Gramowski of the Gestapo not to sell 'goods in short supply' to Jews in the future.

Frau Mannheimer, who was ill, was not questioned until 4 March 1942, when something even more serious was revealed. It turned out that she had made a gift of her house to her former servant Elina Seuss (born 1890). While Frau Mannheimer spent each night in the local Jewish old-age home (and had done so since January 1941), during the day she went back to her former house, where Seuss cooked and looked after her (as she had done for some thirty-four years). Though the gift of the house took place legally and was registered, the Gestapo would not tolerate Seuss working as a servant, put her in gaol for a couple of weeks (7 to 21 March), and gave her a warning. Mannheimer was subsequently confined to the old-age home, while her lifelong servant was detailed for work in agriculture, for which she had neither experience nor, in all probability, much strength.[46]

[46] StA W: Gestapo 14341.

This was a case that began with a denunciation from people who, it seems, were simply after an excessive share of schnapps for themselves. The local gendarme played the role of petty tyrant and Nazi enforcer. Certainly, merchant Hell's courage was put to the test; he swore later to the Gestapo that since the 'events' he had refused to sell anything to the Jews 'because I do not want to have any further unpleasantness'.

The dire consequences which followed were out of all proportion to the pettiness of the complaint. However, once 'opponents' such as the Jews were involved in any case, it ceased to be trivial. The case also shows how racial policy was enforced all the way down the line. The action which formed the basis of the indictment in the first instance—selling schnapps to Jews—had not even found its way into a law or regulation at this time. Two long-term relationships with Frau Mannheimer were broken off, and no doubt the word spread rapidly through the small town. The Pfaff family, 'ordinary' citizens, helped make possible the policing of the spirit of Nazi racism. The whole case took place when Jews were much in need of support—for it was at this time that the deportations were under way. Once the matter was brought to police attention, the network moved into relentless action, with the Gestapo in far-off Würzburg providing the ultimate sanction. While merchant Hell might storm angrily out of the Miltenberg police station, he would not conduct himself thus in the Würzburg Gestapo post.

Numerous other Germans in the employ of Jews or in some kind of business contact with them had brushes with the Gestapo when they persisted in these relations or expressed the mildest kinds of solidarity with the persecuted, such as visiting them or offering some assistance. In November 1941 Mathilde Braun (born 1913) visited Selma Goldstein (born 1878) to whom she had been a servant for ten years, at the old-age home for Jewish people. The servant was spotted in the company of three women in front of the building by the notorious Gestapo official Michael Völkl, who was there by chance on another matter (in all likelihood arranging the deportations of Jews). Braun stood out as the only one not wearing a yellow star. She admitted under questioning that it was known to her 'that that sort of socializing with Jews was forbidden' but that she had felt sorry for her former employer. Braun ended up by spending three weeks in gaol until the matter was cleared up. In September 1942 Frau Goldstein was sent to the Theresienstadt concentration camp.[47]

In January 1942 the Würzburg Kreisleitung of the NSDAP wrote to the Gestapo to say that 'it had been observed' that German 'racial comrade' Elenore Lohmann was seen daily on visits to the home of a Jewish woman, Sarah Stern, and 'because the suspicion exists that Lohmann is providing the Jewish resident with food' a request was made to undertake 'the necessary'

---

[47] Ibid. 12070. Cf. ibid. 16710, from Urspringen (early 1940).

action. Stern (born 1877), had employed Lohmann (about 65 years of age) as housekeeper until 1940; they had known each other for 'about twenty to twenty-five years'. Lohmann and her married daughter, who could not afford to give very much, had on occasions done a kindness. For example, when Stern's son was 'evacuated' in November 1941, he was brought a cooked chicken, for which no money was taken. In the future, the Gestapo made clear, *all* relations between Jews and non-Jews ('Aryans') were to cease, as these were legally 'forbidden'.[48] Here the small comfort provided by an old employee of very humble circumstances was treated by the Gestapo and NSDAP as an extremely serious offence. The case shows just how determined some people were to implement the letter of the law, and, moreover, how such enforcement was dependent on a tip-off about the 'criminal' deeds.[49]

Some merchants caught in the act tried to come up with *ad hoc* justifications for selling goods to Jews. Thus, a report from Kitzingen stated that in mid-1941 a fish-merchant accused of being a 'friend to the Jews' claimed that he was overpricing the fish he sold them. He may well have invented this part of the story for his own protection.[50]

Gestapo files sometimes came into existence when someone noticed 'suspicious mail', whereupon the Gestapo might order a 'postal surveillance'. Needless to say, a careless phrase from a Jewish person who had already emigrated could lead to real trouble.[51] Indeed, post from emigrated Jews seems to have been checked regularly, not by the Gestapo but by the post office, and all were keen to sniff out any deviations.[52] One Würzburg postman was himself denounced in April 1936 for subletting part of his four-room apartment to a Jew *before* 1935.[53] Two men in the wine business, one of them Jewish, who had known each other since 1900 got into trouble in March 1943 when a house-search in Düsseldorf led to the discovery that the German merchant had been asked to send wine to his Jewish colleague's ex-wife. The deed was traced to Würzburg, where the elderly wine-dealer (born 1887) 'had it pointed out to him that every relation with Jews is forbidden'.[54]

When it came to members of the NSDAP, local authorities were determined to enforce Nazi teachings on race as far as possible. Any non-conformity was treated as a grave offence and could result in expulsion from the Party. A 41-year-old farmer from Unteralthertheim who played cards with some Jews was thrown out of the NSDAP in late February 1936.[55] A merchant and Party member, Adolf Baumann, who moved to the town of Willmars towards the

[48] StA W: Gestapo 3705.
[49] See e.g. ibid. 4767, which resulted in a Jewish-owned business being taken over.
[50] Ibid. 6113.
[51] Ibid. 17933.
[52] Ibid. 1607.
[53] Ibid. 17625.
[54] Ibid. Cf. HStAD: Gestapo 7535.
[55] StA W: Gestapo 661.

end of 1937, began almost immediately to have social contacts with local Jewish people. The cell-leader reported that, to no avail, he had reminded Baumann of his duties as a Party member. Baumann's wife, who visited Jewish neighbours, was thrown out of the Nazi women's organization (NS Frauenschaft). Summoned before the cell-leader, the couple were anything but willing to follow their leader's commands. Eventually, in October 1938, some windows were broken in Baumann's store: understandable, said the gendarme's report to the Gestapo, given behaviour which had 'raised a strong anger in the population'. This coded expression signified that the local NSDAP and SA had probably thrown the stones. By 30 August 1939 the man had successfully been kicked out of the Party, which ended the affair for the time being.[56]

These and similar cases of non-compliance with the Nazi stance on isolating the Jews socially and economically, suggest an official paranoid suspicion that, despite all the regime's efforts, the Jews' social and economic privileges persisted. Munich's Gestapo headquarters alerted all branches in Bavaria on 19 November 1936 to watch out for the 'camouflage of Jewish businesses': behind the front of ownership by an old employee, friend, or acquaintance, the Jewish owner might still be continuing as before. Cases were cited where non-Jewish merchants and customers co-operated in the 'camouflage', such as by mailing wares under their name instead of that of the Jewish merchant, and so on.[57] Local authorities out in the provinces seemed fanatical in their efforts to make sure that Jews were not carrying on under some guise or other, and in their zeal do not seem to have required much urging from Berlin or anywhere else. Their efforts could not have succeeded without the co-operation of at least some of the population, and they were definitely assisted by denunciations from people who were moved as much by personal motives as by anti-Semitism.[58]

4. REJECTION OF AND RESISTANCE TO NAZI ANTI-SEMITISM

Care must be taken not to underestimate the number of people who at one point or another may have offered aid and comfort to the Jews. If they were never caught, hence never turned over to the Gestapo, there would be no official record of their activities. In addition, most of the files of those who were caught were destroyed. There is oral testimony, but this kind of documentation is limited, not least because some of the people who provided

[56] Ibid. 2838: cf. ibid. 14843, the case of a factory-owner shut out of the NSDAP in July 1935; and ibid. 3459 (another man in June 1936).

[57] StA W: NSDAP/GL/XII/1 contains relevant correspondence; cf. StA M: NSDAP 437 (GL letter of 17 Nov. 1938).

[58] For various kinds of denunciations of relations with Jews see e.g. StA M: NSDAP 358 (three separate ones from Laufen in 1937: 19 May, 24 June, 6 Dec.; see also ibid. 572 and 578.

assistance would have perished along with those whom they had helped. The combination of these factors means that unknown numbers of stories of resistance to the persecution of the Jews have been lost to history. What is known from survivors is that any Jews who went underground could not have lasted for long without the help of non-Jews.[59] In the Würzburg Gestapo materials one particularly courageous case has come to light, and is worth reviewing, not only because it shows that some people rejected Nazi anti-Semitism and sought to do something about it, but also because it suggests something about the possibilities and limitations of opposition in the dictatorship.

Ilse Sonja Totzke was born in 1913 in Strasburg, then capital of imperial Germany's conquered province of Alsace. When Germany lost the war this area came under the control of France, and her father Ernst, a German citizen (born in Prussia) and music conductor, was forced to leave; young Ilse went with him, first to Mannheim and later to Ludwigshafen, where he subsequently opened his own music school. Ilse's wealthy mother joined them subsequently, but she died in 1921. Although Ilse was supposed to inherit money from her mother's estate, her father, who had remarried in 1924, refused to give up the money; and some time between 1929 and 1931, while at a boarding school in Bamberg, she won a court case against him. On 17 November 1935, as a music student in Würzburg, she was involved in a serious motor-cycle accident in which she suffered a fractured skull, and was hospitalized in Würzburg's Juliusspital until Christmas. In her first interrogation by the Gestapo, on 5 September 1941, she said that after the accident, recurring, week-long headaches had prevented her from finishing her music studies, begun in 1932. Though in 1934, at the age of 21, she had inherited a considerable sum of money (some 42,000 marks), her inability to take up regular employment, the costs of medical care, and her contribution to her stepsisters' schooling had eaten away at her inheritance, so that by 1941 most of it was spent.

Alone and without regular employment, but yet with some means of support, Totzke had stood out from her neighbours, and her suspicious behaviour was subject to repeated, unsolicited denunciations. In her first interrogation she said that she did not particularly care from whom she rented her flat, nor who else lived in the house; she had often sublet from Jewish families, and had been acquainted with a number of Jewish women in Würzburg. For example, she had visits from a Jewish woman and her family whom she had met in 1934–5. She had also socialized with other Jewish women. In the file there is no evidence that she had any association with Jewish men. Had she befriended males, she would have run the risk of being charged with the very serious crime of 'race defilement', an allegation

---

[59] Deutschkron, 109 ff.; Behrend-Rosenfeld, 202 ff.

that could not be brought against the women Ilse befriended.

Totzke's brushes with the Würzburg Gestapo began in 1936, when, for reasons that are not made clear in the file, her letters were placed under surveillance. In all likelihood this began when a neighbour tipped off the Gestapo that something suspicious was afoot. On 3 April 1939 a neighbour of Totzke's (she lived somewhat on the outskirts of Würzburg), Studienrat Dr Ludwig Kneisel, attached to the local university, made a personal appearance at Gestapo headquarters to report a conversation he had had with a neighbour who mentioned her 'suspicious behaviour'. Dr Kneisel said that he 'felt bound by his duty as a reserve officer' to inform the Gestapo, which could contact additional (named) persons for further information. (The same man wrote to the police again in mid-1940 to report that Totzke had been seen near troop movements.) The Gestapo questioned neighbours about Totzke, and, though some had a number of potentially damaging things to say, there was little on which to base a case. One neighbour was specifically asked to keep watch and to telephone the Gestapo if anything turned up.

On 29 July 1940 yet another denouncer appeared at Gestapo headquarters, this time a 22-year-old clerical worker, Gertrud Weiss, who reported that on the numerous occasions on which she and Totzke had spoken to each other Totzke had never used the 'Heil Hitler!' greeting. (As is clear from numerous other files, failure to give this 'German greeting' was taken to indicate reservations about Hitler's Germany, and could be used as evidence of political views.) Weiss said that Totzke seemed always anti-German, pro-French, and sympathetic towards the Jews—and, moreover, claimed to know a lot about armies and such things. While she apparently had no job, she had plenty of money; she stayed home all day, did little shopping, went out at dusk, and returned only at dawn. (The Weiss family's shepherd dog, it was alleged, always barked upon Totzke's return!) Weiss also said that Totzke occasionally had a woman visitor (about 36 years old) who 'looked Jewish'.

All of the above denunciations could be reduced to one or two points. Totzke did not fit into the pattern of the neighbourhood, and had no regular job or family; she was unconventional, did not show any zeal for the Nazi regime, and was reluctant to accept the official line on Jews, the French, or much else. She thus earned the continuing attention of her neighbours, who kept trying to pin something on her. Early in 1941 she was once more denounced, this time by an anonymous letter from 'a close neighbour', who alleged that Totzke visited a young Jewish woman. The note is full of spelling and grammatical errors, but, instructively, ends by saying that 'every German can and must know the laws; only for Miss T. they seem not to exist'.

For whatever reason, the Gestapo waited until August 1941 to bring Totzke in for questioning. Her signed statement is a remarkable document. Apart from some of the personal matters summarized above, Totzke was asked several pointed questions which related to the series of denunciations over the previous years. The most important matter put to her concerned the extent to which she socialized with Jews. Totzke made no effort to deny that since coming to Würzburg she had befriended three Jewish women: all are named, with their dates of birth. When the Gestapo pointed out that this kind of behaviour might show a failure to comply with the regime's official anti-Semitism, she answered:

If it is concluded on the basis of my Jewish acquaintances that I do not have much use for National Socialism, I would say that I do not concern myself with politics. The action against the Jews, however, I believe is not right. I cannot declare myself in agreement with these measures. To that I would add that I am not a Communist. Every decent person is fine with me, regardless of nationality. I chose my living-quarters outside Würzburg in order to be by myself and to hear nothing of the world. My doctor also advised me to live in the open as much as possible.

Totzke was brought in again on 28 October 1941, when she was again formally warned to avoid all Jews or face a spell in a concentration camp. By the time of her interrogation, racial persecution had been very much stepped up, not only in the East but on the home front as well (Jews in Germany had to wear the yellow star on their clothing, even when they were at home, from September 1941).

On 24 November 1941 it officially became a crime for Jews and non-Jews to show friendship for one another by appearing in public together; if they were spotted the Jewish person 'in every case' was to be sent to a concentration camp for an indefinite period, while the 'German-blooded' person who 'still did not seem to grasp the most elementary essential concepts of National Socialism' was to be placed in protective custody and, in the most serious cases, sent to a concentration camp for up to three months for 'educative purposes'.[60] Jews became the more easily identified as social outcasts after they were forced to wear the yellow star. No doubt there was an increased official (and civilian) sensitivity in late November 1941, when the deport-ations of the Jews from Würzburg and Lower Franconia began.

Not until a year later, in December 1942, was Totzke summoned to the Gestapo headquarters in Würzburg. She later said that she knew what was in store for her, precisely because she had maintained the forbidden relations. Upon receiving the summons, she left town immediately for Berlin, where she had some contacts. She renewed a friendship (from a visit there in September 1942) with a Jewish woman, Ruth Basinsky. Totzke stayed in Basinky's apartment for a few days, but for some reason returned to Würz-burg, where she managed to elude the police. By early 1943 she was back in Berlin, and learnt that Basinksy was in a 'Jewish camp' in the August Strasse. Totzke sought out Basinsky, whom she persuaded to flee with her to

[60] See the letter of 3 Nov. 1941 from Gestapo Nuremberg to the Administration in Würzburg: StA W: NSDAP/GL/MF XII/4.

Switzerland. Jews were being systematically rounded up in Berlin at this time and assigned to 'the lists' of those who were to be shipped to the east. In early 1943 no Jew in Berlin was unaware that momentous consequences were involved in the deportations, though few anticipated mass murder. Totzke later remarked to the Gestapo that 'I played with the idea of leaving Germany for a long time, because I do not feel good under the government of Adolf Hitler. More than anything else I find the Nuremberg Laws incomprehensible, and it was because of that that I maintained the relationships with the Jews I knew.'

On 12 or 13 February 1943 she left Berlin with Basinsky for Heidelberg, where they stayed for a week, each renting a different room and trying to remain as inconspicuous as possible. From there they went on to Strasburg, and, after a number of other stops, to Dürmenach—an area known to Totzke—near the Swiss border. They crossed the border illegally into Switzerland on the night of 26–7 February 1943, but were caught almost immediately by Swiss border-guards. Having been detained for several hours until dusk, when they were released at the border area, they tried their luck once again, at a different place. After a few hours of freedom in Switzerland, they were caught and this time turned over by the Swiss to the German customs and to a death sentence. From her signed statement taken down at the German border Totzke stated her primary motive:

I was not ordered by anyone to bring the Jewish person Ruth Sara Basinsky to Switzerland. I simply had pity for the latter and wanted to protect her from the evacuation. I also admit that I was the one who persuaded her to flee. For my efforts I have received compensation neither from Basinsky nor from other persons. I deny that I had previously helped Jews to leave illegally. The escape plan was totally my own, and I was supported by no one . . . I would like to mention once again that I wanted to leave Germany because I reject National Socialism. More than anything else, I cannot agree with the Nuremberg Laws. I planned to get myself interned in Switzerland. I do not want to live further in Germany under any circumstances.

Basinsky was sent back to Berlin and Totzke to Würzburg, where she arrived on 10 March 1943. The Gestapo in Würzburg placed Totzke in 'protective custody', and eventually she was sent to Ravensbrück concentration camp in accordance with the provisions of the decree of 24 September 1941, which prohibited Jews and non-Jews from appearing in public together. The Gestapo concluded the dossier by saying that

Totzke justified her activities on the basis of the fact that she rejected National Socialism, did not feel well under the government of Adolf Hitler, and also found the Nuremberg Laws incomprehensible. She wanted to find refuge for herself and to protect the Jew Basinsky from evacuation, because she felt sorry for the Jews . . . As is evident from the foregoing, Totzke is a person who rejects National Socialism and makes no bones about it. She is a woman of the Jews [*Judenweib*] and according to her revealed behaviour is beyond redemption [*nicht mehr besserungsfähig*].[61]

Ilse Totzke never returned from the concentration camp. That she could tell Gestapo officials to their face in September 1941 that she did not agree with Nazi anti-Semitism betokens great courage. The 'good neighbours' who kept turning her in on the flimsiest of grounds demonstrate the pronounced role of denunciations in the policing of Nazi Germany. Motives for the tip-offs were mixed; some justified their accusations by claiming that they made them out of a sense of 'duty'. It can hardly be doubted that there was also a great deal of envy, resentment, and pettiness.

5. CONCLUSION

Gestapo files registered a network of personal, friendly, sexual, and also business relations between Jews and non-Jews as these had developed over generations. It was precisely this network that the regime sought to dismantle as part of the effort to implement racist ideology. The enforcement of racial policy was heavily dependent upon the voluntary provision of information. Different degrees of co-operation were required to enforce different kinds of policies. Those that pertained to the private and intimate spheres were especially removed from the gaze of the police, and without denunciations from the population the 'crimes' would almost certainly have gone undetected. The process by which the Gestapo, with the help of some 'ordinary citizens', enforced policy simultaneously eliminated the 'more or less protected enclaves' required for people to gather, mobilize, and give expression to disobedience. In spite of the odds, however, some refused to comply with Nazi teaching on race, kept up contacts, and offered help even when it became life-threatening to do so. False accusations, including the exploitation of the situation for private purposes, helped to build barriers between the Jews and everyone else in the country. In this and other chapters of the book an effort has been made to remove the abstract character of the persecution and to show the significance of widespread social co-operation, collaboration, accommodation, and adjustment. Without social co-operation of various kinds, irrespective of motives, the anti-Semitic policies would have remained so many idle fantasies.

[61] For all of the above see StA W: Gestapo 16015.

7

Compliance through Pressure

BAVARIAN popular opinion concerning the 'Jewish question' towards the end of the first six years of the Nazi dictatorship was, according to a recent account, 'largely indifferent and infused with a latent anti-Jewish feeling'.[1] There is good reason to believe that the rural Catholic (and especially Lower Franconian) population as a whole was among the slowest in Bavaria—and thus in all of Germany—to embrace the official line on the Jews. On the other hand, the Jews were a fairly numerous and highly visible minority in the area, and some people were likely to take advantage of the Nazi regime's teachings to demonstrate their commitment to Nazism or merely to reap personal rewards.

In some localities across Germany, even in Bavaria, there was practically no Jewish population to speak of, and so the Gestapo was not faced with enforcing rules concerning relations which crossed the ethnic border. Of course a person could still get in trouble with the law for expressing dissent with the anti-Semitism or some other policy of the regime. There was a greater expenditure of police resources in those areas which had large numbers of Jews, and also in areas like Lower Franconia, where Jews had settled in small clusters and for some time throughout the district. In Lower Franconia countless kinds of social relationships had taken root between Jews and non-Jews, and the local representatives of Nazism took it upon themselves to destroy these bonds. While the general *modus operandi* of the Gestapo tended to be the same across the country, the extent of its efforts and 'success' in enforcing racial policy clearly varied from place to place, and hasty generalizations across the board should be avoided. In all likelihood, the Gestapo found it easier to achieve results in this sphere of its activity where there was a history of anti-Semitism, in smaller cities—even Catholic ones such as Würzburg—and in the rural communities such as those in Lower Franconia. The big city tended to provide greater anonymity, hence some degree of protection from the prying eyes of neighbours. Keeping secrets and maintaining illicit liaisons or frowned-upon contacts are invariably more difficult in the society of a small town or village. Harassment drove many Jews from rural parts, and for some there was a hope that they could find refuge in the bigger cities.

With all due regard to these caveats, it is reasonable to assume that

---

[1] Kershaw, *Popular Opinion*, 277.

instances of accommodation to Nazi racial doctrine in the files of the Würzburg Gestapo, if placed on a scale covering the whole country, would be towards the minimal end of the gauge. Embracing the official line—or co-operating with the authorities as if one embraced it—was almost certainly more enthusiastic, or at least more widespread, in areas which had supported the Nazis to a greater extent before 1933, and which had a more pronounced tradition of anti-Semitism in conjunction with large Jewish populations. Even in Lower Franconia, which had no such pronounced tradition, the readiness of a sufficient number of people to inform made it possible to enforce the policy. More and more people began to turn their backs on the Jews, as is indicated by one report for November 1936 from the Lower Franconian and very Catholic village of Bad Neustadt (population 995 in 1933, of which at least 120 were Jews):

In general the attitude of the population in regard to the Jews has almost completely changed. While earlier an unmistakable stand was taken in favour of the persecuted Jews, now one hears the remark, 'If only they would all soon be gone!' It is solely because of the danger of diminishing the taxable income and thereby damaging the communal finances that the departure of the Jews is regarded as inconvenient.[2]

Many people who had social contacts of one sort or another with the Jews gradually yielded to official and semi-official pressure to comply, and made the appropriate adjustments,[3] not only inside Germany, but later on in the occupied countries of Europe as well.[4] The Gestapo responded to any dissent with policies on the 'Jewish question' by redoubling its efforts in order to obtain compliance through police pressure, where necessary fulfilling its mandate with methods that gained a reputation for utter brutality. Word soon spread that anyone could be summoned to police headquarters or picked up, mistreated, held indefinitely; and, at the whim of the Gestapo, hapless suspects could be sent off to a concentration camp under 'protective custody' orders. When it came to enforcing racial policies designed to isolate the Jews,

---

[2] StA W: LRA Bad Neustadt 21905: report, 1 Dec. 1936; also cited in Kershaw, *Popular Opinion*, 240.

[3] For recent approaches to accommodation see Gruchmann, 84ff.; Proctor, 64ff.; Peukert, *Volksgenossen*, 55ff.; Marssolek and Ott, 131ff.; Peter Hayes, *Industry and Ideology: IG Farben in the Nazi Era* (Cambridge, 1987), 81ff. See the important study of Hitler's role in fostering the acceptance of the new order in Kershaw, *The Hitler Myth*, 48ff.

[4] In general, see Konrad Kwiet and Helmut Eschwege, *Selbstbehauptung und Widerstand: Deutsche Juden im Kampf um Existenz und Menschwenwürde 1933–1945* (Hamburg, 1984), 157ff. For Belgium see Helene Moszkiewiez, *Inside the Gestapo: A Jewish Woman's Secret War* (Toronto, 1985), 43ff.; for France see Tom Bower, *Klaus Barbie, Butcher of Lyons* (London, 1984), 51ff. Bower cites August Moritz, head of section VI in Lyons, who noted that besides the political fanatics there were criminals and others who used the mechanism of the denunciation to remove enemies. According to him, queues formed daily 'at the special kiosks for denunciations... We had so many that we couldn't even check most of them.' Cf. Bertran M. Gordon, *Collaborationism in France During the Second World War* (Ithaca, 1980), 339, and John F. Sweets, *Choices in Vichy France: The French under Nazi Occupation* (Oxford, 1986), 100.

there can be no doubt that the wrath of the Gestapo knew no bounds, often dispensing with even the semblance of legal procedures. It is important to be reminded of the 'legal' and 'extra-legal' terror brought down on the heads of those who would not otherwise comply, and some of the results of the pressure.

1. YIELDING TO PRESSURE: BREAKING PERSONAL BONDS

The Gestapo files often suggest an extraordinary degree and variety of accommodation to the regime's doctrines on race. However, caution is advisable when interpreting such evidence. Understandably, most of those brought in for interrogation did what they could to sound like true believers. For example, when the elderly sister of Würzburg's famous Bishop Ehrenfried was reported for helping an elderly Jewish woman, she denied it emphatically to the police, even though she had certainly provided some help.[5] None the less, the anti-Semitic message got through in countless ways.

Relationships going back many years were broken off. An unmarried clerical worker, Maria Zirkel (born 1907), had known her Jewish friend Karl Staff since the age of 17, and had had an intimate relationship with him which was terminated soon after the 'seizure of power'. In early February 1937 a member of the Nazi Party denounced the two to the Gestapo for allegedly spending a weekend together in the country house of Heinz Zell. Ordered to Gestapo headquarters to answer the charges, both people insisted that they no longer had a sexual relationship. The interrogations provided testimony that was utterly consistent with the couple's claims that since 1933 they had done no more than to greet each other in the street. After further surveillance and questioning, additional witnesses failed to prove the charge and the matter was dropped. Zirkel and Staff had been able to adjust to the new facts of life from the outset of the dictatorship.[6]

Those who had had business contacts with Jews before the 'seizure of power', or who had been employed in Jewish firms, continued to be watched closely. Some were reported for having had personal links before 1933, even where these had almost certainly now disintegrated.[7] The charge of 'race defilement' was itself so grave, and the consequences so disastrous, that prudence dictated the end of some relationships of this kind. One would think that any non-Jew who dared to continue contacts with a Jew was an out-and-out resister or staunch opponent. However, even here the Gestapo files dealing with 'race defilement', although they often reveal evidence of non-

---

[5] StA W: Gestapo 6146. For a discussion of this case see pp. 174–5 above. Cf. Henry, *Victims and Neighbors*, 106.
[6] StA W: Gestapo 7177; cf. ibid. 7597.
[7] Ibid. 10014; cf. ibid. 8871, 8989.

compliance with the letter and spirit of the Nuremberg Laws, also show as much or more evidence of accommodation.

There are many cases in which long-term, intimate involvements were either terminated or deliberately kept short of sexual intercourse. The book-keeper Klara Drehbock (born 1889) had been employed by the same firm, Klau and Sichel, in Würzburg for more than thirty years. She had been on friendly terms with one of the Jewish owners, Alfred Weinstein, for almost as long, and had corresponded with him as far back as the years of the First World War. The two had seen each other outside business hours on occasion, but put a stop to this public display of their affection after the passage of the Nuremberg Laws in September 1935, perhaps until 16 March 1937, when they were seen together and promptly reported. Drehbock maintained that she was a virgin, and was willing to submit to a medical examination to prove that the 'race defilement' charges were without foundation. An examination was not carried out, but she was warned to avoid all contact with Weinstein. The couple either had no further meetings or were sufficiently discreet to avoid suspicion. The case reveals the ways in which people such as these, even as they resisted, had to come to some form of accommodation with the regime's teachings on race.[8]

On 18 May 1936 the Nazi party Kreisleitung in Würzburg forwarded a detailed denunciation from the local economic department of the Schweinfurt NSDAP about the sausage firm of Karl Schübel in Würzburg. Before 1933 the business had been bought out by Ludwig Frankental, a Jewish merchant, who was accompanied by Erika Müller, a non-Jewish associate, when he moved to town from Fulda. They were not well off and, trying to make the little firm prosper, they shared a room at the back of the store as a place to sleep at night. In keeping with business practice, the firm's old name was retained, while the new owners name was printed in small letters on the door. In 1936 Frankental was accused of 'camouflaging' the Jewish-owned business behind its former owner's name, and of having an affair with Müller. Surveillance was instituted immediately—as was usual in such cases, not by the Gestapo itself but by others designated by the police. Most damning was the charge that Müller and Frankental, when they were together outside the immediate neighbourhood, referred to themselves as man and wife and pretended to be an 'Aryan' couple by the name of Schübel (the former owner of the business).

Müller and Frankental were arrested briefly on 12 June 1936. Müller declared her innocence and insisted on a medical examination to verify that she was still a virgin. Tests by the health office supported her claim, and the most serious charge of 'race defilement' was dropped. As in the previous case,

---

[8] StA W: Gestapo 10014: he was deported to Theresienstadt (Terezin) on 23 Aug. 1942 (his file is no. 10305).

this one combined elements of non-compliance with and adjustment to Nazi racism. Both couples had modified their behaviour, and sexual activity could not be proven. To be sure, even in cases where penetrative sexual intercourse did not take place, but it could be shown that couples obtained sexual satisfaction in other ways, charges were laid under the Nuremberg Laws, as (it was maintained) the laws were designed 'for the protection of German blood *and* German honour'.[9]

Once the 'race defilement' charge against Frankental and Müller had failed, the other evaporated. Despite a warning, Müller continued to work in the store, a decision she justified by saying that she hoped to take it over eventually. During the 'night of broken glass' in November 1938, a private citizen called the Würzburg Gestapo headquarters, and the two charges of camouflaging the Jewish business and 'race defilement' were renewed. Just how closely the couple had been watched is made clear in the letter which the Gestapo asked the caller to submit; it was claimed that Müller did Frankental's washing, including pyjamas and handerkerchiefs, and that they ate together. While Müller was arrested, and stayed in gaol until at least the end of the month, Frankental went missing. Some fourteen different witnesses were brought in for what was clearly a massive investigation of the charges against Müller. This time the denouncer was a competitor, a man (born 1890) who had worked for the old firm for eight years before it was taken over by Frankental. At the time of the take-over his position was given to Müller, whereupon he went off to start a rival firm. Material in the dossier indicates that he wanted the business and that he had tipped off the Gestapo when he got wind that Müller was about to take it over. In the end she was cleared. Frankental probably got out of the country.

As was shown in the last chapter, not all accommodation resulted from a direct brush with the terror apparatus. Some did, however, even when the encounter was a relatively minor one. NSDAP Kreisleiter Knaupp, in Würzburg, was given information, which he sent promptly to the Gestapo, that in the Café Kies on 14 March 1938 at 16.15, when dance-music on the radio was interrupted for a speech by the Führer, two men (names unknown) had turned it off. A 'lady' immediately attempted to ascertain their names, whereupon the radio was turned back on. She was not satisfied with this, all the more as there was a suspicion that one or both might be Jewish. Though Maier, the café-owner, and his wife were interrogated, the identity of the men who had turned the radio off was never clarified. The rumour that Jewish persons frequented the café turned out, however, to be true, even though Maier had been in the NSDAP since 1932 and his future son-in-law was in the SS. On the day he was requested to appear at Gestapo headquarters he

---

[9] Ibid. 7989 (emphasis added). For cases where no intercourse took place but convictions were still obtained see Noam and Kropat, 118ff., and Anja Rosmus-Wenninger, *Widerstand und Verfolgung am Beispiel Passaus 1933–1939* (Passau, 1983), 72–3.

placed in the window of his establishment the sign 'Entry to Jews Forbidden'. While there is evidence in this dossier of non-conforming behaviour, one can see how individuals gave in under pressure.[10]

After the pogrom of November 1938 across the country, maintaining contacts with Jews became more difficult and downright dangerous. The tailor Alfons Mantel from Hassfurt (born 1879) had made suits for thirty years for his Jewish business colleague and neighbour, Julius Goldschmidt. Until shortly before Goldschmidt was arrested in November as part of the pogrom, he and Mantel had split the cost of a daily newspaper. Mantel had been a supporter of the Catholic Party (the BVP) and was known to have little time for the Third Reich. The police were told that in addition to this 'undesirable' contact with Goldschmidt, Mantel avoided using the 'Heil Hitler!' greeting 'as far as possible'. Mantel explained in his own defence that he had begun to curtail his business associations with Goldschmidt ever since 1933, 'as the Jewish question grew more acute'. Here, in all likelihood, an old friendship was brought to a close as local police, with the co-operation of an 'ordinary' citizen, intervened to enforce the spirit of the law—for there was nothing in the statutes against this kind of socializing.[11]

Flight from the country and suicide were the ultimate forms of yielding to pressures to comply with Nazi anti-Semitism. Many couples hoped that big cities, such as Berlin and Frankfurt, might provide anonymity and a modicum of protection from denunciations. Others left the country altogether, and some of them were later overtaken by the conquering German armies. One pair, who left for Paris in 1933 and were married there (in 1938), were subsequently tracked down in mid-1942, whereupon the man was sent back to Germany and gaol. It is not clear what happened to the Jewish woman, although, if apprehended, at the very least she would have been placed in 'protective custody'.[12]

Not all personal bonds across the ethnic boundary dissolved under pressure, but all of them had to adjust. 'Mixed marriages' between Jews and non-Jews, still possible before the Nuremberg Laws prohibited any further such unions, presented in microcosm the dilemma of living in a country where 'racial mixing' was anathematized. Mixed marriages were of two basic types, the 'privileged' and 'non-privileged'. Precisely who could qualify for which status changed in the years after the promulgation of the Nuremberg Laws. In general terms, a Jewish partner in a privileged marriage was not subject to most anti-Semitic laws, whereas a Jewish person in a mixed marriage that was labelled as non-privileged was treated as were all other Jews. In September 1941, when Jews in Germany were forced to wear the yellow star, those living in privileged mixed marriages were exempted, which in turn meant

---

[10] StA W: Gestapo 6814.
[11] Ibid. 6916.
[12] Ibid. 14557. See Kwiet and Eschwege, 141 ff.

that the Jewish person was less vulnerable to daily chicaneries and harassments. More importantly, such persons were not (initially) subject to the deportations which began with the 'star' decree. This decree gave special status to a Jew in a mixed marriage on condition that children born of the marriage would not be raised as Jews; it continued to apply if the marriage dissolved or if an only son was killed in the current war. In a childless mixed marriage, a Jewish woman, but not a Jewish man, would enjoy the 'privileges' for the duration of the marriage. The decree only incidentally favoured a Jewish woman and only so long as the marriage lasted; its effect was to protect the 'German' man in a childless mixed marriage from the pain associated with his spouse's having to wear the yellow star. It also ensured that a 'German' woman living in such a union would not be shielded from this indignity. In practice, a Jewish woman legally entitled to 'privileged' status, none the less found herself vulnerable.[13]

By early 1943 there were sixty 'privileged' mixed marriages in Lower Franconia.[14] In Germany proper (the 'Altreich') there were still 12,117 privileged and 4,551 non-privileged marriages.[15] The Gestapo monitored them closely, and a revealing record of what was involved in such relationships has been left by Lotte Paepcke, the Jewish partner in a mixed marriage. She was 'fortunate' because she had a child who did not count as Jewish under the law; even if her marriage had disintegrated she would, in theory, have been exempted from wearing the yellow star.

Paepcke discusses the fate of her friend Lilli, like herself a Jewish woman in a mixed marriage. Lilli and her husband Erich, both medical doctors who married during their university years before 1933, moved to the country, opened a practice, built a house, and had five children. As they lived far from the nearest city, they looked forward to occasional visits from other local notables, such as the pastor, medical colleagues, and the cultivated estate-owner down the road; for culture there were trips to the city, vacations abroad, and so on. With the year 1933 much of this way of living began to change: the local SA band surrounded the house at one point and sought without success to place Lilli in 'protective custody'. Paepcke says that the villagers, while not abandoning the doctors overnight, were not entirely unhappy to see some of the 'high and mighty' taken down a peg or two. One day the estate-owner dropped by to say that in future ('no insult intended to you or your spouse') he and his wife would be avoiding all contact: 'In my exposed position, I simply cannot afford the risk,' he explained. Soon afterwards their medical colleagues made similar statements, and in six months

---

[13] Cf. Adler, 280–1; Raul Hilberg, *The Destruction of the European Jews*, rev. edn. ii (New York, 1985), 417ff.; Ralph Giordano, *Die Bertinis* (Frankfurt, 1982). A Trier Party leader suggested that Jews should also wear a yellow star on the back of their clothing to make them recognizable from behind. See Franz Josef Heyen, *Nationalsozialismus im Alltag* (Boppard, 1967), 152.

[14] Adler, 621.

[15] Ibid. 281.

the pastor had to admit that he dared not visit any more because he had already been warned three times by the Party. This kind of popular accommodation, the result of formal and informal pressure to comply, had an unfortunate impact on Lilli's husband, a man who desperately wanted such things as security, peace, and honour; unwilling to do his part to maintain the marriage, he was more than relieved when Lilli took the children and moved to the city. However, upon registering with the authorities, she neglected to add 'Sara' to her name, as the law then demanded. This oversight was reported to the Gestapo, before whom she was repeatedly ordered to appear. After a fourth visit she served a gaol sentence, and worked in a factory; she was eventually sent to Auschwitz, where she perished. The adjustments of the husband, neighbours, and colleagues had contributed to Lilli's death. This is just one example: the story of the mixed marriages remains to be written.[16]

2. SCRUPULOUSNESS IN POLICING RACE RELATIONS

Many of the allegations that turned out to have some basis were of a trivial nature. Anyone reading through the Gestapo files will inevitably be struck by the scrupulousness of the police in relentlessly following up information on the pettiest accusations.

A 33-year-old servant, Margareta Steinmetz, did not have the courage to appear at Gestapo headquarters herself, but an acquaintance with whom she discussed the defiance of the racial code which she had witnessed brought it to the Gestapo in May 1937. It seems that the tax-inspector Rudolf Schäfer was seen by Steinmetz shaking hands with the Jewish butcher's wife, Renate Mai, on his way to playing chess at the Alhambra Café. Steinmetz was convinced that on another occasion Mai was about to let Schäfer into her apartment, but had stopped when spotted. As it happened, Schäfer had known the butcher and his wife for twenty-five years, and there was nothing more to the case than that he greeted Frau Mai from time to time while passing in the street. The charge was eventually dropped, but not before it was turned over to one of the town's most feared Gestapo officers for his personal attention.[17]

Another case illustrates how far local authorities carried the enforcement of racial policy. On her rounds at various times in the course of 1941, nurse Bettina Werner of the Nazi Welfare Association (the NSV) in Unteraltertheim had on several occasions observed Jewish people in the homes of patients she visited. Suspecting there was more to it than met the eye, she decided to report the matter, incriminating both Jews and their non-Jewish associates.

[16] Lotte Paepcke, *Ich wurde vergessen: Bericht einer Jüdin, die das Dritte Reich überlebte* (Freiburg, 1979), 60ff.
[17] StA W: Gestapo 10822.

One of those she denounced was an elderly Jewish woman, Frau Julier (born 1876), who, it turned out, had recently helped a family at the time of the potato harvest, and had done some other chores. Irmgard Junge, a widow (born in 1876), who had accepted help from Julier as well as from a Jewish man (born in 1878), claimed in her defence that no other labour was available. After lengthy investigation by local police the case was forwarded to the Gestapo in Würzburg, where it was regarded as a serious matter. The case ended with the following note from the Würzburg Gestapo official:

I request that Irmgard Junge, whose behaviour is by all events to be considered as a disregard of government regulations, sign a document relating to this matter in which she is warned under threat of the most drastic state police measures... Furthermore, I point out that Jews are only permitted to be employed by Aryans if beforehand the relevant [Nazi Party] Kreisleitung is informed.[18]

Others denounced by nurse Werner in this case were also interrogated, and, though nothing happened to any of them, Werner was responsible for getting six different people into trouble with the law on the flimsiest of grounds. Her denunciation of the Jews came after the deportations to the east had commenced, so that she could hardly have been unaware of the grave implications of her act. The scrupulousness with which the Gestapo enforced racial policy was shared by others outside police ranks.

The reach of the anti-Semitic newspaper *Der Stürmer* was considerable— it was read not only by hardened Nazis or the Gestapo, but also by local policemen in small towns and villages. Maria Keller, a chemist living in Aschaffenburg from mid-1936, was a candidate for a position with the local administration there. It was necessary to investigate Keller's background in order to make a 'political evaluation'. The police office in town concluded that 'the reputation [of this person] cannot be termed one without problems. She appears in regard to morals to be pretty decadent, because before the National Socialist uprising she entertained relations with Jews about which at the time even the *Stürmer* reported.' Here is a case where nothing was suggested about Keller's behaviour after January 1933, let alone after the promulgation of the Nuremberg Laws. There is nothing more in the file, and she probably did not get the job.[19]

By 23 September 1937 Blockleiter Treu, in Würzburg's Goethestrasse, was determined to catch the widow Frau Cäcile Heim (born 1888) and the Jewish merchant who lived across the street from her, Albert Kuppel (born 1873), in the act of 'race defilement'. Blockleiter Treu, like these two neighbours of his, was a merchant, and they had all lived in the same vicinity for many years. Treu asked his immediate Party boss to request the Gestapo to put the couple under surveillance. Initially a secret agent of the Gestapo was sent

[18] Ibid. 14270; see also ibid. 15978.
[19] Ibid. 8871

(agent number 5127A), on both 16 and 17 November 1937. This person's meticulous journal survives; it records everyone's movements, their coming and going, opening and closing of curtains, switching on and off of a certain light (both thought by Herr Treu to be possible signals, for Heim and Kuppel lived in buildings facing one another). While carrying out this surveillance, from 8.00 a.m. to 6.00 p.m. daily, the agent learnt a great deal from co-operative neighbours, especially from Treu and his wife. The two people had been close before 1933, it was said, and Kuppel had helped settle Heim's estate when her husband died in 1925.

From 1933 both began adjusting their behaviour; visits to each other's apartments had been reduced and had now virtually stopped. Treu's unstinting efforts had been unable to unearth a single instance when anything compromising happened between Frau Heim and Herr Kuppel. The Gestapo, unwilling to let the case rest on the investigative talents of a mere agent, sent two full-time officials—admittedly not very senior ones—on 21 November to see if they could do any better. They were able to see Kuppel actually enter Heim's store. The police decided to wait a spell before breaking in to catch the couple in the act, but within a few minutes Kuppel left the store again. The officials could only report that they had overheard what sounded like an argument. Both agents returned on 22 and 23 November. The surveillance ended when Kuppel died suddenly of natural causes.

This allegation was pursued by the Gestapo to great lengths even though a genuine fear of 'race defilement'—producing a child of mixed ancestry—was out of the question, given the advanced years of both persons under suspicion. The file reveals the remarkably dogged and sometimes ridiculous efforts of the Gestapo and the associated police network.[20]

Hardly less ridiculous was a case involving Walburga Grafenberger (born 1900), who had worked for a Jewish firm as its bookkeeper and, until the emigration of its owner in late 1938, was a loyal employee who helped in the 'Aryanization' of the business. On 12 June 1939 Otto Leucht of the railway police telephoned Gestapo headquarters with the 'news' that 'in the last little while' Grafenberger had been observed 'frequently travelling in the direction of Frankfurt a.M.', and in addition was seen in the company of a man of 'Jewish appearance' at the railway station. The Gestapo had her letters investigated for three months. Eventually it came out that she visited one Harry Meister, 'a student' from Hanover, who was not Jewish, the Gestapo deduced, for in one letter he asked her to help out with the harvesting of the crop. The assumption was that Jews did not work as farmers.[21]

When it came to enforcing racial policy, the Gestapo did not stop at the border. Indeed, even after one trial for 'race defilement' was concluded and

---

[20] StA W: Gestapo 11646 (his file is No. 3776).
[21] Ibid. 12589.

the man (a Jew and Polish citizen) was deported, the 'German' woman was denied a passport when the authorities, informed by the woman's mother, found out that she planned to join the man, whom she had known for ten years, in Poland. The mother apparently approached the Party leader in Laufen (May 1937) in order to 'save' her daughter. (At a trial that had been held back in October 1935, incidentally, no sexual relations could be proven to have taken place after the Nuremberg Laws, so the couple had adjusted to the situation sufficiently to avoid the worst consequences.)[22] In another case a woman from Amberg (born 1915), who in early 1936 applied to emigrate to Chicago to work as a servant to a Jewish family, was prevented from leaving; brought to Gestapo headquarters in Würzburg, she admitted having known a Jewish man who had left for Palestine in mid-1934 (that is, before the Nuremberg Laws). The police suspected that she wanted to join him, and so refused permission on the grounds that it had to prevent 'prohibited relations'.[23] One far-fetched Würzburg case from March 1942 was initiated by an anonymous letter, which spoke of a person's connections with Jews in Basle; that case was checked repeatedly until 10 February 1945, at which time not only were the charges found to be false, but the identity of the original complainant uncovered. The Gestapo said of the latter that 'here was a case of an intriguer'.[24]

Anonymous denunciations alleging 'criminal' activity abroad are not uncommon in the Gestapo files. On 31 March 1937 someone charged that while a soldier was in Spain he had been friendly with both Jews and Marxists. Since the man was still in Spain, no checks could be made and the matter was dropped.[25] Another anonymous tip from 1937 arrived by letter from the United States; the charge was without foundation.[26] While stationed in Cracow, Andreas Kaiser, an engineer from Hammelburg, permitted some of the Jews under his supervision to drive a truck and move about without a (Jewish) identification armband. This behaviour, reported in November 1940, was investigated by the Gestapo in Jaroslau (i.e. Jarosław) in the east, and the file was forwarded to the relevant domestic Gestapo back in Germany.[27] In Würzburg too, anyone in charge of conscripted Jewish labour who was thought to be lenient was liable to be denounced.[28] With the outbreak of the war, and especially from the beginning of the attack on the Soviet Union in June 1941, the spy–counter-spy atmosphere, deliberately played up by the Propaganda Ministry, led to an increase in the number of anonymous tips. The army command post in Bad Kissingen (responsible for Lower Franconia)

---

[22] StA M: NSDAP 358; the woman lived in Fürth.
[23] StA W: Gestapo 15963; cf. ibid. 13534. From elsewhere see HStA D: Gestapo 46339.
[24] StA W: Gestapo 5952; cf. ibid. 7120, from Feb. 1939.
[25] Ibid. 5628.
[26] Ibid. 5860.
[27] Ibid. 11585.
[28] Ibid. 12037.

reported on 13 December 1941, for example, 'an extraordinary increase in anonymous reports. These were radically worked through. It turns out that most of the denunciations are without foundation.'[29] As the next chapter shows, the vast numbers of foreigners in the country added to the siege atmosphere.

3. THE CRACKDOWN ON 'DEGENERACY' IN THE GESTAPO FILES

The racist message was pressed home as part of other campaigns conducted by the Gestapo. Hans Peter Bleuel suggests that the regime was intent upon 'purifying' the country, cleaning up 'degeneracy' of all kinds. The legal principles of Weimar were thrown out in favour of the idea that 'no act should go unpunished' if it contravened the 'dictates of wholesome popular sentiment'.[30]

A number of groups who were subjected to special attention by the regime are registered in the Gestapo files—'anti-social' elements such as homosexuals, and gypsies. People who were branded as having 'loose morals' also turn up, especially when they could be linked to any of the other persecuted groups. Klaus Barbie's first Gestapo assignment was to the Berlin vice squad (in 1936), where, as one recent account put it, he formed a 'sense of his future' in that the 'job involved arresting Jews, homosexuals and prostitutes and gave him his first opportunity to physically attack the "enemy"'.[31] The regime was drawing up plans for the prosecution of all these people, and many more—from the work-shy to alcoholics—in a law which never actually came into being, on the 'enemies of the community' (*Gemeinschaftsfremde*).[32] Even without such a law, however, they were persecuted, all the more so if an informant linked them with Jews. Those Jews who by chance were also habitual criminals, sexual 'deviants', or promiscuous individuals, or who led a boisterous social life, were particularly endangered.

One variety of Nazi anti-Semitism was fuelled by the suspicion that wealthy Jews somehow sexually exploited young women in their employ. It is no accident that the Nuremberg Laws (para. 2) not only explicitly prohibited extra-marital sexual intercourse between Jews and non-Jews, but (para. 3) forbade Jews from employing 'female citizens of German or kindred blood as domestic servants' (this last stipulation was not to come into force until

---

[29] BA/MA: KTB RW 21–65/3.

[30] Hans Peter Bleuel, *Sex and Society in Nazi Germany*, trans. J. Maxwell Brownjohn (Phil., 1973), 208ff.

[31] Erna Paris, *Unhealed Wounds: France and the Klaus Barbie Affair* (New York, 1985), 41.

[32] For an introduction see Jeremy Noakes, 'Nazism and Eugenics: Background to the Nazi Sterilization Law of 14 July 1933', in R. J. Bullen *et al.* (eds.), *Ideas into Politics* (London, 1984), 75ff., and Peukert, *Volksgenossen*, 246ff.

I January 1936).[33] Female employees in Jewish firms or those working for professionals such as doctors and lawyers were not expressly covered in the law. The door was opened to denouncers, however, because of the widespread prejudice that Jews misused their position of authority to obtain sexual favours. Nikolaus Herzl (born 1892), a Jewish merchant from Würzburg, had been in trouble with the law, mainly for swindling, since the beginning of the Third Reich. Denounced in a letter from the DAF in early January 1936, Herz was arrested, placed in 'protective custody', and sent to a concentration camp, and only released in order to emigrate (to China, in July 1939). The impression conveyed by his dossier is that the DAF and the Gestapo capitalized on the chance that Herz, a married man, had had a non-Jewish servant-girl working in his home. That was banned by the Nuremberg Laws. No effort needed to be made to prove 'race defilement'; the mere accusation of employing the non-Jewish girl was enough.[34]

One of the earliest allegations of 'race defilement' to come to the attention of the Würzburg Gestapo after the Nuremberg rally of 1935 (during which the race laws were announced) pertained to an affair in Schweinfurt. Already by 26 November 1935 a denunciation had led to the arrest of the 50-year-old Jewish merchant Ludwig Abramsohn. He had hired Wilhelmina Kohrt as a clerk in 1926, and the interrogations indicated (whether or not correctly) that he had gradually forced his attention on the woman—as, it was alleged, he had done with others before that. Somebody told the police that Abramsohn and Kohrt lived as a married couple, and Abramsohn was initially given two years in jail; when the time came to release him, the Gestapo placed him in 'protective custody', and he only managed to get out of Buchenwald on 6 October 1938 in order to emigrate.[35] There was a firm resolve to 'clean up' relationships of this kind.

In early April 1938 an anonymous letter was sent to the head of the 'food and drink' section of the DAF in Würzburg concerning Hanelore Krieger and her Jewish employers in the firm of M. Hanauer & Son, a liquor factory in Würzburg-Heidingsfeld. Krieger (born 1905), a worker whose apprenticeship had begun in the factory in 1918, had had little formal education, and from what she earned in 1938 (190 marks per month) helped support her elderly parents. In 1927 or 1928 Krieger's boyfriend, she said later, had got into financial difficulties, and she had gone to her boss, Julius Rosenheim, from whom she obtained 200 marks in return for a promise of sexual favours. She continued her visits to the old man for a fee (about 50 marks), and when that source of funds dried up Krieger made similar arrangements with Julius Rosenheim's son, Alfred. In her defence she told the Gestapo that she wanted

[33] See Hirsch, Majer, and Meinck (eds.), 350ff.
[34] StA W: Gestapo 1303. See ibid. 10247 for another example of bringing charges of sexual offences as a means of harassment (in Kleinwallstadt, Jan. 1937).
[35] Ibid. 8792.

the extra money to help her boyfriend, a student, who was also in financial need. Her liaison with Alfred Rosenheim continued until the end of 1936 or so, when, Krieger said, her anxieties led her to turn instead to the firm's bookkeeper, Georg Böhme, a non-Jewish married man. Her behaviour was brought to the attention of the Gestapo when, apparently, the bookkeeper's wife got wind of the affair and sent the anonymous letter mentioned above.

Alfred Rosenheim and Hanelore Krieger were arrested and brought to trial. In court she changed her testimony and said that sexual relations had ended in the summer of 1934; while the court accepted this, and set Rosenheim free, the Gestapo, maintaining that she had probably been bought off by a third party, placed Rosenheim in 'protective custody' anyway, as a corrective to what they saw as a failure of the justice system.[36]

Prostitution was allowed to continue, though it was more stringently controlled, under the Nazi dictatorship. A decree of 9 September 1939 from the Reich Interior Ministry put local police (the Kripo) in charge of proper surveillance of brothels. Charges of anti-social behaviour were to be brought against pimps and others living off the profits of prostitution. Special brothels were created for the armed forces, and there were also such houses, inhabited by foreign women, for the foreign workers in Germany. But prostitutes could get into trouble with the Gestapo if they had Jewish clients; these relations were also subject to the Nuremberg Laws.[37] The Gestapo (and the SD, for that matter) sometimes used prostitutes for the purposes of entrapment. However, no use of prostitutes is explicitly registered in the cases of the Würzburg Gestapo, and the files have to be supplemented with other materials to show how unsuspecting Jews were lured into compromising situations and denounced.[38]

To the extent that prostitutes are mentioned in the files, the point is made to expose the failings of certain men in various Nazi organizations. Otherwise the cases involving prostitution were processed by the regular police. But in Würzburg and other cities there were instances when prostitutes—or people suspected of operating as prostitutes—got into trouble because the client turned out to be Jewish. For example, in March 1936 neighbours observed that a certain woman was receiving people who might be Jews while she was also receiving Party members, SS, and SA; the tip was given to the local Party boss, who, when relaying it to the Gestapo, mentioned that the estranged husband of the woman recently talked about her as now 'plying the trade' [*seine Frau ginge auf den Strich*].[39] At almost the same time a Jewish woman, Friedel Scharf (born 1907), was denounced by the SA Standarte 9, Würzburg.

---

[36] StA W: Gestapo 10266.

[37] For examples of prostitutes hiding 'submerged' Jews see Boehm, 100, and Gerhard Kiersch *et al.*, *Berliner Alltag im Dritten Reich* (Düsseldorf, 1981), 106–7.

[38] See Schellenberg, 18ff., on 'Salon Kitty'.

[39] StA W: Gestapo 2040.

Scharf had recently been discharged from a mental institution and was unable to come to grips with life on the outside, especially the anti-Semitic laws. It was alleged that she was out to sabotage the Nuremberg Laws by deliberately accosting SA men and trying, not unsuccessfully, to seduce them. The complaint was that this woman was living as a prostitute; as the SA leader wanted, the Gestapo put a stop to it.[40]

A number of other cases in the Würzburg files strongly suggest that the woman involved was at least a part-time prostitute or, as in the case of Hanelore Krieger (above), that she supplemented her income by providing sexual favours. Hans Robinsohn discusses another such case in his study of 'race defilement' in Hamburg; a Jewish man and his non-Jewish friend, simply out for a good time one evening, met up with a prostitute, and were denounced; the woman subsequently testified against her Jewish customer that he was not, as he claimed, drunk at the time (which might be used to moderate the seriousness of the 'crime') but merely a little in his cups.[41] Sarah Gordon found 'no cases of open prostitution' in the Düsseldorf files, though it is unclear what is meant by that term.[42] In fact it would be surprising if prostitutes were *entirely* absent from the material, particularly because local police were so keen to follow up complaints in order to harass the Jews. In neighbouring Frankfurt there was a case involving a prostitute in the summer of 1938, and, though sexual intercourse did not take place, the accused was found guilty. The court decided that the law had still been broken, since the concept of forbidden 'sexual relations' (*Geschlechtsverkehr*) within the terms of the Nuremberg Laws involved the protection of German 'honour' as well as German 'blood'. The man was sentenced to two years and two months in gaol after which he was probably placed in 'preventative custody' in a concentration camp.[43]

Promiscuous sexual behaviour involving Jewish males or females and crossing the ethnic barriers was criminalized and, as far as possible, 'cleaned up' after 1933. Bernard Martin, a married truck-driver and 'ordinary citizen'. went to the DAF in Kitzingen in mid-December 1937 to hand in the names of five men who had had sexual relations with Anna Laska, a 44-year-old Jewish woman. Martin also suggested that Laska had probably had an abortion, forbidden under paragraph 218 of the criminal code. Under questioning by the Labour Front's local boss, Martin admitted that he too had had sexual relations with Laska, although only before the promulgation of the Nuremberg Laws, a statement that proved false under investigation, and which cost him a year in gaol (from April 1938).[44] Martin probably calculated

[40] Ibid. 6024; for other cities see Bleuel, 214ff.
[41] Robinsohn,41.
[42] Sarah Gordon, 212.
[43] See Noam and Kropat, 156ff.
[44] StA W: Gestapo 13085.

that he might ward off attention to his own behaviour by turning in the five men.

On 4 November 1938 the welfare office of the Ochsenfurt Kreisleitung of the NSDAP wrote of a wayward husband who was not only neglecting his wife and child, but had for months on end paid no support to his family. He was playing the role of the 'cavalier' in the town and keeping company with a number of women of questionable moral standards—one of whom, Johanna Kemp (born 1906), was both married and Jewish. The man in question, Gerhard Neff (born 1913), had trained to be a tailor, and with his father's financial help opened his own business. Neff did well initially, married in 1934, and took on an apprentice, but within a few years grew bored and restless. In 1937 he bought a powerful motor cycle, had intimate relations with several women of dubious virtue (so his father attested), and made friends with a number of men, one of whom was Stefan Kemp, a German man living in a 'mixed marriage' with Johanna Kemp. Gerhard Neff began to drive her about on his motor cycle, and eventually they had an affair.

Brought to trial, Gerhard Neff seemed to fit the unflattering pictures painted of him by his wife and father; the latter said at one point that his son possessed neither 'any sense of duty nor consciousness of his responsibilities'. In his own defence Neff claimed that the whole affair should be blamed on Johanna Kemp, who seduced him 'in order to ruin my family'. Neff was tried and sentenced to one and a half years in gaol. Johanna Kemp fared much worse. The 32-year-old woman had to face accusations of sexual promiscuity when three of the men with whom she was accused of having had relations at one time or another were interrogated. There was some evidence that she had had a number of such relationships, going as far back as 1930. While Neff was given a gaol term, she was sent to Ravensbrück in 1939, even though she and her husband sought to leave the country. She died there in April 1942.[45]

After the first six or seven years of Nazi Germany, the laws and regulations on race could be stretched almost with impunity by the Gestapo. Proceedings could have been started against Bernard Martin under any number of pretexts, but the Gestapo went after him with particular vehemence because he disregarded the race laws.[46] In another case from 1937, two married men from Aschaffenburg—a restaurant-owner (born 1908) and a market gardener (born 1905)—were accused of having sexual relations with a 20-year-old Jewish woman. They were brought to trial in Aschaffenburg, but the court found it impossible to convict because of the unreliable testimony of the woman, who kept changing and embellishing the story. But the point was

---

[45] StA W: Gestapo 3585, 8440, 14410.
[46] Ibid. 13085.

brought home that, while promiscuity was frowned upon, it had to cease completely between Jews and non-Jews.[47]

Jews who had a criminal record and were promiscuous were in particular danger in Nazi Germany. Two unrelated cases of persons unknown to one another ran a similar course. Both Friedrich Schleier, a Jewish butcher (born 1889), and Samuel Braunthal, a Jewish baker from Würzburg (born 1888), had been in trouble with the law before 1933. Most of the charges had to do with shady business practices of various kinds, but Schleier had been found guilty, in 1924, of sexually assaulting a crippled young woman, and had been sent to prison for three years. He was also said to offer abortions, another serious matter. In early 1936 both men were separately reported to the Gestapo. Schleier was accused of going about Kleinlangheim trying to entice women to sleep with him; the charges against Braunthal were likewise vague, with no names or dates even mentioned, save that the Gestapo asked about his sexual partners before 1933. While there is no evidence of 'race defilement' after 1933, what Schleier and Braunthal had done before the 'seizure of power' sealed their fate. Both were initially placed in 'preventative arrest' (*Vorbeugungshaft*); Braunthal was eventually released and emigrated to the United States, but Schleier was sent to Buchenwald, where he died on 25 April 1940.[48] Such cases illustrate how the Gestapo used the race laws to deal with persons it wanted to get rid of because of their criminal and promiscuous pasts.

Jewish medical doctors were vulnerable, especially if suspected of offering abortions. Dr Max Bloom (born 1894) was a specialist in women's diseases in Würzburg, and in February 1937 was denounced on two serious charges. One was that he provided abortions, but although fifty-two former patients were questioned, nothing conclusive turned up. The other charge, of having an illicit relationship with his ex-secretary, Maria Friedrich, seemed to have some basis. Bloom had wanted to marry her, and in early 1935 had obtained the necessary papers. As she said in her testimony, however, 'further political developments in Germany led to the disappearance of hope for a steady relationship'. From July 1935, when Friedrich left for Munich, until she was interrogated in 1937 she had not seen, written, or spoken to Dr Bloom. Here was a case that showed some initial non-conformity with the spirit of the times, but even before the relations were declared illegal (in September 1935) the pressure to comply had grown irresistible.[49]

Homosexuality was among the most serious morals charges that could be laid in Nazi Germany, and from the outset the regime made it clear that there was going to be a campaign to stop it. The Gestapo was deeply involved in the effort, and as the Würzburg case-files make clear, it went to great lengths

---

[47] Ibid. 9380; 14689 (hers is No. 12562).
[48] Ibid. 7182, 14640.
[49] Ibid. 15622.

to enforce the policy. Within the SS itself, Himmler took decisive steps to combat homosexuality, including expulsion of homosexuals from the organization (by 1937), and frequently banishment to a concentration camp, where they would be 'shot while attempting to escape'.[50]

Already by the autumn of 1934, the Gestapo throughout Germany was requesting that local outposts record and forward to Berlin the names of previously convicted, as well as suspected, homosexuals. That kind of procedure, as Bleuel remarks, 'paved the way for denunciation and arbitrary arrest'.[51] Given the official sensitivity, it is not surprising that numerous homosexuals were discovered, and from Lower Franconia they were shipped off to Dachau. The Gestapo concluded from a case in mid-summer 1935 of a Party member with this 'disposition' that the man 'consciously worked against the interests of the Party ... [and] damaged its image' and the National Socialist state. He not only represented a 'continuing danger for the Party movement in particular, but also for public security and order in general'.[52] Eugen Kogon suggested that the Gestapo took advantage of the looseness of the 'crime' of being homosexual. It 'readily had recourse to the charge of homosexuality if it was unable to find any other pretext for proceeding against Catholic priests or irksome critics. The mere suspicion was sufficient.'[53]

The Gestapo was particularly anxious to crack down on Jews who were accused of being homosexual. One of the cases which came to trial in Würzburg concerned a Jewish wine-merchant, Dr Leopold Isaak Obermayer (born 1892), accused not merely of being a homosexual but also of being a paedophile. Educated and cultivated, with Swiss and German citizenship, Obermayer was not impressed by the Nazi take-over; he had taken the precaution of depositing pictures of his homosexual friends, some of them naked, in his bank for safe keeping. In October 1934, upon learning that his mail was being opened, he appealed to the Police President of Würzburg, an old school colleague, and subsequently to the new Gestapo chief in Würzburg, Josef Gerum, a man who was not only a fanatical Nazi, but was especially zealous in his battle against homosexuality. Gerum had Obermayer arrested for spying and spreading malicious rumours, and there was a suggestion, never really taken seriously, that he may have had contact with illegal Communist circles. When a search turned up the photographs he kept in his safe-deposit box, he was branded an 'enemy of the people' (*Volksschädling*). These pictures would have led to a death sentence had Obermayer not possessed Swiss nationality, but, even so, by early January 1935 he was sent to Dachau.

---

[50] See Bleuel, 222ff.

[51] Ibid. 222.

[52] StA W: Gestapo 17315. Cf. other cases of Party members and the Hitler Youth, ibid. 85, 191, 600, 1030, 1116. Nearly 300 cases deal with homosexuality, and 126 others with 'morals charges'.

[53] Kogon, 50.

Gerum used the findings against Obermayer in his promotion of anti-Semitic and anti-homosexual sentiment in the district, and the local press welcomed the opportunity to publicize the information which he provided. The Gestapo, or at least Gerum, hoped that charges of treason would lead to the death penalty for Obermayer, and probably the confiscation of his business and wealth. The complication remained his Swiss nationality, and in September 1935, under pressure from Munich to press charges or release the prisoner—who was still in Dachau—Gerum had Obermayer charged and brought back to a local gaol. Gerum's determined harassment continued, and though Obermayer managed time after time to escape the inevitable by using all kinds of ploys—such as appealing to the Minister of Justice—on 13 December 1936 the court sentenced him to ten years. Transferred to Mauthausen, Obermayer eventually died in late February 1943.[54] This was not the only Jewish homosexual persecuted to death by the Gestapo in Würzburg, and there were similar, less public, cases throughout the country.[55] The slightest hint of moral turpitude involving Jews of any age was followed up.[56]

4. DIRTY METHODS

The secret police frequently resorted to intimidation, extortion, and blackmail to force hapless victims to sign 'confessions'. Some officials acted with such brutality that some people saw no way out but to sign. There were Gestapo officers who deliberately used demeaning language and the familiar or contemptuous *du*, even with older Jewish women.[57]

For the most part the dirty methods and torture remain unmentioned in Gestapo files, but in one case suicide is registered. On 22 March 1936 a local SA leader in Würzburg noticed that Samual Novak, an older Jewish man (aged 61) from Sommerhausen, near Ochsenfurt, was escorting the much younger Augusta Hauser (27 years old) in a Würzburg restaurant, the Englischer Garten. Both were taken into custody and marched by the SA troop to Gestapo headquarters. Hauser, a married woman, had once been a housemaid in Würzburg, and had been acquainted with Novak as far back as 1929. In January 1934 they met again, and soon commenced a sexual relationship, which was continuing at the time of their detention. Under interrogation, she explained that she found the older man charming and interesting. Novak denied everything. There is evidence of pressure being brought on them both, and, perhaps seeing the hopelessness of the situation, especially after Hauser had confessed, Novak hanged himself in his cell on

---

[54] StA W: Gestapo 8873. See the account in Fröhlich, 76ff., and the press reports in Schultheis, 686–96. See also n. 102 below.

[55] StA W: Gestapo 12037.

[56] Ibid. 8855 (a case from Thailheim, 12 July 1939).

[57] See e.g. Deutschkron, 111ff.

the night of 25–6 March. The whole case ran its tragic course in just over 72 hours.[58]

Police entrapment highlights another side of the *modus operandi* of the Gestapo, and casts additional doubt on Gordon's claims (discussed in Chapter 6) that all those accused of crimes such as 'race defilement' should be regarded as opponents of Nazi anti-Semitism. The larger Gestapo headquarters evidently included a special 'Rassenschande' branch within the Judenreferat. Although most Gestapo posts did not have the personnel to permit such specialization, all certainly had a section concerned with Jews. Evidence from Hamburg and Berlin suggests that where they existed the 'race defilement' subsections were under pressure to come up with a quota of cases, which some apparently decided to fill by entrapment. An ex-Berlin Gestapo man maintained that 'it was the duty of the Rassenschande Department to produce cases ... When the flood of denunciations ebbed—for after all, even private revenge has its fill—they had to invent other methods. A number of unfortunate girls was recruited for this task.' They lured unsuspecting Jews into compromising situations, then denounced them to the police 'or exploited the shameful situation for private blackmail'. The same official maintained that some local Nazis opened a 'minor reign of terror' by utilizing these race laws not only against the Jews, but against fellow citizens whose car, garden, or piece of jewellery they might covet; the laws might be used to repay an old insult, a social slight, or refused favour. While a person might avoid 'politics' with the greatest of care, 'he could always be caught on a technical charge of Rassenschande', a charge the informers sought to establish.[59]

Another well-tried form of entrapment utilized by the Gestapo came into particular prominence after 1942, when in some parts of the country a decision was made to deal with elderly Jewish people (over 65) who had managed to escape deportation, as well as to begin rounding up others, such as the Jewish partners in mixed marriages, who had previously been exempted. The Gestapo began conducting house-searches, whose purpose was to find something that could count as an infraction of a regulation in order to justify an arrest. The names of non-Jews found in the address-book of a Jewish woman in a mixed marriage came to suffice as grounds for suspecting forbidden relations (*Umgang*); when all else failed they were not above planting evidence, a piece of an enemy propaganda leaflet, for example.[60] To local Gestapo officers it was a foregone conclusion that every Jewish person brought to their attention was (or could be) linked with some

---

[58] StA W: Gestapo 15591.

[59] See Hansjuergen Koehler, *Inside Information* (London, 1940), 190. He was able to avoid 'the nauseating task' of serving in the local branch (p. 189). See also his *Inside the Gestapo* (London, 1940), with corroborating evidence in Leonard Gross, 155ff.; Robinsohn, 107, mentions the Hamburg 'Rassenschande-Dezernat'.

[60] See Moritz and Noam, 284ff.

infringement of race regulations.[61] All Jews who were accused of a crime automatically became subject to the Gestapo instead of the criminal police, because their Jewishness gave the alleged crime, whatever it was, a racial and thus 'political' aspect.[62]

The police used all kinds of laws, and not only those on race, to enforce racial policy. For example, when an opportunity arose it would pursue a Jewish citizen suspected of a non-racial crime, such as stealing, or of a 'political' crime, such as malicious gossip.[63] That the Jews were to be singled out for special attention by the justice system in general is evident from the fact that from May 1935 the Reich Ministry of Justice created the office of press specialist in each local and regional appeal court across Germany. This office was responsible for collecting proceedings of all kinds brought against Jews and seeing that these cases received suitable publicity, with the aim of 'educating the people'.[64] There was particular delight in publicizing a bona-fide charge such as stealing or embezzlement, but even minor infractions of the Nuremberg Laws were jumped upon with alacrity and passed on to the press. On 7 December 1935 the Minister of the Interior made a special point in a letter to all local administrations that they were to have the press report on all criminal deeds ('strafbare Handlungen') involving Jews.[65]

The Gestapo's arbitrary and high-handed methods were grist to the rumour-mills which played their part in contributing to the social reinforce-ment of the terror apparatus. That the patently innocent could be charged, with almost complete legal impunity for the accuser, had to be widely known—indeed, was often publicized by the press specialist attached to the court. Apart from making it clear that citizens of 'Aryan' stock were free to bring such charges, the press publicity also fostered compliance with Nazi teachings, since those after a quiet life decided simply to avoid the race issue altogether, and eschew all contact with Jewish citizens.[66]

5. POLICING THE SPOKEN WORD

A separate group of fifty-two case-files of the Würzburg Gestapo deals with remarks by individuals concerning Nazi policies towards the Jews. Most, but not all, of these were made in public places such as restaurants, cafés, pubs,

---

[61] StA W: Gestapo 8989.

[62] See e.g. ibid. 10524.

[63] See Adler, 678ff.

[64] Schütz, 115ff. Regionally directed Gestapo interest at about the same time can be deduced from correspondence in StA Marburg, 180 LRA Wolfhagen, from the Kassel Gestapo (27 Sept. 1935). Cf. the request on 26 Aug. 1938 from the Karlsruhe Kripo to be informed of Jewish indictable activities, whether of a 'political or general criminal nature', reprinted in Paul Sauer (ed.), i. 110.

[65] BAK: R18/3746b.

[66] See Willi Bohn, '*Hochverräter!*' (Frankfurt, 1984), 104ff.

and so forth. These dossiers reveal grumblings and complaints from tongues loosened by alcohol, and some degree of disenchantment with the proceedings against the Jews. The zeal with which the delinquent statements were reported, almost gives the impression that there was one denouncer in the vicinity of every person who ventured anything vaguely resembling a criticism of anti-Semitic policies.

The Jewish community in Lower Franconia was widely dispersed and visible across the district; most communities of any size had at least a handful of Jewish people. As shown above, there was a never-ending public harassment, which peaked during the pogrom of 1938. Many Jews left, but a good many remained in their home towns until their emigration before 1940 or their deportation, beginning in the autumn of 1941. The regime made great efforts to publicize anti-Jewish policies, since it set out to break up established relationships between Jews and non-Jews. Obviously, people in small communities know when merchants are forced to sell out, when cattle-dealers are forbidden the right to sell stock, when Jewish doctors give up their practices, and so on. Apart from specific acts against people in the immediate vicinity, anti-Semitism was conveyed in countless other ways, such as through press, radio, and cinema propaganda.

Over the twelve-year history of Nazi Germany only fifty-two errant statements in regard to what was happening to the Jews could be discovered and reported in all of Lower Franconia.[67] Obviously, the way in which the Gestapo reacted to those who dared to say anything that might imply criticism of some aspect of the regime, let alone sympathy for the Jews, played a role in producing the silence. None the less, given the vigilance of the volunteer denouncers and attentiveness of the Gestapo, it would seem fair to conclude that the relative paucity of negative remarks aimed at the regime's anti-Semitism is an indication of the extent to which citizens accommodated themselves to the official line and, to all intents and purposes, did not stand in the way of the persecution of the Jews. The few critical remarks picked up in the district of Lower Franconia, an area that was no hotbed of Nazism, suggest that the response elsewhere was probably even more muted.

Even in the much larger jurisdiction of the special court in Munich, designed especially to deal with all kinds of critical remarks, there was a total of only just over seventy persons tried between 1933 and 1944 for making comments which in some, often remote, way could be construed as 'negative' concerning the topics of Jews and Jewish policy. (Included in this number were at least three Jewish persons.) Almost half of the cases (thirty-four) were dropped.[68] Of course, the special courts did not handle every case of such 'treasonous' statements; and the police and Gestapo dealt with more than those sent to

[67] See Ralf Dahrendorf's comments in *Society and Democracy in Germany* (London, 1968), 364, on the 'great quiet' of the Germans.
[68] They bear the formula 'Verfahren eingestellt'

trial. Even so, the scale of negative remarks about the regime's approach to the Jews must be termed so small as to be almost insignificant.[69]

Paula Klein from Würzburg stands out as a rare case of someone who refused to buckle under and adjust. A down-to-earth working woman ('without profession'), born in Frankfurt a.M. in 1893, she had long been used to speaking her mind. Reported by a truck-driver in October 1933 for having said that Hitler 'was as much a scoundrel and crook' as the people he had replaced, she was apparently let off, as she was in April 1936, when she was turned in by an NSV nurse for having said she would give nothing to the Nazi charity Mother and Child because 'people who cannot feed children should not have any'. She managed to avoid getting into serious trouble until May 1940, when she was again denounced, this time by her neighbour, who in a letter asked the Gestapo to keep her identity a secret 'because I live in the house'. This time Klein was put in gaol for two months for saying, among many other things, that the Jews should be left in peace, that the cost of living was too high, Germany should get out of the war, the 'bloody' Italians got the coal and Germans did not, and so on. It was bound to be a difficult business to transform the behaviour and habits of such an unconventional person, and had the regime lasted longer she would probably have been declared an 'asocial element' or perhaps 'enemy of the community' and put in a camp somewhere.[70]

Most 'negative' remarks reported to the police hardly represented serious opposition to anti-Jewish policies. Würzburg's theatre-director, overheard in a local restaurant, was turned in to the police on 10 October 1933 for criticizing the government and for having said that the whole anti-Semitic thing was nonsense.[71] On 17 May 1938 the gendarme in Esselbach was informed that in the local pub Peter Meister had said that the boycott against the Jews 'wasn't right either, because Jews have to pay their taxes as well'.[72] Hans Griewalt, a local leader of the Nazi Peasants' Association, turned in a 53-year-old man he overheard in a Thüngersheim café on 10 January 1938 saying that he and his family would continue to visit their Jewish medical doctor in spite of the regime's policies: 'For me it's strictly a matter of his ability.'[73] A Frankenheim woman turned in her neighbour for remarks on the 'Jewish question' she overheard through the kitchen window; while the Gestapo itself felt that the complainant was unreliable, the tip-off was checked and, more or less as expected, found to be a baseless act of hostility aimed at a despised neighbour.[74]

[69] For the records see StA M: Sondergericht.
[70] StA W: Gestapo 6209.
[71] Ibid. 17654.
[72] Ibid. 7100.
[73] Ibid. 17610.
[74] Ibid. 15866.

In several cases handled by the Würzburg Gestapo throughout the period down to 1939 someone suggested that it was possible to get a better deal in Jewish businesses.[75] A statement overheard in a Würzburg restaurant got Wilhelm Knetebeck into trouble. It was claimed that Knetebeck had said, 'I would rather buy from the dirtiest Jews than from the current National Socialists. You can't do business without Jews. Conditions are terrible!' Knetebeck insisted at his interrogation that he had only said, 'I would just as soon purchase from Jews as from a bad peasant or Christian.'[76] Karl Horn stated in an Aschaffenburg pub on 1 September 1937 that you could not hold it against someone who shopped at the Jews' stores, 'because the Jews sell everything cheaper'. Horn was reprimanded for the remarks and tried to get out of responsibility for them by implying that he did not care less about the Jews one way or another, but simply meant that he did not feel like paying for the regime's anti-Semitic policies by being forced to pay higher prices in non-Jewish stores.[77] On 15 October 1938 a Nazi Party member reported having overheard a peasant in a Mosbach pub say that the 'policies against the Jews are not right' because earlier he had had no trouble trading in cows with them, but now they were gone.[78]

Throughout this particular group of files the idea recurs that the persecution of the Jews would, directly or indirectly, be repaid with war and destruction. At the end of May 1937 a man was reported for saying in a Würzburg restaurant that Hitler's persecution of the Jews was making the foreign political situation worse.[79] At a wedding on 27 June 1938 farmer Michael Stechner from Grettstadt, near Schweinfurt, made some incautious remarks which were overheard by the deputy mayor of Grettstadt, who reported them to his superior. Eventually ordered to the police station in Gochsheim, Stechner was accused of having said that it 'was impossible to have any faith in the government' and that 'the entire leadership of the state is built on a completely mixed-up basis. Mishandling the Jews so terribly will lead in no time to chaos in the German Reich. You can see it already in the case of Czechoslovakia.'[80]

On 30 September 1938 a woman in the dairy business reported to the local NSDAP in Castell that one Heinz Auer had said Germany would not be in such a mess if Hitler had not persecuted the Jews, and that Hitler would have to take the responsibility if war came.[81] Two soldiers who had quarters in the home of an Ergoldsbach woman, Betty Kneisel, were reported in mid-March

---

[75] See e.g. StA W: Gestapo 5421: Aschaffenburg, Sept. 1937.
[76] Ibid. 4905.
[77] Ibid. 5421.
[78] Ibid. 17666.
[79] Ibid. 11898.
[80] Ibid. 17505. Stechner was exonerated by the Bamberg special court, for reasons not stated in this file.
[81] Ibid. 5080.

1938 to the NSDAP Ortsgruppe because they had said that 'Hitler made a great mistake when he laid hands on the Jews; they ought to have been left in peace.' Kneisel felt that such attitudes from these people, on their way to Austria, represented a 'danger' to the state.[82] A Würzburg man was reported two days after Christmas 1939 for implying that Germany had enough on its hands already without getting involved in the persecution of the Jews.[83] Even as late as August 1943 some Germans (for example, one woman in Gerolzhofen) were of the opinion that the increasing air attacks against the country were 'a reprisal for the burning of the synagogues and for driving the Jews out of the country'. 'Dear God,' she added, 'we ordinary folk now have to pay the price; we didn't want the war and never had anything against the Jews.'[84]

The one event that did spark off negative comment in Lower Franconia, which is registered in this set of sources, was the 'night of broken glass' of 9–10 November 1938. In fact, the mild reactions to that pogrom, based on all kinds of considerations, spilled over into the following weeks and months, not only in this part of Germany, but in many other areas as well.[85] The charges brought before the Munich special court (above) reflect a similar pattern of reluctance to express reservations about the events. Some Germans were disgusted by it, but they tended to focus primarily on its utter wastefulness. A particularly crass example comes from Augsfeld, near Hassfurt, where Georg Werner was involved in a late-night card-game at the local pub on 23 November 1938. As midnight approached, he said (it was recalled by a witness), 'If they had hanged all the Jews together it wouldn't have bothered me. But property of the people ought not to be destroyed.' Brought in to account for what was said (along with the other five card-players), Werner told the police that 'the Jews belonged in a workhouse', and that he had 'absolutely no sympathy' for them. However, in so far as the pogrom had destroyed their property—which was part of the 'German people's goods', it had gone too far.[86] Similar remarks were attributed to Anton Konrad just after the pogrom during a Sunday-evening visit to a pub in Oberthulba. In a state of considerable agitation, and under the influence of alcohol, this farmer confronted SA man Bruno Schultz over the issue. Schultz promptly reported that Konrad (born 1891, father of eight) had said, 'It should not have been done, destroying 1 billion marks worth of the Jews' stuff. The Sudeten Germans ought to have got the Jews' things; now they won't get it because

---

[82] Ibid. 7220.

[83] Ibid. 7279.

[84] Ibid. 5667. She was tried and given 4 months in gaol. Cf. a case from Geroda, Mar. 1941 (ibid. 13167).

[85] There is a remarkable silence in the long report of events in the Palatinate from Speyer, 30 Nov. 1938, in StA M: Gestapoleitstelle Munich 60.

[86] StA W: Gestapo 10675; he does not seem to have been charged.

it's been wrecked. Just today you saw that the people won't give anything more to your collections.'[87]

In general, across Lower Franconia the reactions to the regime's pogrom were negative, while people still remained hostile to or at least unsupportive of the Jews. In his monthly report on the situation the chief administrative officer of the area wrote that it was 'regretted by a great part of the population, especially in the rural areas, that in the event valuables were destroyed which, in respect to our raw-material situation, might have been put to more useful purposes for the people as a whole'. He also reported that 'many *Volk*-comrades declared, after so much valuable property was aimlessly destroyed, that they could not bring themselves to give anything to the collections. Fears about lack of generosity in giving to the winter assistance work have also been raised in other jurisdictions.'[88]

There are other indications that a few people had begun to feel troubled by the events. Johannes Weber, a worker, entered a Jewish firm in Klingenberg (owned by his neighbour Israel Berliner) on the day following the pogrom, and found a group of acquaintances already there; when the conversation turned to what had happened, Weber stated that he could not get any sleep during the night because of what was happening to his Jewish neighbour, Herr Berliner, who lived across the street. Though Weber 'did not actually say anything', according to one witness, his gestures made it clear that what had happened to the Jews 'did not suit him'. Still another witness insisted that Weber had said, 'What kind of thing is this, destroying everything? Haven't you people read the Führer's decree that nothing more should be done to the Jews?' The next day at work in the local docks he twice said, 'You are scoundrels!'—a reference, according to the denouncer, to Nazis who supported such an action. Weber was arrested and given a warning to watch his step in the future.[89] The Arnstein gendarme was informed on 13 December 1938 that farmer Peter Heinecke (born 1913) yelled at some SA members in the local pub as follows: 'You want to exterminate the Jews, well to hell with you; you're the ones who should be exterminated. I much prefer them. With them you can do something; you people belong against the wall and should be chopped up.' Heinecke was put on trial, but the general amnesty quashed the proceedings.[90] A Würzburg man got into trouble when, on 16 February 1939, upon hearing of a Jewish woman's recent suicide, he exclaimed in the neighbourhood vegetable store, within earshot of the wife of an NSDAP member, 'It's no wonder, seeing how they are treating the Jews: shame on the Third Reich!'[91]

---

[87] StA W: Gestapo 15113. A warning was issued.
[88] Bay HStA: MA106681, also in Broszat *et al.* (eds.), *Bayern in der NS-Zeit*, i. 475.
[89] StA W: Gestapo 9434.
[90] Ibid. 13463.
[91] Ibid. 8043; see also the case of a woman in Wiesentheid, 14 Nov. 1938 (ibid. 14392).

That the 'Jewish question' reached a particularly acute stage after the pogrom can be seen from another case. Two days after Christmas 1938 three different people were denounced in the Hassfurt area: Frau Müller (a restaurant-owner, born 1879), for giving a Jew a loaf of bread; Herr Ringer (mover/shipper, born 1880), for saying to a Jewish man 'Until later' (a normal valediction); and Herr Vogel (a trader, born 1892), because he obtained wares from a Jewish firm. Local officials were even more attentive than usual to the most trivial of accusations in the days following the pogrom.[92] Some Germans were scandalized by the events of the 'night of broken glass', but if these cases are any guide it would seem that the regime decided to clamp down on dissent harder than ever in the aftermath.

6. Deportations of the Jews from Lower Franconia

In early July 1944 a woman was reported by her close friend for saying (in the privacy of the apartment they shared), among other things, that one SS man had told her that he was once up to his knees in blood during the shooting of 40,000 Jews.[93] But it is exceedingly rare for the Gestapo case-files to contain references to the murder of the Jews in the east. There were no reports of reactions to forcing the Jews to wear the yellow star, nor, for that matter, to their deportation.

The Gestapo was the major institution responsible for carrying out the deportations. The ever-tightening guide-lines for conducting them were followed in mind-numbing compliance with eleven separate regulations. Everything was registered, including family pets. Jews were not simply herded together, but the process had to follow precise plans right up to the last-minute checks to see whether they were carrying something prohibited. Making each transport 'ready for shipment' was the task of the Gestapo. All dwellings were to be left in a clean and tidy fashion. Each person to be deported was informed of all these stipulations, and simultaneously assigned a call-up number, which on the appointed day was to be written on a card (4 × 10 cm.) and attached to the upper clothing.[94] On departure (for which two days' notice was given) the Jews—many of them from homes which had been in the family for generations—left behind all they owned, and, to stop any thefts, the police demonstrably sealed the doors.

The first transport from Würzburg left with 202 Jews (including 40 children and young people) on 27 November 1941. Before departure they were assembled and searched and detained for the night; on the day of the transport

---

[92] Ibid. 10672 (all cases are in this file).
[93] Ibid. 2635.
[94] StA W: NSDAP XII/4 (it was called a 'Merkblatt'). For a detailed examination of the deportations from Lower Franconia see Adler, 168ff., and Schultheis, 527ff.

they were marched to the railway station. The next transport, with 208 persons, left on 24 March 1942 from Kitzingen; Jews from fifteen different towns in the area were collected and kept overnight, probably in three different small hotels. Another shipment took place on 25 April 1942, when a large number from all across Lower Franconia, some 850 people, left from Würzburg.[95] Jews were held in the specially lighted 'Platz'schen Garten'; this was a large restaurant and beer-garden, taken over by the Gestapo and reorganized to 'process' the Jews. On 10 and 23 September two further transports left the area; the first had 177 people, the second 562 from more than a dozen cities, including larger numbers of sick and infirm. The last transport, of some 64 persons, departed on 17 June 1943. Altogether some 2,063 Jews had been deported to various destinations in six different transports.[96]

By the time of the second of these forced evacuations it is already obvious that much was known about them. One Würzburg citizen even wrote to the Gestapo to ask if he could pick up a rucksack from one of the deported Jews, as he was badly in need of one.[97] In spite of this knowledge, though, probably neither the Jews nor most other people in Lower Franconia had adequate information concerning what was going on in the east.[98] Taking photographs of the deportations was not permitted, but several taken on behalf of the Gestapo show the sad procession of Jews marching off in orderly fashion down one of Würzburg's main streets and carrying their few permitted goods; one picture shows on the opposite side of the wide street, near a park, many citizens who were quietly watching.[99]

In the smaller cities and villages of Lower Franconia the opportunities for hiding Jews who wanted to go underground were not present to the extent that they were in large cities such as Berlin. In order for Jews to live illegally, they had to be able to count on a network of people who would help by giving shelter—even for a day or two. Small towns, where everybody knows everybody else, made going underground difficult. One study estimates that some 1,402 Jews emerged from the destruction of Berlin at the war's end, but in no other large German city was the figure larger than fifty. It concludes that, of the Jewish population in 1933, about 1 per cent (5,000 persons) survived in Germany with help from non-Jews.[100] No Jews were able to go underground in Lower Franconia.[101]

---

[95] See Schultheis, 564ff.
[96] Ibid. 616.
[97] Ibid. 593.
[98] Ibid. 625.
[99] See Dettelbacher, 142; Schultheis gives a full photographic record, with about 100 pictures of events in Kitzingen and Würzburg.
[100] Kwiet and Eschwege, 150–1.
[101] See the account of Flade, *Würzburger Juden*, 343ff.

7. CONCLUSION

The Gestapo brought enormous pressure to bear in order to enforce the official teachings on race, especially in matters pertaining to the Jews living in the country. The evidence in the case-files suggests that the local Gestapo tended to interpret its mandate in the broadest possible terms, and did not simply wait for orders from Berlin or elsewhere. Josef Gerum, for a time chief of the Gestapo in Würzburg, actually had to be restrained by his superiors on more than one occasion when his enthusiasm in the pursuit of 'opponents', even inside the Nazi movement, threatened to get out of hand.[102] Suspects who were summoned to local Gestapo posts could readily be mistreated, sometimes to such an extent that they were driven to suicide. The brutalities of the Gestapo itself (especially evident in the recent documentary film on Klaus Barbie, *Hotel Terminus*, by Marcel Ophuls), contributed to the atmosphere of foreboding in which compliance appeared more and more advisable.

The Gestapo's reputation for brutality no doubt assisted the police in the accomplishment of its tasks, but brutality alone, as is shown in the next chapter, does not provide a satisfactory explanation for its effective functioning. While the Gestapo certainly intensified the pressure to attain compliance with Nazi anti-Semitism, for example, it could not on its own enforce even the more rudimentary racial policies designed to isolate the Jews. From the case-files it appears that many individuals, especially members of official and semi-official organizations and associations, members of the Nazi Party, and others in positions of authority (such as medical doctors, nurses, welfare officials), collaborated with the Gestapo in the endeavour to enforce racial policy. When it came to separating the Jews from other persons in Germany, a great deal of such volunteered information was forthcoming. Much of this assistance was not required by law or by orders from above. While Gestapo officials intensified their efforts to bring pressure to bear, to achieve National Socialist ends, the Gestapo's operations would have been seriously hampered without the provision from non-official sources of information on suspected deviations from the new behavioural norms.

The last three chapters have resisted any attempt to assess whether or not Nazi racial policies were popular; they have looked instead at what was required to enforce them. In attempting to understand the routine operations

---

[102] See Gerum's large file in the BDC. On taking up his position as Gestapo chief of Würzburg in mid-April 1934, by his own account Gerum found within 'official Party circles' there 'innumerable unclean elements' who had found their way into various offices. By early May 1935 he was writing 15-page letters to his superiors denouncing many members in the 'movement'—among other things, for corruption and 'sexual misconduct' (including homosexuality), charges denied in even longer letters by Gauleiter Otto Hellmuth. His boss, Heinrich Himmler, according to another letter in Gerum's dossier, had little use for him, among other things because he was not above pulling strings to get ahead himself, but also because he was prone to criticism of other Party comrades.

of the Nazi system the question of the popularity of the regime is to a very large extent beside the point, and undue preoccupation with whether or not a given policy was popular can lead down blind alleys. Successful enforcement of Nazi racial policies depended on the actions of enough citizens, operating out of an endless variety of motives, who contributed to the isolation of the Jews by offering information to the Gestapo or other authorities of Party or state. The other side of the coin, the 'astonishingly rare'[103] remarks about the Nazi terror, and especially the few occasions on which people broke their silence on the persecution of the Jews in the country, provide additional, silent testimony as to the effectiveness of the enforcement of racial policy.

[103] Peukert, *Volksgenossen*, 64.

8

'Racially Foreign':
Racial Policy and Polish Workers

DIEMUT MAJER notes, in a book on 'racially foreign people' (*Fremdvölkische*) in the legal and administrative practice of the Third Reich, that the very first piece of anti-Jewish legislation—the law to 'restore' the civil service of early 1933—was to apply to people with 'non-Aryan', rather than simply Jewish, origins. From the very outset, she argues, given the lack of precision of 'Aryan' and 'non-Aryan' (neither was defined), the racism of the regime could spread beyond the Jews to include many others who were considered 'undesirable'. Inside Germany there was a massive sterilization programme aimed at those suffering from 'hereditary diseases', as well as a euthanasia programme and efforts designed to solve the 'gypsy problem'; even the few blacks born in the Rhineland as a result of relationships with the French occupation troops in 1923 were not overlooked.[1] It is in this context that one should understand the experiences of foreign workers, especially all those from the east, in wartime Germany.

At about the time of the deportation of the remaining Jews in the autumn of 1941, the Nazi regime, driven by the exigencies of labour shortages, was—in its own terms—creating a new racial problem as it imported ever-increasing numbers of foreign workers. Even in the later years of peace, but especially

---

[1] Diemut Majer, '*Fremdvölkische*' im Dritten Reich: Ein Beitrag zur nationalsozialistischen Rechtssetzung und Rechtspraxis in Verwaltung und Justiz unter besonderer Berücksichtigung der eingegliederten Ostgebiete und des Generalgouvernements (Boppard, 1981), 125–6. On the gypsies, see Joachim S. Hohmann, Geschichte der Zigeunerverfolgung in Deutschland (Frankfurt, 1981), 178, who sets the number killed at 500,000. See also Reiner Pommerin, 'Sterilisierung der Rheinlandbastarde': Das Schicksal einer farbigen deutschen Minderheit 1918–1937 (Düsseldorf, 1979), 41ff.; Bock, 238, suggests that 400,000 sterilizations took place. See the correspondence (spring 1934) from the head doctor in Oehringen (Württemberg), from which one might deduce popular acceptance of sterilization among the population there: HStA S: E 151.k.VI. A recent study of the Nazi euthanasia programme, first instituted at the beginning of the war in 1939, counts the following numbers of victims: at least 5,000 chronically ill children, an additional 70,000 or so hospital patients (about 1,000 of whom were Jewish), another 20,000 concentration-camp inmates, and 'at least' 30,000 hospital patients were killed after the 'action' had been officially halted in August 1941, most of them Polish and Soviet foreign workers who became mentally ill, or came down with tuberculosis. See Schmuhl, 361–4. For comments on euthanasia of the population in Lower Franconia see StA W: SD 10; report of 13 Feb. 1941: 'A part of the population, in particular the religious, especially Catholic, section, rejects any interference with life, even of the sick ... The majority of the population, however, have already progressed so far that they completely approve the euthanasia of the seriously mentally ill, and are even of the view that in this area more could be undertaken than has been the case thus far.'

by the first winter of the war, new 'racially foreign' peoples were being coaxed or coerced into coming to Germany to work. Close to six million civilian workers and two million prisoners of war were working in Germany by August 1944. Given that the Nazi doctrines on race condemned most of these people to a status of racial inferiority, there was a determination to keep them separate from the German people, and above all to prevent any 'racial mixing'.

This chapter investigates additional aspects of the enforcement of racial policy by focusing on the relationships between the German people and those from Poland, numerically one of the largest groups, consigned to an especially despised place in Nazi thinking. As will become clear, while the enforcement of racial policy with respect to the Poles initially showed signs of success, fairly soon it began to falter. Many factors were at work, but the overriding difficulty faced by the Gestapo was the failure to elicit sufficient co-operation from the population. The chapter draws upon Gestapo case-files on foreign workers, as well as those on Germans accused of being out of step with Nazi teachings, and utilizes local reports of the SD in order to depict the responses of Germans to the strident entreaties of Nazi authorities to avoid all contact (*Umgang*) with foreigners.

I. NAZI POLICY AND THE POLISH PEOPLE

No sooner had the regime cured the massive unemployment it faced when Hitler assumed power than labour shortages began to appear, and these were exacerbated with the rapid expansion of the armed forces in the 1930s. In an effort to cope with the problem, increased numbers of foreign workers were permitted into the country. Polish agricultural workers provided the single biggest contingent before the outbreak of war.

There had been a long tradition of hostile relations between the Germans and the Poles. 'Polnische Wirtschaft' (roughly, 'economics, Polish style') was a term of abuse and derision, and suggested disorganization, clumsiness, and stupidity.[2] Even before 1914 there was a consistent anti-Polish stance in government; Poles were treated with prejudice, and from time to time expelled

---

[2] Jan Tomasz Gross, *Polish Society under German Occupation: The Generalgouvernement* (Princeton, 1979), 47. See also Martin Broszat, *Zweihundert Jahre deutsche Polenpolitik* (1963; Frankfurt, 1972), 234 ff. Cf. Richard C. Lukas, *Forgotten Holocaust: The Poles under German Occupation 1939–1944* (Lexington, 1986), 1 ff. See esp. Jochen August, 'Die Entwicklung des Arbeitsmarkts in Deutschland in den 30er Jahren und der Masseneinsatz ausländischer Arbeitskräfte während des Zweiten Weltkrieges', *Archiv für Sozialgeschichte*, 24 (1984), 305 ff.

from the country.[3] Anti-Polish sentiment even touched people of the stature of Max Weber.[4] Germany also had a long tradition of importing foreign labourers, well before 1914, and many of them were Poles. During the First World War, when the labour shortfall was greater than ever, not only were prisoners of war compelled to work, but in addition each year, except 1917/18, there were never fewer than 300,000 Poles employed in Germany, mostly in agriculture.[5]

The efforts of the Gestapo in racial affairs, far from diminishing with the isolation, emigration, and/or deportation of the Jews to the east, actually had to be stepped up dramatically. Even before the outbreak of war in 1939, the large number of foreign workers in the country and their relations both to their employers and to the people at large had to be policed. In 1938 nearly 100,000 Poles worked in Germany, mostly in agriculture. When mistreated, overworked, or underpaid, these people were capable of causing local commotions that could only be resolved when the police intervened and the Poles were sent home; later on, after their country was defeated in war, Poles working in Germany were more open to exploitation than ever.[6]

An indication of the kinds of things in store for the Poles, whether inside Germany or in the occupied territories, can be seen in a memorandum of the Racial Political Office of the Nazi Party, written by Dr E. Wetzel and Dr G. Hecht in November 1939. The aims were 'first, the complete and final Germanization of the [ethnic] groups of appropriate composition; second, the removal of all foreign elements not to be Germanized; third, a new settlement by Germans. The long-term goal must be the complete destruction of the Polish people.'[7] To bring about the 'solution' to the Polish question, the nation was to be deprived of leaders; the intelligentsia was also to be wiped out, and the workers on the land, 'racially the worst part of the Polish people', were to be kept in a state of slavery, educated sufficiently to be able to carry out the orders of their masters.[8] 'Racially useful' children were to be sent back to

---

[3] Hans-Ulrich Wehler, *The German Empire 1871–1918*, trans. K. Traynor (Leamington Spa, 1985), 113. See Richard C. Murphy, *Gastarbeiter im Deutschen Reich: Polen in Bottrop 1891–1933*, trans. T. Schoenbaum-Holtermann (Wuppertal, 1982), 183 ff. Cf. Christoph Klessmann, *Polnische Bergarbeiter im Ruhrgebiet* (Göttingen, 1978); Dietmar Petzina, 'Soziale Lage der deutschen Arbeiter und Probleme des Arbeitseinsatzes während des Zweiten Weltkriegs', in Wacław Długoborski (ed.), *Zweiter Weltkrieg und sozialer Wandel* (Göttingen, 1981), 65 ff.; Hans Pfahlmann, *Fremdarbeiter und Kriegsgefangene in der deutschen Kriegswirtschaft 1939–1945* (Darmstadt, 1968) 153 ff.

[4] Wolfgang J. Mommsen, *Max Weber and German Politics 1890–1920*, trans. M. S. Steinberg (Chicago, 1984), 21 ff.

[5] Ulrich Herbert, *Geschichte der Ausländerbeschäftigung in Deutschland 1880 bis 1980* (Berlin, 1986), 100. See also Martin Broszat, *Nationalsozialistische Polenpolitik 1939–1945* (Stuttgart, 1961), 9 ff.

[6] See the report of Jan.–Feb. 1938 of the Reich Labour trustee, in Mason, *Arbeiterklasse*, 618 ff.

[7] BAK: R49/75: 25 Nov. 1939, 'Die Frage der Behandlung der Bevölkerung der ehemaligen polnischen Gebiete nach rassenpolitischen Gesichtspunkten', 16, 20.

[8] Ibid. 23.

the fatherland for Germanization. (This was already a prelude to the notorious stealing of children carried out by the SS organization Lebensborn.[9] At the same time, efforts were to be made to save those who could pass Germanization tests, and there began a massive resettlement programme that would involve moving millions of Poles from their homes; a figure of 5.3 million is mentioned in the text.[10] It might be expeditious, according to the memorandum, to treat Jews and Poles in the same way, or to play them off against one another, as the case demanded.,[11]

The 'General Plan East' envisaged several genocides. Formulated on Himmler's inspiration in late 1940 or early 1941, it advocated the following 'solution to the Polish question': 80 to 85 per cent of all Poles would be removed from the German settlement area, and the 20 million or so 'racial undesirables' would be pushed out over a thirty-year period, perhaps to Siberia.[12] The reason given for not 'solving the Pole question' on the model of the 'final solution' to the Jewish question was that neighbouring peoples might become concerned about their own future. Such 'political dangers' had to be avoided, and forced resettlement was the only real alternative. The Poles would be joined in Siberia or elsewhere by 50 per cent of the Czech population, 65 per cent of the Ukrainian population, 75 per cent of the 'white Ruthenians'; and eventually the Russian question itself would have to be faced.[13] According to another memorandum from Himmler (May 1941), Germany would have to rid itself of other ethnic groups, even long-settled peoples, such as the Kaschubians.[14] These 'negative' population policies were to be matched by a 'positive' effort at resettling Germans in the east, where, together with those capable of being 'Germanized', they would give birth to the 'thousand-year Reich'.[15]

As bloodthirsty and genocidal in scope as Nazi theories were, in the short term the acute labour shortage in Germany could only be met by importing at least some of the despised foreigners. Other possible avenues were eschewed. In particular, political considerations and ideological reservations hindered the Nazi leadership from making up the shortfall by forcing longer hours on the existing workforce or having even more women work, or declaring a

---

[9] See BAK: R49/5: decree of 19 Feb. 1942.

[10] Ibid. R49/75: memo of 25 Nov. 1939, p. 25. See also Himmler's decree of 30 Oct. 1939 on 'Einsatz von eindeutschungsfähigen Polen', ibid. R49/11, 3ff.

[11] Ibid. R49/75: memo of 25 Nov. 1939, p. 36. See also ibid. R49/2: Führer decree, 7 Oct. 1939, p. 3; and Jutta Sywottek, *Mobilmachung für den totalen Krieg: Die propagandistische Vorbereitung der deutschen Bevölkerung auf den Zweiten Weltkrieg* (Opladen, 1976), 209ff.

[12] Text, with introduction by Helmut Heiber, in 'Der Generalplan Ost', *VfZ* 6 (1958), 306–9.

[13] Ibid. 319, 309, 310.

[14] Text, with introduction by Helmut Krausnick, in 'Denkschrift Himmlers über die Behandlung der Fremdvölkischen im Osten (Mai 1940)', *VfZ* 5 (1957), 194ff. Full text in BAK: R49/2, 76ff.

[15] Cf. Robert L. Koehl, *RKFDV: German Resettlement and Population Policy 1939–1945. A History of the Reich Commission for the Strengthening of Germandom* (Cambridge, Mass., 1957), 41ff.; and Jan Gross, 29ff.

'total war', in which all resources would be fully mobilized.[16] Hitler felt it was important that Germans should not be asked to sacrifice too much. As Timothy Mason has pointed out, great care was taken on the home front, so that the experiences of the First World War would not be repeated.[17] In order for Germans to enjoy at least some 'butter'—consumer goods and reasonable living conditions—along with the 'guns', foreign labour would be exploited even inside Germany.[18]

The decision to tap the reservoir of Polish labour was taken as part of a long-term plan for Poland, reaching into the anticipated post-war phase. Just how draconian that exploitation was going to be was made clear at a conference involving Hitler, Hans Frank, Martin Bormann, and others on 2 October 1939. Bormann's memorandum of the discussion reflects Hitler's wish that the Poles be kept in a position of inferiority relative to the Germans. For example, when 'normal times' returned, the German worker was never to work more than eight hours each day, while a Pole, even if he or she worked fourteen, should still be paid less than the German.[19] According to a decree from Hitler of 12 October 1939, Poland was not going to be incorporated into the Reich as were Austria and Czechoslovakia; its western areas were to be 'Germanized'—cleansed of Poles and 'returned' to Germany—while for the time being its eastern territory was to go to the Soviet Union. What was left, the central section, was turned into the General Government under Hans Frank.[20] On 20 October 1939, at a meeting between Hitler and Keitel, it was decided that the Poles there were only to be given the lowest level of subsistence: no effort was to be made to turn the General Government into a 'model state along the lines of German order'; quite the contrary, the area was to be kept leaderless and in a state of confusion. Among other things, the region was to become a kind of dumping-ground for groups deported from the Fatherland proper; in that regard 'it should enable us to cleanse the Reich of Jews and Poles'.[21]

The threat of war between Poland and Germany, and its outbreak in

---

[16] Ingrid Schupetta, *Frauen- und Ausländererwerbstätigkeit in Deutschland von 1939 bis 1945* (Cologne, 1983), 39ff. The average working week increased only slightly from 46 hours in 1929 to 47.8 in 1939: Karl Hardach, *Wirtschaftsgeschichte Deutschlands im 20. Jahrhundert* (Göttingen, 1976), 95ff. See Claudia Koonz, *Mothers in the Fatherland: Women, the Family and Nazi Politics* (New York, 1987), 196ff.; Jill Stephenson, *The Nazi Organisation of Women* (London, 1981), 178ff.; Dörte Winkler, *Frauenarbeit im 'Dritten Reich'* (Hamburg, 1977), 187ff.; Ludolf Herbst, *Der totale Krieg und die Ordnung der Wirtschaft: Die Kriegswirtschaft im Spannungsfeld von Politik, Ideologie und Propaganda 1939–1945* (Stuttgart, 1982), 150ff.

[17] Mason, *Arbeiterklasse*, 1ff. See also his 'Women in Germany, 1925–1940: Family, Welfare and Work', *History Workshop Journal*, 1, 2 (summer and autumn 1976), 120ff.

[18] See Richard Overy, 'Germany, "Domestic Crisis" and War in 1939', *Past and Present* (1987), 138ff.

[19] IMT, xxxix. 425, doc. 172 USSR.

[20] See Horst Rohde, 'Hitlers erster "Blitzkreig" und seine Auswirkungen auf Nordosteuropa', in *Das Deutsche Reich und der Zweite Weltkrieg*, ii (Stuttgart, 1979), 139ff.

[21] IMT, xxvi. 377ff., doc. 864-PS.

September, had already disrupted the flow of Polish labour recruited to help with the harvest that year. Immediate relief was provided by employing some 300,000 Polish prisoners of war and an additional 110,000 civilians by the end of October.[22] Brought to Germany, the prisoners were used in groups of fifty or so, supervised by the military, in agriculture in the first instance, but also in public works. This initial exploitation of the Poles, however, was simply on an *ad hoc* basis. As Jan Gross makes clear, utilization of Poles and many others from the east as slave labour 'was a residual goal, adopted as a temporary measure, in view of unavoidable delay before reaching—through resettlement, extermination, or Germanization—the final desired state of the intended polity: the racially pure Great German Reich. In its extreme form, employed in the concentration camps, this goal was known as the policy of "extermination through labour".'[23]

There were few attractive options open to the 15 million or so Poles crowded into the General Government on the defeat of their country. Not only were all labour organizations abolished and welfare legislation suspended, but the new regulations of 26 October made all Poles between the ages of 18 (soon reduced to 14) and 60 'subject to compulsory public labour'.[24] Given the possibilities of employment in Germany proper, something like 100,000 Poles tried to make the best of a bad situation.[25] Even had they been treated kindly, however, given the numbers which Nazi authorities were demanding, compulsion would almost certainly have been called for sooner or later. By early 1940 the Reich was asking Governor Hans Frank for over one million workers, male and female, for work in agriculture and industry. This number was to be sent in 1940 alone.[26]

Alongside the general labour shortage in Germany, there had been a flight from the land of essential labour and domestics. Poles were to help fill this gap. Initially, 780,000 were wanted for agricultural work—with 100,000 for Bavaria alone.[27] Domestics were to be consigned to rural areas, where, besides helping out with household chores, they were to provide agricultural labour. Frank was right to doubt the feasibility of such plans because of the sheer numbers involved. In early 1940 an effort to advertise the opportunities for work in Germany met with some success, because word had spread that Polish workers had been treated relatively decently there before the war; but by mid-March compulsion was being used.[28] According to stories told by

---

[22] Edward L. Homze, *Foreign Labor in Nazi Germany* (Princeton, 1967), 23.

[23] Jan Gross, 50.

[24] Alfred Konieczny and Herbert Szurgacz, *Praca przymusowa polaków pod panowaniew hitlerovskim 1939–1945* (Poznań, 1976), 319 (p. 325 for the decrees); cf. Homze, 29.

[25] Figure cited from Jan Gross, 79 n. 27.

[26] *Das Diensttagebuch des deutschen Generalgouverneurs in Polen 1939–1945*, ed. Werner Präg and Wolfgang Jacobmeyer (Stuttgart, 1975), 96–7 (19 Jan. 1940).

[27] Konieczny and Szurgacz, 326ff.

[28] See IMT, xxix. 391, doc. 2233-PS (remarks by Frank, 16 Mar. 1940). Cf. Konieczny and Szurgacz, 354ff. (2 May 1940).

Poles in Germany, many were simply pressed into coming and round-ups were often carried out by Nazi 'recruiters' and their Polish helpers.[29] Certainly by 1944 few would go unless subjected to compulsion of one kind or another.[30] One recent estimate suggests that probably 'no more than 15 per cent' departed voluntarily.[31] Rumours were circulating about what was in store in Germany, as is obvious from the ways in which Poles would do everything in their power to escape the round-ups.[32]

From the start Governor Frank was bothered about the use of force to fill the quotas, but he also thought it counter-productive for Poles to be treated so badly once they had arrived.[33] 'If the people are supposed to work in Germany, they should not at the same time be kept under as parasites.'[34] The money that Poles managed to scrape together from their work in Germany, he remarked, was worth practically nothing by the time it was sent home and converted.[35] He complained later that 'we would have been able to send at least 50 per cent more volunteer workers to the Reich if they had been better treated'.[36] Efforts to attract workers, he said on many occasions, were 'constantly hampered by the fact that the Poles and the Jews were placed on the same level' inside Germany. In February 1944 he finally got Himmler to agree to drop the expression 'Jews and Poles' in ordinances and police regulations, since the Poles considered it a defamation to be thus lumped together in the same category.[37]

By March 1943 one million Poles had been recruited for work.[38] Because some people returned home (pregnant women, people suffering from some infirmity, for example), there was a constant fluctuation in the total number at any one time, but the tally never dropped back below one million. (The precise statistics are, however, difficult to analyse in view of the many official changes in the border of Poland.) On 30 September 1944 some 1,701,412 people were registered, of whom just over a third were women.[39] In the summer of 1944 approximately three-quarters of all the women worked in agriculture, compared with just over two-thirds of the Polish men.[40]

Initially the overwhelming majority of all Poles were in agriculture (90 per

---

[29] Dürkefälden, 119; Herbert Spaich, *Fremde in Deutschland: Unbequeme Kapitel unserer Geschichte* (Weinheim, 1981), 169ff.

[30] See esp. August, 'Arbeitsmarkt', 342ff. Cf. Konieczny and Szurgacz, 420ff.

[31] Jan Gross, 79.

[32] Ibid. 79ff.

[33] *Diensttagebuch des Generalgouverneurs*, 293 (27 Oct. 1942).

[34] Ibid. 153 (12 Mar. 1940).

[35] Ibid. 511 (22 June 1942).

[36] Ibid. 587 (9 Dec. 1942).

[37] Ibid. 796. Cf. Fritz Sauckel's testimony in IMT, xv. 164ff.

[38] *Diensttagebuch des Generalgouverneurs*, 631 (13 Mar. 1943).

[39] See Ulrich Herbert, *Fremdarbeiter: Politik und Praxis des 'Ausländer-Einsatzes' in der Kriegswirtschaft des Dritten Reiches* (Berlin, 1986), 272. Cf. Czesław Łuczak, *Położenie polskich robotników przymusowych w Rzeszy 1939–1945* (Poznań, 1975), 201, and Homze, 195.

[40] Schupetta, 97.

cent in mid-1940), but in time German industry also showed an interest in
Polish technical and industrial workers. By November 1942 the percentage
in agriculture went below 75 per cent for the first time, and continued to
decline slowly thereafter.[41] But in view of the initial concentration on agriculture it is not surprising that their geographic distribution coincided with
Germany's major agriculture sectors. The eastern states consistently
employed most Polish labour; the figures for September 1944 (for example)
are: Brandenburg, 162,391; East Prussia, 144,511; Lower Silesia, 132,496;
Pomerania, 116,105. At the same time, the west German state of Westphalia
had 91,590, and Bavaria a total of 71,711.[42]

Within Bavaria Polish men and women were usually distributed in small
clusters or sent directly to the homes of farmers; as a rule there were fewer
than ten per village. Because many either worked as domestics or had quarters
in the same house, social interaction was virtually unavoidable. Surveillance
and separation were easier in the cities, where larger groups could be kept
in camps near railway stations or in the proximity of a factory. Bavaria's
Catholic rural population was reluctant to support Nazism before 1933 and,
especially in Lower Franconia, slow to come round thereafter. By June 1940
there were already some 3,000 Poles in the Würzburg district alone (2,400
men, 600 women).[43] Almost without exception, these people were Catholic,
and often they were rural folk themselves. How was the Gestapo to go about
enforcing the stringent policies on non-fraternization in such circumstances?

2. GESTAPO CONTROL OF THE FOREIGN WORKERS

The recruitment of Polish citizens in the 1930s was accompanied by a concern
about 'racial mixing',[44] and this was reflected in the creation of a special
department within the personal staff of Reichsführer SS Himmler. Werner
Best, in a letter of 13 August 1937 to local authorities, had made it clear
that 'every police measure must be taken' to ensure that, after completing
their jobs in agriculture, these workers left Germany again.[45] The Poles who
came were protected under the terms of a treaty of November 1927, and
were allowed to attend church and celebrate religious holidays, and generally
were to be respected.[46] A wholly new situation arose after the defeat of Poland
in September 1939.

Throughout the autumn and into the winter, as more and more Poles were
brought to Germany, a whole series of policies were being formulated to

---

[41] Eva Seeber, *Zwangsarbeiter in der faschistischen Kriegswirtschaft* (Berlin (East), 1964), 152.
[42] See the table in Łuczak, p. lxxiv.
[43] StA W: SD 9 (27 June 1940).
[44] BAK:R58/1030, 1 ff.: Group Arbeitseinsatz of Göring's staff to Minister of War (12 Apr.
1937).
[45] Ibid. 6–7.
[46] Ibid. 7–8.

regulate their every move. A long communication sent on 8 March 1940 instructed the Gestapo posts concerning their enforcement. The memorandum set out guide-lines for dealing with all eventualities: (1) insubordination, disobedience, and shirking were to be dealt with immediately (recalcitrant cases were to be sent to the rock-quarry in Mauthausen, and perhaps given 'special handling'); (2) 'undesirable' sexual behaviour, was also to be subject to 'special handling', and the German person involved was to be arrested; (3) security risks were to be watched by the Gestapo, which was to censor letters; (4) the Gestapo was also to co-ordinate the hunt for workers who left their workplace without permission. Finally, (5) ordinary citizens' behaviour would in future also have to be policed more closely in order to protect the 'honour and dignity' of the Germans. Specifically, anyone caught aiding and abetting Poles in not fulfilling their duties would have to be 'warned'; also to be warned were those who encouraged Poles in 'unfortunate' behaviour, such as frequenting bars and restaurants not set aside for them, or who helped them by purchasing tickets, passing on letters, collecting money and clothes for them, and so on. If a warning did not suffice, trangressors should be sent to a concentration camp.[47] These stipulations, given somewhat more precision in the weeks and months that followed, were an open invitation to local Gestapo officials to take measures as they saw fit. As the Poles left the transports they were registered; a file, with photograph attached, was opened on each person.[48]

The 'duties of male and female civilian workers of Polish nationality during their stay in Germany' were written up in nine short paragraphs. Translated where necessary, these were to be read and, some local police insisted, even signed by each person and kept on file. These regulations institutionalized the Poles' inequality. Henceforth, confined to their workplace and to their billets after curfew, excluded from using public transport except with special permission, they were at all times to wear an identification badge—a purple 'P' sewn to all their clothing on the right breast. Even when they worked indoors in a household, the 'P' was still mandatory. Paragraph 6 prohibited 'all social contact with the German people'. 'Visits to theatres, cinemas, dances, bars, and churches in company with Germans' were explicitly forbidden. Paragraph 7 stated bluntly that 'anyone who has sexual intercourse with a German man or woman, or approaches them in any other improper manner, will be punished by death'.[49] In other words, 'race defilement' of Germans by Poles, which had been serious enough when it involved Jews and non-Jews, was turned into a capital offence.

[47] Ibid. 28–35: Himmler to all police (8 Mar. 1940).

[48] For examples of surviving files see StA NadD and BGLK. See also Christoph U. Schminck-Gustavus, 'Zwangsarbeitsrecht und Faschismus: Zur "Polenpolitik" im "Dritten Reich"', *Kritische Justiz*, 13 (1980), 1–27, 184–206.

[49] BAK: R58/1030, 42–3.

Another letter from Himmler on 8 March 1940 indicates that even before
the adoption of these measures, in the provinces harsh consequences already
ensued wherever sexual relations between Poles and Germans were discovered. Writing to Rudolf Hess in Munich, Himmler remarked on the practice
of on-the-spot justice. His plea for immediate arrests was not, he claimed,

to prevent expressions of the justified anger of the German people about such shameful
behaviour. On the contrary, I believe the impact of public defamation to be a most
effective deterrent; I have no reservations if, for example, a German woman, in the
presence of the female youth of the village or such, has her hair shaved off or is led
through the village with a sign telling of her act. Still, the defamation must be kept
roughly within these bounds and ought not to lead to the injury of the persons
involved.

As another of his letters to local authorities made clear, it was expected that
some public demonstration should take place as a means of instruction for
Germans and Poles alike.[50] It would seem that the police brutality which
gradually developed in dealing with the 'Jewish question' inside Germany
was applied from the start when it came to the Poles. That there was now a
state of war contributed further to the brutality.

The Gestapo was to make sure that even in the workplace German managers saw to it that contact between Poles and Germans be kept to a minimum.
Managers were to be informed that they would be watched to make sure that
they did not forget that 'all social relations between Poles and Germans' were
forbidden. 'Friendliness' towards the Poles, they were reminded, would not
be tolerated.[51] In addition, larger firms employing great pools of foreign labour
were encouraged to establish their own punishment systems in the vicinity
of the plant; there are indications that some of these approached the Dachau
model in cruelty, and of course, many more groups were represented in them
besides the Poles.[52]

Just as many of the lessons learnt from experiences gathered during the
persecution of the Jews were applied to the Poles, in turn the methods used
in dealings with the Poles were later applied to other groups brought from
eastern Europe. Similar stipulations, including the death penalty for sexual
relations and a distinctive sign ('Ost') that was to be worn on their clothing,
were imposed on the workers brought into Germany from the occupied Soviet
territories after the beginning of the war in the east in June 1941. If anything,
even greater efforts were expended to keep them apart from the German

[50] BAK: 53: Himmler to Hess.
[51] Ibid. 46ff. The 'Ost'-badge decree was issued on 20 Feb. 1942; see *Allgemeine Erlaßsammlung*, 24ff.
[52] See Klaus J. Bade, 'Transatlantic Emigration and Continental Immigration: The German Experience Past and Present', in Klaus J. Bade (ed.), *Population, Labour and Migration in 19th and 20th Century Germany* (Leamington Spa, 1987), 143ff.

population—not only because of the danger of racial mixing, but out of fear of ideological pollution from those exposed to Communism.[53]

The arrival of Polish workers has been described by Wendelgard von Staden (née von Neurath), who as a young woman lived on a large farm to the north of Stuttgart. What she has to say no doubt applies to other rural areas such as Lower Franconia. The first experience of the Poles which the family had was the dozen prisoners of war sent to them at the conclusion of the Polish campaign in 1939. Only some of these (Josef and Szigmund) stayed on. Because everyone in the village fit enough to serve in the military was drafted, even fields which the von Neuraths had leased out were returned to them, and there was insufficient local labour to cultivate all the land that was available. Even before mass conscription this area had witnessed extreme labour shortages on the land, as many had left for the better prospects offered by industry.[54] In 1940 and into 1941 'trainloads of forced female labourers from Poland' arrived.[55] In time the relatives of some of the Poles also came— 'that was possible if you knew how to get along with the officials'.[56] After the winter of 1941–2, she went on,

trainloads of forced workers were sent from the occupied Russian territories. Whoever needed workers—and that was everyone, farmers and businessmen, craftsmen and factory owners alike—could go to the railway station and collect them as the trains came in. Since we had more and more vegetable fields under cultivation and could not possibly get the work done by ourselves, we went with Szigmund on the tractor to the Stuttgart station.

Trains from the east were rolling into the huge concourse. It was evening. Guards were standing on the platform. With white billows of steam, large locomotives still crusted with snow came puffing to a halt on the tracks. Out of the boxcars poured hundreds of women. 'A slave market', muttered my mother. Holding themselves erect, the women cautiously stepped down from the cars; they wore long skirts and heavy padded jackets over loose blouses. Bundles were balanced on their heads.

The guards allotted us ten workers, all young girls. We learned from their documents that they came from a village in the Ukraine called Vilika Vovnianka. We settled the girls in the house by the nursery. They had a large room with beds and washbasins on one side and benches and tables where they could eat on the other. At first mother worried about them because of the great numbers of Polish and Russian male workers in the area. But the girls did not let anyone near them, at least not until Josef was admitted after Michalina's death. The girls from Vilika Vovnianka stayed with us until the end of the war.[57]

---

[53] Herbert, *Fremdarbeiter*, 154ff.

[54] See SD reports for 1938 in StA L: K110/44; cf. LA Speyer: H33 1268 III, reports from Frankental (29 Nov. 1939).

[55] Wendelgard von Staden, *Darkness over the Valley*, trans. M. C. Peters (Harmondsworth, 1982), 39.

[56] Ibid. 40.

[57] Ibid. 42–3.

The SD's first report of any significance concerning the reception of the Poles, in early December 1940, sounded a note that would be struck many times in the next years: 'It is reported unanimously from all parts of the Reich to which Polish prisoners of war or Polish farm-workers have been sent that the simple people have yet to adopt the appropriate attitude that will be necessary in the future.' There was a case reported from a village near Breslau (i.e. Wrocław) where Poles, along with all the farmers of the area, turned out for the Saturday-night dance. As if that was not 'alarming' enough, the Poles were encouraged to dance with German women.[58]

According to the SD report, this friendliness towards the Poles (*Polen-freundlichkeit*) 'especially in rural areas finds crucial support from Catholic clerics'. In Erlangen sympathy for the Poles reached such proportions that the Church took up collections of books, food, money, and clothes to be sent to Poland.[59] Early Labour Front accounts from Bavaria showed that it conformed to the national trend; in fact, because of the large Catholic population there was even more solidarity with the Poles.[60] The usual note struck in local Bavarian reports was that the work of the Polish labourers and prisoners of war was 'satisfactory', but that, in the words of a report of December 1939 from Gauleiter Hellmuth's office in Würzburg,

the attitude of the population leaves much to be desired. Apparently rural districts have been offering Sunday clothes for church-going. One priest gave out 3 marks to the guard, to pick up cigarettes for the prisoners. According to the record, the guard, who shares guilt in the affair, has been strenuously set straight by his headquarters. The proceedings against the priest are being followed up by the Secret State Police.[61]

Other acts of Christian charity were reported from neighbouring Cronheim, near Gunzenhausen, similarly resulting in intervention of the Gestapo.[62]

3. GESTAPO CASE-FILES AND 'FRIENDLINESS TOWARDS THE POLES'

Across Germany the Gestapo took immediate steps to police the foreign workers, and soon it had to devote an increasing share of its resources to that effort. Between May and August 1942, the Gestapo made 107,960 arrests, 79,821 of which dealt with foreigners; in addition there were 4,962

---

[58] Heinz Boberach (ed.), *Meldungen aus dem Reich: Die geheimen Lageberichte des Sicherheitsdienstes der SS 1938–1945* (Herrsching, 1984), 528 (4 Dec. 1939) [cited henceforth as *Meldungen aus dem Reich*].

[59] Ibid. The report concluded that the German population was also not 'reserved enough' when it came to Czech farm-workers.

[60] StA B, in IfZ: MA 541 (Aug. 1940).

[61] *KLB* vi. 163.

[62] Ibid. ii. 345–6 (Mar. 1940).

cases where Germans were caught in forbidden relations.[63] Both represented approximately 300 per cent increases from the same period the year before. The figures for July to September 1943 indicate that the overall trend continued upwards—of the 146,217 arrests, 105,262 concerned foreigners. The biggest offence was the ill-defined category of refusal to work or shirking. There were, in addition, 4,637 arrests of Germans for breaking regulations by socializing with foreign workers.[64] These statistics suggest a dramatic change of orientation in the Gestapo's enforcement undertakings, the vast majority of which were now directed at the foreigners—keeping them at work and racially segregated. As indicated below, these figures probably underestimate the involvement of the Gestapo, because in 1944 and 1945, as the war was brought to Germany, not all dealings with these workers were registered.

Already in the early spring of 1940 numerous instances were brought to the Würzburg Gestapo's attention. Even before Himmler's regulations were formulated, an anonymous letter of denunciation to the SD in Aschaffenburg on 15 January 1940 claimed that the owner of a pub stopped two men from drinking beer together; because one of the men was a Pole, it was brought to the attention of the Gestapo. Both were duly warned.[65] This complaint pertained to two males, so there really was no question of any racial mixing or 'race defilement'. But the accusation, like many others, named the Poles as the new 'untouchables', permanent outsiders present only to be exploited.

A native farm-worker who bought schnapps for two male Polish colleagues in early May 1940 was denounced and eventually fined; the instructions issued by Himmler in March had criminalized such behaviour. Drinking the schnapps with the two Poles compounded the 'crime' because it showed friendship.[66] Another early incident came to light when gendarme Wilhelm Noller from Mainbernheim reported to the local magistrate that he and the local Nazi peasants' leader Hans Pfeuffer had witnessed a crime on 3 March 1940. They noticed the birthday celebrations going on in the next room in the pub; though someone kept trying to close the connecting door they saw that a Polish male was there as well. This 'raised the ire' of both Noller and Pfeuffer who made the illegality of this fraternization quite clear to those assembled. Someone was bold enough to suggest that if drinking with Poles was not allowed, perhaps the Poles would not be so interested in working in Germany. If the peasants had to work in the fields how could Germany win the war? More arguments followed. This complaint was passed on to the

---

[63] See Wolfgang Schumann *et al.*, *Deutschland im zweiten Weltkrieg*, ii (Berlin, (East), 1975), 412.

[64] Ibid. iv (1985), 407. For further exploration of the Gestapo's arrest statistics and their implications see my 'Surveillance and Disobedience'.

[65] StA W: Gestapo 14819.

[66] Ibid. 11453 (Obernbreit).

Gestapo, and warnings were subsequently issued.[67] Another tip was relayed to the police in July 1940. Frank Schnitzler, from Fröhstockheim, near Kitzingen, invited Jan Kurzawa to a birthday party, which was against the law; he claimed later that he did not know that 'social relations with Poles were forbidden and punishable'. He and another celebrant had to be taught otherwise, as was Kurzawa.[68] There was also a case where the police were informed when Poles loitered 'suspiciously' near the house of someone who was not their employer.[69]

Not all Party members felt about the Poles as did Herr Pfeuffer. For example, the village peasant-leader Karl Jooss, from Westheim, gave Poles permission to dance at a birthday party in a closed-off room in a local pub. This was reported to the local magistrate at the end of March 1941. Whoever passed on the information quoted Jooss as saying, 'Come on! After all it's the end of carnival and the Poles should be allowed to dance as well; they want to have some fun too.'[70] Apprised of this behaviour, the local magistrate passed the information on to the Gestapo, with the comment that he was already investigating this 'politically irresponsible and inappropriate' behaviour of Herr Jooss and the pub-owner who went along with it. More than one publican was turned in for allowing Poles in his establishment when it had not been specifically designated for that purpose.[71] Joachim von Münster was the Ortsbauernführer in Pfändhausen. In mid-June 1940 he 'took his Polish farm-worker with him to see a film presentation'. The Pfändhausen Nazi Party cell-leader who was in attendance took umbrage, and told von Münster that such a thing was forbidden. The latter left the room immediately 'with his Pole', and soon after called for his two German farm-workers to follow. The cell-leader felt compelled to inform the Gestapo, and von Münster was given a 'sharp warning'.[72]

There were other 'dangerous' settings besides pubs and places of entertainment. One was the church. Bettina Kahn (aged 23), from Römershag, invited Teresa Stecko, a Polish domestic in her employ, to attend mass with her at the end of September 1940. This was forbidden, and Kahn was denounced to the Gestapo. Poles were not allowed to attend church with a German, and could go to mass only once a month in places set aside for them; the Polish language could not be used in public prayer or hymn-singing, not even in the confessional, nor could Germans serve as altar-boys at a Polish service. Any event which brought Catholics together—a christening, for example—could be an occasion for denunciation. In addition, Poles were not

---

[67] StA W: Gestapo 568.
[68] Ibid. 7596; 16606.
[69] Ibid. 16460.
[70] Ibid. 2762 (this was Shrove Tuesday).
[71] See e.g. ibid. 12073: Würzburg (Apr. 1941).
[72] Ibid. 8271.

to be buried between two Germans. In August 1942 the NSDAP Kreisleitung in Ochsenfurt complained that upon the death of a Pole wreaths had been sent by the German families for whom he and his mother had worked. This gesture was condemned as a 'base and insidious' act by people who were expressly forbidden by the Gestapo from attending the funeral.[73]

Foreign workers could even give offence at the beauty salon. From Dettelbach in late 1943 came a report that Polish women, as well as some from the Ukraine and the Soviet Union ('Ost' workers), got 'perms' at a local establishment. While it was true 'that no official prohibition existed' against this, the magistrate felt bound to point out that the Reich Beauticians' Guild considered such a practice 'undesirable': 'Only a hair-cut and hair-wash are acceptable, the latter, however, only if German customers are not inconvenienced by a long wait.' The hairdresser was 'instructed' by the police, and reminded of the Guild's guide-lines.[74]

A denunciation might simply come from an unknown passer-by in the street. In May 1940 18-year-old Heinz Knuter, who had been in the Hitler Youth since 1935, was seen walking with a Polish girl in Rieneck. He and the young woman were advised of the seriousness of the matter and given a warning. At this point (Spring 1940) there was still some leniency, and Knuter's behaviour was attributed to 'youthful rashness and ignorance'.[75]

Information from the persons unknown to the Gestapo could be stimulated by the slightest incident. On a visit to a laundry in Würzburg someone heard an employee, Wally Martschenko, from eastern Europe, calling her German colleague, the elderly Maria Precht, 'an idiot and old pig!' Such boldness was cause for suspicion, and a little digging produced some evidence. It seems that the employer, Frau Johanna Römm, had taken Martschenko to the cinema on one occasion, and even let her turn on the radio. This was a matter investigated in full by the Gestapo, with warnings issued all round. All Römm could say in her defence was that 'in agreement with the local labour office I exchanged two Polish women for Martschenko', but that when she did so, the labour office neglected to pass on a copy of the guide-lines about the treatment of eastern workers. This was now put right.[76]

Like all tips to the Gestapo, the accusation of being 'friendly' to the Poles could be used for all the 'wrong' reasons. In July 1940 Albertshofen Party

---

[73] Ibid. 5361; cf. 16397. Though not prosecuted for sending the wreath (the man had worked for her for three years), the woman was brought in for interrogation. The latter case and the whole issue of enforcement of policies in the religious sphere are discussed in Anton Grossmann, 'Fremd- und Zwangsarbeiter in Bayern 1939–1945', in Klaus J. Bade (ed.), *Auswanderer—Wanderarbeiter—Gastarbeiter: Bevölkerung, Arbeitsmarkt und Wanderung in Deutschland seit der Mitte des 19. Jahrhunderts* (Ostfildern, 1984), 614ff. For the law see *Allgemeine Erlaßsammlung*, 150ff. (10 Sept. 1943).

[74] StA W: Gestapo 6297.

[75] Ibid. 4280; 9631.

[76] Ibid. 10865.

member Paul Hellman turned in his neighbours, the Klostermanns—Christoph, another Party member (born 1899), and Babette (born 1903)—for being 'particularly friendly' to 'their Pole', the domestic Janka. Not only did the Klostermanns let their house be used as a place where Poles of the area gathered, but, Hellman insisted, they let them rest inside at noon when it was hot, while their German workers continued to toil in the sun. Almost without exception, the neighbours were uncertain about the validity of the charges, but one after another they made potentially damning statements. Margarete Ludwig (born 1908), for example, was of the opinion that the Poles made many 'visits' to the Klostermanns 'purely for entertainment purposes'; some of these lasted until 1.00 a.m. 'The whole neighbourhood was upset by this.' Frau Ludwig had protested to the Klostermanns, but was told to mind her own business. The Gestapo, after a 'wide-ranging' investigation, concluded its case with the notation that 'hostile neighbourly relations' existed between Hellmann, the original complainant, and the Klostermanns. These were caused in part because of business competition (both were involved in market gardening), and because Hellmann simply felt that Babette Klostermann was something of 'a big mouth', who rubbed many people the wrong way. The only thing that could be established for certain was that on occasion (first recorded for 27 May 1940) the Klostermanns had permitted Poles to meet in their home, once until 10.00 p.m. The Klostermanns were warned that the next time they could expect to be sent to a concentration camp.[77]

Being brought in for interrogation by the police or the Gestapo was, by late 1940, a prospect laden with anxiety and danger: the Gestapo had an evil reputation by that date, and there was always the possibility of arbitrary arrest and detention. An appearance in court could no longer be assumed and, regardless of a trial's outcome, the Gestapo could place whomever it wished in 'protective custody'.

One form of 'friendly' relations which came in for special surveillance by local authorities and their amateur helpers concerned the generosity of Germans to the Poles. The sight of a Pole riding about the countryside on a bicycle, even if he had been given permission to do so, was thought intolerable by some citizens.[78] Attention was devoted to making sure that guide-lines regulating food, clothing, and other provisions for the Polish workers were not exceeded. (It has to be remembered that Germans themselves were subject to rationing and complained bitterly about cut-backs as they were introduced.[79]) Exactly what the Poles were allowed was vague, and the rules were constantly changing; this very uncertainty worked as a deterrent to generosity precisely because *any* open-handedness was potentially 'criminal'

[77] StA W: Gestapo 16179.
[78] Ibid. 463.
[79] See *Meldungen aus dem Reich*, 1873–4 (Dec. 1940); 2148 (Mar. 1941); 3496ff. (Mar. 1942).

in that it might indicate 'friendliness'. If a German woman was involved and the Poles were male, the possibility of sexual relations was also checked.[80]

Similar strictures were in place with regard to other workers from the east; not only were their rations intentionally kept shorter than those of Germans, but they were prevented from purchasing supplementary food and clothing not on the rationed lists. While some people were prepared to risk being informed upon, others showed willingness to inform and to express 'legitimate' outrage at the very idea of a German giving a Pole an extra drink of alcohol, or an extra portion of food. Local officials could also demonstrate their 'commitment' to the cause by zealously following up the complaint. An impression of how far things could go may be gathered from the following illustrations.[81]

Michael Linz, owner of a wholesale fruit and gardening business in Würzburg, upon visiting a restaurant on a Sunday evening in early August 1941 with his nephew and family, asked for cigarettes but was told by the waitress, Else Mores (born 1888), that there were none to be had. Satisfied momentarily by this answer, Linz saw soon enough that this was not the case. 'After about ten minutes two Polish farm-workers from the Keesburg estate came into the pub. Not enough that these scoundrels got beer, but the waitress took a packet of Eckstein cigarettes out of her pocket and offered them to the Poles. Shortly before a German had been told that there wasn't one in the place. That has to be wiped out, the spot blown to pieces, and the whole bunch sent to a concentration camp.' This outraged citizen sent his complaint to the Würzburg Kreisleitung, who passed it to the Gestapo. Frau Mores was fined 10 marks. In her defence she insisted that she did not know the Poles, and that as she never had enough cigarettes to go around, she tried to give them out to her customers as fairly as possible. For Linz, and the Gestapo, it appeared criminal that Poles should get the cigarettes while Germans went without.[82]

In early 1941 someone told the magistrate in Obernburg that Titus Schumacher (born 1879), a butcher and restaurant-owner in Eschau, had given an excessive amount of alcohol to Jaros Mynarek, a Polish civilian, 'around the turn of the year in 1941'. The Pole not only got drunk, but Schumacher, it was alleged, permitted him to stay the night. An investigation showed that Schumacher had earlier sent this same man, who turned out to be an ex-employee, 'used clothes and also cigars or cigarettes, a piece of Wurst, and a small number of baked goods'. While nothing could be proven in regard to the alcohol, and a reasonable explanation was found for Mynarek's spending

---

[80] Herbert, *Fremdarbeiter*, 125.

[81] For an early analysis of conditions see Patricia Harvey, 'Labour', in Arnold Toynbee (ed.), *Survey of International Affairs 1939–1946: Hitler's Europe* (London, 1954), 249ff.; cf. International Labour Office, *The Exploitation of Foreign Labour by Germany* (Montreal, 1945), 90ff.

[82] StA W: Gestapo 6963.

the night, the generosity was condemned as 'un-German behaviour', and Schumacher was warned.[83]

The village gendarme in Thüngen was keen to do his duty. At the end of January 1942 it was observed that 'in the last few days' Poles had been seen (by persons not named in his letter) sending more packages than usual to Poland.

This gave rise to a suspicion that either stolen goods or bought goods that were subject to the war measures' ordinances were being sent to Poland. On that basis I stopped a Pole I met in the street, who was on the way to the post office with a package under his arm, and brought him to the gendarmerie post in order to investigate the contents. In this way I was able to determine that the package contained 4 pounds of wheat flour.

'The Pole Andryszak' said he had been able to make the purchase because 'an old lady' had given him the necessary ration coupon, but the gendarme was having none of it. He tracked down the crime to the baker's shop. Indeed, it was the baker—a member of the Nazi Party 'in good standing and with a good reputation'—who had given Andryszak the flour in lieu of wages for unloading a wagon.[84] The assumption that when Poles shipped something home it must have been stolen or acquired illegally can be seen in other cases, and reinforces the impression of the lowly existence they faced inside Germany.[85] Such cases also show that local village policemen knew what was expected and did the bidding of the Gestapo without having to be prompted.

4. POLICING SEXUAL RELATIONS WITH POLISH WORKERS

Sexual relations between Germans and Poles, as between 'Aryans' and Jews, was highest on the list of 'sins against the blood', as conceived by Hitler and other leaders in Nazi Germany. In August 1940 the RSHA wanted to apply the same measures against workers and prisoners of war from western Europe, but little came of that intention because of the fear of negative reactions from collaborationist governments, such as the one in Vichy France.[86] No such reservations affected the Gestapo when it came to taking steps at the slightest suggestion that Poles were misbehaving, or even that Germans were being too 'friendly' towards them. It was particularly keen when it came to charges of forbidden sexual relations. As was stated unequivocally in paragraph 7 of the regulations of 8 March 1940 concerning the behaviour of the Poles, this

---

[83] StA W: Gestapo 4946.

[84] Ibid. 13464.

[85] Cf. ibid. 14102; Würzburg case (26 June 1940).

[86] Cf. Herbert, *Fremdarbeiter*, 125–6, and Therkel Straede, 'Dänische Fremdarbeiter in Deutschland während des Zweiten Weltkrieges', *Zeitgeschichte*, 13 (1986), 397ff.

would result in the execution of the man or woman who had such relations with a German person.[87]

Instances such as one reported near Würzburg in July 1940 caused some modification in the regulations concerning the punishment of the woman. A 57-year-old farmer took advantage of his domestic servant, a Polish girl (aged 16) in his employ. It is unclear from the file how the word got out, but the testimony suggests sexual assault. His son, a soldier on leave, was actually charged with rape, but it seems that he was allowed to return to his troop. His father, in the meantime, apparently not well enough for a gaol term, was given a warning and told that he would not be trusted to employ foreign workers again.[88]

Reinhard Heydrich wrote to the Gestapo posts on 3 September 1940 that some revisions to the guide-lines were necessary, especially when it came to sexual relations between a German man and Polish woman. The reports of such events showed, according to his letter, that the sexual contacts were often sought by the German and that

frequently the Polish women are in a condition of dependence on these German men. Often the farmers' sons, or immediate bosses, in some cases even the owners themselves, initiate the sexual relations. And it is precisely those Polish women who fulfil their duties at work, and who want to retain their place of work, who become readily inclined to bend to the demands of their employers. For these reasons, sexual relations between German men and women workers of Polish nationality are not to be dealt with by special handling.[89]

'Special handling' in this context was the code-word for execution, which was now to be reserved for Polish men. According to the new policy, Polish women were to be arrested for up to three weeks, forced to change their place of work, and, in cases of recidivism, especially if they 'tempted' young men, sent to a concentration camp. The German was to be sent to a concentration camp for three months and, depending upon the seriousness of the case, further 'state police measures' might be taken.[90] Yet, as another case from Lower Franconia in early 1941 indicates, the new regulations did not stop the sexual exploitation of young Polish women. A Nazi Party member and wholesale baker from the Aschaffenburg area had repeatedly forced his attentions on his 15-year-old domestic. Even though the baker already had a criminal record, and notwithstanding the seriousness of the crime, he was not shipped to Dachau—as the guide-lines on the matter prescribed—but was

[87] Grossmann, 'Fremd- und Zwangsarbeiter', 618, maintains that the law applied initially only to Bavaria and only later (5 July 1941) to the country as a whole. This is not borne out by correspondence in BAK: R/58 1030, 42–3.
[88] StA W: Gestapo 5645.
[89] BAK: R58/1030, 88ff.
[90] Ibid. 90.

let off thanks to the intervention of the local mayor and district magistrate.[91]

The SD in Würzburg reported with consternation in November 1940 that German men, especially the farm-workers in rural areas, 'did not have the slightest sensitivity' when it came to sexual relations with their female Polish workmates, some of whom were getting pregnant and having to return to Poland. All the relevant authorities should be instructed, the report went on, to impress on the German workers that such behaviour was not acceptable. 'All cases in which contraventions have been established must be dealt with by draconian measures, because only thus will the necessary deterrent be achieved. Often more effective than a sentence are the measures of popular justice, with heads shaved and a marching about with placards in the village.'[92]

Polish women (and female eastern ('Ost') workers) who became pregnant were sent home; they could not stay beyond the sixth month of the pregnancy. On the one hand, there was the problem of the children: if permitted to remain in Germany, as the magistrate in Krumbach said (February 1943), 'the danger of their mixing with German children when they reached the age when they must attend school would become unavoidable'.[93] Pregnant women were considered 'unusable' after the sixth month and were sent back along with the physically or mentally ill.[94] One historian has suggested that, as the situation got increasingly tense in the course of the war, some women from eastern Europe used pregnancy as a method of getting out of Germany.[95]

German women in rural areas, often left to fend for themselves, established friendly and sometimes sexual relations with the foreign workers and prisoners of war. There was trouble even if a Frenchman or Italian were involved.[96] But a sexual liaison with a German woman was punishable by death if the foreigner came from eastern Europe. A German woman from the Ochsenfurt area, denounced by anonymous letter in mid-1943, was picked up and brought to Würzburg, along with the Polish man; the latter hanged himself in his cell on the night of 27 August 1943.[97]

German women caught in a sexual relationship with a Polish civilian or prisoner of war, especially if they became pregnant, presented the racist regime with something of a dilemma when the man appeared 'suitable for Germanization'. Such cases were discussed in a special letter of 10 March

[91] StA W: Gestapo 17008; this case is also discussed in Anton Grossmann, 'Polen und Sowjetrussen als Arbeiter in Bayern 1939–1945', *Archiv für Sozialgeschichte*, 29 (1984), 382–3.
[92] StA W: SD 9 (22 Nov. 1940).
[93] StA NadD: Reg. 17377.
[94] BAK: R58/1030, 91 ff.: Heydrich to Gestapo (3 Sept. 1940). See also the reference to the fate of Polish and Soviet workers in note 1, p. 215 above.
[95] Grossmann, 'Polen', 387.
[96] See StA W: Gestapo 2062, for an example of a woman arrested on suspicion of sexual relations with an Italian internee in Aug. 1944. For a case where all that happened was that a woman gave an Italian a piece of bread and an apple (30 Dec. 1943) see ibid. 5101.
[97] The case is discussed in Grossmann, 'Polen', 386.

1942 from Müller in Berlin to all Gestapo posts. If, in an initial judgment, both parties were deemed 'racially acceptable', and if the 'racially foreign' man wanted to marry the woman, no further proceedings would be taken against her. The Pole would be placed in gaol and 'his potential for Germanization' assessed. In the event of a 'positive result', pictures were to be sent to the RSHA in Berlin, both persons were set free, and the case was dismissed; if it were negative, the 'usual special handling' was to be applied to the Polish male worker.[98]

This was the fine print, and came too late to save Kasimer Jankovski and Eduard Koncik. Their troubles came to light when 15-year-old Cäcilie Bauer was brought by her father (Richard) to St Josef hospital in Schweinfurt in mid-August 1941. His daughter's pregnancy of three months was confirmed by Dr Brasch, to whom it was confided that the father was a Pole. Upon hearing this, Brasch disregarded his doctor's oath of confidentiality and wrote a letter to the magistrate in town. As he put it, 'I felt myself duty-bound to make this report in order to protect the remaining youth of the village'. The village in question was nearby Holzhausen. The Bauer family lived there, and for thirteen months, so had the Polish prisoners of war Jankovski (aged 26) and Koncik (aged 25). Jankovski had struck up a relationship with Cäcilie Bauer during the first weekend of May 1941, in the company of her friend Elfriede Kort (also 15 years old), who, it seems, had relations with Koncik. All four were in serious trouble. Given their age, Cäcilie Bauer and Elfriede Kort were arrested briefly, sent to Würzburg, and released. Instead of dealing with the Poles on the spot with public hanging, as regulations permitted, the authorities sent Jankovski and Koncik to a concentration camp for execution: 'otherwise there can be no doubt that great agitation would have resulted among the Catholic population of Mainfranken'.[99]

Jankovski and Koncik were among the first Poles in Bavaria to be executed for having sexual relations with German women, but they certainly were not the last. The exact number of the executed is not known. Anton Grossman hints that in Bavaria the number approached several dozen, but this figure is certainly much too low. An insufficient number of local reports of the SD and/or other Nazi organizations survive for historians to be able to establish the number of executions (whether carried out in public or behind prison walls) with any precision. However, the few records of public reactions that exist create the distinct impression that many more executions took place in Bavaria than Grossman suggests. Not only were the documents detailing such executions destroyed, but many cases were never written up in the files in the first place. According to one set of documents which were recently

[98] BAK: R58/1030, 168–70.
[99] StA W: Gestapo 6961; 8548. (Bauer eventually had a miscarriage.)

discovered, more than 900 executions (mostly of Poles) took place in Hamburg alone.[100]

The most detailed accounts of popular reactions to the various punishments meted out both to Poles and to the Germans involved were written by the SD as part of the continuing concern to monitor public opinion. The SD analysed the effects on public relations, and offered suggestions for improvements. What follows draws upon the few SD reports which survive in Würzburg, and supplements these with an examination of others from surrounding districts.

One of the first instances when 'popular justice' was employed against a German woman occurred in distant Oschatz, near Leipzig. The detailed note from the SD in Oschatz to Berlin explained how on 18 September 1940 Kreisleiter Albrecht saw to it that Frau Dora von Calbitz was publicly punished because she had 'sought and had sexual relations' with a Pole. Her punishment, it needs to be remembered, was inflicted on countless other German women (but no men) in the last years of the Third Reich.

Frau von Calbitz, married, with a husband at the front, was described simply as a 'rural farm-worker'. She was questioned on the evening of 19 September 1940 in ·the presence of the Kreisleiter and a gendarme, and admitted that she had had small 'skirmishes' with a Polish prisoner of war. This case was handled mainly by the leader of the local Nazi Party—the Gestapo is not even mentioned here—which indicates a trend, remarked upon in the literature, whereby the NSDAP began to reclaim much of the influence and importance it had not really had since the 'seizure of power'.[101] Kreisleiter Albrecht had von Calbitz taken into custody in the evening and intended to have a public display the next day.

Already in the early morning hours word spread that a German woman was supposedly going to be placed in a pillory. From 9.00 o'clock onwards the scene in the city was already changing, and until roughly 11.00 innumerable people gathered in front of the Oschatz town hall; they wanted to see this dishonourable German woman. At 11, on the stroke of the hour, von Calbitz appeared, with head shaven bald, greeted by spontaneous derisive calls from the assembled crowd of people, and was placed in the caged pillory. On the front of the pillory hung a sign which bore the following words:

> I have been a dishonourable German woman in that I sought and had relations with Poles. By doing that I excluded myself from the community of the people.
>
> *Signature*: Dora von Calbitz

Without interruption new crowds of Oschatz inhabitants, on foot and bicycle, streamed by the city hall so that from time to time police action was necessary to

---

[100] See Grossmann, 'Polen', 384–5, and C. U. Schminck-Gustavus, *Das Heimweh des Walerjan Wroble: Ein Sondergerichtsverfahren 1941/42* (Berlin, 1986), 142.

[101] See e.g. Beck, 151 ff.

direct the crowd along an orderly path. 'The proper thing—I hope the others will learn; the dirty pig deserves nothing better.' These were the kinds of statements made by the populace in their comments on this filth.

By 2.00 p.m., when von Calbitz was released, no less than 95 per cent of the Oschatz population had appeared at the pillory... The success of this measure from the propaganda point of view was complete. The attitude of the entire town towards this defiling urge was one of unanimous rejection.[102]

In broad outline, this was the method used nearly everywhere to deter sexual and social relations with the Poles. The reception, however, was not always as acclamatory. The SD reports from Würzburg offer many interesting insights into the attitude of the Lower Franconian population to the Poles, and to the punishments inflicted on anyone breaking the strict codes. In general terms, according to a report of 27 June 1940, 'the native population does not maintain the necessary distance and often there exists false pity with the foreign workers. One has the impression that some national comrades express their rejection of the Party and state by way of a particularly loving treatment of the Poles.' Numerous examples are cited to show the absence of 'national pride' amongst Lower Franconians. The custom of treating the Poles better than required would appear to have been the norm in this area, and was attested by reports from all over the district.[103] While there were individual farmers who wanted to get rid of their Poles once the crops were in, and to trick them out of what was legitimately owed to them, the population continued, for the most part, to be kindly towards the Poles.[104] Popular sympathy was based in part on religious affiliations and social bonds, reinforced by living in close proximity on isolated farms.

The first public punishment was mentioned in the SD report on 27 June 1940, referred to above, and many more were to follow. There is brief reference to the rape of a young German (aged 16) from the village of Kleinrinderfeld, near Würzburg, and to the intimidation and virtual rape of another (aged 17) by Polish prisoners of war. Despite being 'victims', the young women had their heads shaven—which was carried out by the SA with the permission of the local magistrate and Kreisleiter—and were paraded through the village. In a follow-up report of 7 September 1940 the unsurprising reaction of the townsfolk, at least the Catholic part, was said to be one of 'complete rejection' of this treatment. The injustice of shaving the heads of the two young women was established legally when a court subsequently ruled that they were innocent of all guilt.[105]

At the end of 1940, the first full year of the programme of bringing Poles to Germany, the SD in Berlin wanted to learn about experiences to date. More

[102] BAK: NS 29/4, 103–4.
[103] St A W: SD (5 Oct., 8 Nov. 1940).
[104] Ibid. (10 Sept. 1940).
[105] Ibid. (7 Dec. 1940).

particularly, the survey was concerned with (1) the number of hangings of Polish men for forbidden sexual relations, and (2) the number of public defamations of German women. In answer to the survey, it was reported that in a small town near Würzburg an 18-year-old woman who had returned from gaol in Würzburg after being caught having relations with a Polish man was taken from her home, had her head shaved, and was paraded through the streets.[106] From the Schweinfurt SD outpost came word that no hangings had been carried out, but that one woman had had her head shaved and had been led through the village of Brebersdorf. 'Our experience of the local attitude is that while Party circles strenuously uphold the absolute importance of the regulations, the average village inhabitant feels more genuine sympathy for these people, particularly if the affected person is known to be industrious or has a decent appearance, judged from a racial point of view.'[107] SD reports from Ebern, Bad Brückenau, Karlstadt, Königshofen, Bad Neustadt, Bad Kissingen, and Würzburg also indicated no hangings.

The summary of the year 1940 by the Würzburg SD pointed to the injustice in the rape case of Kleinrinderfeld, but instead of taking that as a reason to suggest that 'popular justice' should cease, the SD officer Fellrath reached an opposite conclusion. He took the case as 'proof of the extraordinary moral effect' this kind of demonstration had. He was impressed that the parents and family of the young women had told the magistrate that it would have been better to have had the women punished by the courts than to have them suffer the 'shame' of being shaved and led through the village. The father of one had gone into a fit when he removed the hat covering his daughter's head. Such revulsion, according to Fellgrath, proved that whereas the ordinary system of justice had lost something of its deterrence, 'popular justice' carried far greater 'moral' impact. Moreover, 'for weeks' afterwards word of the events circulated throughout the district. 'The salutary effect' was the fear that such a thing could happen again, so that 'for the indefinite future' women would consider it prudent to avoid relationships with Poles.[108]

Obviously these reports from Würzburg reflect the double standard current in Nazi Germany. German men caught having relations with Polish women were to be warned, while German women were put in the pillory.[109] One example of what happened to a German woman who had sexual relations with a Frenchman is worth looking at both in order to show the double standard in operation and to illustrate how others besides the Poles were subject to Nazi regulations on socializing between Germans and foreigners. A married woman from Bramberg, near Ebern, who had relations with a French prisoner had her head shaved and was marched through the town

---

[106] StA W: Gestapo 5352 (May/June 1940).
[107] StA W: SD (2 Dec. 1940).
[108] Ibid. (7 Dec. 1940).
[109] Ibid. (22 Nov. 1940).

with a sign which said, 'I have sullied the honour of the German woman.' Some of the women in town muttered about the double standard openly, and wondered if German men who had sexual relations with French women in France were treated this way. But while 'most women'—even those in the Party—criticized the punishment, 'a greater part of the population welcomed the measure, and some demanded that a beating be added.' The religious, especially the Catholic population, felt that these punishments were unacceptable, and someone was overheard to remark: 'Thumb-screw and torture chambers are all that is needed; then we shall be fully back in the Middle Ages.' No mention is made of the fate of the French prisoner, though in all likelihood he was sent for a time to a concentration camp; in contrast to the fate of a Pole in a similar situation, he was probably not executed.[110]

The Jena Supreme Court President noted somewhat earlier (March 1940) that the practice in Thuringia, even before a woman was charged with having prohibited sexual relations, was to parade her with shaved head and placards through the village; citizens there were no less divided on the issue, with some declaring it to be 'out of the Middle Ages', while others considered it appropriate.[111] One memorandum (July 1941) by a propaganda leader to the Party Chancellery suggested that when public defamation failed to deter German women, the death penalty should be introduced for them as well, but nothing came of that.[112]

After the spate of early reports, all mention of the foreign workers (Poles and everyone else) falls off in the files of the Würzburg SD. Most of the SD reports from the Würzburg area (not, of course, the Gestapo case-files), like those elsewhere in the country, were destroyed during the fighting, or deliberately burnt by Nazi functionaries at the end of the war. The few that can now be consulted in the local archives were painstakingly reconstructed from the blackened remains of the fire and pieced together.

They are all singed around the outer perimeter, and are in places very difficult to read. In any case, the gaps in the documentation are likely to remain, and even the best efforts of the massive research project in Bavaria have been unable to come up with more. By chance, however, there are some relevant SD records (again with enormous gaps) from neighbouring Bavarian districts.

The SD in Bayreuth, responsible for the Bavarian 'Ostmark' (which included the Upper Palatinate, Lower Bavaria, and part of Upper Franconia), wrote several important reports in mid-1942 which deal with foreign workers and their relationships with Germans. The SD was most unhappy to note that even workers from the Soviet areas were received well in the countryside, because farmers regarded them as workers first, and not as 'racially foreign';

[110] Ibid. (14 Mar. 1941).
[111] BAK: R22/3369, 12: OLGP (30 Mar. 1940).
[112] Herbert, *Fremdarbeiter*, 126.

many were Catholic, so they were especially welcomed by Catholics because the religious factor 'served to erase the boundaries' between the peoples. Indeed, some of them were better regarded (in this area) than other foreigners, such as the Poles or even the French. It was a shock both to the SD and to most Germans that the Russians did not fit the picture painted of them by Nazi propaganda. For the SD this meant that much would have to be done to overcome these impressions gained from actual contact.[113]

A report of August 1942 showed not merely the continuation of forbidden sexual relations between German women and 'racially foreign' males, but a considerable increase. The SD recorded that fully twice as many cases would be registered in 1942 as in 1941. Some 257 German women were reported for forbidden relations with the 'racially foreign' prisoners of war in the Regensburg area alone in the first six months of 1942; another 39 women and girls were reported for having relations with civilian Poles. The SD felt that in more pronounced Catholic locations (such as around Landshut) the situation was probably worse. The report cited a combination of factors, including a failure to communicate 'to the simple classes of the people', feelings of pity for the foreigners forced from their homes to work in Germany, far from family and loved ones, close contacts at the workplace, and the influence of the Catholic Church.[114] The report at the end of the month reiterated the view that it was particularly in Catholic areas that forbidden relations were prevalent, and that the rural population was most involved. As far as the SD was concerned, the main culprit was the Church itself, the institution that made so much of the 'brotherhood of man'. The priests, by dropping hints here and there, were doubtlessly sowing seeds of dissent.[115]

The Gestapo sometimes carried out the execution of Poles without due process, as is indicated already in July 1941 in a mildly phrased letter of complaint by the Nuremberg Supreme Court President to the Minister of Justice in Berlin. It seems that near Michelsneukirchen the Gestapo hanged Julian Majlca for having an affair with a German woman, who became pregnant (she was given ten months in gaol). After the execution all the Poles in the vicinity were marched past the body. The same letter mentioned a case where the Gestapo in Regensburg went to the court gaol, picked up a Pole who was being held for having forbidden relations, took him out, and executed him. In November this procedure was followed in the forest near Eschlbach, where the Pole Jarek was hanged for having relations with a 20-year-old woman. Again, 100 or so Poles from the area were led past.[116] A report of mid-1942 suggests that the Gestapo wanted to handle all matters pertaining to the Poles, especially when the death penalty was to be applied. The justice

---

[113] StA B: M30/1049 SD (20 July 1942).
[114] Ibid. (17 Aug. 1942).
[115] Ibid. (31 Aug. 1942).
[116] BAK: R22/3381, 76–7, 88ff.: OLGP Nuremberg.

authorities were left in the dark.[117] The report of 4 September 1942 said that 'some Poles' had been hanged by the Gestapo, but that nothing more was known.[118] In view of these actions, it seems likely that the preoccupation of the Gestapo with the foreign workers was greater than suggested by the statistics mentioned above, for almost certainly such executions were never reported.

That matters were not much different elsewhere is suggested by correspondence from other areas in Germany. Thus, a report from the Supreme Court President in Jena as early as 31 May 1940 noted that two courts had been supposed to deal with a Polish man who was accused of having sexual relations with a German woman; he was given seven years by one court, and there was a proposal to send him before a 'special court'. But before that could happen 'an official of the Secret State Police appeared, took the files, and declared that the Security Main Office in Berlin had issued orders to hang the Pole'.[119] In a case from the same area in September 1940 the Gestapo hanged a Polish man at the side of the road between Hörselgau and Fröttstadt; the body remained there for twenty-four hours.[120] A similar letter of complaint came from the Hessian Supreme Court President in March 1942. On 24 January, it stated, a Polish woman near Fulda killed her employer's child with a cleaver and injured another. She was hanged by the Gestapo on its own authority, and in the presence of 200 Poles brought to see the spectacle; there were no court proceedings. The Court President had no doubt that the Pole deserved what she got, and believed that the courts would have delivered the same verdict, but lamented that the Gestapo, with its 'lynch justice', was undermining what was left of the justice system. He was particularly disturbed that the Gestapo had permitted some 500 German citizens to witness the hanging, along with the 200 Poles brought to see it as a deterrent. The Gestapo was inclined to the view that an execution should take place as close as possible to the scene of the 'crime', but when local officials felt that the people of the area were not 'schooled' enough, or that they were too committed to religious faith, in which case a public execution could misfire by outraging their sensibility, the condemned person was sent to a concentration camp for 'special handling'.[121]

'The opinion of the German population on the execution of Poles still varies greatly': so began a special section of an SD report of 17 August 1942 in Bayreuth.[122] In view of the increasing incidence of forbidden contact between Germans and foreign workers, especially those from Poland, some suggestions

[117] Ibid. (11 Aug. 1942).
[118] Ibid. 119.
[119] BAK: R22/3369, 9ff.
[120] Ibid. 28.
[121] BAK: R22/3371, 71: OBLGP Kassel (5 Mar. 1942). See also examples in Aurel Billstein, *Fremdarbeiter in unserer Stadt* (Frankfurt, 1980), 36ff.
[122] For what follows see StA B: M30/1049, SD (17 Aug. 1942).

about how to deal with the situation were offered. The SD provided observations on the reaction of the German people on the basis of experiences from
'the execution of Poles over the course of time in virtually all parts of the
district'. Considerable importance was attributed to the selection of the place
of execution. An example of a poor choice was a case in the Straubing area
where the local Party boss selected a spot only a few hundred metres from a
youth-camp which housed 100 young girls. In the Lichtenfels district another
unfortunate choice was made when the Polish man was hanged in a place
favoured as a nice spot to go for a walk. Some villagers now thought that
this picturesque hill was spoilt and they wondered aloud why a 'less beautiful
site' could not have been found. In Rottenburg (Lower Bavaria) an execution
was carried out on a piece of private land without the permission of its
shocked owner, who vowed he would lodge a complaint. The choice in the
Zwiesel district was not much better: local women were worried about going
past it in the evening for fear it might now be haunted.

The SD believed that German citizens should be kept from witnessing the
executions. For the most part this recommendation had been followed, in
order to prevent the execution from turning into a sensation, or a farce.
In Hildburghausen (Gau Thuringia), when 'twenty Poles were executed,
numerous German national comrades, soldiers and civilians, were present at
the site. The figure of between 800 and 1,000 spectators has been mentioned.
Besides that, the police kept back an additional 600 to 700 women and
children in the forest.' The SD maintained that 'this kind of mass execution'
should not be allowed to turn into a show for hundreds of Germans. That
such large-scale executions of Poles took place this early in the war, well
before the tide really turned and the war was brought back to the German
homeland, means in all likelihood that many more deaths occurred than is
usually suggested in the literature. Perhaps further research in Polish sources
will settle the matter.

The SD report analyses the widely varying reactions of the German people
to the executions into different categories. Whenever a Polish man was
executed for having sexual relations with a German woman, the response of
the people was 'much clearer and unambiguous' if he happened to be evidently 'racially inferior'. A similar stance was taken if the murder of a
gendarme had taken place. In the Lichtenfels district popular opinion was in
agreement with the fate of Poles held responsible for murdering a gendarme,
as it was when it came to the 'ratio of ten Poles for one German'. It was
regarded as 'self-evident' that 'special handling' was called for in cases of
sexual assaults on German women; the usual distinction in attitudes between
the Nazi and non-Nazi population then 'disappeared'. Many people who had
daily contact with the Poles agreed with 'sharp measures' when they were
needed, but there were the 'exceptions', notably the religious Germans.
'Women of this category' were known to have muttered 'To do such a thing

to a poor Pole: he's also a person, and just to hang him!' Another remark 'not seldom' heard was 'Why just up and hang so many? After all, they are people too!' In such religious circles there was also a questioning of the practice of hanging a Pole without a court hearing.

But how, if at all, should the German woman who willingly engaged in illicit sexual relationships with a Polish man be punished? That, according to the document, was the 'most important' issue exercising all national comrades of all social classes. Party members insisted that the woman was every bit as guilty as the man, and should be hanged as well. The remarks cited by the SD were, 'And what was done with the Miss?', or 'She ought to have been hanged next to him', and so on. Such opinions were in fact common in all circles. 'Reflections that the woman is German-blooded, and as such ought to be handled more mildly, are foreign to the population.' In Regensburg it had been reported that 'the larger part of the city population actually apportioned the greater guilt to the German girl'. The reason for this view was that 'the Polish man was simply satisfying his sexual need, while the German girl, from whom more could be expected than from the Pole, had damaged the honour of the nation'. Local Nazi Kreisleiters took the view that, at the very least, the German woman should be forced to attend the execution.

If the German woman became pregnant and the Polish man was judged 'racially inferior' he was promptly hanged; but there remained the problem of what ought to be done with the mother and child. As the policy stood, according to the SD, the population saw a contradiction. While one woman might have to bear the shame alone, with her child—who would learn soon enough that its father was hanged as a criminal—another woman, if her Polish friend passed the appropriate racial examination, would be spared the shame and under some circumstances be able to marry him. Just how far ordinary German people had come to identify with Nazi racial policies is suggested in their implicit and explicit acknowledgement that both women 'forgot their honour'. What was bothering them was the different—unjust— effects that the same 'crime' could produce. While one woman paid too heavily, the other got off and could even beat the system.

Some German women committed suicide when they found out that they had been reported for having sexual relations with foreign workers. How frequently this happened cannot be established, but the SD made special mention of it in a report of August 1942.[123] Two young women in the Münchberg district, whose husbands were in the army, took their own lives, events which caused some consternation among other women of the area; however, they tended to place blame on the state and the authorities for letting foreigners in the country move about with far too much freedom.

[123] Ibid. (21 Aug. 1942). Not only Nazi zealots felt that the German woman should be punished; cf. the magistrate in Mühldorf, Feb. 1941, cited in Grossmann, 'Fremd- und Zwangsarbeiter', 618–19.

The population was found to express great pity when the Polish person who was executed was very young. There was also some dissatisfaction, especially in Party circles, when the man to be executed was obviously suitable for 'Germanization', even though he may have failed the racial 'tests'. Further criticism pertained to the long interval which sometimes occurred between the deed and the punishment. Hearings could drag on for nearly a year (as happened in Lichtenfels), whereas 'in a straightforward case the punishment should, if possible, follow immediately'. According to regulations from Berlin, the Polish workers in the area were to witness any execution, and one of them had to carry out the hanging. 'The impression created by the spectators', the SD said, 'is on the whole best characterized as "indifference". The Poles accept the event with stoic quiet. The same is true for the lecture which follows from the translator. Remarks from the Poles indicate a basic rejection of the execution, although there are variations in the sharpness of this rejection.' The SD maintained that doubtlessly the executions were a deterrent—an expression of conviction rather than a calculation based on hard evidence. They were on firmer ground when they acknowleged that 'hatred of the Germans' increased as a result.[124] In Bavaria executions were organized by Gestapo commandos from Munich, Nuremberg, or Regensburg.[125]

Notwithstanding the dire consequences in store for offenders, and in spite of the belief that executions, as the ultimate form of punishment, would check prohibited sexual relations, many foreign workers were able to find sympathetic German women who were themselves willing to risk public humiliation and personal tragedy. The Attorney-General's office in Munich continued to complain in June 1944 that German women had not ceased having intimate relations with foreigners of all kinds, and that in fact the illicit acts had increased in volume. The Party in particular stepped up its efforts to get through to the women in public meetings. 'Hitherto the particularly heavy punishments have, unfortunately, not achieved an overwhelmingly successful result.'[126]

5. GERMANS AND FOREIGNERS ON THE HOME FRONT IN THE LAST YEARS

Even before word about the disastrous outcome of the battle at Stalingrad reached Germany (at the end of January 1943) there was widespread concern on the home front about the millions of foreigners on German soil.[127] As early

---

[124] StA B: M30/1049, SD (17 July 1942); also for what follows.
[125] Grossmann, 'Polen', 384.
[126] BAK: R22/3379, 115: GSA b. OLGP, Munich (10 June 1944).
[127] *Meldungen aus dem Reich*, 4750 (4 Feb. 1943).

as 1942 this anxiety was given limited expression in some areas with the establishment of a volunteer police force (a 'Landwacht') that would help out in the event of an uprising.[128] After Stalingrad, however, the attitude of foreigners inside Germany began to change. Already in February 1943 Poles began to stop wearing the obnoxious 'P' required by law, and to make alarming 'advances' to German women.[129] One statement of a foreign worker quoted by the SD was, 'In the last while we've had to run around in rags, but soon you'll have to run around in rags and we'll put on the nice clothes.'[130] Other nationalities, especially the French, made no secret of their joy (*Schadenfreude*) about Stalingrad. Discipline among 'east' workers began to break down, as they reckoned with a victory of the Russians and the beginnning of reprisals; most Germans could count on 'having their throats cut'.[131] The impact of Stalingrad inside Germany made the policing of all foreign workers more difficult for the Nazi authorities.[132]

People in Lower Franconia and rural Bavaria, like those in most parts of Germany, regarded the events in the eastern campaign with grave concern. In their midst, the foreign workers constantly served to remind them of what was in store. The lowly Ukrainian servant who had worked for a number of years for a family in Augsburg now assured them—in broken German—that, since they had been kind to her, she would be putting in a good word for them when the Russians came.[133] The SD reported from Würzburg in early March 1943 'hopelessness and demoralization in all circles of society'.[134] At the same time Friedberg's SD post observed that

in conversation with the people in rural areas [there was] palpable anxiety concerning general security. The large number of foreign workers, the waves of conscription, and the small number of official surveillance persons are the main causes of this manifestation. 'If the foreigners only could, they would ring all our necks. They are all over the place, meet with one another, and hatch their tricks. If things were to go badly over there, then our goose would be cooked!' It is also pointed out that in some villages not a single gun is available, and that this is known by the farm-workers.[135]

Similar reports came from all over the country.[136]

Discovery of the murders of thousand of Poles shot by Soviet troops and buried at Katyn (March 1940) was played up by Nazi propaganda for all it

---

[128] Beck, 15.
[129] *Meldungen aus dem Reich*, 4849 (25 Feb. 1943).
[130] Quoted ibid.
[131] Ibid.
[132] Cf. BAK: R22/3381, pp. 126ff.: OLGP Nuremberg (31 Mar. 1943). Cf. the popular outrage (even among Party members) in Weisingen, near Dillingen/Donau, when a French prisoner of war was shot in Dec. 1942: StA NadD: GL Schwaben 2/27.
[133] StA NadD: SD Friedberg (8 Feb. 1943).
[134] StA W: SD (8 Mar. 1943).
[135] StA NadD: SD Friedberg (1 Mar. 1943).
[136] BGLK: Abt. 465d, GL Baden 8. Cf. the mixed reports in *Meldungen aus dem Reich*, 5295 ff. (May 1943); 5861ff. (Oct. 1943); 6349 ff. (Feb. 1944).

was worth.[137] Out in the German countryside, however, there was talk that other mass graves, this time of Jews, would soon be found. Given those deeds, and the persecutions of the Poles inside Germany, country people thought it prudent not to make too much of the atrocities of the Russians.[138]

Worries about the foreigners within the country, coupled with war-weariness and increasing doubts and scepticism about eventual victory, grew throughout 1943. There was also fear of being bombed, and even in the rural parts of Bavaria this concern was fuelled daily. Lower Franconians' first direct experience of the bombing came on 17 August 1943, when 376 US 'Flying Fortresses' attacked Schweinfurt in a daylight raid, followed by 291 on 14 October. While losses were heavy among the bombers (60 on the first attack, 77 on the second one, with an additional 121 aeroplanes damaged on the second raid alone), this was little comfort to the people on the ground, all the more so as the Allied forces felt confident enough to carry out these raids, and many others, by day.[139] Following the second raid, Würzburgers grew disturbed by the rumour that some of Schweinfurt's industry would be brought to the city, thereby turning it into a military target.[140] They were also upset that hardly any precautions had been taken in case of an attack on the city; though Würzburg was not a military target, how long would it be overlooked?[141]

As the chances of a German victory dwindled and the war was brought increasingly to the home front, the foreign workers began to flex their muscles. The SD in Friedberg noted in early February 1944 how the situation was deteriorating:

The behaviour of the Poles and other foreign workers in regard to the development of the war has become almost unmanageable. An informer reports that particularly the Poles begin to rule whole villages, and that farmers, out of anxiety that they might lose their workers, do not dare to say anything. Pfaffenhofen a.d. Glon reports: 'The regulation that Poles must be home by 8.00 p.m. is hardly followed. The farmers themselves say that they cannot really see to this, because otherwise the Poles will not work any more or would engage in passive resistance. In this regard, men of the Landwacht maintain that this year more sabotage and partisan acts are likely to be reckoned with. Farsighted farmers bring forth the suggestion that strict controls should be introduced and not just the Poles but also the careless farmers forced to adhere strictly to the regulations.'[142]

The volume of Gestapo records in Würzburg pertaining to Germans who broke rank with the regime by socializing with the Poles shows a noticeable

---

[137] Cf. Steinert, 143.

[138] StA NadD: SD Friedberg (23 Apr. 1943). Cf. the SD in Würzburg to the same effect, quoted in Kershaw, *Popular Opinion*, 365.

[139] Figures in Beck, 72; 84–5.

[140] StA W: SD (26 Oct. 1943).

[141] Ibid. (11 Apr. 1944).

[142] StA NadD: SD (6 Feb. 1944).

decline beginning in 1944; so far not a single case has turned up for 1945. A combination of factors were at work. For its part, the Gestapo attempted to enforce policy to the bitter end, so the lack of cases does not testify to waning of interest or official concern. Moreover, the law-breakers were often summarily dealt with and no files written up. Authorities in Nuremberg believed that the decline in the numbers of Poles being brought to court for various misdemeanours could be traced to the Gestapo and the police, who wanted to deal with the matters themselves and on the spot.[143] At the very end, all kinds of people were simply shot out of hand, left in ditches or hanging from trees and lamp-posts at the side of the road. Law-enforcement and justice authorities in both the civilian and military spheres, far from becoming lax, grew more vicious.[144]

The falling off of documentary evidence cannot be entirely explained by the practice of summary justice, however. As has been seen,[145] the statistics gathered by the authorities at the time led to alarm that there were more 'criminal' acts in this sphere than even before. The conclusion is unavoidable that the absence of records on forbidden contact with the Poles was also a consequence of the unwillingness, for whatever reason, of ordinary citizens to denounce. While such co-operation had never been exclusively based on loyalty to the regime as such, with defeat looming nearer participation of this kind in the terror system must have appeared increasingly imprudent.

Because the treatment of the Poles in Germany reflected the fate of Germany's armed forces on the battlefront, when victories were reported on all fronts not only were many local officials inclined to be stricter, but according to the recollections of some Poles, German citizens with whom they had contact shared in the euphoria and were inclined to be harsher towards these foreigners, even in the absence of specific justification in Nazi regulations. After the war a Polish worker, for example, reported that in the early summer of 1940, following the victories in western Europe, his (female) employer on the farm in Pomerania where he and other Poles worked suddenly informed them that they could no longer draw water from the well. They were told that 'for the Poles there is enough water in the river'. A number of other Polish workers state how their treatment changed in Germany after Stalingrad. Until then, using the Polish language in public had been discouraged, though the authorities had had no choice but to tolerate its use, given that many Poles could not speak German, and a minimum of communication between workers was needed at the job site. There had been some official concern about the use of the Polish language, as indicated above, and there was even worry

---

[143] For earlier complaints see BAK: R22/3381, 69; OLGP, Nuremberg (6 May 1941).

[144] Manfred Messerschmidt and Fritz Wüllner, *Die Wehrmachtjustiz im Dienste des National-sozialismus* (Baden-Baden, 1987), 63ff. Reports ('Anzeigen') to the 'People's Court' greatly increased after July 1944; see Schumann *et al.*, vi (1985), 266.

[145] See above pp. 226ff.

about Polish-speaking priests addressing Sunday service in Polish, as there was that foreigners speaking their own languages might foment strikes or even resistance. After Stalingrad, at least some of the informal proscriptions on the use of Polish began to disappear, although Polish workers remained aware that at the very least it was inadvisable to use it in front of Nazis, especially those in the SS.[146]

Certainly, any German employer, such as a farmer, would also take practical considerations into account before running to the authorities to report breaches of regulations, not least because there was little prospect of getting a replacement for an arrested Pole or other foreign worker. Even sullen and potentially rebellious help on the farm was better than nothing.[147] In Bavaria, as early as mid-1942, a full six months before Stalingrad, justice authorities were already complaining that 'in order not to lose the assistance of the foreign workers, the rural population in several places were neglecting to denounce all crimes, so that in truth the foreigners reign on the farm. That has emerged especially in the neighbourhood around Donauwörth.'[148] However, at the same time there were even a few official initiatives designed to mitigate at least some of the oppressive regulations concerning foreign workers.[149]

But if some convinced Nazis grew increasingly desperate, for many Germans war-weariness, reinforced by bombings and shortages of the bare necessities, inclined them to accept that a day of reckoning was not far off. Especially after the Allied landings in June 1944, there was a precipitous decline in the willingness of ordinary citizens to provide denunciations of 'criminal' behaviour. As some of the SD reports cited above indicate, the sense of impending doom and fear of reprisals just round the corner grew all across the district of rural Bavaria which employed Poles, and especially workers from the 'enemy states' whose armies were gaining the upper hand. Straining to keep going day after day, fearing that the foreign workers might get out of hand, and trying to keep their personal record as clean as possible, people now found it possible to overlook suspicious behaviour. As a consequence, the enforcement process ground to a halt.

In late 1944 justice authorities in Bamberg attributed the failure of citizens to take seriously the official imperatives about the danger of 'blood-mixing' to the 'guilelessness of the Germans': 'The racially foreign person in many cases lives with the German national comrade—especially in the country-side—under the same roof; the national comrade does not see in him the

---

[146] Jochen August, 'Erinnern an Deutschland: Berichte polnischer Zwangsarbeiter', in Jochen August et al., *Ausländische Arbeiter und Deutsche 1939–1945* (Berlin, 1986), 124–5.

[147] BAK: R22/3379, 118: GSAWb. OLGP, Munich (31 July 1944).

[148] BAK: R22/3379, 76: OBLGP (29 July 1942).

[149] BAK: R55/1233, 149: Propaganda Ministry memorandum (25 Aug. 1944). See Grossmann, 'Fremd- und Zwangsarbeiter', 601.

member of a foreign or enemy state, but a valuable fellow worker at a time of labour shortage. Pity and charity are the products of this false point of view and German sentimentalism.'[150]

The historian Max Domarus, resident of Würzburg during these stormy last years, points to specific experiences that turned people such as those in his native city and the surrounding district away from supporting the efforts of the regime. In October and November 1944 all able-bodied men, from pensioners to raw youths, were recruited to work on the 'Westwall', the border fortifications in the Saar area, where they dug tank-traps by hand. At almost the same time there was a call by Hitler to create a popular people's army of men between the ages of 16 and 60, the 'Volkssturm', which would be thrown into battle. Not only was this a prospect few could relish, but what was even more worrying was whether or not the Allied armies would treat members of the Volkssturm as regular soldiers subject to the conventions of war, or simply look upon them as partisans who could be shot out of hand. Another factor contributing to the fall of morale in cities behind the lines, like Würzburg, was the influx of evacuees from the front-line areas. Far from being grateful, the latter tended to disparage natives for not having contributed to the war effort for which they had sacrificed so much. There was also a return to religion. According to witnesses, the churches were once again filled to overflowing. The reputation of the NSDAP in Lower Franconia suffered discredit not only because the war was turning out badly, but also because local Nazi boss Hellmuth was both personally unpopular and known as a staunch anti-Catholic.

To make matters worse, the alarming sight of massive numbers of bombers flying over the area with impunity on their way to targets in the east or to Schweinfurt, even the occasional crash of a bomber in town or the unloading of a small number of bombs on to a target there (as on 21 July 1944), made tangible the destructive power that was imminent, even as it simultaneously fuelled the hope that somehow Würzburg might be spared. There were wild rumours that Würzburg would be designated a 'hospital city, and that Winston Churchill had a special place in his heart for it because he had allegedly attended the local university and befriended its beloved Bishop Ehrenfried. Under the circumstances, it is not so surprising that fewer and fewer people were willing to provide the Gestapo or Nazi organizations with the tips which made enforcing Nazi teachings of any kind possible.[151]

To the relief of many Germans, the rampage of the foreign workers inside

---

[150] BAK: R22/3355, 103: Bamberg OBLGP (1 Dec. 1944).

[151] For the above see Max Domarus, *Der Untergang des alten Würzburgs im Luftkrieg gegen die deutschen Großstädte* (Würzburg, 1985), 14ff. Würzburg was bombed with devastating results only weeks before American troops arrived; at least 5,000 people perished; 90% of the old city, and about 70% of the rest, was destroyed. See Heinrich Dunkhase, 'Würzburg, 16. März 1945 21.25 Uhr–21.42 Uhr: Hintergründe, Verlauf und Folgen des Luftangriffs der No. 5 Bomber Group', *Mainfränkisches Jahrbuch*, 32 (1980), 1ff.

Germany did not assume the proportions many had expected from early 1943 onwards.[152] According to Wendelgard von Staden's recollections, introduced above, the Poles and Russians who worked on their farm near Stuttgart did not seek revenge. Instead, they behaved as if not much had happened. No doubt this reserve can be partially explained by their apprehension about having to return to lands liberated by the Red Army and now in the Soviet sphere. To be sure, von Staden notes how, when time dragged on and they were allowed to wander about, some Russians became dangerous, especially if refused something like a bicycle they wanted to take back with them.[153] The scattered 'bands' of foreign workers in the Rhine–Ruhr area were also relatively quiet, and were far from having any political aims, as the Gestapo feared, or acting like the partisan armies in the east. Most of them had simply been bombed out, and, driven by hunger and the need for shelter, tried to survive in the ruins, either on their own or in combination with Germans who were living there illegally as well.[154]

Even during the chaotic days of April and May 1945, inside Germany the Poles and eastern workers did not seek revenge on the ordinary people. Henryk Grygiel, a Polish forced labourer for three years, recounts his experiences of those months. He conveys the impression that the regime, even if only with conscripted Hitler Youth boys, managed to keep control of the situation, not least by shooting and hanging German deserters. The grip of the Nazis was replaced almost overnight, at least in the western sections of the country, by that of the Allies. Vigilante justice broke out here and there, but a full-scale massacre was avoided.[155]

6. CONCLUSION

Foreign workers, regarded as a necessary evil and temporary expedient caused by acute labour shortages, came to Germany in massive numbers beginning in the winter of 1939–40. On their arrival, Polish workers and others from the east were explicitly made aware of the racist policies that had been designed to regulate their every move. Publicized for the purpose of popular 'education' across Germany as well, the policies aimed at segregating 'racially

---

[152] Cf. BAK: R22/3374, 95ff: OLGP, Cologne (1 Apr. 1943); the same tone is in all the reports. See also Wolfgang Domarus, *Nationalsozialismus, Krieg und Bevölkerung: Untersuchungen zur Lage, Volksstimmung und Struktur in Augsburg während des Dritten Reiches* (Munich, 1977), 158ff.

[153] Von Staden, 106ff.

[154] Herbert, *Fremdarbeiter*, 331ff. See also Wolfgang Jacobmeyer, *Vom Zwangsarbeiter zum heimatlosen Ausländer: Die Displaced Persons in Westdeutschland* (Göttingen, 1985), 48ff.

[155] Christoph U. Schminck-Gustavus (ed.), *Hungern für Hitler: Errinnerungen polnischer Zwangsarbeiter im Deutschen Reich 1940–1945* (Reinbek bei Hamburg, 1984), 120ff. See also Barbara Kasper et al.,*Arbeiten für den Krieg: Deutsche und Ausländer in der Rüstungsproduktion bei Rheinmetall-Borsig 1943–1945* (Hamburg, 1987), 92ff.

foreign peoples' as far as possible. Germans were encouraged to adopt the official line on the racial inferiority of these people, but at the very least they were warned to have no truck with the new racial 'peril' within. Any forgetfulness was answered in no uncertain terms.

As its case-files on those who did 'forget' indicate, the Gestapo took seriously its imperative to enforce racial policy, and, as long as there was information—whether from official sources or the population at large—it was willing and able to press home Nazi behavioural codes. It was hardly less scrupulous in regard to the Poles than it had been with the Jews, and initially it received a great deal of information about the slightest infraction of the strict rules. As its record of arrests makes clear, the Gestapo had to devote an increasing amount of time to policing the foreigners, and after the opening of hostilities against the Soviet Union in the summer of 1941 this activity consumed the great majority of all the Gestapo's work. Efforts to deal with the Communists, Socialists, and other such resistance paled in comparison. In response to the increased pressure on its limited resources from the new arrivals, the Gestapo adopted far more brutal methods than it had hitherto applied (inside Germany, that is) against the Jews or anybody else.

In spite of the draconian measures, and the strenuous efforts devoted to policing contacts across the ethnic borders out in the countryside, there were limitations on what could be achieved. Undoubtedly, one of the key factors which restricted what could be accomplished concerned the reluctance to denounce the 'criminal' deeds, a reluctance that by 1944 nearly turned to silence. It would seem that there was greater reticence to offer information concerning foreign workers than there had been earlier when it came to enforcing Nazi anti-Semitism. Curiously, it had been easier to get popular co-operation with the isolation of established residents in Germany—the Jews and those who tolerated them or showed signs of rejecting the regime's teachings—than to police the new outsiders streaming into the country. Without exaggerating that difference, enough has been said on the topic already to indicate that a major cause of the unwillingness to inform can be traced to the turn for the worse taken by the war, with the many painful and daily consequences for most Germans. But other factors were at work as well.

On the one hand, committed Nazis saw little or nothing to choose between Poles and other Slavic people and the Jews; there was a long-standing prejudice against the Poles, especially as they were perceived as having posed a threat in some way over the decades, such as in the eastern parts of Prussia and even in some parts of the Rhineland, where they settled. However, anti-Slavism was not nearly as widespread as anti-Semitism. It is clear that religion played an important part in eliciting some sympathy for the Poles. Most of them who were brought to Germany were Catholic, and all of them Christian. As members of the community of the faithful that the Nazis never managed to disassemble, and unlike the Jews, who had no such refuge, they could count on some understanding, especially from the more devoutly religious parts of the country.[156] Individual priests, as shepherds of the flock, also found it easier to speak out on the 'Polish question' than they had on the question of the Jews; such messages must have influenced popular opinion. The Jews had no such spokesmen, and some religious teachings even fuelled anti-Semitism.

Social status and usefulness were also a factor in popular responses to the 'Polish question'. Many Poles were rural folk, from the humbler social classes. Their efforts, especially on the farms in the countryside where they worked and were quartered, were appreciated, all the more so as German men were called up, or (from autumn 1944) marched off for work on fortifications, or conscripted into the 'People's Army'. The Jews had been predominantly from the middle classes, and there were countless ways in which one might gain psychological and/or material satisfaction from denunciations involving them. It was not as obvious how one might take advantage of Poles and other downtrodden foreigners for private purposes, especially as the war dragged on. (It also needs to be borne in mind that anti-Semitic teachings themselves had tended to find a less favourable response in areas where Jews performed useful economic tasks for which there was no non-Jewish alternative. Even some Nazis were far from pleased to see the end of Jewish cattle-merchants, for example.)

The persecution of the Jews inside Germany occurred during the heyday of the regime, when many Germans found it possible to accommodate themselves in some way to the new regulations. That the Gestapo had to take more 'illegal' or arbitrary steps to enforce racial policies against the Poles in part indicates that the enforcement process was faltering. Some of the incentives that had fuelled denunciations no longer existed, and the initial show of support for policing the foreign workers fell off sharply as the deepening crisis of the final months of the regime saw everyone scurrying for cover— except the Gestapo, which, now devoid of its contacts, hacked away to the bitter end.

---

[156] See the report in *Meldungen aus dem Reich*, 4266ff. (Oct. 1942).

Conclusion

PART I of the book suggested that historians and political scientists must bear part of the responsibility for misperceptions concerning the functioning of the police state. In spite of many works on the SS and concentration-camp system, we have been reluctant to deal in detail with the routine operation of the Gestapo outside the gaols and camps. Chapter 1 was intended to help correct some of our questionable impressions of the Gestapo by showing how it emerged by building on the traditions of the political police in the country, to a very large extent drawing the bulk of its personnel from the various police forces of the Weimar Republic. From these beginnings the Gestapo was able to attain central control of the country under Himmler and Heydrich, and was granted virtually complete freedom from the traditional constraints of the law, administration, and police. In Chapter 2 we saw that at the local level the Gestapo was far from being a numerically large body. It simply did not have the physical resources to accomplish the tasks assigned to it, especially as these increased in number and scope. And this point stands even when one includes the help it could count on from other organizations of the Nazi Party and German state.

Some historians have argued that the 'perversion' of the Gestapo resulted not because of the existence of the political police as such, but from external factors—the bosses in Berlin who issued criminal orders. However, a responsible account must also consider the internal dynamic of this police force, which led it to trample underfoot the civil and legal rights of citizens. Ambitious members in a secret or political police, given the ability to act almost with impunity, to detain suspects indefinitely, and to extort information from them at will, can hardly be expected to resist such temptations for long. Beginning in early 1933, it proved to be an alarmingly simple matter to turn the existing political police into the dreaded Gestapo.

The transformation from the old decentralized political police forces across the individual German states did not require a widespread cleansing of the ranks or purge of the old political police. In a word, the police became Nazis or at least adjusted to Nazi conceptions of the police; there was no wholesale expulsion of the old custodians in favour of Nazi Party members, the Brownshirts (SA), or SS radicals. That said, there was some shuffling in some quarters; but, as we have seen, there is a considerable difference of opinion concerning the nature and extent of any 'purge'. The only way to settle the issue would be to carry out a full-scale quantitative analysis of Germany's various political police forces before 1933 (perhaps as far back as 1930), and then to trace what happened in the following years. This will be no simple task, because, unfortunately, while the individual records of all those who served in the Gestapo at one time or another are preserved in the Berlin Document Centre, their files have not been categorized separately but are scattered amongst all the Nazi Party members (over 10 million index-cards), SS leaders (over 60,000 files), and various other groupings. Only when a researcher has the specific names and birth-dates of the men who served in the Gestapo (or Kripo or SD, for that matter) is it possible to track down the data in the Berlin Centre.

With due regard to these difficulties, we saw that members of the Gestapo were not simply political appointees, or just fanatical Nazis who benefited from political patronage after the 'seizure of power'. While there was some 'cleansing', we concluded that it was too little to be termed a purge.[1] In some places, such as Würzburg, there was simply no purge at all, while in other areas the changes were minimal. The not surprising pattern among the political police (and other police forces, for that matter) was to stay on and make the adjustment; that propensity is consistent with the much wider pattern in German society by which various occupational groups came to terms with the new regime. Moreover, given the expressed desires of those in charge of the police, and the intentions of the new holders of power—especially after the burning of the Reichstag buildings at the end of February 1933—to establish law and order and to support the police, it was particularly tempting for policemen to turn to National Socialism. Obviously, some of the old political police and others in the justice system were going to be sacked, either because they had alienated local Nazis too much before the 'seizure of power', or because their views were too opposed or too well known for them to be able to work under the Nazis. For the most part, however, the inescapable conclusion is that the old political police tended to stay at their desks, and, in the Gestapo, played the part of loyal enforcers of the dictatorship's will.

Many career policeman did not 'stay at their desks' merely in order to 'prevent the worst', but took advantage of the greatly expanded opportunities offered under the dictatorship. Whether they joined the Nazi Party (as most eventually did) or the SS (in a minority of cases), these men hunted down opponents and acted with the greatest brutality towards the unfortunates

---

[1] Adrian Lyttelton may be right to maintain that in Italy the State police constituted 'the central and dominant instrument of control', but he is on less firm ground when he adds that 'in Germany, the police administration fell into the hands of an ideologically inspired elite, originating in the ranks of the party. In Italy, it remained under the control of trained bureaucrats, and this was a fact of decisive importance.' *The Seizure of Power: Fascism in Italy 1919–1929*, 2nd edn. (Princeton, 1987), 297. There were differences in the terror systems, but the personnel in the political police of each regime do not account for them alone. For a critical introduction see Geoff Eley, 'What Produces Fascism: Pre-Industrial Traditions or a Crisis of the Capitalist State?', in his *From Unification to Nazism: Reinterpreting the German Past* (Boston, 1986), 254 ff.; MacGregor Knox, 'Conquest, Foreign and Domestic, in Fascist Italy and Nazi Germany', *Journal of Modern History*, 56 (1984), 1–57.

caught up in their web. It would be less than accurate to suggest that these men remained the 'apolitical experts' they are alleged to have been. Many of them had, or at least developed, definite political views, and they found the powers of the police over suspects much more palatable than the far more restricted ones of the old Weimar democracy. They were every bit as interested in 'cleaning up the country' as their masters, and certainly needed little prodding to move with brutality and violence against the ever-increasing numbers of people who were declared opponents and criminals.

The effectiveness of any police is to some extent dependent upon co-operation from the society of which it is a part. Inside Germany the relations between the people and the police were varied. The routine operation of the Gestapo in Würzburg and Lower Franconia, for example, needs to be situated within this local context. It would be one thing if the area was a hotbed of Nazism, where widespread co-operation with the police could perhaps be taken for granted, but quite another if the population was known to have had reservations about Nazism before 1933, and continued to harbour doubts thereafter.

As we saw in Part II, Würzburg and Lower Franconia should not be equated with all of Franconia or 'Franken'—the latter usually identified with the two Protestant districts of Upper and Middle Franconia, and linked to a stronger tradition of anti-Semitism and support of Nazism. Würzburg and Lower Franconia were largely unsympathetic to Hitler and the Nazi Party before 1933. Here was one of Germany's 'blackest' districts because of the population's overwhelming Catholicism and tradition of voting for the Catholic Party; it was among the most reluctant to vote for the NSDAP or join the Nazi Party. After the 'seizure of power', however, this area gradually—if perhaps only partially—fell into line, very much like the rest of the country. Indeed, as Peter Hoffmann remarks, 'on the whole, at all times from 1933 to 1945 the majority of German voters, indeed of the entire population, sup-ported the government, albeit with varying degrees of willingness'.[2]

Although Würzburg and Lower Franconia were thus not immune to the appeals of Nazism after 1933, it is reasonable to suggest that the support there probably remained at the lower end of the scale, and that by extension the Gestapo attained minimal co-operation. In all likelihood the police had an easier time of it in areas which were more prone to Nazism before 1933 and thus more outspoken in support of the regime thereafter. It is also reasonable to suggest that the Gestapo was able to count on more co-operation from the population when it came to enforcing anti-Semitic policies of all kinds in districts known to have traditions of anti-Semitism, such as in neighbouring Middle Franconia, where Gauleiter Julius Streicher set the tone, at least until he lost his post in 1939. Without pressing the point, it might

[2] Hoffmann, 51.

be suggested that popular co-operation with the Gestapo in enforcing anti-Semitic policies was at least as great elsewhere. Although the Gestapo was operating in less than an optimal environment from its post in Würzburg, as the rest of the book makes clear, the police were able to enforce racial policy there without great difficulty until the latter part of the war.

One ought to be cautious, however, in extrapolating from Würzburg to the rest of the country. Enforcement may have been easier to achieve in smaller cities and towns in rural districts. Keeping secrets or maintaining illicit and 'dangerous' liaisons is always more difficult in such milieux. In addition, it would have been more hazardous to express any sympathy one might have felt for the plight of Jewish neighbours and friends. The big cities tended to provide greater anonymity, hence relatively more protection from the prying eyes of neighbours, and it was precisely for that reason that many Jews were increasingly drawn to larger urban centres after 1933. Going underground was at least a possibility in the metropolis, whereas not a single Jewish person managed to find refuge through the war years in all of Lower Franconia.

What could the people of the district have known about the persecution of the Jews? This question was raised in order eventually to evaluate the extent and significance of co-operation with the Gestapo on the 'Jewish Question' in the area around Würzburg. We saw in Chapter 4 that the anti-Semitic excesses were widespread, public, and almost impossible to overlook, not least because Jews were scattered in numerous small clusters across the district. Given this pattern of settlement, Jews were known to many people, and, when anti-Semitism was stepped up, the people of the district had to bear witness. Everyday harassment was not uncommon, and the brutalities, especially during the pogrom of November 1938, were impossible to ignore. It was also clear what was in store for anyone who sympathized with the Jews or questioned official policy. Being turned in to the authorities for the smallest sign of non-compliance was too common not to have struck anxiety in the hearts of anyone who might under other circumstances have found no fault with the Jews.

It should also be kept in mind that the pattern of Jewish settlement in Lower Franconia was not typical for Germany as a whole. Some districts, even in Bavaria itself, had no Jewish population to speak of in the first place; in those areas the Gestapo was not faced with policing relations across the ethnic border at all.

In Part III we turned to the question of enforcement of Nazi racial policy. In Chapter 5 we examined political denunciations, or the provision of information from the population at large about suspected 'political' criminality. In the Gestapo case-files several kinds of phrases stand out. Some proceedings opened with remarks such as 'It has been reported that', or 'An anonymous telephone-caller said', or 'The Security Service in Aschaffenburg wishes investigated', and so on. In 1983, when I began this study, many books were being published on popular forms of resistance and dissent. It was beginning to appear as if German society under Nazism was a seething mass of discontent and disillusion, and one could only wonder how the Gestapo managed to function at all. Yet, reading through the Gestapo files, one could see many examples of what might count as some Germans' *positive* disposition towards or at least co-operation with the regime. Obviously some people had made the necessary adjustments and accommodated themselves to the new system, and some were clearly reaping personal advantages from the 'terror system'. Denunciations turned out to be the key link in the three-way interaction between police, people, and policy. This is the theme followed up in detail throughout the remainder of the book.

Some historians are reluctant to label as denunciation all information on suspected 'criminality' which made its way into official channels, and was eventually passed on to the Gestapo. Ulrich Herbert, for example, prefers to characterize much of it as 'gossip and twaddle' ('Klatsch und Tratsch').[3] The label we attach to this information is quite beside the point. As we have seen, all information from the population passed on to the authorities *functioned* as system-supportive, whether it originated as 'harmless' neighbourhood gossip or otherwise. It also did not matter all that much if, or when, the motive for informing was utterly self-serving. In fact, although the question of motives is bound to arise, the Gestapo did not greatly trouble itself about the source of information or the motives of informers. Reinhard Mann's study of 825 randomly selected files from the materials of the Düsseldorf Gestapo shows just how little the police worried about such matters. It will be recalled that Mann found no information on how or why the Gestapo began a file in 39 per cent of the cases, and that for an additional 37 per cent of his sample 'private' or instrumental motives were at work. In other words, a total of 76 per cent of his sample of Gestapo cases began when the motive, if known by the Gestapo, was presumably not important enough to have been noted, and/or when it was *clearly* based on personal or instrumental reasons rather than on 'proper' Nazi ones. He considered that only 24 per cent of all the cases in his sample were based on 'system-loyal' motives.[4] If the Gestapo were to have delayed its routine operation until it received this kind of properly motivated information, its work-load—and presumably effectiveness—would have been reduced considerably.

Normally, if information turned up on suspicious behaviour, especially if it pertained to important 'opponents' such as Jews, Communists, or Socialists, then the wheels of the police machine moved into motion. As we have seen, right at the highest political and administrative levels in Berlin, the leaders of the country could not make a firm decision about how to deal with the

[3] Herbert, *Fremdarbeiter*, 124.
[4] R. Mann, *Protest und Kontrolle*, 295.

flood of denunciations, even when many turned out to be either carelessly laid or downright false.

From Chapter 5 throughout the rest of the book, the sense conveyed is that there developed a kind of auto-policing, or at least an auto-surveillance system in Nazi Germany. There are hints in the literature, especially on Vichy France, to indicate that a similar pattern developed there as well.[5]

Chapter 6 examined how the Gestapo went about enforcing anti-Semitic policies designed to separate the Jews from others. In the first instance, the official endeavour was to isolate the Jews socially, but, especially with the Nuremberg Laws of September 1935, efforts increased to ensure that sexual contacts across the ethnic borders ceased. In order to police these intimate spheres of social and sexual life, the Gestapo required the co-operation of citizens who suspected transgressions.

Different degrees of co-operation were evidently required by the Gestapo to enforce different kinds of policies, and the more private spheres were infiltrated with the help of neighbours, friends, acquaintances, or customers in shops and pubs. If the Würzburg (and Düsseldorf) Gestapo files are any guide, there was little difficulty in attaining information. Not everyone gave up on the Jews and broke off social contacts with them. However, as the ease with which such non-compliance or dissent could be picked up by the regime, helped by vigilant citizens, became clear, bonds of solidarity were either broken or driven underground.

But as Chapter 6 showed, in spite of the massive anti-Semitic campaigns, the deluge of propaganda, and official and semi-official pressures to break off all contacts with the Jews, some people would not comply. The odds against detection were small. Just as care must be taken not to overestimate the numbers of opponents of Nazi anti-Semitism, in fairness it must also be remembered that some people, at great risk, provided aid and assistance, and there were individuals, such as Ilse Totske, who paid with their lives in their effort to help Jews.

Although non-compliance and some resistance to Nazi anti-Semitism show up in the Gestapo files, as Chapter 7 points out, the Gestapo responded to such behaviour by redoubling efforts to obtain compliance through police pressure, including the use of methods that soon brought it a reputation for brutality. When it came to enforcing racial policies designed to isolate the Jews, there can be no doubt that the Gestapo was particularly brutal, and often dispensed with even the semblance of legal procedures. Towards the

---

[5] André Halimi, *La Délation sous l'occupation* (Paris, 1983), 7, suggests that between 3 and 5 million letters (signed or anonymous) of denunciation were sent to various authorities in Vichy France. Even if he exaggerates the number, his examples make clear that this kind of denunciation was far from uncommon in France, that the motives of the writers were not always 'system-loyal' but frequently 'instrumental', and that the regime reaped the benefits in terms of surveillance and control. See also Sweets, 246.

end of the war, the Gestapo applied even harsher methods to the foreign workers in the country, especially those from Poland. The knowledge spread that anyone could be summoned to police headquarters, mistreated, and held almost indefinitely before being sent to a concentration camp under 'protective custody' orders, and it is not difficult to see how a reputation for ruthlessness and brutality contributed to 'successful' enforcement practices. An examination of the case-files suggests, however, that such methods do not in themselves provide a satisfactory explanation of how the Gestapo was able to carry out its broad mandate. From the very beginning of the regime, it is clear that, brutal or not, the Gestapo's own resources—measured in institutional terms—never allowed it the independence it might have wished to accomplish the tasks assigned to it. In the first instance it had to rely on the collaboration of other police organizations, and organizations such as the SD and other official 'informers'. However, in the sphere of racial policies, especially ones that sought to encroach into the most private areas of social and sexual life, the Gestapo was very much dependent upon the collaboration of individuals in a whole range of official and semi-official organizations and associations. Other people provided information they obtained in their professional capacity, such as medical doctors, nurses, and even priests. In the enforcement of racial policies designed to isolate the Jews, the success of the Gestapo's efforts was especially tied to the readiness of German citizens to provide information on suspected deviations from the new behavioural norms.

The 'successful' enforcement of Nazi anti-Semitism was not dependent on its acceptablity to the population as a whole, nor on its positive reception by them or even their schooled indifference. It mattered not so much whether the activities of Hitler and his henchmen were popular. It certainly was not necessary for Germans to become raucous in their anti-Semitism, let alone violent towards the Jews. It can also be argued that the functioning of the Gestapo could survive popular indifference. The enforcement of Nazi anti-Semitic policies required—once the regime set the tone or official 'line' on the 'Jewish question' and could count on enough zealous officials in place to press anti-Semitism home—that a sufficient number of people come forward, for whatever reason, to offer information when they witnessed non-compliant acts of any kind. Nazi anti-Semitic policy would in all likelihood have remained impossible to enforce if this requirement had not been met.[6] The rarity of

---

[6] Anti-Semitic measures could not be enforced nearly as 'successfully' in Fascist Italy. Nevertheless, Susan Zuccotti points out that at least some assistance from civilians was received, and that some Jews 'were betrayed by Italian informers—individual citizens motivated by general anti-Semitism and pro-Nazism, private quarrels and vendettas, their own personal involvement in illegal activities, or just plain greed. The Nazis offered rewards for information leading to the arrests of Jews, and several Italians collected. More often, the Germans received anonymous letters': *The Italians and the Holocaust: Persecution, Rescue, Survival* (New York, 1987), 136–7. Meir Michaelis, *Mussolini and the Jews: German–Italian Relations and the Jewish Question in Italy 1922–*

'oppositional' or 'treasonous' remarks on the issue brought to the attention of the police and court system—even when it came to the open pogroms and terror aimed at the Jews—offers silent or indirect testimony as to the effectiveness of the enforcement of anti-Semitic policies.

Chapter 8 turned to the enforcement of racial policies which were designed to isolate and segregate the Polish foreign workers who, from late 1939, were brought to Germany in increasing numbers to help meet acute labour shortages. The presence in Germany of these foreigners, whom Nazi ideology condemned as a 'racially foreign' peril, posed an enormous problem for a regime determined to prevent all sexual or even friendly relations from developing across the ethnic lines. In order to police these foreigners, several approaches were adopted. Some people were consigned to work-camps, or to specific factories which created special camps right on the premises—even, as at the Volkswagen Works, complete with a special Gestapo post of its own.[7] However, enforcing racial policy was much more difficult in respect of the Polish workers in rural areas, such as the district around Würzburg. It was one thing for the police and Nazi officials to issue strict guide-lines which laid down exactly what was and was not permitted, but how were these guide-lines to be policed and the rigid separation of the Poles from the Germans guaranteed? As far as concerns the functioning of the Gestapo there was little or no difference between prosecuting those thought guilty of 'race defilement' when the 'racially foreign' person involved was Jewish, and when a Pole was implicated. The police used the same terminology in both cases.

That the regime was able to elicit co-operation from the population in policing the foreigners, not only in Lower Franconia but across the country, is suggested by the rapidly expanding numbers of Poles (and other foreign workers) brought to Gestapo attention and registered in arrest statistics. No reliable figures of Gestapo arrests from 1933 to 1945 appear to have survived. There are indications in the fragmentary and flawed statistics on its arrests during the war years which suggest that a major transformation took place in its activities. It may well be, as Reinhard Mann's figures for Düsseldorf make clear, that after 1941 the *absolute* number of new Gestapo cases declined.[8] However, national figures for several war years show that the Gestapo began to devote increasing energy to controlling the army of foreign workers,

---

1945 (Oxford, 1978), 389, adds that 'while it is true that at least four-fifths of the Jews living in Italy succeeded in eluding the grasp of the SS and that most of these were saved by Italian Aryans of all classes, it is no less true that such successes as Bosshammer [Eichmann's expert in Italy] was able to achieve were largely due to (willing and unwilling) Italian collaborators.'

[7] See Klaus-Jörg Siegfried (ed.), *Rüstungsproduktion und Zwangsarbeit im Volkswagenwerk 1939–1945: Eine Dokumentation* (Frankfurt, 1986), 92ff., and his *Das Leben der Zwangsarbeiter im Volkswagenwerk 1939–1945* (Frankfurt, 1988), 61 ff.

[8] See R. Mann, *Protest und Kontrolle*, 182, 241, 252, 294, 296.

whose *relative* importance to the Gestapo increased dramatically.[9] In order to supervise these workers and segregate them from the German population, especially when they were employed outside camps, the police were to a large extent dependent upon the provisions of information from attentive citizens, and in the first years of the programme apparently had no difficulty in obtaining it. While not all those arrested were informed upon by a civilian—a supervisor or Labour Front official in a camp, or a Nazi Party official detailed to watch them, could readily call upon the Gestapo—local studies suggest that a substantial proportion probably resulted from tip-offs from the public. It is also clear from fragmentary evidence that the Gestapo continued to make special efforts (not without some success) to recruit informers inside even the smallest clusters of foreign workers scattered around the country.[10]

In short, the bulk of the Gestapo's efforts soon went into dealing with the new 'racially foreign' threat inside the country. The police continued to uncover various kinds of German 'opposition', but in relative terms such arrests represented a declining percentage of the Gestapo's work-load. In all likelihood opposition, (broadly defined) dissent, and (criminalized) malicious gossip were growing, so it is plausible to suggest that a large part of the reason for the failure to turn up more cases of these 'crimes' is that citizens were becoming less inclined to inform. Evidently, in the district around Würzburg the people grew increasingly unwilling to inform on delinquent Poles or Germans, especially from 1944; in 1945 Gestapo files which pertain to the racial persecution of the Poles disappear completely. No doubt, as Chapter 8 indicated, there were numerous factors which contributed to the silence. As the war was literally brought home to Germany the Gestapo grew more ruthless than ever, and there are scattered indications from elsewhere in the country that it began to dispense with even the semblance of regulations, to cease recording its activities, and to shoot large numbers of foreign workers who might otherwise be able to testify about witnessed misdeeds in the threatened post-war trials.[11]

[9] This is analysed in more detail in my 'Surveillance and Disobedience: Comments on the Political Policing of Nazi Germany', in Francis R. Nicosia and Lawrence D. Stokes (eds.), *Opposition and Resistance to National Socialism in Germany, 1925–1945* (Berg Publications, forthcoming).

[10] See HStA D: RW 58, 25283, 1–12.

[11] See esp. Herbert, *Fremdarbeiter*, 336ff. Cf. Herbert Obenaus, '"Sei stille, sonst kommst Du nach Ahelm!" Zur Funktion der Getapostelle in der ehemaligen israelitischen Gartenbauschule von Ahlem (1943–1945)', offprint from *Hannoversche Geschichtsblätter*, NF 41 (1987), 1–32. Note also Klaus Bästlein, 'Die Akten des ehemaligen Sondergerichts Kiel als zeitgeschichtliche Quelle', *Zeitschrift der Gesellschaft für Schleswig-Holsteinische Geschichte*, 113 (1988), 157ff.

EPILOGUE

It seems appropriate to end with a brief word about the fate of Gestapo officials and key Nazi leaders in Würzburg after the war. The following letter, here translated in full, summarizes most of what happened. It may not typify all the trials, but shows that most of the accused were able to exonerate themselves. Gestapo members charged with participation in the deportations of Jews from Germany got off because it could not be proven that they knew what went on in the extermination camps in Poland; those held responsible for killing foreign workers in Germany were also exonerated, as these acts 'took place because of an infringement of prescribed rules and regulations (e.g. insulting or physically attacking German superiors or employers, indulging in illicit sexual intercourse with German women etc.'.[1] The letter was sent to me in response to an inquiry I made on 15 August 1988 to the Zentrale Stelle der Landesjustizverwaltungen (Central Office of *Land* Judicial Authorities) in Ludwigsburg.

Dear Professor,

Proceedings (1 Js 1/48) were carried out by the Würzburg public prosecutor's office against former members of the Gestapo post Würzburg. Subject of the proceedings was the participation of the accused in the deportations of the Jews from Franconia (among other places to Riga, Trawniki [Travnik], Izbica, Theresienstadt [Terezin], and Auschwitz [Oświęcim]).

The proceedings against those members of the Gestapo post in Würzburg to which your inquiry referred, had the following results:

In regard to the accused Karl Bauer, Ernst Gramowski, Oswald Gundelach, and Michael Völkl, proceedings were suspended.

---

[1] See Adalbert Rückerl, *The Investigation of Nazi Crimes 1945–1978: A Documentation*, trans. D. Rutter (Hamden, Conn., 1980), 112–13. By the same author see *Nationalsozialistische Vernichtungslager im Spiegel deutscher Strafprozesse*, 3rd edn. (Munich, 1979); also Herbert Jäger, *Verbrechen unter totalitärer Herrschaft* (Frankfurt, 1982) 22ff. For similar outcomes in the post-war trials see Adolf Diamant, *Gestapo Frankfurt a.M.* (Frankfurt, 1988), 299ff. He could find evidence of only 7 accused having served any sentences, out of a total of 180 persons who were members of the Frankfurt Gestapo at one time or another (p. 300). This book arrived too late to be included in my analysis as a whole, but Diamant's reconstruction of the workings of the Gestapo, including its organization and methods of operation, its relatively small numbers especially of those actually engaged in police work, and the absence of a purge, supports my conclusions. For an introduction to the role of denunciations in the denazification of Germany see e.g. Krüger, 97, 101–2; Niethammer, *Die Mitläuferfabrik*, 593ff.; James F. Tent, *Mission on the Rhine: Reeducation and Denazification in American-Occupied Germany* (Chicago, 1982), 91. See also Edward N. Peterson, *The American Occupation of Germany: Retreat to Victory* (Detroit, 1977), 138ff.; Dietrich Güstrow, *In jenen Jahren: Aufzeichnung eines 'befreiten' Deutschen* (Munich, 1985), 30–1, 96–7.

Charges were preferred by the Würzburg public prosecutor's office before the criminal division of the Würzburg superior court (KLs 63/48 of the Würzburg superior court) against the accused Georg Baumann, Stefan Göss, Helmut Heisig, Franz Keil, Georg Krapp, Friedrich Krauß, Hans Laub, Balthasar Lutz, August Pössinger, Franz Schäffer, Hans Schilling, Georg Stolz, Georg Vogel, Franz Wittmann, and Josef Zwingmann. In these criminal proceedings before the Würzburg superior court the accused Helmut Heisig, August Pössinger, and Franz Wittmann were exonerated in the judgment of 30 April 1949.

The remaining accused were sentenced by the criminal division of the Würzburg superior court for criminally abetting the crime of false imprisonment as follows:

The accused Bauer and Lutz each to a gaol term of 6 months, the accused Baumann, Krapp, and Zwingmann each to a goal term of 9 months, the accused Vogel to a gaol term of 10 months, the accused Göss, Laub, Schäffer, and Schilling each to a gaol term of 11 months, and the accused Keil, Krauss, and Stolz each to a gaol term of 1 year and 2 months.

There was an appeal on the basis of further denials by the convicted accused.

On the basis of an appeal launched by the convicted, the judgment of the criminal division of the Würzburg superior court on 30 April 1949 was overturned by the decision of the Bavarian supreme court on 15 November 1950. The matter was sent back by the Bavarian supreme court for further discussion and decision to the appeal court at the Nuremberg-Fürth superior court. In the trial 213 Ks 1/51 of the appeal court at the Nuremberg-Fürth superior court, all of the convicted in the Würzburg trial were exonerated, with the exception of Krauss, who in the mean time had died.

With regard to the persons mentioned by you beyond this, the following trials have come to light here:

Josef Gerum

Trial 1b Js 1862/57 of the public prosecutor's office Munich I (basis of this trial unknown; the proceedings were suspended as per decision of 10 December 1958);

Trial 1 Js 6665/52 of the Würzburg public prosecutor's office, because of false imprisonment leading to the death of the Jewish lawyer Dr Adler from Würzburg (the proceedings were suspended as per decision of 25 July 1953;

Trial 1 Js 151/48 of the Würzburg public prosecutor's office, because of the arrest of the writer Nebuschka (the proceedings were suspended as per decision of 23 January 1950);

Trial 1 Js 55/49 of the Würzburg public prosecutor's office, among other things because of extorting testimony from political prisoners. In these proceedings charges were brought against Gerum by the criminal division of the Würzburg superior court (KLs 44/56 of the Würzburg superior court). Gerum was exonerated in the verdict of 22 October 1956;

Trial 1 Js 404/52 of the public prosecutor's office Munich I (the basis of the trial unknown; the proceedings were suspended at some point not known here).

Ernst Gramowski

Trial 1 Js 33/70 of the Würzburg public prosecutor's office, because of mass shootings carried out by members of the Task Force I/3 of the Commander of the

Security Police Lublin in the period from September to December 1939 (proceedings were suspended as per decision of 15 July 1970);

Trial 1a Js 275/70 of the Schweinfurt public prosecutor's office, because of selecting so-called intolerable Russian prisoners of war in the officers' camp at Hammelburg (proceedings were suspended as per decision of 27 November 1970);

Trial 1 Js 34/70 of the Würzburg public prosecutor's office against Ernst Gramowski and Oswald Gundelach, because of participation in the deportations of the Jews in the area of the Gestapo post Würzburg during the years 1941 to 1943 (proceedings were suspended as per decision of 18 September 1970);

Trial 11 Js 24/70 of the Nuremberg-Fürth public prosecutor's office against Karl Eibl and Gramowski, because of the killing of a Polish foreign worker on 8 July 1942 by members of the Gestapo main branch Nuremberg and the Gestapo post Würzburg (proceedings against Karl Eibl were suspended as per decision of 19 September 1974; proceedings against Ernst Gramowski were dropped upon his death on 11 January 1973);

Trial 7 Js 233/62 of the Wiesbaden public prosecutor's office, because of being an accessory to murder (more on the accusation is not known here; the proceedings were suspended as per decision of 15 February 1974);

Trial 3c Js 1110–18/50 of the Nuremberg-Fürth public prosecutor's office against Ernst Gramowski and eight others, because of being an accessory to murder (selection of Soviet prisoners of war; the proceedings were temporarily suspended as per decision of 9 June 1950 because of unknown whereabouts).

Oswald Gundelach

Trial 1 Js 34/70 of the Würzburg public prosecutor's office; see above (as with Ernst Gramowski);

In the verdict of the US Military court in Landsberg on 3 April 1947, Oswald Gundelach was sentenced to life imprisonment, and on 14 March 1953 was released to Versbach (the basis of the conviction in unknown).

Balthasar Lutz

The [justice] authorities in Dortmund brought proceedings 45 Js 3/61 against Lutz and eighteen others. Basis of the charge was the mass shooting of at least 7,000 Jews in the period from March to September 1942 by former members of the Commando of the Security Police Minsk, outer branch Wilejka [Vileyka]. The proceedings with respect to Lutz were suspended.

Besides that, the [justice] authorities in Dortmund brought proceedings 45 Js 16/73 against Lutz and others for the killing of between 20,000 and 30,000 Jews in the area of Weisruthenien [Belorussia], where measures for the 'final solution of the Jewish question' were carried out in the years 1941 to 1944 by former members of the Main Outer Post Wilejka of the Commander of the Security Police and of the SD in Minsk, as well as by members of several gendarme posts and of a gendarme expedition. In regard to Lutz, the proceedings were stopped because of his death.

Hans Schilling

Trial 1 Js 55/49 of the Würzburg public prosecutor's office was commenced against him and others for, among other things, extorting testimony. This proceeding was suspended.

Georg Vogel

Trial 1 Js 55/49 of the Würzburg public prosecutor's office was commenced against him and others for, among other things, extorting testimony. In these proceedings the criminal division of the Würzburg superior court brought charges against Georg Vogel and Franz Wittmann (KLs 46/50 of the superior court Würzburg). In the verdict of the superior court Würzburg of 12 May 1951 Vogel was exonerated. The verdict for Franz Wittmann was a gaol sentence of 1 year and 3 months.

Franz Wittmann

Trial 1 Js 55/49 (KLs 46/50 of the Würzburg superior court); see above (with Georg Vogel).

Dr Otto Hellmuth

Trial 1 Js 151/48 of the Würzburg public prosecutor's office, because of the arrest of the writer Nebuschka (proceedings suspended as per decision of 23 January 1950);

Trial Js 2711/50 of the Würzburg public prosecutor's office' because of breach of the public peace (proceedings suspended);

Trial 1 Js 586/62 of the Würzburg public prosecutor's office because of Nazi violence (proceedings suspended);

Trial 1 Js 127/48 of the Würzburg public prosecutor's office because of serious breach of the public peace (proceedings suspended).

Dr Karl Wicklmayr

Dr Wicklmayr was sentenced to one year in gaol (Ks 11/50 superior court Würzburg) according to the verdict of the appeal court at the superior court Würzburg on 17 May 1952. In the verdict of the superior court Munich II of 3 July 1951 he was sentenced to 6 years in gaol for killing five prisoners in the period from March to May 1933 in the Dachau concentration camp (12 Js 1649/48 StA Munich II, 12 Ks 5/51 LG Munich II).

Besides that, proceeding II Js 100/60 of the public prosecutor's office Landshut was brought against Dr Wicklmayr (the basis of the trial unknown), but was suspended.

No criminal proceedings have been found against Theo Albin Memmel.

With friendly greetings,

Biemüller
(County Court Judge)

BIBLIOGRAPHY

LIST OF ARCHIVES CONSULTED

Unpublished materials were consulted in the following archives. Only the most important file-groups are specifically mentioned.

1. *Archiv der sozialen Demokratie (Friedrich-Ebert Stiftung), Bonn*
2. *Badisches Generallandesarchiv, Karlsruhe* (BGLK)
3. *Bayerisches Hauptstaatsarchiv, Abt. 1, Allgemeines Staatsarchiv, Munich* (Bay HStA)

4. *Bayerisches Hauptstaatsarchiv, Abt. 2, Geheimes Staatsarchiv, Munich* (Bay HStA)

Bayerische Politische Polizei
Government Presidents' and Police Reports
Polizeidirektion Augsburg
Polizeidirektion München

5. *Berlin Document Centre* (BDC)
6. *Bundesarchiv Koblenz* (BAK)

NS 6	Parteikanzlei
NS 29	SD Lageberichte
R 7	Reichswirtschaftsministerium
R 18	Reichsministerium des Innern
R 22	Reichsjustizministerium
R 43 II	Reichsministerium für Volksaufklärung und Propaganda
R49	Reichskommissar für die Festigung deutschen Volkstums
R 58	Reichssicherheitshauptamt

7. *Bundesarchiv, Militärarchiv, Freiburg* (BA/MA)

Rüstungsinspektion/Kommandos

8. *Geheimes Staatsarchiv Preußischer Kulturbesitz Dahlem, Berlin* (GSA)

HA/Rep. 90P Gestapo Lageberichte

9. *Hauptstaatsarchiv Düsseldorf* (HStA D)

RW 18	Stapoleitstelle Düsseldorf
RW 34	Stapoleitstelle Köln
RW 36	Stapostelle Düsseldorf, Außenstellen
RW 58	Gestapo-Personalakten (cited as Gestapo with file-number)

10. *Hauptstaatsarchiv Stuttgart* (HStA S)
11. *Hessisches Hauptstaatsarchiv, Wiesbaden* (HHStA)
12. *Institut für Zeitgeschichte Munich* (IfZ)

13. *Landeshauptarchiv Koblenz* (LHA Ko)
Gestapo, SD

14. *Landesarchiv Speyer* (LA Speyer)
Polizeibehörden
Gestapo case-files

15. *Leo Baeck Institute, New York*
Autobiographies of survivors

16. *'Myers Collection', University of Michigan, Ann Arbor*
Eisenach NSDAP files

17. *National Archives, Washington, DC*

18. *Staatsarchiv Bamberg* (StA B)

19. *Staatsarchiv Ludwigsburg* (StA L)

20. *Staatsarchiv Marburg*
Gestapo Kassel reports

21. *Staatsarchiv München* (StA M)
Gestapo
Sondergericht München

22. *Staatsarchiv Neuburg an der Donau (StA NadD)*

23. *Staatsarchiv Nürnberg*

24. *Staatsarchiv Würzburg* (StA W)
Gauleitung Mainfranken (NSDAP GL)
Gestapo case-files (cited as Gestapo with file-number)
Landratsamt (LRA)
SD-Hauptaußenstelle

25. *Wiener Library, London*
Eye witness reports.

26. *Yivo Institute for Jewish Research, New York*

LIST OF PUBLISHED WORKS CITED

ADAM, UWE DIETRICH, *Judenpolitik im Dritten Reich* (Düsseldorf, 1972).
——'Wie spontan war der Pogrom?', in Pehle (ed.), *Judenpogrom*.
ALDER, H. G., *Der verwaltete Mensch: Studien zur Deportation der Juden aus Deutschland* (Tübingen, 1974).
ALDER-RUDEL, S, *Ostjuden in Deutschland 1880–1940* (Tübingen, 1959).
ALLEN, WILLIAM SHERIDAN, 'Die deutsche Öffentlichkeit und die "Reichskristallnacht" Konflikte zwischen Werthierarchie und Propaganda im Dritten Reich', in Peukert and Reulecke (eds.), *Die Reihen fast geschlossen*.
——*The Nazi Seizure of Power: The Experience of a Single German Town 1922–1945*, rev. edn., (New York, 1984).

Allgemeine Erlaßsammlung, pt. 2, ed. RSHA (1944) (in IfZ).

Alltagsgeschichte der NS-Zeit: Neue Perspektive oder Trivialisierung? Kolloquien des Instituts für Zeitgeschichte (Munich, 1984).

ALY, GÖTZ, and ROTH, KARL HEINZ, *Die restlose Erfassung: Volkszählen, Identifizieren, Aussondern im Nationalsozialismus* (Berlin, 1984).

ANDREAS-FRIEDRICH, RUTH, *Der Schattenmann: Tagebuchaufzeichnungen, 1938–1945* (1947; Berlin, 1983).

ARENDT, HANNAH, *The Origins of Totalitarianism* (New York, 1966).

——*Eichmann in Jerusalem: A Report on the Banality of Evil*, rev. edn. (New York, 1965).

ARONSON, SHLOMO, *Reinhard Heydrich und die Frühgeschichte von Gestapo und SD* (Stuttgart, 1971).

AUGUST, JOCHEN, 'Die Entwicklung des Arbeitsmarkts in Deutschland in den 30er Jahren und der Masseneinsatz ausländischer Arbeitskräfte während des Zweiten Weltkrieges', *Archiv für Sozialgeschichte*, 24 (1984).

——'Erinnern an Deutschland: Berichte polnischer Zwangsarbeiter', in August *et al.*, *Ausländische Arbeiter*.

——*et al.*, *Ausländische Arbeiter und Deutsche 1939–1945* (Berlin, 1986).

AYASS, WOLFGANG, 'Vagrants and Beggers in Hitler's Reich', in Evans (ed.), *The German Underworld*

AYÇOBERRY, PIERRE, *The Nazi Question: An Essay on the Interpretations of National Socialism (1922–1975)*, trans. R. Hurley (New York, 1981).

BACH, H. I., *The German Jew: A Synthesis of Judaism and Western Civilization, 1730–1930* (Oxford, 1984).

BADE, KLAUS J., 'Transatlantic Emigration and Continental Immigration: The German Experience Past and Present', in Bade (ed.), *Population*.

——(ed.), *Auswanderer—Wanderarbeiter—Gastarbeiter: Bevölkerung, Arbeitsmarkt und Wanderung in Deutschland seit der Mitte des 19. Jahrhunderts*, 2 vols. (Ostfildern, 1984).

——(ed.), *Population, Labour and Migration in 19th and 20th Century Germany* (Leamington Spa, 1987).

BÄSTLEIN, KLAUS, 'Die Akten des ehemaligen Sondergerichts Kiel als Zeitgeschichtliche Quelle', *Zeitschrift der Gesellschaft für Schleswig-Holsteinische Geschichte*, 113 (1988).

BAYLEY, DAVID. H., 'The Police and Political Development in Europe', in Tilly (ed.), *Formation of National States*.

BECK, EARL R., *Under the Bombs: The German Home Front 1942–1945* (Lexington, 1986).

BEHREND-ROSENFELD, ELSE R., *Ich stand nicht allein: Leben einer Jüdin in Deutschland 1933–1944* (1945; Munich, 1988).

BESSEL, RICHARD, *Political Violence and the Rise of Nazism: The Storm Troopers in Eastern Germany 1925–1934* (New Haven, 1984).

BEST, WERNER, *Die deutsche Polizei* (Darmstadt, 1941).

BIELENBERG, CHRISTABEL, *Ride Out the Dark: The Experiences of an Englishwoman in Wartime Germany* (1968; Boston, 1984).

BILLSTEIN, AUREL, *Fremdarbeiter in unserer Stadt* (Frankfurt, 1980).

BIRN, RUTH BETTINA, *Die Höheren SS- und Polizeiführer: Himmlers Vertreter im Reich und in den besetzten Gebieten* (Düsseldorf, 1986).

BLACK, PETER R., *Ernst Kaltenbrunner: Ideological Soldier of the Third Reich* (Princeton, 1984).

BLAU, BRUNO, *Das Ausnahmerecht für die Juden in Deutschland 1933–1945* (Düsseldorf, 1954).

BLEUEL, HANS PETER, *Sex and Society in Nazi Germany*, trans. J. Maxwell Brownjohn, (Phil., 1973).

BOBERACH, HEINZ (ed.), *Meldungen aus dem Reich: Die geheimen Lageberichte des Sicherheitsdienstes der SS 1938–1945*, 17 vols. (Herrsching, 1984).

——(ed.), *Richterbriefe: Dokumente zur Beeinflussung der deutschen Rechtsprechung 1942–1944* (Boppard, 1975).

BOCK, GISELA, *Zwangssterilisation im Nationalsozialismus: Studien zur Rassenpolitik und Frauenpolitik* (Opladen, 1986).

BOEHM, ERIC H. (ed.), *We Survived: Fourteen Histories of the Hidden and Hunted of Nazi Germany* (Santa Barbara, 1985).

BOHN, WILLI, *'Hochverräter!'* (Frankfurt, 1984).

BOWDEN, TOM, *Beyond the Limits of the Law* (Harmondsworth, 1978).

BOWER, TOM, *Klaus Barbie, Butcher of Lyons* (London, 1984).

BOYLE, KAY, *The Smoking Mountain: Stories of Germany During the Occupation* (New York, 1963).

BRACHER, KARL DIETRICH, *Die deutsche Diktatur: Entstehung, Struktur, Folgen des Nationalsozialismus*, 2nd edn. (Cologne, 1969).

——'Stufen der Machtergreifung', in Bracher, Sauer, and Schulz, *Machtergreifung.*

——SAUER, WOLFGANG, and SCHULZ, GERHARD, *Die nationalsozialistische Machtergreifung: Studien zur Errichtung des totalitären Herrschaftssystems in Deutschland 1933/34* (Cologne, 1962).

BRAMSTEDT, E. K., *Dictatorship and Political Police: The Technique of Control by Fear* (1945; New York, 1976).

BRENNATHAN, ESRA, 'Demographische und wirtschaftliche Struktur der Juden', in Mosse (ed.), *Entscheidungsjahr.*

BROSZAT, MARTIN, 'Nationalsozialistische Konzentrationslager 1933–1945' in Buchheim *et al., SS-Staat*, vol. ii.

——*Nationalsozialistische Polenpolitik 1939–1945* (Stuttgart, 1961).

——'Politische Denunziationen in der NS-Zeit: Aus Forschungserfahrungen im Staatsarchiv München', *Archivalische Zeitschrift*, 73 (1977).

——*Der Staat Hitlers: Grundlegung und Entwicklung seiner inneren Verfassung* (Munich, 1971).

——*Zweihundert Jahre deutsche Polenpolitik* (1963; Frankfurt, 1972).

——*et al.* (eds.), *Bayern in der NS-Zeit*, 6 vols. (Munich, 1977–83).

BROWDER, GEORGE C., 'Die Anfänge des SD: Dokumente aus der Organisationsgeschichte des Sicherheitsdienstes des Reichsführers SS', *VfZ* 27 (1979).

——'The SD: The Significance of Organization and Image', in Mosse (ed.), *Police Forces.*

——'*Sipo* and SD, 1931–1940: Formation of an Instrument of Power' (University of Wisconsin Ph.D. thesis; Madison, 1968).

BRÜCKNER, PETER, *Das Abseits als sicherer Ort* (Coburg, 1980).

BUCHHEIM, HANS, 'Die SS: Das Herrschaftsinstrument', in Buchheim *et al., SS-Staat*, vol i.

——*et al.*, *Anatomie des SS-Staates*, 2 vols. (Olten, 1965).

BULL, HEDLEY (ed.), *The Challenge of the Third Reich* (Oxford, 1986).

BULLEN, R. J., *et al.* (eds.), *Ideas into Politics* (London, 1984).

CAHNMANN, WERNER, 'Village and Small-Town Jews in Germany: A Typological Study', *YLBI* 19 (1974).

CAPLAN, JANE, *Government without Administration: State and Civil Service in Weimar and Nazi Germany* (Oxford, 1988).

——'Politics and Polyocracy: Notes on a Debate', in Maier *et al.* (eds.), *The Rise of the Nazi Regime*.

CHAPMAN, BRIAN, *Police State* (London, 1970).

CHILDERS, THOMAS, *The Nazi Voter: The Social Foundations of Fascism in Germany, 1919–1933* (Chapel Hill, 1983).

COBB, RICHARD, *The Police and the People: French Popular Protest 1789–1820* (Oxford, 1970).

CRANKSHAW, EDWARD, *Gestapo: Instrument of Tyranny* (London, 1956).

DAHRENDORF, RALF, *Society and Democracy in Germany* (London, 1968).

DEBUS, KARL HEINZ, 'Die Reichskristallnacht in der Pfalz: Schuldbewußtsein und Ermittlung', *Zeitschrift für die Geschichte des Oberrheins*, 129 (1981).

DELARUE, JACQUES, *Geschichte der Gestapo*, trans. Hans Steinsdorff (Düsseldorf, 1964).

DESROCHES, ALAIN, *La Gestapo: Atrocités et secrets de l'inquisition nazie* (Paris, 1972).

DETTELBACHER, WERNER, *Damals in Würzburg* (1971; Würzburg, 1982).

Das deutsche Reich und der Zweite Weltkrieg, ed. Militärgeschichtliches Forschungsamt, 5 vols. (Stuttgart, 1979–88).

DEUTSCHKRON, INGE, *Ich trug den gelben Stern* (1978; Cologne, 1983).

Deutschland-Berichte der Sozialdemokratischen Partei Deutschlands 1934–1940, 7 vols. (Frankfurt, 1980). [Cited as *Sopade*.]

DIAMANT, ADOLF, *Gestapo Frankfurt a.M.* (Frankfurt, 1988).

DICKINSON, JOHN K., *German and Jew: The Life and Death of Sigmund Stein* (Chicago, 1967).

DIEHL-THIELE, PETER, *Partei und Staat im Dritten Reich* (Munich, 1969).

DIELS, RUDOLF, *Lucifer ante Portas . . . Es spricht der erste Chef der Gestapo* (Stuttgart, 1950).

Das Diensttagebuch des deutschen Generalgouverneurs in Polen 1939–1945, (ed.) Werner Präg and Wolfgang Jacobmeyer (Stuttgart, 1975).

DŁUGOBORSKI, WACŁAW (ed.), *Zweiter Weltkrieg und sozialer Wandel* (Göttingen, 1981).

DOMARUS, MAX, *Der Untergang des alten Würzburgs im Luftkrieg gegen die deutschen Großstädte* (Würzburg, 1985).

DOMARUS, WOLFGANG, *Nationalsozialismus, Krieg und Bevölkerung: Untersuchungen sur Lage, Volksstimmung und Struktur in Augsburg während des Dritten Reiches* (Munich, 1977).

DOMRÖSE, ORTWIN, *Der NS-Staat in Bayern von der Machtergreifung bis zum Röhm-Putsch* (Munich, 1974).

DÖRING, HANS-JOACHIM, *Die Ziegeuner im NS-Staat* (Hamburg, 1964).

DRÖGE, FRANZ, *Der zerredete Widerstand; Zur Soziologie und Publizistik des Gerüchts im 2. Weltkrieg* (Düsseldorf, 1970).

DUNKHASE, HEINRICH, 'Würzburg, 16 März 1945 21.25 Uhr–21.42 Uhr: Hintergründe, Verlauf und Folgen des Luftangriffs der No. 5 Bomber Group', *Mainfränkisches Jahrbuch*, 32 (1980).

DÜWELL, KURT, *Die Rheingebiete in der Judenpolitik des Nationalsozialismus vor 1942* (Bonn, 1968).

EBBINGHAUS, ANGELIKA, et al., *Heilen und Vernichten im Mustergau Hamburg* (Hamburg, 1984).

ELEY, GEOFF, 'What Produces Fascism: Pre-Industrial Traditions or a Crisis of the Capitalist State?', in id., *From Unification to Nazism: Reinterpreting the German Past* (Boston, 1986).

ELTON, G. R., *Policy and Police: The Enforcement of the Reformation in the Age of Thomas Cromwell* (Cambridge, 1972).

EMSLEY, CLIVE, *Policing and its Context 1750–1870* (London, 1983).

ENGELMANN, BERNT, *Im Gleichschritt marsch* (Cologne, 1981).

EPSTEIN, KLAUS, *The Genesis of German Conservatism* (Princeton, 1966).

EVANS, RICHARD J., 'Introduction: The "Dangerous Classes" in Germany from the Middle Ages to the Twentieth Century', in Evans (ed.), *The German Underworld.*

——(ed.), *The German Underworld: Deviants and Outcasts in German History* (London, 1988).

FALTER, JÜRGEN W., 'Der Aufstieg der NSDAP in Franken bei den Reichstagswahlen 1924–1933: Ein Vergleich mit dem Reich unter besonderer Berücksichtigung landwirtschaftlicher Einflußfaktoren', *German Studies Review*, 9 (1986).

FANGMANN, HELMUT, REIFNER, UDO, and STEINBORN, NORBERT, *Parteisoldaten: Die Hamburger Polizei im 'Dritten Reich'* (Hamburg, 1987).

FAUST, ANSELM, *Die Kristallnacht im Rhineland: Dokumente zum Judenpogrom im November 1938* (Düsseldorf, 1987).

FEIN, HELEN, *Accounting for Genocide: Victims—and Survivors—of the Holocaust* (New York, 1976).

FISCHER, CONAN, *Stormtroopers: A Social, Economic and Ideological Analysis 1929–35* (London, 1983).

FLADE, ROLAND, *'Es Kann sein, daß wir eine Diktatur brauchen': Rechtsradikalismus und Demokratiefeindschaft in der Weimarer Republik am Beispiel Würzburg* (Würzburg, 1983).

——*Juden in Würzburg 1918–1933* (Würzburg, 1985).

——*Die Würzburger Juden: Ihre Geschichte vom Mittelalter bis zur Gegenwart* (Würzburg, 1987).

FOUCAULT, MICHEL, *Discipline and Punish: The Birth of the Prison*, trans. A. Sheridan (New York, 1979).

——'Nietzsche, Genealogy, History', in Paul Rabinow (ed.), *The Foucault Reader* (New York, 1984).

——'Politics and Reason', in *Michel Foucault: Politics, Philosophy, Culture. Interviews and other Writings 1977–1984*, ed. Lawrence D. Kritzman (New York, 1988).

——'The Subject and Power', in Herbert L. Dreyfus and Paul Rabinow, *Michel Foucault: Beyond Structuralism and Hermeneutics*, 2nd ed. (Chicago, 1983).

FRIES, BRUNO, et al., *Würzburg im III. Reich* (Würzburg, 1983).

FRÖHLICH, ELKE, 'Die Herausforderung des Einzelnen: Geschichten über Widerstand und Verfolgung', in *Bayern in der NS-Zeit*, vi.

GALLO, MAX, *The Night of the Long Knives*, trans. L. Emmet (New York, 1972).

GEHRING-MÜNZEL, URSULA, 'Emanzipation', in Flade, *Würzburger Juden.*

GELLATELY, ROBERT, 'Enforcing Racial Policy in Nazi Germany', in Thomas Childers and Jane Caplan (eds.), *Re-Evaluating the 'Third Reich': Interpretations and Debates* (New York: Holmes and Meier, forthcoming).

——'The Gestapo and German Society: Political Denunciation in the Gestapo Case Files', *Journal of Modern History*, 60 (1988).

——*The Politics of Economic Despair: Shopkeepers and German Politics, 1890–1914* (London, 1974).

——'Surveillance and Disobedience: Comments on the Political Policing of Nazi Germany', in Francis R. Nicosia and Lawrence D. Stokes (eds.), *Opposition and Resistance to National Socialism in Germany, 1925–1945* (Berg Publications, forthcoming).

——'Terror System, Racial Persecution and Resistance in Nazi Germany: Remarks on the Historiography', *German Studies Review* (forthcoming).

GENSCHEL, HELMUT, *Die Verdrängung der Juden aus der Wirtschaft im Dritten Reich* (Göttingen, 1966).

GEYER, MICHAEL, 'National Socialist Germany: The Politics of Information', in May (ed.), *Knowing One's Enemies*.

GILES, GEOFFREY J., *Students and National Socialism in Germany* (Princeton, 1985).

GIORDANO, RALPH, *Die Bertinis* (Frankfurt, 1982).

GISEVIUS, HANS BERND, *To the Bitter End*, trans. R. and C. Winstone (London, 1948).

GOEBBELS, JOSEPH, *My Part in Germany's Fight*, (1940), trans. K. Fiedler (New York, 1979).

GORDON, BERTRAN M., *Collaborationism in France During the Second World War* (Ithaca, 1980).

GORDON, SARAH, *Hitler, Germans, and the 'Jewish Question'* (Princeton, 1984).

GOTTO, KLAUS, and REPGEN, KONRAD (eds.), *Kirche, Katholiken und Nationalsozialismus* (Mainz, 1980).

GRAF, CHRISTOPH, *Politische Polizei zwischen Demokratie und Diktatur* (Berlin, 1983).

GRAML, HERMANN,'Die Behandlung der Anfällen von sogenannter Rassenschande Beteiligten "Deutschblütigen" Personen', in *Gutachten des Instituts für Zeitgeschichte*, vol. i (Stuttgart, 1958).

——*Der 9. November 1938: 'Reichskristallnacht'*, 4th edn. (Bonn, 1956).

GREIVE, HERMANN, *Geschichte des modernen Antisemitismus in Deutschland* (Darmstadt, 1983).

GRIEB-LOHWASSER, BIRGITT, 'Jüdische Studenten und Antisemitismus an der Universität Würzburg in der Weimarer Republik', in Schultheis (ed.), *Streifzug durch Frankens Vergangenheit*.

GROSS, JAN TOMASZ, *Polish Society under German Occupation: The Generalgouvernement* (Princeton, 1979).

GROSS, LEONARD, *The Last Jews in Berlin* (Toronto, 1983).

GROSSMANN, ANTON, 'Fremd- und Zwangsarbeiter in Bayern 1939–1945', in Bade (ed.), *Auswanderer*.

——'Polen und Sowjetrussen als Arbeiter in Bayern 1939–1945', *Archiv für Sozialgeschichte*, 29 (1984).

Gruchmann, Lothar, *Justiz im Dritten Reich: Anpassung und Unterwerfung in der Ära Gürtner* (Munich, 1988).

GRUNBERGER, RICHARD, *A Social History of the Third Reich* (Harmondsworth, 1974).

GÜSTROW, DIETRICH, *In jenen Jahren: Aufzeichnung eines 'befreiten' Deutschen* (Munich, 1985).

GÜSTROW, DIETRICH, *Tödlicher Alltag: Strafverteidiger im Dritten Reich* (Berlin, 1981).

Gutachten des Instituts für Zeitgeschichte (Struttgart, 1958).

GUTTERIDGE, RICHARD, *Open thy Mouth for the Dumb: The German Evangelical Church and the Jews 1870–1950* (Oxford, 1976).

HAHN, FRED, *Lieber Stürmer! Leserbriefe an das NS-Kampfblatt 1924 bis 1945* (Stuttgart, 1978).

HALIMI, ANDRÉ, *La Délation sous l'occupation* (Paris, 1983).

HAMBRECHT, RAINER, *Der Aufstieg der NSDAP in Mittel- und Oberfranken (1925–1933)* (Nuremberg, 1976).

HAMILTON, RICHARD, *Who Voted for Hitler?* (Princeton, 1982).

HANNOVER, HEINRICH, and HANNOVER-DRÜCK, ELISABETH, *Politische Justiz 1918–1933* (Bornheim-Merten, 1987).

HARDACH, KARL, *Wirtschaftsgeschichte Deutschlands im 20. Jahrhundert* (Göttingen, 1976).

HARRIS, FREDERICK J., *Encounters with Darkness: French and German Writers on World War II* (Oxford, 1983).

HARVEY, PATRICIA, 'Labour', in Arnold Toynbee (ed.), *Survey of International Affairs 1939–1946: Hitler's Europe* (London 1954).

HAY, GERHARD, 'Das Jahr 1938 im Spiegel der NS-Literatur', in Knipping and Müller (eds.), *Machtbewußtsein*.

HAYES, PETER, *Industry and Ideology: IG Farben in the Nazi Era* (Cambridge, 1987).

HEHL, ULRICH VON (ed.), *Priester unter Hitlers Terror: Eine biographische und statistische Erhebung*, 2nd edn. (Mainz, 1985).

HEIBER, HELMUT (intro.) 'Der Generalplan Ost ', *VfZ* 6 *(1958)*.

HELMREICH, ERNST CHRISTIAN, *The German Churches under Hitler: Background, Struggle, and Epilogue* (Detroit, 1979).

HENNIG, EIKE, *Bürgerliche Gesellschaft und Faschismus in Deutschland: ein Forschungsbericht*, 2nd edn. (Frankfurt, 1982).

——(ed.), *Hessen unterm Hakenkreuz: Studien zur Durchsetzung der NSDAP in Hessen*, 2nd edn. (Frankfurt, 1984).

HENRY, FRANCIS, *Victims and Neighbors: A Small Town in Nazi Germany Remembered* (South Hadley, Mass., 1984).

HERBERT, ULRICH, '"Die guten und die schlechten Zeiten"': Überlegungen zur diachronen Analyse lebensgeschichtlicher Interviews', in Niethammer (ed.), *'Die Jahre'*.

——*Fremdarbeiter: Politik und Praxis des 'Ausländer-Einsatzes' in der Kriegswirtschaft des Dritten Reiches* (Berlin, 1986).

——*Geschichte der Ausländerbeschäftigung in Deutschland 1880 bis 1980* (Berlin, 1986).

HERBST, LUDOLF, *Der totale Krieg und die Ordnung der Wirtschaft: Die Kriegswirtschaft im Spannungsfeld von Politik, Ideologie und Propaganda 1939–1945* (Stuttgart, 1982).

HEYEN, FRANZ JOSEF, *Nationalsozialismus im Alltag* (Boppard, 1967).

HIDEN, JOHN and FARQUHARSON, JOHN, *Explaining Hitler's Germany: Historians and the Third Reich* (Totowa, NJ, 1983).

HIGONNET, MARGARET RANDOLPH, et al. (eds.), *Behind the Lines: Gender and the Two World Wars* (New Haven, 1987).

HILBERG, RAUL, *The Destruction of the European Jews*, rev. ed., 3 vols. (New York, 1985).

HIRSCH, MARTIN, MAJER, DIEMUT, and MEINCK, JÜRGEN (eds.), *Recht, Verwaltung und*

Justiz im Nationalsozialismus: Ausgewählte Schriften, Gesetze und Gerichtsentscheidungen von 1933 bis 1945 (Cologne, 1984).

HIRSCHFELD, GERHARD (ed.), *The Policies of Genocide: Jews and Soviet Prisoners of War in Nazi Germany* (London, 1986).

——and KETTENACHER, LOTHAR (eds.), *Der 'Führerstaat': Mythos und Realität. Studien zur Struktur und Politik des Dritten Reiches* (Stuttgart, 1981).

HOCH, GERHARD, *Zwölf wiedergefundene Jahre: Kaltenkirchen unter dem Hakenkreuz* (Bad Bramstedt, [1980]).

HOCHHUTH, ROLF, *Eine Liebe in Deutschland* (Reinbek bei Hamburg, 1980).

HOFFMANN, PETER, *German Resistance to Hitler* (Cambridge, Mass., 1988).

HOHMANN, JOACHIM S., *Geschichte der Zigeunerverfolgung in Deutschland* (Frankfurt, 1981).

HÖHNE, HEINZ, *The Order of the Death's Head: The Story of Hitler's SS*, trans. R. Barry (1966; London, 1972).

HOMZE, EDWARD L., *Foreign Labor in Nazi Germany* (Princeton, 1967).

HÜTTENBERGER, PETER, 'Heimtückefälle vor dem Sondergericht München 1933–1939', in Broszat *et al.* (eds.), *Bayern in der NS-Zeit*, iv.

INTERNATIONAL LABOUR OFFICE, *The Exploitation of Foreign Labour by Germany* (Montreal, 1945).

JÄCKEL, EBERHARD, and ROHWER, JÜRGEN (eds.), *Der Mord an den Juden im Zweiten Weltkrieg* (Stuttgart, 1985).

JACOBMEYER, WOLFGANG, *Vom Zwangsarbeiter zum heimatlosen Ausländer: Die Displaced Persons in Westdeutschland 1945–1951* (Göttingen, 1985).

JÄGER, HERBERT, *Verbrechen unter totalitärer Herrschaft* (Frankfurt, 1982).

JAMIN MATHILDE, 'Zur Rolle der SA im nationalsozialistischen Herrschaftssystem', in Hirschfeld and Kettenacher (eds.), *Führerstaat*.

——*Zwischen den Klassen: Zur Sozialstruktur der SA-Führerschaft* (Wuppertal, 1984).

JARAUSCH, KONRAD H., *Students, Society, and Politics in Imperial Germany: The Rise of Academic Illiberalism* (Princeton, 1982).

JOCHMANN, WERNER, 'Die Ausbreitung des Antisemitismus', in Mosse (ed.), *Deutsches Judentum*.

Justiz und NS-Verbrechen: Sammlung deutscher Strafurteile wegen ns. Tötungsverbrechen 1945–1966, 24 vols. (Amsterdam, 1968).

KAMMLER, JÖRG, 'Nationalsozialistische Machtergreifung und Gestapo—am Beispiel der Staatspolizeistelle für den Regierungsbezirk Kassel', in Hennig (ed.), *Hessen unterm Hakenkreuz*.

KASPER, BARBARA, *et al.*, *Arbeiten für den Kreig: Deutsche und Ausländer in der Rüstungsproduktion bei Rheinmetall-Borsig 1943–1945* (Hamburg, 1987).

KATER, MICHAEL H., 'Begrifflichkeit und Historie: "Alltag", "Neokonservatismus" und "Judenfrage" als Themen einer NS-bezogenen Sozialgeschichtsschreibung', *Archiv für Sozialgeschichte*, 23 (1983).

——'Die ernsten Bibelforscher im Dritten Reich', *VfZ* 17 (1969).

——*The Nazi Party: A Social Profile of Members and Leaders, 1919–1945* (Cambridge, Mass., 1983).

——'Nazism and the Third Reich in Recent Historiography', *Canadian Journal of History*, 20 (1985).

——*StudentenschaftundRechtsradikalismusinDeutschland1918–1933*(Frankfurt, 1975).

KATZ, JACOB, *From Prejudice to Destruction: Anti-Semitism, 1700–1933* (Cambridge, Mass., 1980).

——*Out of the Ghetto: The Social Background of Jewish Emancipation 1770–1870* (Cambridge, Mass., 1973).

KENRICK, DONALD and PUXON, GRATTAN, *The Destiny of Europe's Gypsies* (New York, 1972).

KERSHAW, IAN, 'German Popular Opinion and the "Jewish Question", 1939–1943: Some Further Reflections', in Arnold Paucker (ed.), *Die Juden im Nationalsozialistischen Deutschland/The Jews in Nazi Germany 1933–1945* (Tübingen, 1986).

——*The 'Hitler Myth': Image and Reality in the Third Reich* (Oxford, 1987).

——*The Nazi Dictatorship: Problems and Perspectives of Interpretation* (London, 1985; 2nd edn. forthcoming).

——*Popular Opinion and Political Dissent in the Third Reich: Bavaria 1933–1945* (Oxford, 1983).

KIERSCH, GERHARD, *et al.*, *Berliner Alltag im Dritten Reich* (Düsseldorf, 1981).

Die Kirchliche Lage in Bayern nach den Regierungspräsidentenberichten 1933–1943, ed. Helmut Witetschek *et al.*, 6 vols (Mainz, 1966–81); i: Helmut Witetschek, *Regierungsbezirk Oberbayern* (1966); ii: Helmut Witetschek, *Regierungsbezirk Ober- und Mittelfranken* (1967); iii: Helmut Witetschek, *Regierungsbezirk Schwaben* (1971); iv: Walter Ziegler, *Regierungsbezirk Niederbayern und Oberpfalz* (1973); v: Helmut Prantl, *Regierungsbezirk Pfalz* (1978); vi: Klaus Wittstadt, *Regierungsbezirk Unterfranken* (1981). [Cited as *KLB*.]

KIRSCHNER, KLAUS, ' "Da brennt's in Ermreuth!" Juden und Nazis in einem fränkischen Dorf', *Frankfurter Hefte*, 10 (1979).

KLEE, ERNST, *'Euthanasie' im NS-Staat: Die 'Vernichtung lebensunwerten Lebens'* (Frankfurt, 1983).

KLEIN, THOMAS, *Die Lageberichte der Geheimen Staatspolizei über die Provinz Hessen-Nassau 1933–1936*, 2 vols. (Cologne, 1986).

KLEMPERER, VICTOR, *LTI: Lingua Tertii Imperii. Die Sprache des Dritten Reichs* (Frankfurt, 1982).

KLENNER, JOCHEN, *Verhältnis von Partei und Staat 1933–1945: Dargestellt am Beispiel Bayerns* (Munich, 1974).

KLESSMANN, CHRISTOPH, *Polnische Bergarbeiter im Ruhrgebiet (Göttingen, 1978)*.

——and PINGEL, FALK, (eds.) *Gegner des Nationalsozialismus* (Frankfurt, 1980).

KNIPPING, FRANZ, and MÜLLER, KLAUS-JÜRGEN (eds.), *Machtbewußtsein in Deutschland am Vorabend des Zweiten Weltkrieges* (Paderborn, 1984).

KNOX, MACGREGOR, 'Conquest, Foreign and Domestic, in Fascist Italy and Nazi Germany', *Journal of Modern History*, 56 (1984).

KOEHL, ROBERT LEWIS, *The Black Corps: The Structure and Power Struggles of the Nazi SS* (Madison, Wis., 1983).

——*RKFDV: German Resettlement and Population Policy 1939–1945. A History of the Reich Commission for the Strengthening of Germandom* (Cambridge, Mass., 1957).

KOEHLER, HANSJUERGEN, *Inside Information* (London, 1940).

——*Inside the Gestapo* (London, 1940).

KOGON, EUGEN, *Der SS-Staat: Das System der deutschen Konzentrationslager* (1946; Munich, 1974).

KOHLER, ERIC D., 'The Crisis of the Prussian Schutzpolizei 1930–32', in Mosse, (ed.), *Police Forces*.

KONIECZNY, ALFRED, and SZURGACZ, HERBERT, *Praca przymusowa polaków pod panowanien hitlerovskim 1939–1945* (Poznań, 1976).

KOONZ, CLAUDIA, *Mothers in the Fatherland: Women, the Family and Nazi Politics* (New York, 1987).

KORDT, ERICH, *Wahn und Wirklichkeit* (Stuttgart, 1948).

KOSELLECK, REINHARD, *Preußen zwischen Reform und Revolution* (Stuttgart, 1975).

KRAUSNICK, HELMUT, (intro.) 'Denkschrift Himmlers über die Behandlung der Fremdvölkischen im Osten (Mai 1940)', *VfZ* 5 (1957).

KRÜGER, WOLFGANG, *Entnazifiziert!* (Wuppertal, 1982).

KULKA, OTTO DOV, 'Die Nürnberger Rassengesetze und die deutsche Bevölkerung im Lichte Geheimer NS-Lage- und Stimmungsberichte', *VfZ* 32 (1984).

——'"Public Opinion" in National Socialist Germany and the "Jewish Question"', *Zion*, 40 (1975).

——'"Public Opinion" in Nazi Germany and the "Jewish Question"', *The Jerusalem Quarterly*, 25 (1982).

——and Rodrique, Aron, 'The German Population and the Jews in the Third Reich: Recent Publications and Trends in Research on German Society and the "Jewish Question"', *Yad Vashem Studies*, 16 (1984).

KUNZE, MICHAEL, *Highroad to the Stake: A Tale of Witchcraft*, trans. W. E. Yuill (Chicago, 1987).

KWIET, KONRAD and ESCHWEGE, HELMUT, *Selbstbehauptung und Widerstand: Deutsche Juden im Kampf um Existenz und Menschenwürde 1933–1945* (Hamburg, 1984).

LANG, JOCHEN VON (ed.), *Das Eichmann Protokoll* (Berlin, 1982).

LAQUEUR, WALTER (ed.), *Fascism: A Reader's Guide* (Berkeley, 1976).

LARSEN, STEIN UGELVIK, et al. (eds.), *Who were the Fascists? Social Roots of European Fascism* (Bergen, 1980).

LATOUR, C. F., 'Goebbels' "Außerordentliche Rundfunkmaßnahmen" 1939–1942', *VfZ* 11 (1963).

LAUBER, HEINZ, *Judenpogrom 'Reichskristallnacht' November 1938 in Großdeutschland* (Gerlingen, 1981).

LEHR, STEFAN, *Antisemitismus: Religiöse Motive im sozialen Vorurteil* (Munich, 1974).

LIANG, HSI-HUEY, *The Berlin Police Force in the Weimar Republic* (Berkeley, 1970).

LINZ, JUAN J., 'Some Notes towards a Comparative Study of Fascism in Sociological Historical Perspective', in Laqueur (ed.), *Fascism*.

LOHALM, UWE, *Völkischer Radikalismus: Die Geschichte des Deutschvölkischen Schutz- und Trutz-Bundes* (Hamburg, 1970).

ŁUCZAK, CZESŁAW, *Położenie polskich robotników przymusowych w Rzeszy 1939–1945* (Poznań, 1975).

LUKAS, RICHARD C., *Forgotten Holocaust: The Poles under German Occupation 1939–1944* (Lexington, 1986).

LYTTELTON, ADRIAN, *The Seizure of Power: Fascism in Italy 1919–1929*, 2nd edn. (Princeton, 1987).

McKALE, DONALD M., *The Nazi Party Courts* (Lawrence, Kan., 1974).

MAIER, CHARLES S., *The Unmasterable Past: History, Holocaust, and German National Identity* (Cambridge, Mass., 1988).

MAIER, CHARLES S., *et al.* (eds.), *The Rise of the Nazi Regime: Historical Reassessments* (Boulder, Colo., 1986).

MAIER, JOACHIM, 'Die katholische Kirche und die Machtergreifung', in Michalka (ed.), *Machtergreifung*.

MAJER, DIEMUT, *'Fremdvölkische' im Dritten Reich: Ein Beitrag zur nationalsozialistischen Rechtssetzung und Rechtspraxis in Verwaltung und Justiz unter besonderer Berücksichtigung der eingegliederten Ostgebiete und des Generalgouvernements* (Boppard, 1981).

MANN, ERIKA, *School for Barbarians: Education under the Nazis* (London,1939).

MANN, GOLO, *Deutsche Geschichte des 19. und 20. Jahrhunderts* (Frankfurt, 1967).

MANN, REINHARD, *Protest und Kontrolle im Dritten Reich: Nationalsozialistische Herrschaft im Alltag einer rheinischen Großstadt* (Frankfurt, 1987).

——(ed.), *Die Nationalsozialisten: Analysen faschistischer Bewegungen* (Stuttgart, 1980).

MARGALIOT, ABRAHAM, 'The Reaction of the Jewish Public in Germany to the Nuremberg Laws', *Yad Vashem Studies*, 12 (1977).

MARRUS, MICHAEL R., *The Holocaust in History* (Hanover and London, 1987).

MARSSOLEK, INGE, and OTT, RENÉ, *Bremen im Dritten Reich: Anpassung, Widerstand, Verfolgung* (Bremen, 1986).

MASCHMANN, MELITA, *Fazit: Mein Weg in der Hitler-Jugend* (Munich, 1981).

MASON, TIMOTHY W., *Arbeiterklasse und Volksgemeinschaft: Dokumente und Materialien zur deutschen Arbeiterpolitik 1936–1939* (Gütersloh, 1975).

——'Intention and Explanation: A Current Controversy about the Interpretation of National Socialism', in Hirschfeld and Kettenacher (eds.), *Führerstaat*.

——'The Third Reich and the German Left: Persecution and Resistance', in Bull (ed.), *Challenge of the Third Reich*.

——'Women in Germany, 1925–1954: Family, Welfare, and Work'. *History Workshop Journal*, 1, 2 (Summer and Autumn 1976).

MAY, ERNEST R. (ed.), *Knowing One's Enemies: Intelligence Assessment before the two World Wars* (Princeton, 1986).

MAYER MILTON, *They Thought they were Free* (Chicago, 1955).

MEHRINGER, HARTMUT, 'Die bayerische Sozialdemokratie bis zum Ende des NS-Regimes: Vorgeschichte, Verfolgung und Widerstand', in Broszat *et al.* (eds.), *Bayern in der NS-Zeit*, v.

——'Die KPD in Bayern 1919–1945: Vorgeschichte, Verfolgung und Widerstand', in Broszat *et al.* (eds.), *Bayern in der NS-Zeit*, v.

MEISNER, MICHAEL, *Bekenntnisse eines Außenseiters* (Würzburg, 1985).

Meldungen aus dem Reich: see Boberach.

MEMMING, ROLF B., 'The Bavarian Governmental District Unterfranken and the City Burgstadt 1922–1939: A Study of the National Socialist Movement and Party–State Affairs' (University of Nebraska Ph.D. thesis; Lincoln, 1974).

MENZE, ERNEST A. (ed.), *Totalitarianism Reconsidered* (Port Washington, NY, 1981).

MERKL, PETER H., *The Making of a Stormtrooper* (Princeton, 1980).

MERSON, ALLAN, *Communist Resistance in Nazi Germany* (London, 1985).

MESSERSCHMIDT, MANFRED and WÜLLNER, FRITZ, *Die Wehrmachtjustiz im Dienste des Nationalsozialismus* (Baden-Baden, 1987).

METTERNICH TATIANA, *Purgatory of Fools* (New York, 1976).

MEYER, GERTRUD, *Nacht über Hamburg: Berichte und Dokumente* (Frankfurt, 1971).

MICHAELIS, MEIR, *Mussolini and the Jews: German–Italian Relations and the Jewish Question in Italy 1922–1945* (Oxford, 1978).

MICHALKA, WOLFGANG (ed.), *Die nationalsozialistische Machtergreifung* (Paderborn, 1984).

MOMMSEN, HANS, *Beamtentum im Dritten Reich* (Stuttgart, 1966).

——'The Realization of the Unthinkable: The "Final Solution of the Jewish Question" in the Third Reich', in Hirschfeld (ed.), *Policies of Genocide.*

——'The Reichstag Fire and its Political Consequences', in Hajo Holborn (ed.), *Republic to Reich: The Making of the Nazi Revolution* (New York, 1973).

MOMMSEN, WOLFGANG J., *Max Weber and German Politics 1890–1920*, trans. M. S. Steinberg (Chicago, 1984).

MOORE, BARRINGTON, jun., *Injustice; The Social Bases of Obedience and Revolt* (White Plains, NY, 1978).

——*Terror and Progress USSR* (Cambridge, Mass., 1954).

MORITZ, KLAUS, and NOAM, ERNST, *NS-Verbrechen vor Gericht 1945–1955: Dokumente aus hessischen Justizakten* (Wiesbaden, 1978).

MOSSE, GEORGE L., *Toward the Final Solution: A History of European Racism* (New York, 1978).

——(ed.), *Police Forces in History* (London, 1975).

MOSSE, WERNER E. (ed.), *Deutsches Judentum in Krieg und Revolution 1916–1923* (Tübingen, 1971).

——(ed.), *Entscheidungsjahr 1932: Zur Judenfrage in der Endphase der Weimarer Republik* (Tübingen, 1966).

MOSZKIEWIEZ, HELENE, *Inside the Gestapo: A Jewish Woman's Secret War* (Toronto, 1985).

MÜLLER, ARND, *Geschichte der Juden in Nürnberg 1146–1945* (Nuremberg, 1968).

MÜLLER-CLAUDIUS, MICHAEL, *Der Antisemitismus und das deutsche Verhängnis* (Frankfurt, 1948).

MURPHY, RICHARD C., *Gastarbeiter im Deutschen Reich: Polen in Bottrop 1891–1933*, trans. T. Schoenbaum-Holtermann (Wuppertal, 1982).

NEUFELDT, H.-J., HUCK, J., and TESSIN, G., *Zur Geschichte der Ordnungspolizei* (Koblenz, 1957).

NEUMANN, FRANZ, *Behemoth: The Structure and Practice of National Socialism* (New York, 1966).

NIETHAMMER, LUTZ, *Die Mitläuferfabrik: Die Entnazifizierung am Beispiel Bayerns* (Berlin, 1982).

——(ed.), *'Die Jahre weiß man nicht, wo man die heute hinsetzen soll': Faschismus-Erfahrungen im Ruhrgebiet* (Berlin, 1983).

NIPPERDEY, HANS CARL, 'Die Haftung für politische Denunziation in der Nazizeit', in H. C. Nipperdey (ed.), *Das deutsche Privatrecht in der Mitte des 20. Jahrhunderts: Festschrift für Heinrich Lehmann zum 80. Geburtstag*, i (Berlin, 1956).

NOAKES, JEREMY, 'Nazism and Eugenics: Background to the Nazi Sterilization Law of 14 July 1933', in Bullen *et al.* (eds.), *Ideas.*

NOAM, ERNST and KROPAT, WOLF-ARNO, *Juden vor Gericht 1933–1945: Dokumente aus hessischen Justizakten* (Wiesbaden, 1975).

NOLAN, MARY, 'The *Historikerstreit* and Social History', *New German Critique*, 44 (Spring–Summer 1988).

NOWAK, KURT, *'Euthanasie' und Sterilisierung im 'Dritten Reich'* (Weimar, 1980).

OBENAUS, HERBERT, *'"Sei stille, sonst kommst Du nach Ahlem!" Zur Funktion der Gestapostelle in der ehemaligen israelitischen Gartenbauschule von Ahlem* (1943–1945)', offprint from *Hannoversche Geschichtsblätter*, NS 41 (1987).

——and OBENAUS, SIBYLLE, (eds.), *'Schreiben wie es wirklich war!' Aufzeichnungen Karl Dürkefäldens aus den Jahren 1933–1945* (Hannover, 1985).

OPHIR, BARUCH Z., and WIESEMANN, FALK (eds.), *Die jüdischen Gemeinden in Bayern 1918–1945* (Munich, 1979).

ORB, HEINRICH, *Nationalsozialismus: 13 Jahre Machtrausch* (Olten, 1945).

ORLOW, DIETRICH, *History of the Nazi Party: 1933–1945* (Pittsburgh, 1973).

OVERY, RICHARD, 'Germany, "Domestic Crisis" and War in 1939', *Past and Present*, 116 (1987).

——*Goering: The Iron Man* (London, 1984).

PAEPCKE, LOTTE, *Ich wurde vergessen: Bericht einer Jüdin, die das Dritte Reich überlebte* (Freiburg, 1979).

PARIS, ERNA, *Unhealed Wounds: France and the Klaus Barbie Affair* (New York, 1985).

PÄTZOLD, KURT, *Faschismus, Rassenwahn, Judenverfolgung: Eine Studie zur politischen Strategie und Taktik des faschistischen deutschen Imperialismus (1933–1935)* (Berlin (East), 1975).

PEHLE, WALTER H. (ed.), *Der Judenpogrom 1938* (Frankfurt, 1988).

PETERSON, EDWARD, N., *The American Occupation of Germany: Retreat to Victory* (Detroit, 1977).

——*The Limits of Hitler's Power* (Princeton, 1969).

PETZINA, DIETMAR, 'Soziale Lage der deutschen Arbeiter und Probleme des Arbeitseinsatzes während des Zweiten Weltkriegs', in Długoborski (ed.), *Zweiter Weltkrieg*.

PEUKERT, DETLEV J. K., *Die KPD im Widerstand: Verfolgung und Untergrundarbeit an Rhein und Ruhr 1933 bis 1945* (Wuppertal, 1980).

——*Volksgenossen und Gemeinschaftsfremde: Anpassung, Ausmerze und Aufbegehren unter dem Nationalsozialismus* (Cologne, 1982).

——'Widerstand und "Resistenz": Zu den Bänden V und VI der Publikation "Bayern in der NS-Zeit" ', *Archiv für Sozialgeschichte*, 24 (1984).

——and BAJOHR, FRANK, *Spuren des Widerstands: Die Bergarbeiterbewegung im Dritten Reich und im Exil* (Munich, 1987).

——and REULECKE, JÜRGEN (eds.), *Die Reihen fast geschlossen: Beiträge zur Geschichte des Alltags unterm Nationalsozialismus* (Wuppertal, 1981).

PFAHLMANN, HANS, *Fremdarbeiter und Kriegsgefangene in der deutschen Kriegswirtschaft 1939–1945* (Darmstadt, 1968).

POMMERIN, REINER, *'Sterilisierung der Rheinlandbastarde': Das Schicksal einer farbigen deutschen Minderheit 1918–1937* (Düsseldorf, 1979).

PRIDHAM, GEOFFREY, *Hitler's Rise to Power: The Nazi Movement in Bavaria 1923–33* (London, 1973).

PROCTOR, ROBERT H., *Racial Hygiene: Medicine under the Nazis* (Cambridge, Mass., 1988).

RAAB, HELMUT, *Der Arbeiter im Reich des Hakenkreuzes: Widerstand und Verfolgung in Würzburg* (Würzburg, [1983]).

RAMME, ALWIN, *Der Sicherheitsdienst der SS* (Berlin, 1970).

REBENTISCH, DIETER, 'Die "politische Beurteilung"als Herrschaftsinstrument der NSDAP', in Peukert and Reulecke (eds.), *Die Reihen fast geschlossen.*

——and RAAB, ANGELIKA, *Neu-Isenburg zwischen Anpassung und Widerstand* (Neu-Isenburg, 1978).

RECK-MALLECZEWEN, FRIEDRICH PERCYVAL, *Diary of a man in Despair*, trans. P. Rubens (1966; New York, 1970).

REICHE, ERICH G., *The Development of the SA in Nürnberg 1922–1934* (Cambridge, 1986).

REITER, HERMANN, *Die Revolution von 1848/49 in Altbayern: Ihre sozialen und mentalen Voraussetzungen und ihr Verlauf* (Munich, 1983).

REITLINGER, GERALD, *The SS: Alibi of a Nation 1922–1945* (1956; Englewood Cliffs, NJ, 1981).

RICHARDSON, JAMES F., 'Berlin Police in the Weimar Republic: A Comparison with Police Forces in Cities in the United States', in Mosse (ed.), *Police Forces.*

RICHARZ, MONIKA (ed.), *Jüdisches Leben in Deutschland: Selbstzeugnisse zur Sozialgeschichte 1918–1945*, ii–iii (Stuttgart, 1979, 1982).

ROBINSOHN, HANS, *Justiz als politische Verfolgung: Die Rechtsprechung in 'Rassenschandefällen' beim Landgericht Hamburg 1936–1943* (Stuttgart, 1977).

ROCKENMAIER, DIETER W., *Das Dritte Reich und Würzburg: Versuch einer Bestandsaufnahme* (Würzburg, 1983).

ROHDE, HORST, 'Hitlers erster "Blitzkrieg" und seine Auswirkungen auf Nordosteuropa', in *Das Deutsche Reich und der Zweite Weltkrieg*, ii (1979).

ROSMUS-WENNINGER, ANJA, *Widerstand und Verfolgung am Beispiel Passaus 1933–1939* (Passau, 1983).

RÜCKERL, ADALBERT, *The Investigation of Nazi Crimes 1945–1978: A Documentation*, trans, D. Rutter (Hamden, Conn., 1980).

——*Nationalsozialistische Vernichtungslager im Spiegel deutscher Strafprozesse*, 3rd edn. (Munich, 1979).

RÜRUP, REINHARD, *Emanzipation und Antisemitismus: Studien zur 'Judenfrage' der bürgerlichen Gesellschaft* (Göttingen, 1975).

——(ed.), *Topographie des Terrors: Gestapo, SS und Reichssicherheitshauptamt auf dem 'Prinz-Albrecht-Gelände'. Eine Dokumentation* (Berlin, 1987).

RUSCHE, GEORG, and KIRCHHEIMER, OTTO, *Punishment and Social Structure* (1939; New York, 1968).

SAUER, PAUL, *Württemberg in der Zeit des Nationalsozialismus* (Ulm, 1975).

——(ed.), *Dokumente über die Verfolgung der jüdischen Bürger in Baden-Württemberg durch das nationalsozialistische Regime 1933–1945*, 2 vols. (Stuttgart, 1966).

SAUER, WOLFGANG, 'Die Mobilmachung der Gewalt', in Bracher, Sauer, and Schulz, *Machtergreifung.*

SCHADT, JÖRG (ed.), *Verfolgung und Widerstand unter dem Nationalsozialismus in Baden* (Stuttgart, 1976).

SCHELLENBERG, WALTER, *The Labyrinth: The Memoirs of Walter Schellenberg*, trans. L. Hagan (New York, 1956).

SCHEWICK, BURKHARD VAN, 'Katholische Kirche und nationalsozialistische Rassenpolitik', in Gotto and Repgen (eds.), *Kirche.*

SCHLEUNES, KARL A., *The Twisted Road to Auschwitz: Nazi Policy towards German Jews 1933–1939* (Urbana, Ill., 1970).

SCHMIDT, ERNST, *Lichter in der Finsternis: Widerstand und Verfolgung in Essen 1933–1945*, 2nd edn. (Frankfurt, 1980).

SCHMINCK-GUSTAVUS, CHRISTOPH U., *Das Heimweh des Walerjan Wroble: Ein Sondergerichtsverfahren 1941/42* (Berlin, 1986).

——'Zwangsarbeit und Faschismus: Zur "Polenpolitik" im "Dritten Reich"', *Kritische Justiz*, 13 (2 parts) (1980).

——(ed.), *Hungern für Hitler: Errinnerungen polnischer Zwangsarbeiter im Deutschen Reich 1940–1945* (Reinbek bei Hamburg, 1984).

SCHMUHL, HANS-WALTER, *Rassenhygiene, Nationalsozialismus, Euthanasie: Von der Verhütung zur Vernichtung 'lebensunwerten Lebens'* (Göttingen, 1987).

SCHOENBAUM, DAVID, *Hitler's Social Revolution: Class and Status in Nazi Germany 1933–1939* (London, 1967).

SCHOLDER, KLAUS, *Die Kirchen und das Dritte Reich*, i (Frankfurt, 1977).

SCHOLL, INGE, *Die weiße Rose* (1955; Frankfurt, 1985).

SCHULTHEIS, HERBERT, *Juden in Mainfranken 1933–1945* (Bad Neustadt a.d. Saale, 1980).

——(ed.), *Ein Streifzug durch Frankens Vergangenheit* (Bad Neustadt a.d. Saale, 1982).

SCHUMANN, WOLFGANG, et al., *Deutschland im zweiten Weltkrieg*, 6 vols. (Berlin (East), 1974–85).

SCHUPETTA, INGRID, *Frauen- und Ausländererwerbstätigkeit in Deutschland von 1939 bis 1945* (Cologne, 1983).

SCHÜTZ, Dr [HANS], *Justiz im 'Dritten Reich': Dokumentation aus dem Bezirk des Oberlandesgerichts Bamberg* (Bamberg, 1984).

SCHWARZ, STEFAN, *Die Juden in Bayern im Wandel der Zeiten* (Munich, 1963).

Das Schwarzbuch: Tatsachen und Dokumente. Die Lage der Juden in Deutschland 1933, ed. Comité des Délégations Juives (Paris 1934; repr. Frankfurt, 1983).

SCHWARZE, JOHANNES, *Die bayerische Polizei und ihre historische Funktion bei der Aufrechterhaltung der öffentlichen Sicherheit in Bayern von 1919–1933* (Munich, 1977).

SCHWARZWÄLDER, HERBERT, *Geschichte der freien Hansestadt Bremen*, iv. *Bremen in der NS-Zeit (1933–1945)* (Hamburg, 1985).

SEEBER, EVA, *Zwangsarbeiter in der faschistischen Kriegswirtschaft* (Berlin (East), 1964).

SEIDLER, HORST, and RETT, ANDREAS, *Das Reichssippenamt entscheidet: Rassenbiologie im Nationalsozialismus* (Vienna, 1982).

SHIRER, WILLIAM L., *Berlin Diary* (New York, 1941).

SIEGFRIED, KLAUS-JÖRG, *Das Leben der Zwangsarbeiter im Volkswagenwerk 1939–1945* (Frankfurt, 1988).

——(ed.), *Rüstungsproduktion und Zwangsarbeit im Volkswagenwerk 1939–1945: Eine Dokumentation* (Frankfurt, 1986).

SIEMANN, WOLFRAM, *'Deutschlands Ruhe, Sicherheit und Ordnung': Die Anfänge der politischen Polizei 1806–1866* (Tübingen, 1985).

SOMBART, NICOLAUS, *Jugend in Berlin* (Munich, 1984).

SPAICH, HERBERT, *Fremde in Deutschland: Unbequeme Kapitel unserer Geschichte* (Weinheim, 1981).

SPINDLER, MAX, *Bayerische Geschichte im 19. und 20. Jahrhundert 1800–1970*, 2 vols. (Munich, 1978).

SPITZNAGEL, PETER, *Wähler und Wahlen in Unterfranken, 1919–1969* (Würzburg, 1979).

STACHURA, PETER D. (ed.), *The Nazi Machtergreifung* (London, 1983).

STADEN, WENDELGARD VON, *Darkness over the Valley*, trans. M. C. Peters (Harmondsworth, 1982).

STEGMANN, DIRK, *Die Erben Bismarcks: Parteien und Verbände in der Spätphase des Wilhelminishen Deutschlands* (Cologne, 1970).

STEIN, GEORGE H., *The Waffen SS: Hitler's Elite Guard at War, 1939–1945* (Ithaca, 1966).

STEINBACH, LOTHER, *Ein Volk, Ein Reich, Ein Glaube? Ehemalige Nationalsozialisten und Zeitzeugen berichten über ihr Leben im Dritten Reich* (Berlin, 1983).

STEINER, GEORGE, 'Enormities beyond Measure', *Times Literary Supplement* (13 July 1984).

STEINERT, MARLIS G., *Hitler's War and the Germans: Public Mood and Attitude During the Second World War*, ed. and trans. T. E. J. de Witt (Athens, Ohio, 1977).

STEPHENSON, JILL, *The Nazi Organisation of Women* (London, 1981).

——Review of Gordon, *Hitler, Germans and the 'Jewish Question'*, in *History*, 71 (1986).

STERN, FRITZ, *Dreams and Delusions: The Drama of German History* (New York, 1987).

STOKES, LAWRENCE D., *Kleinstadt und Nationalsozialismus: Ausgewählte Dokumente zur Geschichte von Eutin, 1918–1945* (Neumünster, 1984).

——'The *Sicherheitsdienst* (SD) of the *Reichsführer* SS and German Public Opinion, September 1939–June 1941' (Johns Hopkins University Ph.D. thesis; Baltimore, 1972).

——'Zur Geschichte des "wilden" Konzentrationslagers Eutin', *VfZ* 27 (1979).

STRAEDE, THERKEL, 'Dänische Fremdarbeiter in Deutschland während des Zweiten Weltkrieges', *Zeitgeschichte*, 13 (1986).

STRAUSS, HERBERT A., and KAMPKE, NORBERT (eds.), *Antisemitismus; Von Der Judenfeindschaft zum Holocaust* (Frankfurt, 1985).

STUCKART, WILHELM, and GLOBKE, HANS, *Kommentare zur deutschen Rassengesetzgebung*, i (Munich, 1936).

SWEETS, JOHN F., *Choices in Vichy France: The French under Nazi Occupation* (Oxford, 1986).

SYWOTTEK, JUTTA, *Mobilmachung für den totalen Krieg: Die propagandische Vorbereitung der deutschen Bevölkerung auf den Zweiten Weltkrieg* (Opladen, 1976).

TENT, JAMES F., *Mission on the Rhine: Reeducation and Denazification in American-Occupied Germany* (Chicago, 1982).

THALMANN, RITA, and FEINERMANN, EMMANUEL, *Crystal Night 9–10 November 1938* (New York, 1974).

THEVOZ, ROBERT, *et al.*, *Die Geheime Staatspolizei in den preußischen Ostprovinzen 1934–1936*, 2 vols. (Cologne, 1974).

THRÄNHARDT, DIETRICH, *Wahlen und politische Strukturen in Bayern 1848–1953* (Düsseldorf, 1973).

TILLY, CHARLES, *The Contentious French: Four Centuries of Popular Struggle* (Cambridge, Mass., 1986).

——(ed.), *The Formation of National States in Western Europe* (Princeton, 1975).

——TILLY, LOUISE, and TILLY, RICHARD, *The Rebellious Century 1830–1930* (Cambridge, Mass., 1975).

TIMPKE, HENNING (ed.), *Dokumente zur Gleichschaltung des Landes Hamburg 1933* (Frankfurt, 1964).

Trials of the Major War Criminals before the International Military Tribunal, 42 vols. (Nuremberg, 1947–9). [Cited as IMT.]

TRÖGER, ANNEMARIE, 'German Women's Memories of World War II', in Higonnet *et al.* (eds.), *Behind the Lines.*

TUCHEL, JOHANNES, and SCHATTENFROH, REINOLD, *Zentrale des Terrors: Prinz-Albrecht-Straße 8. Das Hauptquartier der Gestapo* (Berlin, 1987).

TURNER, HENRY A., jun. (ed.), *Reappraisals of Fascism* (New York, 1975).

UHLIG, HEINRICH, *Die Warenhäuser im Dritten Reich* (Cologne, 1956).

UNGER, ARYEH L., *The Totalitarian Party: Party and People in Nazi Germany and the Soviet Union* (Cambridge, 1974).

VASSILTCHIKOV, MARIE, *Berlin Diaries, 1940–1945* (New York, 1987).

VOLLMER, B. (ed.), *Volksopposition im Polizeistaat: Gestapo- und Regierungsberichte 1934–1936* (Stuttgart, 1957).

WALK, JOSEPH (ed.), *Das Sonderrecht für die Juden im NS-Staat* (Heidelberg, 1981).

WALKER, MACK, *German Home Towns: Community, State, and General Estate 1648–1871* (Ithaca, 1971).

WEHLER, HANS-ULRICH, *The German Empire 1871–1918*, trans. K. Traynor (Leamington Spa, 1985).

WEHNER, BERND, *Dem Täter auf der Spur: Die Geschichte der deutschen Kriminalpolizei* (Bergisch Gladbach, 1983).

WEISENBORN, GÜNTHER, *Der lautlose Aufstand: Bericht über die Widerstandsbewegung des deutschen Volkes 1933–1945*, 4th edn. (Frankfurt, 1974).

——'Reich Secret', in Boehm (ed.), *We Survived.*

WENKE, BETTINA, *Interviews mit Überlebenden: Verfolgung und Widerstand in Südwestdeutschland* (Stuttgart, 1980).

WEYRAUCH, WALTER OTTO, 'Gestapo Informants: Facts and Theory of Undercover Operations', *Columbia Journal of Transnational Law*, 24 (1986).

WIESEMANN, FALK, *Die Vorgeschichte der nationalsozialistischen Machtübernahme in Bayern 1932/1933* (Berlin, 1975).

WINKLER, DÖRTE, *Frauenarbeit im 'Dritten Reich'* (Hamburg, 1977).

WINKLER, HEINRICH AUGUST, *Mittelstand, Demokratie und Nationalsozialismus* (Cologne, 1972).

WRIGHT, J. R. C., *'Above Parties': The Political Attitudes of the German Protestant Church Leadership 1918–1933* (Oxford, 1974).

WULF, JOSEPH, *Presse und Funk im Dritten Reich: Eine Dokumentation* (Frankfurt, 1983).

ZAHN, GORDON, C., *German Catholics and Hitler's Wars* (New York, 1969).

ZIPFEL, FRIEDRICH, 'Gestapo and SD: A Sociographic Profile of the Organizers of the Terror', in Larsen *et al;* (eds.), *Who were the Fascists?*

——'Gestapo und SD in Berlin', *Jahrbuch für die Geschichte Mittel- und Ostdeutschlands*, 9–10 (1961).

——*Gestapo und Sicherheitsdienst* (Berlin, 1960).

ZOFKA, ZDENEK, *Die Ausbreitung des Nationalsozialismus auf dem Lande* (Munich, 1979).

ZUCOTTI, SUSAN, *The Italians and the Holocaust: Persecution, Rescue, Survival* (New York, 1987).

INDEX